Test of English as a Foreign Language

PREPARATION GUIDE

by

Michael A. Pyle, M.A.

and

Mary Ellen Muñoz, M.A.

Series Editor

Jerry Bobrow, Ph.D.

Cliffs Notes

INCORPORATED

LINCOLN, NEBRASKA 68501

ACKNOWLEDGMENTS

We are indebted to many for providing us incentive and support during the time that we were writing this manuscript. We dedicate this book to our families, including María, María Elena, Rita, Louie, and our parents; their understanding and support during the many months of writing was essential.

We are also grateful to Dr. Clyde C. Clements, Jr., Dean of Community Education at Santa Fe Community College, for providing us the opportunity to organize a class for test preparation and supporting us in our quest to write this book. Special thanks are due Dr. Patricia Byrd, Assistant Director of the University of Florida's English Language Institute, for providing us classroom space, equipment, students, publicity, and encouragement. We wish to thank Dr. Manuel López Figuera, María López de Pyle, Dr. Felipe Sierra, Dr. José Zaglul, and Paul F. Schmidt for writing materials for the practice tests.

We also wish to thank Jerry Bobrow of Bobrow Test Preparation Services for recommending our book and Michele Spence of Cliffs Notes, Inc., for her invaluable assistance in editing.

Finally, we are indebted to our students, who acted as our critics while we were preparing the materials.

Thanks are also due to our friends at Educational Testing Service. We are not affiliated with Educational Testing Service nor with the development or the administration of TOEFL tests. Directions to sample tests are reprinted by permission of Educational Testing Service. However, the sample test questions were neither provided nor approved by Educational Testing Service.

CONTENTS

PART III: SUBJECT AREA REVIEWS
with
Exercises and Mini-Tests

PART IV: PRACTICE-REVIEW-ANALYZE-PRACTICE
Six Full-Length Practice Tests

PART V:
LISTENING COMPREHENSION SCRIPTS, ANSWERS, AND EXPLANATIONS FOR PRACTICE TESTS 1 THROUGH 6

PART VI: THE WRITING TEST

Ability Tested • Basic Skills Necessary
• General Information •

PREFACE

Your TOEFL scores make the difference! And better scores result from thorough preparation. Therefore, your study time must be used most effectively. You need the most comprehensive test preparation guide that you can realistically complete in a reasonable time. It must be thorough, direct, precise, and easy to use, giving you all the information you need to do your best on the TOEFL.

In keeping with the fine tradition of Cliffs Notes, leading experts in the field of test preparation and teaching English as a second language have developed this guide as part of a series to provide excellent test preparation materials. The testing strategies, techniques, and materials have been researched, tested, and evaluated, and are presently used at Santa Fe Community College and the University of Florida's English Language Institute.

Part I of this guide gives you basic information on the TOEFL and a Successful Overall Approach to taking the test.

Part II includes a thorough analysis of all question types for the three sections of the test, test-taking techniques and strategies, and a Patterned Plan of Attack for each area.

Part III provides an intensive grammar review, review of style problems in written English, and a survey of problem vocabulary and prepositions. Make full use of the six mini-tests and the fifty-nine exercises that are included with the reviews to chart your progress and your understanding.

Part IV contains six full-length practice tests, very similar in format to the Institutional administration of TOEFL. Take these tests under testing conditions, exactly as you will on the day of the actual test. Follow time allotments carefully.

Part V includes cross-referenced answer keys, scoring sheets, listening comprehension scripts, and answers and explanations for the six practice tests. Use the cross-referenced answer keys to guide you to review sections. After each practice test, be sure to review those areas in which you had difficulty. For vocabulary sections, you will best learn the words by using a good dictionary to look them up. The listening comprehension scripts will give you quick reference for any question with which you had a problem. Use all of the techniques and study tools provided. Your ability and confidence will grow with each practice test.

Part VI: If you will be taking the TOEFL at an administration that includes an essay writing section, review all of the material in Part VI. Practice writing essays on the sample topics provided. Have the practice essays graded by a composition teacher.

Allow yourself as much study time as possible. Study over several months, if you can, slowly and methodically, in conjunction with your regular study of English.

STUDY GUIDE CHECKLIST

_____ 1. Read the TOEFL Bulletin of Information (see page 9 for address).

_____ 2. Become familiar with the Format of Recent TOEFL Exams, page 3.

_____ 3. Familiarize yourself with the answers to Questions Commonly Asked about the TOEFL, page 7.

_____ 4. Learn the techniques of a Successful Overall Approach, page 10.

_____ 5. Carefully study the Analysis of Exam Areas for each of the three test sections, beginning on page 13.

_____ 6. Begin your study of the review material in Part III, do the accompanying exercises, take the mini-tests for each section, and restudy sections that give you trouble.

_____ 7. Strictly observing time allotments, take Practice Test 1, in its entirety, beginning on page 247.

_____ 8. Check your answers and analyze your results, beginning on page 377.

_____ 9. Fill out the Analysis-Scoring Sheet to pinpoint your mistakes, page 382.

_____ 10. While referring to each item of Practice Test 1, study ALL the answers and explanations as well as the listening comprehension script, beginning on page 383. Replay the cassette and listen carefully for questions you missed. Use the cross-referenced answer keys.

_____ 11. Continue your study of the review material given in Part III.

_____ 12. Repeat this process with Practice Tests 2, 3, 4, 5, and 6.

_____ 13. If your TOEFL administration includes an essay section, review all of Part VI and write practice essays as directed.

_____ 14. Go over "Final Preparation," page 481.

PART I: Introduction

FORMAT OF RECENT TOEFL EXAMS

LENGTH AND NUMBER OF QUESTIONS

Administration	Subject Area	Time	Number of Questions
Institutional	Listening Comprehension	35 Minutes	50 Questions
	Structure and Written Expression	25 Minutes	40 Questions
	Reading Comprehension and Vocabulary	45 Minutes	60 Questions
International and Special	Listening Comprehension	35 Minutes	50 Questions
	Structure and Written Expression	35 Minutes	60 Questions
	Reading Comprehension and Vocabulary	65 Minutes	90 Questions
Total Time 1 Hour 45 Minutes to 2 Hours 15 Minutes			150 to 200 Questions

NOTE: Consult the student handbook that you receive from Educational Testing Service. Time limits may change from time to time. It is possible that an International or Special TOEFL will be the same length as an Institutional TOEFL.

All three administrations of TOEFL have the same form. Only the cost, number of questions, and time limits are different.

FORM OF TOEFL

Section I: Listening Comprehension
Part A: Single sentences for which you must choose another sentence in the test book which means *most nearly the same* as the sentence that you hear.
Part B: Short conversations. The conversations are between two people. After each conversation, a third voice will ask a question about what was said. You must find the answer to the question in the test book.
Part C: Oral readings or long conversations. These may be about any subject. There are several questions about each reading or conversation.

Section II: Structure and Written Expression
Part A: Multiple choice answers to complete sentences. You must choose the best way to complete the sentence *in formal written English.*
Part B: Sentences have four words or phrases underlined. You must choose the *one* underlined part that is *incorrect* in formal written English.

Section III: Reading Comprehension and Vocabulary
Part A: Vocabulary. You must choose the *one* word or phrase among four choices which means *most nearly the same* as the underlined word or phrase in each sentence.
Part B: Reading comprehension. You must read selections in the test book and answer questions based on what is *stated or implied* in the readings.

3

GENERAL DESCRIPTION

Use of TOEFL by Colleges and Universities

TOEFL, Test of English as a Foreign Language, is probably the most often used examination in the admissions process of foreign students to colleges and universities in the United States. However, these schools often do not consider the TOEFL score as the only criterion for admission. They may also consider the student's grades in schools which he or she previously attended and the records from any intensive English program in which the student was enrolled. All this depends on the school's admission criteria.

The score which is acceptable to a given school also depends on the regulations for that particular school. Some schools require 450, some 500, some 550 or 600. If you find that a school requires no TOEFL score, or a very low score, it is probable that the school does not have extensive experience with foreign students, and you may find that it would be better to attend a different school. Remember that admission to a school is not the end of the battle, but the beginning. You must be able to understand enough English to make good grades in competition with native English-speaking students. This is what TOEFL tests, and this is why schools consider TOEFL a valuable examination.

Administration of TOEFL

There are three different administrations of TOEFL: Institutional, Special, and International. The format is basically the same; however, the length and uses may be different.

Institutional TOEFL

This administration is generally given only to students in intensive English programs. It is a service offered by these programs to their students, but is an actual TOEFL just like the International and Special administrations.

Registration for an Institutional TOEFL can be done only at a program in which this type of TOEFL is offered. You *cannot* register for this administration of TOEFL through Educational Testing Service.

Scores for this type of TOEFL are generally delivered only to the test taker approximately a week after the exam. Scores are *not* sent to any college or university. Also, scores from the Institutional TOEFL are not accepted by all colleges or universities. You should ask the authorities at any school to which you are applying if they will accept an Institutional TOEFL score from a given institution.

Special and International TOEFL

Any foreign student can take these examinations. Applications are available from Educational Testing Service. With the application, you will receive a booklet explaining when and where you can take these examinations. Some test centers give only the Special or the International, while others give both.

You may not register for either of these tests at the school in which the exam is given; instead, you must send the application to Educational Testing Service. Generally, the deadline for application is about six weeks before the exam, but it is wise to register well in advance because the testing centers are often full before the deadline.

Scores for these administrations are sent to the test taker and to any colleges or universities to which the student is applying approximately five weeks after the exam. Any school in the United States that requires TOEFL for admission will accept the score for either of these administrations.

The Determination of the TOEFL Score

Your test score is determined by adding the total number of correct answers in each section and then changing these "raw scores" into "converted scores." The raw score is the total number correct in each section. The converted score is different for each examination. It is based on the difficulty of the test. There is no way that you can use any simple mathematics to determine the converted score.

The "total converted score" is then determined by adding the three converted scores and multiplying the result by $3\frac{1}{3}$ (or multiplying by 10 and dividing by 3).

In Part V of this guide, there is a scale to convert your practice test scores from raw scores to converted scores. The scale is NOT one that has been produced by Educational Testing Service, but is very similar to one that was used on a recent test. It is intended only to give you a *general idea* of what your total score might be. *Do not assume that it is exactly like that of the TOEFL that you are going to take.*

Sections of the TOEFL

There are now only three sections on the TOEFL. An additional section may be added in the future. There have been experimental sections on the examination recently. ETS uses these experimental sections to determine how well a given type of question tests a student's knowledge of English. When there is such a section, the score for that section is *not* included in the computation of your TOEFL score.

The Writing Test

Beginning with the July, 1986, administration of TOEFL, a separate writing test will be given as part of certain administrations throughout the year. If the school to which you intend to apply requests that you take the writing test, you must apply well in advance for one of the administrations that does offer the writing test. Please see your current TOEFL Bulletin for information and application. Strategies and practice material for the writing test are presented in Part VI of this book.

QUESTIONS COMMONLY ASKED
ABOUT THE TOEFL

Q: WHO ADMINISTERS THE TOEFL?

A: The TOEFL is written and administered by Educational Testing Service (ETS) of Princeton, New Jersey.

Q: IS THERE A DIFFERENCE BETWEEN THE INTERNATIONAL, SPECIAL, AND INSTITUTIONAL ADMINISTRATIONS OF TOEFL?

A: They are the same in difficulty and subject matter tested. However, as the Format of Recent TOEFL Exams indicates, they differ in time, number of questions, and cost.

Q: CAN I TAKE THE TOEFL MORE THAN ONCE?

A: Yes. Previous scores will be reported, but most schools consider only the most recent score. Many students take TOEFL more than once.

Q: WHAT MATERIALS MAY I BRING TO THE TOEFL?

A: Bring your registration confirmation ticket, positive identification (passport or alien registration card), a watch, three or four sharpened Number 2 pencils, and a good, clean eraser.

Q: WHAT MATERIALS MAY I NOT BRING?

A: You may not bring any paper, food, calculators, dictionaries (or any other books), tape recorders, or cameras.

Q: IF NECESSARY, MAY I CANCEL MY SCORE?

A: Yes. You may cancel your score on the day of the test by informing the test center supervisor, or you may contact ETS no later than seven days after the test date. Your score report will record your cancellation as well as completed test scores.

Q: SHOULD I GUESS ON THE TOEFL?

A: Yes. There is no penalty on TOEFL for incorrect answers, so DO NOT LEAVE ANY SPACES BLANK on your answer sheet. Of course, it is best to eliminate the answers that you are sure are not correct, and then choose among the remaining answers. Some educators suggest that if you have many spaces blank when time is almost up on a section, you *may* slightly improve your score by choosing one letter and filling in all the spaces with that answer rather than randomly choosing answers.

Q: HOW SHOULD I PREPARE FOR THE TOEFL?

A: You should study all the material in this book, and complete all the exercises and practice tests. Also, be sure that you know the directions for each section and know the format of the test. Be sure to consult the TOEFL bulletin in case of changes in format.

Q: WHEN IS THE TOEFL ADMINISTERED?

A: The TOEFL is administered every month in some areas. Consult the TOEFL bulletin for the administration dates of areas near you.

Q: IS TOEFL ADMINISTERED ONLY IN THE UNITED STATES?

A: No. TOEFL is administered in many countries. You can receive information on foreign locations by writing to the TOEFL office and asking for the Overseas Edition of the TOEFL bulletin.

Q: HOW AND WHEN SHOULD I REGISTER FOR TOEFL?

A: Most schools with foreign students have copies of the TOEFL bulletin and application form. If your school does not, write to the TOEFL office and request the application form. Remember to register as early as possible before the deadline date in the bulletin. There are a limited number of seats in the testing center. When you fill out the application form, be sure you make a note of your registration number, (printed in red at the top right of the application form.) You will need this number if you need to contact the TOEFL office about your registration.

Q: SHOULD I ORDER THE "SAMPLE TEST" AND "TEST KIT" MENTIONED ON THE APPLICATION FORM?

A: Yes. For additional practice after you have finished using this textbook, it would be a very good idea to order these items.

Q: IS WALK-IN REGISTRATION PROVIDED?

A: No. You MUST register in advance.

Q: ONCE I HAVE RECEIVED MY CONFIRMATION TICKET, MAY I CHANGE THE DATE?

A: Changes in test dates are *not* allowed. If you decide to take the test on a day other than the one that you originally applied for, you must submit a new application with the total fees. You may then request a partial refund for the original amount within sixty days of the original test date.

Q: CAN I CHANGE THE TEST CENTER ONCE MY APPLICATION HAS BEEN CONFIRMED?

A: You may request a change of test center by filling out the form found on the back cover of the TOEFL bulletin and attaching a $5 check. Do *not* fill out another application or return the registration confirmation ticket. If your request is received before the application closing date, every effort will be made to accommodate you.

Q: CAN I RECEIVE A REFUND IF I DO NOT TAKE THE TEST?

A: If you did not enter the test center and did not take the test, you are eligible for a partial refund. Consult the TOEFL bulletin for details.

Q: IF I FINISH A SECTION BEFORE TIME IS CALLED, CAN I GO TO ANOTHER SECTION?

A: No. During the time allotted for a given section, you must work only on questions in that section. If you are found working on another section, your score may be cancelled.

Q: WHAT SHOULD I DO IF I MISPLACE ANSWERS ON MY ANSWER SHEET?

A: To avoid this problem, you should check your answer sheet every ten questions to be sure that if you have skipped a question in the test booklet, you have also skipped it on the answer sheet. If you find that you have misplaced a number of answers, DON'T ERASE THEM. Simply raise your hand and ask for another answer sheet to finish the test beginning in the place that you realized the mistake. After the examination, a proctor will assist you in correcting your answer sheet.

Q: CAN I ERASE AN ANSWER THAT I FEEL IS WRONG?

A: Yes, but it is very important to erase mistakes completely. Before you go to the test, be sure that your erasers are clean so that they will not smudge the paper. If there are two marks for one question on the answer sheet, even if you have tried to erase the incorrect one, the question will not be counted.

Q: HOW SHOULD I MARK MY ANSWER SHEET?

A: Be sure to fill in the answer spaces correctly and completely and to fill in only one answer for each question.

Correct—	Ⓐ ● Ⓒ Ⓓ
Incorrect—	Ⓐ Ⓑ Ⓔ Ⓓ
Incorrect—	Ⓐ Ⓧ Ⓒ Ⓓ

Q: HOW CAN I CONTACT EDUCATIONAL TESTING SERVICE?

A: Test of English as a Foreign Language
Box 899
Princeton, N.J. 08541 U.S.A.
Telephone: (609) 882-6601

TAKING THE TOEFL: A SUCCESSFUL OVERALL APPROACH

Every second counts when you are taking a standardized test such as the TOEFL. Avoid wasting that time. One way that you can save time is by not reading the directions for each section. If you know the directions for each section, and the format looks similar to the format of that section in this guide and the TOEFL handbook, it is suggested that you begin work immediately. While the other examinees are reading the directions, you can answer several questions. Of course, if the section looks at all unfamiliar, check the directions to be sure there has not been a change.

Many who take the TOEFL don't get the score that they are entitled to because they spend too much time dwelling on hard questions, leaving insufficient time to answer the easy questions they can get right. Don't let this happen to you. Use the following system to mark your answer sheet:

1. Answer easy questions immediately.
2. Place a "+" next to any problem that seems solvable but is too time-consuming.
3. Place a "−" next to any problem that seems impossible. Act quickly. Don't waste time deciding whether a problem is a "+" or a "−."

After working all the problems you can do immediately, go back and work your "+" problems. If you finish them, try your "−" problems (sometimes when you come back to a problem that seemed impossible you will suddenly realize how to solve it).

Your answer sheet should look something like this after you finish working your easy questions:

    1. Ⓐ ● Ⓒ Ⓓ
+2. Ⓐ Ⓑ Ⓒ Ⓓ
    3. Ⓐ Ⓑ ● Ⓓ
−4. Ⓐ Ⓑ Ⓒ Ⓓ
+5. Ⓐ Ⓑ Ⓒ Ⓓ

MAKE SURE TO ERASE YOUR "+" AND "−" MARKS BEFORE YOUR TIME IS UP. The scoring machine may count extraneous marks as wrong answers.

By using this overall approach, you are bound to achieve your best possible score.

PART II: Analysis of Exam Areas

This section is designed to introduce you to each TOEFL area by carefully reviewing the

1. Ability Tested
2. Basic Skills Necessary
3. Directions
4. Suggested Approach with Samples

This section features the PATTERNED PLAN OF ATTACK for each subject area and emphasizes important test-taking techniques and strategies and how to apply them to a variety of problem types.

SECTION I: LISTENING COMPREHENSION

The listening comprehension section is always first in the examination and it is in three parts. It typically lasts 30 to 35 minutes and contains 50 questions.

Ability Tested

This section tests your ability to understand and interpret spoken English.

Basic Skills Necessary

It is necessary to have a good "ear" for English, which can only be obtained with a great deal of practice. You must be able to distinguish between words that sound similar and be able to comprehend entire sentences, not just single words or phrases.

PART A

DIRECTIONS

For each problem in Part A, you will hear a short statement. The statements will be *spoken* just one time. They will not be written out for you, and you must listen carefully in order to understand what the speaker says.

When you hear a statement, read the four sentences in your test book and decide which one is closest in meaning to the statement you have heard. Then, on your answer sheet, find the number of the problem and mark your answer.

Suggested Approach with Samples

You will hear: We had expected fifty people to come to the party,
                but only thirty showed up.

You will read: (A) Fifty people came to the party.
                    (B) Thirteen people came to the party.
                    (C) Thirty people came to the party.
                    (D) The party was cancelled because nobody showed up.

Answer (C) means most nearly the same as the sentence that you heard because it says that only thirty people actually came to the party (showed up). Therefore, you should choose answer (C).

Several types of questions often appear in this section, but you should be prepared for any type. Listed here are some areas that you should study in order to improve your score in the listening comprehension sections.

- *Idiomatic expressions:* These are items that are common in English speech although there may be no specific grammatical rules for them. You will be able to learn these by conversing with native English speakers often. (Study verbal idioms, p. 215.)

- *Conditional sentences:* Be sure that you know the meaning of conditional sentences when they are negative or positive. (p. 92)

- *Modals + perfectives:* Be sure that you know the meanings of such expressions as *should have gone* and *must have gone.* (p. 104)

- *Clauses of concession:* Be sure that you know the meanings of such expressions as *although, even though, though, despite,* and *in spite of.* (p. 145)

- *Numbers:* Remember that numbers such as *fifty* and *fifteen* and *sixty* and *sixteen* differ in the placement of stress on the syllables. *Examples:* fifty, fiftéen, síxty, sixtéen. You will also have to do some simple addition, subtraction, or multiplication in this section. Be sure that you know such expressions as *twice as many* and *half as many.*

For Part A questions you should

1. Always look at the answer choices before you hear the question.
2. Be careful of words that sound alike but have different meanings.
3. Strive to understand the entire sentence, not individual words.

PART B

DIRECTIONS

In Part B you will hear fifteen short conversations between two speakers. At the end of each conversation, a third voice will ask a question about what was said. The question will be *spoken* just one time. After you hear a conversation and the question about it, read the four possible answers and decide which one would be the best answer to the question you have heard. Then, on your answer sheet find the number of the problem and mark your answer.

Suggested Approach with Samples

You will always hear three different voices in this section, generally, but not always, alternating between male and female. *Sample:*

You will hear:	Man:	I don't feel like going out tonight. Let's just stay home instead.
	Woman:	OK, but I was looking forward to seeing that new movie about Alcatraz.
	Third Voice:	What does the man want to do tonight?
You will read:		(A) go to a party
		(B) stay home
		(C) see a movie
		(D) sleep

Answer (B) means most nearly the same as what the man said he would like to do. Therefore, you should choose answer (B).

Remember that it is best to glance at the four possible answers *before* you hear the conversation. In this way, you can often listen specifically for the particular information that you know will answer the question. Several types of questions often appear in this section.

1. Where did this conversation most probably take place?
2. What time _____?
3. How much did/does _____ cost?
4. What is the probable relationship between the two speakers?
5. What do we learn from this conversation?
6. Which of the following was *not* mentioned?

Sample: You see that the answers to a question are

　　(A) 3:00　　(B) 3:15　　(C) 3:45　　(D) 4:00

You know that the question will be about time, and you should listen for that.

PART C

DIRECTIONS

In this part of the test, you will hear several short talks and/or conversations. After each talk or conversation, you will be asked some questions. The talks and questions will be *spoken* just one time. They will not be written out for you, so you will have to listen carefully in order to understand and remember what the speaker says.

When you hear a question, read the four possible answers in your test book and decide which one would be the best answer to the question you have heard. Then, on your answer sheet, find the number of the problem and fill in (blacken) the space that corresponds to the letter of the answer you have chosen.

Suggested Approach with Samples

In this section, you will hear long conversations, weather reports, stories, news stories, and reading selections about any topic. You will be asked several questions about each selection.

Again, it is best to glance at the possible answer choices before you hear the reading in order to get an indication of the topic of the reading. Before the mini-talk, the speaker will tell you which question numbers will refer to that particular selection.

1. As in Part B, try to decide what types of questions will be asked.
2. If there are several short answers for any questions, be prepared to put a check mark next to any of those words which are mentioned in the reading. In this way, you will be prepared for a question such as: Which of the following items was *not* mentioned?

Sample: The answer choices are

(A) bread   (B) milk   (C) ice cream   (D) beer

If you put a check mark next to each thing as it is mentioned, the one that is not checked will be the one that was not mentioned. NOTE: *Don't forget to erase the check marks before turning in your answer booklet.*

HOW TO PREPARE FOR THE LISTENING COMPREHENSION SECTION

Besides the methods mentioned here, there is actually no way to "study" for listening comprehension. It is necessary to tune your ear to English. Speak to native English speakers as often as possible. Also you should

1. Watch news and weather reports on television or listen to them on the radio.
2. Make telephone calls to recorded messages such as weather reports, time of day, or movie theaters.
3. Attend lectures at your school or in your city.
4. Make use of the language laboratory if your school has one.

Practice for the listening comprehension section is included in this guide in the practice tests. Use the cassette included with this book to take practice tests 1 through 3. For practice tests 4 through 6, you may order an additional cassette (see ordering information page 463) or you may have friends read the script for you as you take the test. All scripts are included in Part V. Remember the suggestions listed here when you take these tests. If you miss a question, ALWAYS study the script. Look up any words you don't know and study grammatical expressions that have caused you trouble.

A PATTERNED PLAN OF ATTACK

Listening Comprehension

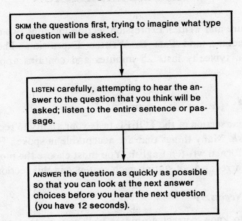

SKIM the questions first, trying to imagine what type of question will be asked.

LISTEN carefully, attempting to hear the answer to the question that you think will be asked; listen to the entire sentence or passage.

ANSWER the question as quickly as possible so that you can look at the next answer choices before you hear the next question (you have 12 seconds).

SECTION II: STRUCTURE AND WRITTEN EXPRESSION

The structure and written expression section includes two question types, Part A, Structure, and Part B, Written Expression. The Institutional administration typically lasts 25 minutes and contains approximately 40 questions.

Ability Tested

The grammar section of the TOEFL tests your ability to recognize *formal written English*. Many things that are acceptable in spoken English are *not* acceptable in formal written English. You must choose the most economical, mature, and correct way of stating each sentence in this section.

Basic Skills Necessary

You need to know correct grammar well enough that an error will be immediately evident.

PART A

DIRECTIONS

This section is designed to measure your ability to recognize language that is appropriate for standard written English. There are two types of questions in this section, with special directions for each type. Part A questions are incomplete sentences. Four words or phrases, marked (A), (B), (C), (D), are given beneath each sentence. You are to choose the *one* word or phrase that best completes the sentence. Then, on your answer sheet, find the number of the problem and mark your answer.

Suggested Approach with Samples

● Notice that the directions call for recognition of language that is appropriate for standard WRITTEN English.
● Notice that you are to choose the ONE word or phrase that BEST completes the sentence. There might be other possible ways of completing the sentence, but only one way is the *best* way.

For Part A questions you should

1. Read the entire sentence, inserting the (A) answer.
2. If that is not correct, try to discover WHY it is incorrect.

3. If you can discover why (A) is incorrect, proceed to answer (B), (C), and (D).
4. If you still are not sure, try to remember a formula for the sentence.
5. If you cannot find the correct answer, eliminate the obviously incorrect answers and GUESS.

Samples:

1. I wish you would tell me _____.
   (A) who is being lived next door
   (B) who does live in the next door
   (C) who lives next door
   (D) who next door was living

When you read the sentence with (A), you can immediately eliminate that answer because *is being lived* is an impossible verbal structure when used with *who*. A *life* may be lived. A *person* may not. *Live* usually does not take a complement and therefore cannot be passive. (B) can also be eliminated because *does* and *in the* are not necessary in this sentence. You will realize by now that the required phrase must be [subject + verb + (complement) + (modifier)]. (D) is incorrect because it does not follow that order. (C) is correct (it has no complement because *live* does not require a complement).

2. During the Daytona 500, the lead car _____, leaving the others far behind.
   (A) forwarded rapidly
   (B) advanced rapidly
   (C) advanced forward quickly
   (D) advanced in a rapidly manner

When you read the sentence with (A), you see that a verb is necessary after *the lead car,* but you know that *forward* is not a verb here. Thus (A) is incorrect. If you realize that *advanced* in (B) is a suitable verb for the sentence, and it is correctly modified by the adverb *rapidly,* you will not have to look further for the correct answer. If you do not realize that (B) is correct and go on to (C), you will see that *advanced forward* is redundant (that is, *advance* means *move forward,* so it is not necessary to use the two words together). (D) is also incorrect because *rapidly* is used in the position of an adjective.

Be sure to review the additional strategies for elimination of incorrect answers in style questions beginning on page 172.

PART B

DIRECTIONS

In Part B questions each sentence has four words or phrases underlined. The four underlined parts of each sentence are marked (A), (B), (C), (D).

You are to identify the *one* underlined word or phrase that should be corrected or rewritten. Then, on your answer sheet, find the number of the problem and mark your answer.

Suggested Approach with Samples

- Again, remember that you are looking for correct WRITTEN English.
- Notice that you are looking for the one word or phrase that is INCORRECT, and thus must be changed to make the sentence correct.

For Part B questions you should

1. Read the entire sentence.
2. If an error does not become immediately evident, remember the formulas from this book and be sure that portions of the sentence fit the correct pattern.

Samples:

1. In <u>the</u> United States, <u>there</u> are <u>much</u> holidays throughout <u>the</u> year.
       A   B   C   D

You should immediately notice that *much* modifies non-count nouns and that *holidays* is a count noun. Therefore, *much* is incorrect, and *many* would be correct. Therefore, (C) is the correct answer.

2. <u>Tomatoes</u> <u>grows</u> <u>all</u> year long <u>in</u> Florida.
      A   B C   D

If you made a hasty decision before reading the entire sentence, you could choose answer (A) assuming that it must be singular because the verb *grows* is singular. But you see by the context of the entire sentence that the sentence is not speaking of a single tomato, and therefore (A) is not the correct answer. (B), then, is incorrect because it is a singular verb; it should be *grow*.

A PATTERNED PLAN OF ATTACK

Structure and Written Expression

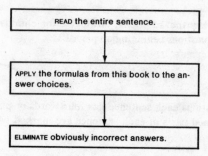

SECTION III: READING COMPREHENSION AND VOCABULARY

This section of the test is divided into two parts. Part A contains problems in vocabulary. Part B contains reading selections and questions based on them. The section contains approximately 30 questions of each type, and you will have 45 minutes to complete it on an Institutional TOEFL. There are more questions and there is a proportionately longer time limit on the International and Special administrations.

PART A: VOCABULARY

Ability Tested

This section tests your knowledge of English vocabulary. You must find synonyms among four answer choices.

Basic Skills Necessary

This section requires a strong college-level vocabulary. A strong vocabulary cannot be developed instantly. It grows over a long period of time spent reading widely and learning new words. Knowing the meanings of prefixes, suffixes, and roots will help you to derive word meanings on the test.

DIRECTIONS

In Part A each sentence has a word or phrase underlined. Below each sentence are four other words or phrases. You are to choose the *one* word or phrase which would *best keep the meaning* of the original sentence if it were substituted for the underlined word.

Suggested Approach with Samples

● Remember that you are looking for the word that means most nearly the same as the underlined word *as it is used in the sentence*. Some words may have several definitions, but only one will fit the meaning of the sentence.
● Read the entire sentence, trying to understand the meaning of the underlined word or phrase from context. Many times, you can understand the meaning of the word from the words around it.

Samples:

1. Because of Angela's <u>antagonistic</u> nature, she finds it difficult to make friends.

   (A) cordial   (B) quarrelsome   (C) talkative   (D) outgoing

21

Even if you do not know the meaning of *antagonistic,* you should be able to assume from the fact that Angela finds it difficult to make friends that it is not a positive quality. (A) and (D) are generally thought of as positive qualities and are therefore incorrect. (C) may be a positive or negative quality, but would not necessarily make it difficult for her to make friends. If you have eliminated these three answers, you will choose the correct answer, (B).

2. The State's Attorney thought that piece of evidence was <u>insignificant</u> early in the investigation, but it turned out to be vital in convicting the criminal.

    (A) important   (C) unalterable
    (B) unclassifiable   (D) unimportant

The first thing that you should notice here is that the word *insignificant* begins with the prefix *in-,* which is often an indicator of a negative idea. However, that will help you to eliminate only answer (A). If you understand the entire sentence, you will know that the piece of evidence was actually quite important (vital). The contrasting conjunction *but* should tell you that the word *insignificant* is actually the opposite of *important;* thus the answer is (D), *unimportant.*

3. The supply of silver in the mines had <u>dwindled</u>, causing great concern among the people of the town.

    (A) diminished   (B) increased   (C) extended   (D) devalued

You know that something happened to the supply of silver. You also know that it caused concern among the people; in other words, it worried them. It does not seem likely that answers (B) and (C) would cause the people to worry, so you can eliminate them. If you understand the meaning of devalued, answer (D), you will probably be able to understand that while *silver* can devalue, it is not usual that one would say that a *supply* had devalued. If you have eliminated (B), (C), and (D), you will arrive at the correct answer, (A).

It is not always easy to answer a vocabulary question when you do not know the meaning of the underlined word or words in the answer. However, this method will help you with some of the questions in this section. At times it will not help, so it is important to have a wide vocabulary. Try to improve your vocabulary at every opportunity. Do the vocabulary exercises in Part III. Try to use these methods when they help you, but as always, if you do not know the correct answer, eliminate and guess. Make a list of any words in the practice exercises that you do not know and study them. Do the same with all vocabulary that you do not know in the practice tests in Part IV. Remember that a good English-English dictionary is indispensable.

A PATTERNED PLAN OF ATTACK

Vocabulary

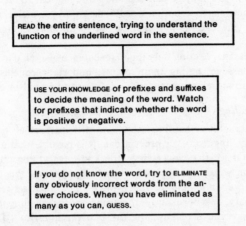

READ the entire sentence, trying to understand the function of the underlined word in the sentence.

USE YOUR KNOWLEDGE of prefixes and suffixes to decide the meaning of the word. Watch for prefixes that indicate whether the word is positive or negative.

If you do not know the word, try to ELIMINATE any obviously incorrect words from the answer choices. When you have eliminated as many as you can, GUESS.

PART B: READING COMPREHENSION

Ability Tested

This section tests your ability to understand, interpret, and analyze reading passages on a variety of topics. The TOEFL is now beginning to stress readings that are typical of those you will read in colleges and universities. Advertisements, directions, and telephone listings will be phased out. You should still be aware that they may appear on a TOEFL, however, and for that reason examples are given here.

Basic Skills Necessary

You must be able to read a selection containing rather complicated constructions and vocabulary and answer questions based on what you have read.

DIRECTIONS

In Part B, the questions are based on a variety of reading material (single sentences, paragraphs, advertisements, and the like). You are to choose the *one* best answer, (A), (B), (C), or (D), to each question. Then, on your answer sheet, find the number of the problem and mark your answer. Answer all questions following a passage on the basis of what is *stated* or *implied* in that passage.

Suggested Approach with Samples

• Be sure to answer questions based on what is *stated* or *implied* in the passage even if it is a subject that you know a great deal about.

• Skim the questions first, noting words which give you a clue about what to look for when you read the passage. Do not spend more than a few seconds doing this.

• Skim the passage, reading only the first sentence of each paragraph.

• Read the passage, noting main points, important conclusions, names, definitions, places, and numbers.

• *Factual Readings:*

The majority of the reading selections will be factual readings from science, history, linguistics, or other areas. It is possible that a reading will show up on TOEFL that you believe you know everything about. Perhaps something from your major field of study will appear. If this happens, you are lucky, but do not assume that you do not have to read it. Some information may not be exactly the same in the reading as you have supposed. Before you read anything, *look at the questions.* Do not spend time looking at all of the answer choices; simply glance at the answer choices so that you have an idea of what to look for. Do not try to look at an answer choice and then skim the reading looking for the answer. Generally, the words in the question and in the reading itself will not be the same and you will lose valuable time using this method. Look at the following example (remember to glance at the questions first).

Questions 1 through 4 are based on the following reading.

Athens and Sparta were the two most advanced Greek cities of the Hellenic period (750–338 B.C.). Both had a city-state type of government, and both took slaves from the peoples they conquered. However, the differences outweigh the similarities in these two ancient civilizations. Sparta was hostile, warlike (constantly fighting the neighboring cities), and military, while Athens catered more towards the democratic and cultural way of life. The latter city left its mark in the fields of art, literature, philosophy, and science, while the former passed on its totalitarianism and superior military traditions. The present system of a well-rounded education followed in the United States is based on the ancient Athenian idea. The Spartan system, on the other hand, was concerned only with military education.

1. Which of the following is *not* true?
   (A) Both cities had city-state types of government.
   (B) Both cities took slaves.
   (C) Both cities were advanced, but in different areas.
   (D) Both cities developed a well-rounded education.

2. Which of the following was *not* mentioned as part of Athens' cultural heritage?
   (A) totalitarianism   (C) art
   (B) well-rounded education   (D) philosophy

3. Which of the following was borrowed from Athens by the United States?
   (A) well-rounded education   (C) totalitarianism
   (B) military might   (D) slavery

4. It can be inferred from this reading that
   (A) Athens and Sparta were friendly with each other
   (B) Athens was attacked by other warlike nations
   (C) Athens never fought other people
   (D) the cultural aspects of Athenian culture made a great impression on the world

Answers:

1. (D) You know from the second sentence that (A) and (B) are true. You know from the entire reading that (C) is also true. The correct answer is (D). The reading said that Sparta was hostile and warlike, with no mention of its having a well-rounded education. The sixth sentence tells you that Athens had a well-rounded education that had an influence on the United States.

2. (A) You must know the meanings of *the former* and *the latter*. Sentence 4 in this reading mentioned Sparta first and Athens second. Thus, if a subsequent sentence speaks of the former and the latter, the former is Sparta (the first) and the latter is Athens (the second). You will see from sentence 5 that the latter (Athens) left its mark in the fields of art and philosophy. Sentence 6 tells you that it was also important in the theory of well-rounded education. Sparta, not Athens, was involved in the idea of totalitarianism. Thus (A) is the answer as it was *not* mentioned as part of Athens' cultural heritage.

3. (A) This question is answered in sentence 6.

4. (D) Inference questions are difficult, but appear occasionally on TOEFL. You must decide which of the answer choices you can assume to be true from the facts given in the reading selection. Again, it is important to eliminate answer choices which are obviously not correct. (A) may be true, but there is nothing in the reading selection to cause you to assume that it is. (C) is definitely not true. Sentence 2 says that both cities took slaves from the people they conquered. If they conquered people, they must have fought. (D) can be inferred from the statement in sentence 5 that the latter (Athens) *left its mark.*

Questions 5 through 9 are based on the following reading.

Finnish-born botanist William Nylander taught at the University of Helsinki for a number of years and later moved to Paris, where he lived until his death at the end of the nineteenth century. During the second half of the last century, he became a prominent figure in the field of lichenology.

Botanists from all over the world sent samples to his laboratory to be analyzed and classified. It can be said without exaggeration that four out of five lichens bear his name.

He was the first to realize the importance of using chemical reagents in the taxonomy of lichens. He selected the most common reagents used by the chemists of his time. Lichenologists all over the world still use these reagents, including tincture of iodine and hypochlorite, in their laboratories. During the first half of the twentieth century, a Japanese named Arahina added only one chemical product—P-Phenol diamines.

Nylander was also responsible for discovering that the atmosphere of big cities hindered the lichens' development and caused them to disappear. Now they are used to detect atmospheric pollution.

Nevertheless, he considered lichens to be simple plants and vehemently opposed the widely accepted modern theories that lichens are a compound species formed by two discordant elements: algae and fungi.

5. Internationally renowned scientists sent lichen samples to Nylander because
    (A) he considered them to be simple plants
    (B) he used reagents to determine their use
    (C) he analyzed and classified them
    (D) he collected and preserved them

6. Which of the following is *not* true?
    (A) Nylander accepted his colleagues' theories on the composition of lichens.
    (B) Eighty percent of lichens bear Nylander's name.
    (C) Today lichens are used to detect atmospheric pollution.
    (D) Most botanists consider lichens to be a compound species.

7. All of the following are true about Nylander, *except*
    (A) he was the first to use chemical reagents in the taxonomy of lichens
    (B) he believed that lichens were simple plants
    (C) he was an esteemed lichenologist
    (D) he taught botany at the University of Paris

8. According to accepted nineteenth-century theories, which two elements form the composition of lichens?
   (A) iodine and chemical reagents
   (B) algae and fungi
   (C) hypochlorite and iodine
   (D) chemical reagents and atmospheric chemicals

9. How could William Nylander best be described?
   (A) degenerate   (C) ingenious
   (B) domineering   (D) anxious

Answers:

5. (C) Choice (B) is an incorrect statement because Nylander used reagents to *identify* lichens, not to determine their *use*. Choices (A), (C), and (D) are correct. Yet, only answer (C) answers the question *why* other scientists sent lichen samples to Nylander. This is explained in sentence 3. (C) is the correct answer.

6. (A) Choices (C) and (D) are true, and mentioned specifically in the reading. (B) is true because the reading says four out of five (80%) of lichens bear Nylander's name. However, (A) is not true, and is therefore the correct answer. The last paragraph states that he vehemently opposed the theories that lichens are a compound species.

7. (D) Choices (A), (B), and (C) are specifically stated in the reading. Sentence 1 says he taught at the University of Helsinki and then moved to Paris, but it does not say that he ever taught in Paris. Therefore, (D) is *not* true and is the correct answer.

8. (B) The last sentence of the reading verifies (B) as the correct answer.

9. (C) This is the correct answer because *ingenious* means *clever* or *showing great practical knowledge or intelligence*. Nylander was first to realize the importance of using chemical reagents and he discovered that atmospheric pollution hindered the development of lichens. (A), (B), and (D) do not describe him as this reading does.

● *Directions:*

It is possible that you will find directions for how to do something or use something on the TOEFL. You may see a recipe, directions for using medication, or any other type of description of a process. Again, look at the questions first.

Questions 10 through 14 are based on the following recipe.

SNOWFLAKE CAKE

2 cups plus 2 tbsp. sifted flour	½ cup soft shortening
1½ cups sugar	1 cup milk
3½ tsp. baking powder	1 tsp. flavoring
1 tsp. salt	4 egg whites unbeaten

Heat oven to 350°. Grease and flour two layer pans, 8 or 9 × 1½″, or an oblong pan, 13 × 9½ × 2″. Sift together into bowl flour, sugar, baking powder, and salt. Add shortening, milk, and flavoring. Beat 2 minutes, medium speed on mixer, or 300 vigorous strokes by hand. Scrape sides and bottom of bowl constantly. Add egg whites. Beat 2 more minutes, scraping bowl frequently. Pour into prepared pans. Bake layers 35 to 40 minutes, oblong 40 to 45 minutes, or until cake tests done. Cool.

10. Which of the following ingredients is measured by a tablespoon?
    (A) flour   (B) baking powder   (C) salt   (D) flavoring

11. If you were using an oblong pan to bake this cake, how long would you bake it?
    (A) 35 to 40 minutes   (C) 40 to 45 minutes
    (B) 45 to 50 minutes   (D) 50 to 55 minutes

12. Which of the following ingredients is *not* called for in this recipe?
    (A) baking powder   (B) milk   (C) salt   (D) egg yolks

13. What is the total amount of time that this cake must be beaten using an electric mixer?
    (A) 2 minutes   (C) 4 minutes
    (B) 35 minutes   (D) 13 minutes

14. Which of the following is added after the mixture has been beaten one time?
    (A) egg whites   (B) salt   (C) shortening   (D) flour

Answers:

10. (A) Even if you do not know the abbreviation for tablespoon. you can see that the baking powder, salt, and flavoring are measured by a *tsp.* (teaspoon). There can only be one item that is measured by tablespoon. Notice that the flour is not measured by a *tsp.*, but by a *tbsp.* This must be the abbreviation for tablespoon since it is the only one spelled in this way.

11. (C) This question is answered in the last sentence, (oblong 40 to 45 minutes). Thus the answer is (C).

12. (D) This question may trick you if you do not know what an egg yolk

is. The yolk is the yellow part of the egg, and the recipe calls for egg whites. Thus answer (D) is the correct answer. It is *not* called for in the recipe.

13. (C) Sentences 5 and 8 indicate that there are two times that the cake mix is beaten, each time for 2 minutes. Thus, the total time is 4 minutes, answer (C).

14. (A) The egg whites aren't added until sentence 7, and the cake has already been beaten in sentence 5. Thus the egg whites, answer (A), are added *after* the mixture has been beaten.

● *Classified advertisements:*

The difficult part about reading classified advertisements is understanding the numerous abbreviations. These advertisements are made as small as possible because one must pay by the line to have them put in a newspaper. The best way to prepare yourself for this type of question is to look at classified advertisements in newspapers, and when you see an abbreviation or word that you don't know, ask somebody the meaning. Look at the questions and then read the following ad.

Questions 15 through 18 are based on the following advertisement.

For Sale: 1972 Estrella, auto., 2 dr. convert., A/C, AM/FM, tape deck, built-in CB, good mpg, red/black, power steer & brks., tilt wheel, $2600 negot. Call 672-6970 after 8.

15. What feature would make this car seem economical?
    (A) A/C   (C) good mpg
    (B) power steer & brks.   (D) built-in CB

16. Which of the following is *not* true?
    (A) The price is firm.
    (B) The steering wheel shaft is movable.
    (C) The car has automatic transmission.
    (D) The top can be lowered.

17. What is the model of this car?
    (A) tilt wheel   (B) Estrella   (C) convert.   (D) CB

18. Which of the following is true?
    (A) The car has a manual transmission.
    (B) The car has four doors.
    (C) The car does not have a radio.
    (D) The car has air conditioning.

Answers:

15. (C) You must understand the abbreviations in order to get the questions right. (A) A/C = air conditioning; (B) power steer & brks. = power steering and brakes; (C) good mpg = good miles per gallon (good gas mileage); (D) CB = citizens' band radio. (A), (B), and (D) would not make the car seem economical. Answer (C), good miles per gallon, indicates that one will not have to spend much money on gasoline and thus is the correct answer.

16. (A) Again, abbreviations are important. (A) is not true because the price is not firm. The ad says $2600 negot. (negot. = negotiable). This means that the owner may accept another price. Therefore, (A) is the correct answer, since the question asks "which of the following is *not* true." Answer (B) is true because a tilt wheel is one which can be moved for additional comfort when one enters or leaves a car. Answer (C) is true because auto. = automatic transmission. Answer (D) is true because convert. = convertible, which means the top can be lowered.

17. (B) The model is the name of the type of car, and begins with a capital letter. Estrella, answer (B), is correct.

18. (D) (A) is not true; the car has automatic transmission, not manual. (B) is not true; 2dr. = 2 doors, so it does not have four doors. (C) is not true; AM/FM refers to a type of radio, so it does have a radio. (D) is the correct answer. A/C = air conditioning.

● *Yellow pages advertisements:*

On the TOEFL, there may be an advertisement from the yellow pages of a telephone book. The best way to prepare for this type of question is to study the yellow pages of your telephone book to see if you understand what everything means. Look at the questions, and then read the following example.

Questions 19 through 23 are based on the advertisement on the following page.

19. Which phrase indicates that the company is an established firm?
    (A) More Than a Quarter of a Century Serving Holly Heights
    (B) Registered Opticians
    (C) One-Day Prescription Service
    (D) Call for an Immediate Appointment

20. In what city would you find this firm?
    (A) Broadview   (C) Holly Heights
    (B) Registered Opticians (D) Vision Center

LET THERE BE LIGHT VISION CENTER
1451 Broadview Rd.
661-9281

More Than a Quarter of a Century Serving
Holly Heights

Registered Opticians

One-Day Prescription Service
Custom-Fitted Glasses to Suit Your Individual Needs

Hard and Soft Contact Lenses

HRS.   M 10–9
                        T–F 8:30–5
                        Sat 10–4

Call for an Immediate Appointment

21. Which evenings will this establishment be open?
    (A) Tuesday through Friday   (C) Saturday only
    (B) Monday only   (D) Monday and Saturday

22. Who would most likely go to this establishment?
    (A) a person needing surgery for an eye disease
    (B) a person who has a prescription for antibiotics to be filled
    (C) a person who does not have an appointment
    (D) a person who needs a new pair of contact lenses

23. Which of the following is *not* true about this business?
    (A) It is closed on Sundays.
    (B) It is open later in the evening on Monday than on other days.
    (C) It has the same hours from Tuesday through Saturday.
    (D) It does not open as early in the morning on Monday and Saturday
        as it does on the other days.

Answers:

19. (A) An established firm is one that has been in business for a long
time. Answer (A) tells you that the business has been in Holly Heights for
more than 25 years. Therefore, it is the correct answer.

20. (C) This is a very easy question. Holly Heights (C) is, of course, the
city.

21. (B) This business closes at 5:00 on Tuesday through Friday. It closes at 4:00 on Saturdays. The only day it is open later is Monday. Therefore, (B) is the correct answer.

22. (D) An optician fills prescriptions for glasses and contact lenses, not for drugs. An optician does not do surgery. The correct answer is (D).

23. (C) Choices (A), (B), and (D) are true. (C) says the business has the same hours from Tuesday through Saturday. This is not true. It has the same hours from Tuesday through *Friday*. Thus, (C) is the correct answer.

● *Lists from white pages of a telephone book:*

Occasionally, TOEFL will have a list of names and telephone numbers from the white pages of a telephone book. The numbers will be for businesses and the questions will ask you to decide which number you would call for a given problem.

Questions 24 through 28 are based on the following list.

Toskes Henry R. MD
 Harris Medical Center 358-2398
 Nights, weekends, holidays 358-9765
Total Energy Insulation
 25 N. Broadway 354-7512
Total Security Systems
 3540 N.W. 23rd Ave. 358-7893
Town Tire Co.
 456 S.W. 6th St. 357-4829
Toyland, Inc.
 3800 N. Grandview 358-9658
Trane Janitorial Center
 3428 Sunland Rd. 767-3829

24. Which number would you probably call to locate a present for a child?
 (A) 767-3829   (C) 354-7512
 (B) 358-9658   (D) 358-9765

25. Which number would you probably call to have a burglar alarm installed in your business?
 (A) 358-7893   (C) 767-3829
 (B) 354-7512   (D) 358-9658

26. Which number would you call if a friend were ill?
 (A) 358-2398   (C) 357-4829
 (B) 767-3829   (D) 358-7893

27. Which number would you probably call if your wheels were out of alignment?
(A) 354-7512   (C) 767-3829
(B) 357-4829   (D) 358-9658

28. Which of the following is most probably *not* a local number?
(A) 358-7893   (C) 357-4829
(B) 354-7512   (D) 767-3829

Answers:

24. (B) If you are trying to locate a present (gift) for a child, you would probably call Toyland, where they probably sell toys. The answer is (B).

25. (A) To have a burglar alarm installed, you would probably call a security business. The correct answer is (A).

26. (A) If somebody were ill, you would probably call an MD (Medical Doctor). The correct answer is (A).

27. (B) If your wheels were out of alignment, you would probably call a tire company or other automobile repair establishment. The only possible answer from this list would be (B), as it is the only number that is connected with automobiles.

28. (D) To find out if a number is local, look at the first two or three digits. The first two will probably be the same, but the third may be different. All the numbers begin with 35 with the exception of answer (D), which begins with 76.

● *Single sentence readings:*

Some of the most difficult questions in the reading comprehension section are short readings of only one sentence. You must choose the answer choice that means most nearly the same as the original sentence. Watch the placement of adjectives and other modifiers. If they do not modify the same noun or verb as they do in the original sentence, they are not correct.

29. Spain has changed over the years, but the fascination and enchantment still remain for the susceptible romantic to savor and treasure.
(A) Susceptible romantics are swept up by the fascinating and enchanting changes being made in Spain today.
(B) Spanish treasures are fascinating and enchanting for the susceptible romantic.
(C) Despite the changes in Spain, susceptible romantics are still enchanted and fascinated by its culture.
(D) The changes in Spain are fascinating and enchanting to the savor of susceptible romantics.

Answers:

(A) There is nothing in the original sentence to indicate that the *changes* are fascinating and enchanting. And the original sentence is not talking about changes that are being made now, but changes that have occurred over a period of years. (A) is not correct.

(B) *Treasure* in the original sentence is a verb. In (B) it is a plural noun. There is nothing to indicate that treasures are fascinating and enchanting. (B) is not correct.

(C) This is the correct answer. The sentence has been reversed and *but* has been replaced by another word that indicates contrast, *despite*.

(D) Again, this sentence says that the *changes* are fascinating and enchanting. (D) is not correct.

30. Tort laws differ from criminal laws in the ends they achieve—the former offer civil remedies in the form of monetary compensation for the injured individual, while the latter are concerned primarily with punishment for the satisfaction of the State.

   (A) In former times, tort laws and criminal laws were the same, but now they are quite distinct in the methods of compensation.

   (B) A tort law is intended to punish a wrongdoer, while a criminal law is intended to offer monetary remedies.

   (C) Tort laws and criminal laws are quite the same because they both are intended to compensate the State with money and to punish the criminal.

   (D) Tort laws are remedial and intended to benefit the individual who has been harmed, but criminal laws are punitive and intended to benefit the State.

Answers:

(A) The original sentence says nothing about former times. Also, it says nothing about the criminal laws' offering any compensation. This answer is not correct.

(B) This sentence is actually the opposite of the original sentence. Be careful of the use of the words *former* and *latter*.

(C) The original sentence tells how the two types of laws are different. Only criminal laws are for the benefit of the State, but they do not offer money to the State. Also, tort laws are not intended to punish the criminal.

(D) This is the correct answer. It and the original sentence say that a tort law is intended to offer money to the individual who has been injured, and a criminal law is intended to be punitive (offering punishment) and intended to benefit the State.

A PATTERNED PLAN OF ATTACK

Reading Comprehension

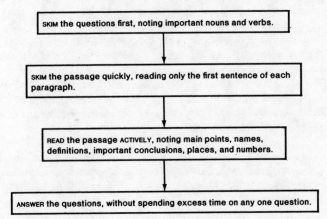

SKIM the questions first, noting important nouns and verbs.

SKIM the passage quickly, reading only the first sentence of each paragraph.

READ the passage ACTIVELY, noting main points, names, definitions, important conclusions, places, and numbers.

ANSWER the questions, without spending excess time on any one question.

PART III: Subject Area Reviews
with
Exercises and Mini-Tests

The following pages are designed to give you an intensive review in English grammar, style in written English, problem vocabulary, and prepositions. Pace yourself. Learn a predetermined amount of material each week, depending on the study time you have available before the actual TOEFL. Do all the exercises and take all the mini-tests that follow each review section.

Be sure that you use the cross-referenced answer keys provided with each of the practice tests to refer back to this review to restudy rules and concepts that give you trouble. You will find also that the table of contents and answer key will direct you quickly to sections you need to go over again.

PART III: Subject Area Reviews
with
Exercises and Mini-Tests

GRAMMAR REVIEW

1. Rules

A rule in grammar is a generalization. It is a formula that one makes to account for how a given grammatical construction *usually behaves*. A rule is *not* necessarily true in every instance. It is *generally* true. Don't be concerned if you see or hear something that does not coincide with a rule in this book.

In this guide:

Parentheses ( ) indicate optional usage when used in a rule.

Braces { } indicate either one choice or the other.

$\begin{Bmatrix} has \\ have \end{Bmatrix}$ = either *have* or *has*

2. Method of Study

The best method of improving your use of English grammar with this guide is to study the formulas and sample sentences. Then do the practice exercise at the end of each section. After each group of lessons, there is an exercise using grammatical points from the preceding explanations. If you still make errors, the practice test answer keys and the index give you the page number of the explanation to study again.

3. Normal Sentence Pattern in English

subject	verb	complement	modifier
John and I	ate	a pizza	last night
We	studied	"present perfect"	last week

● *Subject:* The subject is the agent of the sentence in the active voice; it is the person or thing that does the action of the sentence, and it normally precedes the verb. NOTE: *Every sentence in English must have a subject.* (In the case of commands, the subject is understood.) The subject may be a single noun.

<u>Coffee</u> is delicious.   <u>Milk</u> contains calcium.

The subject may be a noun phrase. A noun phrase is a group of words ending with a noun. (It CANNOT begin with a preposition.)

<u>The book</u> is on the table.   <u>That new, red car</u> is John's.

Examples of subjects:

> <u>We girls</u> are not going to that movie.
> <u>George</u> likes boats.
> <u>Mary, John, George, and I</u> went to a restaurant last night.
> <u>The weather</u> was very bad yesterday.
> <u>The chemistry professor</u> cancelled class today.
> <u>The bank</u> closed at two o'clock.

In some sentences there is not a true subject. However, *it* and *there* can often act as pseudo-subjects and should be considered as subjects when rules call for moving the subject of a sentence.

> <u>It</u> is a nice day today.
> <u>There</u> was a fire in that building last month.
> <u>There</u> were many students in the room.
> <u>It</u> is raining right now.

- *Verb:* The verb follows the subject; it generally shows the action of the sentence. NOTE: *Every sentence must have a verb.* The verb may be a single word.

> John <u>drives</u> too fast.
> They <u>hate</u> spinach.

The verb may be a verb phrase. A verb phrase consists of one or more auxiliaries and one main verb. The auxiliaries always precede the main verb.

> John <u>is going</u> to Miami tomorrow.   (auxiliary–*is*; main verb–*going*)
> Jane <u>has been reading</u> that book.   (auxiliaries–*has, been;* main verb–*reading*)

Examples of verbs and verb phrases:

> She <u>will go</u> to Boston next week.
> Jane <u>is</u> very tall.
> She <u>must have gone</u> to the bank.
> Joe <u>has gone</u> home.
> Mary <u>is watching</u> television.
> It <u>was raining</u> at six o'clock last night.

- *Complement:* A complement completes the verb. It is similar to the subject because it is usually a noun or noun phrase; however, it generally follows the verb when the sentence is in the active voice. NOTE: *Every sentence does not require a complement.* The complement CANNOT begin with a preposition. A complement answers the question what? or whom?

Examples of complements:

John bought <u>a cake</u> yesterday.	(*What* did John buy?)
Jill was driving <u>a new car</u>.	(*What* was Jill driving?)
He wants to drink <u>some water</u>.	(*What* does he want to drink?)
She saw <u>John</u> at the movies last night.	(*Whom* did she see at the movies?)
They called <u>Mary</u> yesterday.	(*Whom* did they call?)
He was smoking <u>a cigarette</u>.	(*What* was he smoking?)

● *Modifier:* A modifier tells the time, place, or manner of the action. Very often it is a prepositional phrase. A prepositional phrase is a group of words that begins with a preposition and ends with a noun. NOTE: A modifier of time usually comes last if more than one modifier is present.

Examples of prepositional phrases:

<u>in the morning, at the university, on the table</u>

A modifier can also be an adverb or an adverbial phrase.

<u>last night, hurriedly, next year, outdoors, yesterday</u>

NOTE: *Every sentence does not require a modifier.* A modifier answers the question when? where? or how?

Examples of modifiers:

John bought a book <u>at the bookstore</u>. (*Where* did John buy a book?)
   modifier of place

Jill was swimming <u>in the pool</u> <u>yesterday</u>. (*Where* was Jill swimming?)
  modifier of *modifier of* (*When* was Jill swimming?)
   place *time*

He was driving <u>very fast</u>. (*How* was he driving?)
   modifier of manner

The milk is <u>in the refrigerator</u>. (*Where* is the milk?)
  modifier of place

She drove the car <u>on Main Street</u>. (*Where* did she drive?)
  modifier of place

We ate dinner <u>at seven o'clock</u>. (*When* did we eat dinner?)
  modifier of time

NOTE: The modifier normally follows the complement, but not always. However, the modifier, especially when it is a prepositional phrase, usually cannot separate the verb and the complement.

Incorrect: She <u>drove</u> on the street <u>the car</u> .
    verb   *complement*

Correct: She <u>drove</u> <u>the car</u> on the street.
    verb *complement*

Exercise 1: Subject, Verb, Complement, and Modifier

Identify the subject, verb, complement, and modifier in each of the following sentences. Remember that not every sentence has a complement or modifier. *Examples:*

Jill / is buying / a new hat / in the store.
subject   verb phrase   complement   modifier of place

Betty / is shopping / downtown.
subject   verb phrase   modifier of place

1. George is cooking dinner tonight.
2. Henry and Marcia have visited the president.
3. We can eat lunch in this restaurant today.
4. Pat should have bought gasoline yesterday.
5. Trees grow.
6. It was raining at seven o'clock this morning.
7. She opened a checking account at the bank last week.
8. Harry is washing dishes right now.
9. She opened her book.
10. Paul, William, and Mary were watching television a few minutes ago.

4. The Noun Phrase

The noun phrase is a group of words that ends with a noun. It can contain determiners (*the, a, this,* etc.), adjectives, adverbs, and nouns. It CANNOT begin with a preposition. Remember that both subjects and complements are generally noun phrases.

- *Count and non-count nouns:* A count noun is one that *can* be counted.

  book–one book, two books, three books, . . .
  student–one student, two students, three students, . . .
  person–one person, two people, three people, . . .

A non-count noun is one that *cannot* be counted.

  milk–you cannot say: one milk, two milks, . . .

It is possible, however, to count some non-count nouns if the substance is placed in a countable container.

  glass of milk–one glass of milk, two glasses of milk, . . .

Some determiners can be used only with count or non-count nouns, while others can be used with either. Memorize the words in the following chart.

WITH COUNT NOUNS	WITH NON-COUNT NOUNS
a, the, some, any	the, some, any
this, that, these, those	this, that
none, one, two, three, . . .	none
many a lot of a {large / great} number of (a) few fewer . . . than more . . . than	much (usually in negatives or questions) a lot of a large amount of (a) little less . . . than more . . . than

It is very important to know if a noun is count or non-count. Students often make mistakes with the following nouns. Be sure that you know the plurals of irregular count nouns. The following list contains some irregular count nouns that you should know.

person–people   child–children   tooth–teeth
foot–feet   mouse–mice

The following list contains some non-count nouns that you should know.

sand	food	information	air	mathematics	money
news	soap	economics	meat	politics	
measles	mumps	physics	advertising*	homework	

*NOTE: Although *advertising* is a non-count noun, *advertisement* is a count noun. If you wish to speak of one particular advertisement, you must use this word.

There are too many advertisements during television shows.

Some non-count nouns, such as *food, meat, money,* and *sand,* may be used as count nouns in order to indicate different types.

This is one of the foods that my doctor has forbidden me to eat.
    (indicates a particular type of food)
He studies meats.
    (for example, beef, pork, lamb, etc.)

The word *time* can be either countable or non-countable depending on the context. When it means an occasion, it is countable. When it means a number of hours, days, years, etc., it is non-countable.

> We have spent too much time on this homework. (non-count)
> She has been late for class six times this semester. (count)

To decide if a noun that you are not sure of is countable or non-countable, decide if you can say: *one* _____ or *a* _____. For example, you can say "one book" so it is a count noun. You cannot say "one money" so it is not a count noun. Also, of course, by the very nature of non-count nouns, a non-count noun can never be plural. Remember that, while some of the nouns in the list of non-count nouns appear to be plural because they end in –s, they are actually not plural.

Exercise 2: Count and Non-Count Nouns

Identify the following nouns as count nouns or non-count nouns according to their *usual* meaning.

television	atmosphere	food	cup
car	person	tooth	money
news	water	soap	hydrogen
geography	pencil	soup	minute

Exercise 3: Determiners

Choose the correct determiners in the following sentences.

1. He doesn't have (many/much) money.
2. I would like (a few/a little) salt on my vegetables.
3. She bought (that/those) cards last night.
4. There are (less/fewer) students in this room than in the next room.
5. There is (too much/too many) bad news on television tonight.
6. I do not want (these/this) water.
7. This is (too many/too much) information to learn.
8. A (few/little) people left early.
9. Would you like (less/fewer) coffee than this?
10. This jacket costs (too much/too many).

• *A* and an: *A* or *an* can precede only singular count nouns; they mean *one*. They can be used in a general statement or to introduce a subject which has not been previously mentioned.

> A baseball is round.   (general–means all baseballs)
> I saw a boy in the street.   (We don't know which boy.)

An is used before words that begin with a vowel sound. *A* is used before words that begin with a consonant sound.

a book   an apple

Some words can be confusing because the spelling does not indicate the pronunciation.

a house   (begins with a consonant sound)
an hour   (begins with a vowel sound)
a university   (begins with a consonant sound)
an umbrella   (begins with a vowel sound)

The following words begin with a consonant sound and thus must *always* be preceded by *a*.

house	home	heavy	half
uniform	university	universal	union

The following words begin with a vowel sound and thus must *always* be preceded by *an*.

uncle	umbrella	hour	heir

The initial sound of the word that immediately follows the indefinite article will determine whether it should be *a* or *an*.

an umbrella   a white umbrella
an hour   a whole hour

● *The:* *The* is used to indicate something that we already know about or something that is common knowledge.

The boy in the corner is my friend.   (The speaker and the listener
                                       know which boy.)

The earth is round.   (There is only one earth.)

With non-count nouns, one uses the article *the* if speaking in specific terms, but uses no article if speaking in general.

Sugar is sweet.   (general–all sugar)
The sugar on the table is from Cuba.   (specific–the sugar that is
                                         on the table)

Normally, plural count nouns, when they mean everything within a certain class, are not preceded by *the*.

Oranges are green until they ripen.   (all oranges)
Athletes should follow a well-balanced diet.   (all athletes)

Normally a proper noun is not preceded by an article unless there are several people or things with the same name and the speaker is specifying one of them.

There are three Susan Parkers in the telephone directory.
The Susan Parker that I know lives on First Avenue.

Normally words such as *breakfast, lunch, dinner, school, church, home,* and *college* do not use any article unless to restrict the meaning.

We ate breakfast at eight o'clock this morning.
We went to school yesterday.

Use the following generalizations as a guide for the use of the article *the.*

USE THE WITH	DON'T USE THE WITH
oceans, rivers, seas, gulfs, plural lakes the Red Sea, the Atlantic Ocean, the Persian Gulf, the Great Lakes	*singular lakes* Lake Geneva, Lake Erie
mountains the Rocky Mountains, the Andes	*mounts* Mount Vesuvius, Mount McKinley
earth, moon the earth, the moon	*planets, constellations* Venus, Mars, Orion
schools, colleges, universities when the phrase begins with school, etc. the University of Florida, the College of Arts and Sciences	*schools, colleges, universities when the phrase begins with a proper noun* Santa Fe Community College, Cooper's Art School, Stetson University
ordinal numbers before nouns the First World War, the third chapter	*cardinal numbers after nouns* World War One, chapter three
wars (except world wars) the Crimean War, the Korean War	
countries with more than one word (except Great Britain) the United States, the Central African Republic	*countries with one word* China, Venezuela, France
	continents Europe, Africa, South America

USE THE WITH	DON'T USE THE WITH
	states Florida, Ohio, California
historical documents the Constitution, the Magna Carta *ethnic groups* the Indians, the Aztecs	
	sports baseball, basketball *abstract nouns* freedom, happiness *general areas of subject matter* mathematics, sociology *holidays* Christmas, Thanksgiving

Exercise 4: Articles

In the following sentences supply the articles (*a, an,* or *the*) if they are necessary. If no article is necessary, leave the space blank.

1. Jason's father bought him _____ bicycle that he had wanted for his birthday.
2. _The_ Statue of Liberty was a gift of friendship from _θ_ France to _The_ United States.
3. Rita is studying _θ_ English and _θ_ math this semester.
4. _The_ judge asked _The_ witness to tell _the_ truth.
5. Please give me _a_ cup of _θ_ coffee with _θ_ cream and _θ_ sugar.
6. _The_ big books on _The_ table are for my history class.
7. No one in _θ_ Spanish class knew _a_ correct answer to _θ_ Mrs. Perez's question.
8. My _θ_ car is four years old and it still runs well.
9. When you go to _the_ store, please buy _a_ bottle of _____ chocolate milk and _a_ dozen oranges.
10. There are only _a_ few seats left for _____ tonight's musical at _____ university.
11. John and Marcy went to _____ school yesterday and then studied in _____ library before returning home.
12. _____ Lake Erie is one of _____ five Great Lakes in _____ North America.

13. On our trip to ___ Spain, we crossed _The_ Atlantic Ocean.

14. _____ Mount Rushmore is the site of _____ magnificent tribute to _The_ four great American presidents.

15. What did you eat for ___ breakfast this morning?

16. Louie played _____ basketball and _____ baseball at _____ Boys' Club this year.

17. Rita plays _____ violin and her sister plays _____ guitar.

18. While we were in _____ Alaska, we saw _____ Eskimo village.

19. Phil can't go to _____ movies tonight because he has to write _____ essay.

20. David attended ___ Princeton University.

21. Harry has been admitted to _The_ School of Medicine at ___ midwestern university.

22. Mel's grandmother is in _____ hospital, so we went to visit her _____ last night.

23. _____ political science class is taking _____ trip to _The_ Soviet Union in ___ spring.

24. _____ Queen Elizabeth II is _____ monarch of _____ Great Britain.

25. _____ Declaration of Independence was drawn up in 1776.

26. Scientists hope to send _____ expedition to _____ Mars during _____ 1980s.

27. Last night there was _____ bird singing outside my house.

28. _____ chair that you are sitting in is broken.

29. _____ Civil War was fought in _____ United States between 1861 and 1865.

30. ___ Florida State University is smaller than _The_ University of Florida.

● *Other:* The use of the word *other* is often a cause of confusion for foreign students. Study the following formulas.

WITH COUNT NOUNS	WITH NON-COUNT NOUNS
an + *other* + singular noun (one more)	xxxxx
another pencil = one more pencil	
the other + singular noun (last of the set)	xxxxx
the other pencil = the last pencil present	
other + plural noun (more of the set)	*other* + non-count nouns (more of the set)
other pencils = some more pencils	other water = some more water
the other + plural noun (the rest of the set)	*the other* + non-count noun (all the rest)
the other pencils = all remaining pencils	the other water = the remaining water

NOTE: *Another* and *other* are nonspecific while *the other* is specific. If the subject is understood, one can omit the noun and keep the determiner and *other* so that *other* functions as a pronoun. If it is a plural count noun that is omitted, *other* becomes *others*. The word *other* can NEVER be plural if it is followed by a noun.

I don't want this book. Please give me another.
(*another* = any other book–not specific)
I don't want this book. Please give me the other.
(*the other* = the other book–specific)
This chemical is poisonous. Others are poisonous too.
    (*others* = other chemicals–not specific)
I don't want these books. Please give me the others.
    (*the others* = the other books–specific)

NOTE: Another way of substituting for the noun is to use *other* + *one* or *ones*.

I don't want this book. Please give me another one.
I don't want this book. Please give me the other one.
This chemical is poisonous. Other ones are poisonous too.
I don't want these books. Please give me the other ones.

Exercise 5: **Other**

Fill in the blanks with the appropriate form of *other*.

1. This pen isn't working. Please give me _____. (singular)
2. If you're still thirsty, I'll make _another_ pot of coffee.
3. This dictionary has a page missing. Please give me _The other_. (the last one)
4. He does not need those books. He needs _The other_ (all the remaining)
5. There are thirty people in the room. Twenty are from Latin America and _The other_ are from _other_ countries.
6. Six people were in the store. Two were buying meat. _another_ was looking at magazines. _another_ was eating a candy bar. _The other_ were walking around looking for more food. (notice the verbs)
7. This glass of milk is sour. _The other_ glass of milk is sour too.
8. The army was practicing its drills. One group was doing artillery practice. _another_ was marching; _____ was at attention; and _The other_ was practicing combat tactics.
9. There are seven students from Japan. _others_ are from Iran, and _The other_ are from _other_ places.
10. We looked at four cars today. The first two were far too expensive, but _The other_ ones were reasonably priced.

NOTE: It is also possible to use the demonstrative articles *this, that, these,* and *those* as pronouns. It is correct to say *this one* and *that one;* however, it is not correct to say *these ones* or *those ones.* Simply use *these* or *those* as pronouns without adding *ones.*

This elevator is broken. That one is also broken. (*that one* = that elevator)
These glasses are dirty. Those are dirty also. (*those* = those glasses)

5. The Verb Phrase

As mentioned in item 3, the verb phrase consists of the main verb and any auxiliaries.

- *Tenses and aspects:*

simple present–He walks to school every day.
simple past–He walked to school yesterday.
present progressive (continuous)–He is walking to school now.
past progressive (continuous)–He was walking to school when he saw Jane.
present perfect–He has walked to school several times.
past perfect–He had walked to school before he hurt his foot.

Given here is a list of some of the common irregular verbs in English. It is very important that you know whether a verb is regular or irregular. You will notice that regular verbs are the same in the past tense and past participle; however, irregular verbs are very often different in these forms.

SIMPLE PRESENT TENSE	SIMPLE PAST TENSE	PAST PARTICIPLE	PRESENT PARTICIPLE
beat	beat	beaten	beating
begin	began	begun	beginning
bind	bound	bound	binding
bite	bit	bitten	biting
blow	blew	blown	blowing
break	broke	broken	breaking
bring	brought	brought	bringing
build	built	built	building
buy	bought	bought	buying
catch	caught	caught	catching
choose	chose	chosen	choosing
do	did	done	doing
drink	drank	drunk	drinking
drive	drove	driven	driving
eat	ate	eaten	eating
fall	fell	fallen	falling

SIMPLE PRESENT TENSE	SIMPLE PAST TENSE	PAST PARTICIPLE	PRESENT PARTICIPLE
feel	felt	felt	feeling
find	found	found	finding
fly	flew	flown	flying
forget	forgot	forgotten	forgetting
get	got	gotten	getting
give	gave	given	giving
hear	heard	heard	hearing
hide	hid	hidden	hiding
keep	kept	kept	keeping
know	knew	known	knowing
lead	led	led	leading
leave	left	left	leaving
lose	lost	lost	losing
make	made	made	making
meet	met	met	meeting
pay	paid	paid	paying
ride	rode	ridden	riding
run	ran	run	running
say	said	said	saying
see	saw	seen	seeing
sell	sold	sold	selling
send	sent	sent	sending
sing	sang	sung	singing
sink	sank	sunk	sinking
sit	sat	sat	sitting
speak	spoke	spoken	speaking
spend	spent	spent	spending
stand	stood	stood	standing
steal	stole	stolen	stealing
strive	strove (strived)	striven (strived)	striving
swim	swam	swum	swimming
take	took	taken	taking
teach	taught	taught	teaching
tear	tore	torn	tearing
tell	told	told	telling
think	thought	thought	thinking
throw	threw	thrown	throwing
understand	understood	understood	understanding
wear	wore	worn	wearing

You should also know that there is no change in the following verbs to indicate the different tenses.

SIMPLE PRESENT TENSE	SIMPLE PAST TENSE	PAST PARTICIPLE	PRESENT PARTICIPLE
bet	bet	bet	betting
bid	bid	bid	bidding
cost	cost	cost	costing
cut	cut	cut	cutting
fit	fit	fit	fitting
hit	hit	hit	hitting
put	put	put	putting
quit	quit	quit	quitting
read*	read	read	reading
shut	shut	shut	shutting
spread	spread	spread	spreading

Read is pronounced differently in the past tense and participle, but is spelled the same.

• *Simple present tense:* This tense is usually not used to indicate present time. However, it is used to indicate present time (now) with the following stative verbs.

know	believe	hear	see	smell	wish
understand	hate	love	like	want	sound
have	need	appear	seem	taste	own

NOTE: The verbs listed above are almost never used in the present or past progressive (continuous), although it is possible in some cases.

Simple present is used to indicate a regular or habitual action.

John walks to school every day.

Examples of simple present tense:

They understand the problem now.	(stative verb)
Henry always swims in the evening.	(habitual action)
We want to leave now.	(stative verb)
The coffee tastes delicious.	(stative verb)
Mark usually walks to school.	(habitual action)
Your cough sounds bad.	(stative verb)

● *Present progressive (continuous):* Use the following rule to form the present progressive.

$$\text{subject} + \begin{Bmatrix} am \\ is \\ are \end{Bmatrix} + [\text{verb} + ing] \ldots$$

The present progressive is used to indicate present time (now) with all but the stative verbs listed previously.

John is eating dinner now.

It is also used to indicate future time.

We are leaving for the theater at seven o'clock.

Examples of present progressive:

The committee members are examining the material now.	(present time)
George is leaving for France tomorrow.	(future time)
Henry is walking to school tomorrow.	(future time)
The president is trying to contact his advisors now.	(present time)
The secretary is typing the letter now.	(present time)
We are flying to Venezuela next month.	(future time)

Exercise 6: Simple Present and Present Progressive

Choose either the simple present or present progressive in the following sentences.

1. Something _____ (smell) very good.
2. We _____ (eat) dinner at seven o'clock tonight.
3. He _____ (practice) the piano every day.
4. They _____ (drive) to school tomorrow.
5. I _____ (believe) you.
6. Maria _____ (have) a cold.
7. Jorge _____ (swim) right now.
8. John _____ (hate) smoke.
9. Jill always _____ (get) up at 6:00 A.M.
10. Jerry _____ (mow) the lawn now.

● *Simple past tense:* The simple past is used for a *completed* action that happened at *one specific time* in the past. The italicized words are important because they show that simple past is not the same as past progressive or present perfect.

John <u>went</u> to Spain <u>last year</u>.
Bob <u>bought</u> a new bicycle <u>yesterday</u>.
Maria <u>did</u> her homework <u>last night</u>.
Mark <u>washed</u> the dishes <u>after dinner</u>.
We <u>drove</u> to the grocery store <u>this afternoon</u>.
George <u>cooked</u> dinner for his family <u>Saturday night</u>.

● *Past progressive (continuous):* Use the following rule to form the past progressive.

$$\text{subject} + \begin{Bmatrix} was \\ were \end{Bmatrix} + [\text{verb} + ing] \dots$$

The past progressive is used to indicate:

(1) An action which was occurring in the past and was interrupted by another action. In this case, the general rule is:

when + subject$_1$ + simple past tense + subject$_2$ + past progressive . . .

OR

subject$_1$ + past progressive + *when* + subject$_2$ + simple past tense . . .

<u>When</u> Mark <u>came</u> home, Martha <u>was watching</u> television.

OR

Martha <u>was watching</u> television <u>when</u> Mark <u>came</u> home.

(2) Two actions occurring at the same time in the past. In this case, the following rules usually apply.

subject$_1$ + past progressive + *while* + subject$_2$ + past progressive . . .

OR

while + subject$_1$ + past progressive + subject$_2$ + past progressive . . .

Martha <u>was watching</u> television <u>while</u> John <u>was reading</u> a book.

OR

<u>While</u> John <u>was reading</u> a book, Martha <u>was watching</u> television.

NOTE: The following construction is also possible, but it is not as common as the preceding two.

> while + subject₁ + past progressive + subject₂ + simple past . . .

While Martha was watching television, John read a book.

(3) An action which was occurring at some specific time in the past.

Martha was watching television at seven o'clock last night.
What were you doing at one o'clock this afternoon?

Examples of past progressive:

John was walking to class when he lost his pen.
The student was reading while the professor was speaking.
George was watching television when his brother called.
Henry was eating a snack at midnight last night.
When Mary came home, her husband was cooking dinner.
Mark was driving on Main Street when his car broke down.

Exercise 7: Simple Past Tense and Past Progressive

Use either the simple past tense or the past progressive in the following sentences as appropriate.

1. Gene _____ (eat) dinner when his friend called.
2. While Maria was cleaning the apartment, her husband _slept_ _____ (sleep).
3. At three o'clock this morning, Eleanor _____ (study).
4. When Mark arrived, the Johnsons _____ (have) dinner, but they stopped in order to talk to him.
5. John _____ (go) to France last year.
6. When the teacher _____ (enter) the room, the students were talking.
7. While Joan was writing the report, Henry _____ (look) for more information.
8. We _____ (see) this movie last night.
9. At one time, Mr. Roberts _____ (own) this building.
10. Jose _____ (write) a letter to his family when his pencil _____ (break).

● *Present perfect:* Use the following rule to form the present perfect.

> subject + $\begin{Bmatrix} has \\ have \end{Bmatrix}$ + [verb in past participle] . . .

The present perfect is used to indicate:

(1) An action that happened at an indefinite time in the past.

John has traveled around the world. (We don't know when.)

(2) An action that happened more than once in the past.

George has seen this movie three times.

(3) An action that began in the past and is still occurring in the present.

John has lived in the same house for twenty years. (He still lives there.)

OR

John has lived in the same house since 1962. (He still lives there.)

If it is now 1982:

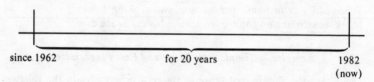

since 1962   for 20 years   1982
(now)

● *For/since:* Use *for* + duration of time: *for five hours, for thirty years, for ten minutes.* Use *since* + beginning time: *since 1972, since five o'clock, since January.*

● *Yet/already:* The adverbs *yet* and *already* are used to indicate that something has happened (or hasn't happened) at an unspecified time in the past. These adverbs are often used with the present perfect.

> *already*–affirmative sentences
> *yet*–negative sentences and questions

NOTE: *Already* usually appears between the auxiliary and the main verb; however, it can appear at the beginning or end of the sentence. *Yet* appears at the end of the sentence.

subject + $\begin{Bmatrix} has \\ have \end{Bmatrix}$ + *already* + [verb in past participle] . . .

subject + $\begin{Bmatrix} has \\ have \end{Bmatrix}$ + *not* + [verb in past participle] . . . + *yet* . . .

Examples of *yet* and *already*:

We have already written our reports.
We haven't written our reports yet.
Gabriel has already read the entire book.
The president hasn't decided what to do yet.
Sam has already recorded the results of the experiment.
Maria hasn't called her parents yet.

NOTE: Another option with the use of *yet* is sometimes possible. In this case, the verb is positive and the adverb *yet* does not appear at the end of the sentence.

$$\text{subject} + \begin{Bmatrix} has \\ have \end{Bmatrix} + yet + \text{[verb in infinitive]} \ldots$$

John has yet to learn the material. = John hasn't learned the material yet.
We have yet to decide what to do with the money. = We haven't decided what to do with the money yet.

• *Present perfect progressive (continuous):* For category (3) of the present perfect rules only, it is also possible to use the present perfect progressive (continuous). Use the following rule to form this aspect.

$$\text{subject} + \begin{Bmatrix} has \\ have \end{Bmatrix} + been + \text{[verb} + ing] \ldots$$

John has been living in the same house for twenty years. = John has lived in the same house for twenty years.

Examples of present perfect:

Jorge has already walked to school.	(indefinite time)
He has been to California three times.	(more than once)
John has worked in Washington for three years.	
OR	(not yet completed)
John has been working in Washington for three years.	
Mary has seen this movie before.	(indefinite time)
They have been at home all day.	(not yet completed)
We haven't gone to the store yet.	(indefinite time)

Exercise 8: Present Perfect and Simple Past

Use either the present perfect or the simple past in the following sentences.

1. John _____ (write) his report last night.
2. Bob _____ (see) this movie before.
3. Jorge _____ (read) the newspaper already.
4. Mr. Johnson _____ (work) in the same place for thirty-five years, and he is not planning to retire yet.
5. We _____ (begin; negative) to study for the test yet.
6. George _____ (go) to the store at ten o'clock this morning.
7. Joan _____ (travel) around the world.
8. Betty _____ (write) a letter last night.
9. Guillermo _____ (call) his employer yesterday.
10. We _____ (see; negative) this movie yet.

- *Past perfect:* Use the following rule to form the past perfect.

> subject + *had* + [verb in past participle] . . .

The past perfect is used to indicate:

(1) An action that happened before another action in the past; there usually are two actions in the sentence.

John <u>had gone</u> to the store <u>before</u> he went home.
    1st action   *2nd action*

Jack <u>told</u> us yesterday that he <u>had visited</u> England in 1970.
  2nd action   *1st action*

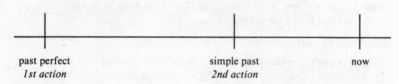

past perfect	simple past	now
1st action	*2nd action*	

The past perfect is usually used with the adverbs *before, after,* or *when.* Study the following formulas.

> subject + past perfect + *before* + subject + simple past tense

John <u>had gone</u> to the store <u>before</u> he <u>went</u> home.

> subject + simple past tense + *after* + subject + past perfect

John went home after he had gone to the store.

> *before* + subject + simple past tense + subject + past perfect

Before John went home, he had gone to the store.

> *after* + subject + past perfect + subject + simple past tense

After John had gone to the store, he went home.

NOTE: The adverb *when* can be used in place of *before* or *after* in any of these four formulas without change in meaning. We still know which action happened first because of the use of past perfect.

(2) A state which continued for a time in the past, but stopped before now. This is similar to rule number (3) for present perfect, but in this case, there is no connection with the present.

Abdu had lived in New York for ten years before he moved to California.

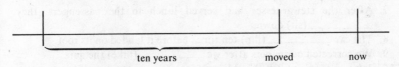

ten years   moved   now

● *Past perfect progressive (continuous):* For category (2) of past perfect only, we can also use the past perfect progressive (continuous). Study the following rule.

> subject + *had* + *been* + [verb + *ing*] . . .

Abdu had been living in New York for ten years before he moved to California.

Examples of past perfect:

The professor had reviewed the material before he gave the quiz.
After Henry had visited Puerto Rico, he went to St. Thomas.
Before Ali went to sleep, he had called his family.

George had worked at the university for forty-five years before he retired.

OR

George had been working at the university for forty-five years before he retired.

After the committee members had considered the consequences, they voted on the proposal.

The doctor had examined the patient thoroughly before he prescribed the medication.

Exercise 9: Past Perfect and Simple Past

Supply the past perfect or simple past in the following sentences.

1. The policeman read the suspect his rights after he ___had___ (arrest) him.
2. After John ___had___ (wash) his clothes, he began to study.
3. George ___had___ (wait) for one hour before the bus came.
4. Maria ___entered___ (enter) the university after she had graduated from the community college.
5. Jeanette ___washed___ (wash) the pipettes after she had completed the experiment.
6. Jane sent a letter to her university after she _____ (receive) her scholarship check.
7. After the stewardesses had served lunch to the passengers, they _____ (sit) down.
8. The car _____ (flip) ten times before it landed on its roof.
9. We corrected our papers after we _____ (take) the quiz.
10. John ___had___ (live) in Miami for one year when his parents came to visit.

6. Subject-Verb Agreement

Remember that the subject and verb in a sentence must agree in person and number.

The elevator works very well.   The elevators work very well.
   singular singular   *plural plural*

● *Subject separated from the verb:* When taking the TOEFL, you must always check the subject and verb to be sure they agree. However, sometimes it is difficult to decide exactly what the subject is if the subject and verb are separated.

The boys in the room are studying.
  plural   plural

Very often, if the subject and verb are separated, they will be separated by a prepositional phrase. The prepositional phrase has no effect on the verb.

```
subject + [prepositional phrase] + verb
```

The study of languages is very interesting.
<u>singular subject</u>   <u>singular verb</u>

Several theories on this subject have been proposed.
<u>plural subject</u>   <u>plural verb</u>

The view of these disciplines varies from time to time.
<u>singular subject</u>   <u>singular verb</u>

The danger of forest fires is not to be taken lightly.
<u>singular subject</u>   <u>singular verb</u>

The effects of that crime are likely to be devastating.
<u>plural subject</u>   <u>plural verb</u>

The fear of rape and robbery has caused many people to flee the cities.
<u>singular subject</u>   <u>singular verb</u>

The following expressions also have no effect on the verb.

```
together with        along with
accompanied by       as well as
```

The actress , along with her manager and some friends, is going to
<u>singular subject</u>   <u>singular verb</u>

a party tonight.

Mr. Robbins , accompanied by his wife and children, is arriving tonight.
<u>singular subject</u>   <u>singular verb</u>

NOTE: If the conjunction *and* is used instead of one of these phrases, the verb would then be plural.

The actress and her manager are going to a party tonight.
<u>plural subject</u>   <u>plural verb</u>

Exercise 10: Subject-Verb Agreement

Choose the correct form of the verb in parentheses in the following sentences.

1. John, along with twenty friends, (is/are) planning a party.
2. The picture of the soldiers (bring/brings) back many memories.
3. The quality of these recordings (is/are) not very good.
4. If the duties of these officers (isn't/aren't) reduced, there will not be enough time to finish the project.
5. The effects of cigarette smoking (have/has) been proven to be extremely harmful.

6. The use of credit cards in place of cash (have/has) increased rapidly in recent years.
7. Advertisements on television (is/are) becoming more competitive than ever before.
8. Living expenses in this country, as well as in many others, (is/are) at an all-time high.
9. Mr. Jones, accompanied by several members of the committee, (have/has) proposed some changes of the rules.
10. The levels of intoxication (vary/varies) from subject to subject.

● *Words that always take singular verbs and pronouns:* Some words are often confused by students as being plural. The following words must be followed by singular verbs and pronouns in formal written English:

any + singular noun		some + singular noun	every	each
anybody	nobody	somebody	everybody	either*
anyone	no one	someone	everyone	neither*
anything	nothing	something	everything	

*either and neither are singular if they are not used with *or* and *nor*.

Everybody who has not purchased a ticket should be in this line.
Something was under the house.
If either of you takes a vacation now, we will not be able to finish the work.
Anybody who has lost his ticket should report to the desk. (note the singular pronoun)
No problem is harder to solve than this one.
Nobody works harder than John does.

● *None/no: None* can take either a singular or plural verb depending on the noun which follows it.

> *none + of the + non-count noun + singular verb*

None of the counterfeit money has been found.

> *none + of the + plural count noun + plural verb*

None of the students have finished the exam yet.

No can take either a singular or plural verb depending on the noun which follows it.

$$no + \begin{Bmatrix} \text{singular noun} \\ \text{non-count noun} \end{Bmatrix} + \text{singular verb}$$

No <u>example</u> <u>is</u> relevant to this case.

$$no + \text{plural noun} + \text{plural verb}$$

No <u>examples</u> <u>are</u> relevant to this case.

● *Either/neither:* When *either* and *neither* are followed by *or* and *nor* the verb may be singular or plural depending on whether the noun following *or* and *nor* is singular or plural. If *or* or *nor* appears alone, the same rule applies. Study the following formulas.

$$\begin{Bmatrix} neither \\ either \end{Bmatrix} + \text{noun} + \begin{Bmatrix} nor \\ or \end{Bmatrix} + \text{plural noun} + \text{plural verb}$$

<u>Neither</u> John <u>nor</u> <u>his friends</u> <u>are going</u> to the beach today.
plural noun   plural verb

<u>Either</u> John <u>or</u> <u>his friends</u> <u>are going</u> to the beach today.
plural noun   plural verb

$$\begin{Bmatrix} neither \\ either \end{Bmatrix} + \text{noun} + \begin{Bmatrix} nor \\ or \end{Bmatrix} + \text{singular noun} + \text{singular verb}$$

<u>Neither</u> John <u>nor</u> <u>Bill</u> <u>is going</u> to the beach today.
singular   singular
noun   verb

<u>Either</u> John <u>or</u> <u>Bill</u> <u>is going</u> to the beach today.
singular   singular
subject   verb

Examples:

<u>Neither</u> John <u>nor</u> <u>Jane</u> <u>is going</u> to class today.
singular   singular

<u>Neither</u> Maria <u>nor</u> <u>her friends</u> <u>are going</u> to class today.
plural   plural

John <u>or</u> <u>George</u> <u>is bringing</u> the car.
singular   singular

<u>Neither</u> Alecia <u>nor</u> <u>Carmen</u> <u>has seen</u> this movie before.
singular   singular

<u>Neither</u> the director <u>nor</u> <u>the secretary</u> <u>wants</u> to leave yet.
singular   singular

● *Gerunds as subjects:* If a sentence begins with [verb + *ing*] (gerund), the verb must also be singular.

Knowing her has made him what he is.
Dieting is very popular today.
Not studying has caused him many problems.
Washing with a special cream is recommended for scalp infections.
Being cordial is one of his greatest assets.
Writing many letters makes her happy.

● *Collective nouns:* Also many words indicating a number of people or animals are singular. The following nouns are *usually singular*. In some cases they are plural if the sentence indicates that the individual members are acting separately.

Congress	family	group	committee	class
organization	team	army	club	crowd
government	jury	majority*	minority	public

*Majority can be singular or plural. If it is alone it is usually singular; if it is followed by a plural noun, it is usually plural.

The majority believes that we are in no danger.
The majority of the students believe him to be innocent.

Examples of collective nouns:

The committee has met, and it has rejected the proposal.
The family was elated by the news.
The crowd was wild with excitement.
Congress has initiated a new plan to combat inflation.
The organization has lost many members this year.
Our team is going to win the game.

The following nouns are used to indicate groups of certain animals. It is not necessary to learn the nouns; however, they mean the same as *group* and thus are considered singular.

flock of birds, sheep	school of fish
herd of cattle	pride of lions
pack of dogs	

The flock of birds is circling overhead.
The herd of cattle is breaking away.
A school of fish is being attacked by sharks.

Collective nouns indicating time, money, and measurements used as a whole are singular.

Twenty-five dollars is too much to pay for that shirt.
Fifty minutes isn't enough time to finish this test.
Twenty dollars is all I can afford to pay for that recorder.
Two miles is too much to run in one day.

- *A number of/the number of:*

> a number of + plural noun + plural verb . . .

> the number of + plural noun + singular verb . . .

A number of students are going to the class picnic. (*a number of* = many)
The number of days in a week is seven.
A number of the applicants have already been interviewed.
The number of residents who have been questioned on this matter is quite small.

- *Nouns that are always plural:* The following nouns are always considered plural. They cannot be singular. In order to speak of them as singular, one must say: "a pair of _____"

scissors	shorts	pants	jeans	tongs
trousers	glasses	pliers	tweezers	

The pants are in the drawer.
A pair of pants is in the drawer.
The pliers were on the table.
The pair of pliers was on the table.
These scissors are dull.
This pair of scissors is dull.

- *There is/there are:* Remember that with sentences beginning with the existential *there,* the subject is actually after the verb.

> there is
> there was   + singular subject . . .
> there has been   (or non-count)

$$\left.\begin{array}{l} \textit{there are} \\ \textit{there were} \\ \textit{there have been} \end{array}\right\} \ + \text{plural subject} \ldots$$

There is a storm approaching.
    singular   *singular*

There have been a number of telephone calls today.
        plural   *plural*

There was an accident last night.
    singular   *singular*

There were too many people at the party.
    plural   *plural*

There has been an increase in the importation of foreign cars.
    singular   *singular*

There was water on the floor where he fell.
    singular   *non-count*

Exercise 11: Subject-Verb Agreement

Choose the correct form of the verb in the following sentences.

1. Neither Bill nor Mary (is/are) going to the play tonight.
2. Anything (is/are) better than going to another movie tonight.
3. Skating (is/are) becoming more popular every day.
4. A number of reporters (was/were) at the conference yesterday.
5. Everybody who (has/have) a fever must go home immediately.
6. Your glasses (was/were) on the bureau last night.
7. There (was/were) some people at the meeting last night.
8. The committee (has/have) already reached a decision.
9. A pair of jeans (was/were) in the washing machine this morning.
10. Each student (has/have) answered the first three questions.
11. Either John or his wife (make/makes) breakfast each morning.
12. After she had perused the material, the secretary decided that everything (was/were) in order.
13. The crowd at the basketball game (was/were) wild with excitement.
14. A pack of wild dogs (has/have) frightened all the ducks away.
15. The jury (is/are) trying to reach a decision.
16. The army (has/have) eliminated this section of the training test.
17. The number of students who have withdrawn from class this quarter (is/are) appalling.
18. There (has/have) been too many interruptions in this class.
19. Every elementary school teacher (has/have) to take this examination.
20. Neither Jill nor her parents (has/have) seen this movie before.

7. *Pronouns*

There are five forms of pronouns in English: subject pronouns, complement pronouns (object pronouns), possessive pronouns, possessive adjectives, and reflexive pronouns.

● *Subject pronouns:* Subject pronouns occur in the subject position of a sentence or after the verb *be*. Study the following list of subject pronouns.

I	we
you	you
he	
she	they
it	

NOTE: Also use the subject pronoun after *than, as,* and *that.*

<u>I</u> am going to the store.
subject

<u>We</u> have lived here for twenty years.
subject

It was <u>she</u> who called you. (after the verb *be*)

<u>She and I</u> have seen this movie before.
    subject

<u>George and I</u> would like to leave now.
     subject

<u>We students</u> are going to have a party.
   subject

NOTE: *We, you,* and *us* can be followed directly by a noun. In the above sentence *we students* makes it more clear exactly who *we* refers to.

● *Complement pronouns:* Complement pronouns occur in complement position or after prepositions unless the preposition introduces a new clause. Study the following list.

me	us
you	you
him	
her	them
it	

NOTE: *You* and *it* are the same for subject or complement position. The others are different.

They called <u>us</u> on the telephone.
    complement

The teacher gave <u>him</u> a bad grade.
complement
John told <u>her</u> a story.
complement
The policeman was looking for <u>him</u>.
after
preposition
To <u>us</u>, it seems like a good bargain.
after
preposition
Mary is going to class with <u>me</u>.
after
preposition

However, remember that if the preposition introduces a new clause, the pronoun will be subject form because it is actually in the subject position of the second clause.

We will leave after <u>he comes</u>.
second clause

● *Possessive adjectives:* Possessive adjectives are *not the same as possessive pronouns*. These simply modify, rather than replace, nouns; possessive pronouns replace nouns. Possessive forms indicate ownership. Study the following adjectives.

my	our
your	your
his	
her	their
its	

NOTE: Possessive adjectives are used to refer to parts of a body.

John is eating <u>his dinner</u>.
This is not <u>my book</u>.
The cat has injured <u>its foot</u>.
The boy broke <u>his arm</u> yesterday.
She forgot <u>her homework</u> this morning.
<u>My food</u> is cold.

NOTE: *Its* is not the same as *It's*. *It's* means *it is*.

● *Possessive pronouns:* These pronouns cannot precede a noun. They are pronouns and thus replace the noun. The noun is understood from the context and is not repeated. Study the following pronouns.

NOTE: mine = *my* + noun; for example, *my book*
         yours = *your* + noun; for example, *your pen*
         hers = *her* + noun; for example, *her dress*

mine	ours
yours	yours
his	
hers	theirs
its	

NOTE: *His* and *its* are the same whether they precede a noun or not.

Examples of possessive pronouns:

This is my book.   This is mine.
Your teacher is the same as his teacher.   Yours is the same as his.
Her dress is green and my dress is red.   Hers is green and mine is red.
Our books are heavy.   Ours are heavy.
Their coats are too small.   Theirs are too small.
I forgot my homework.   I forgot mine.

• *Reflexive pronouns:* These pronouns usually follow the verb and indicate that the subject is both giving and receiving the action. Study the following list.

myself	ourselves
yourself	yourselves
himself	
herself	themselves
itself	

NOTE: In the plural, the *self* changes to *selves*.

NOTE: Most forms are made by adding the suffix to the possessive adjective; however, *himself, itself* and *themselves* are made by adding the suffix to the complement form. The forms *hisself* and *theirselves* are ALWAYS INCORRECT.

NOTE: John bought him a new car. (*him* = another person)

John bought himself a new car.   (*himself* = John)

Examples of reflexive pronouns:

I washed myself.
He sent the letter to himself.
She served herself in the cafeteria.
We hurt ourselves playing football.
They were talking among themselves.
You can see the difference for yourselves.

Reflexive pronouns can also be used for emphasis. This means that the subject did the action alone. In this case, it normally follows the subject.

I myself believe that the proposal is good.
He himself set out to break the long distance flying record.

She herself prepared the nine-course meal.
The students themselves decorated the room.
You yourself must do this homework.
John himself bought these gifts.

NOTE: *by* + reflexive pronoun can also mean *alone*.

John washed the dishes by himself = John washed the dishes *alone*.

Exercise 12: Pronouns

Circle the correct form of the pronoun or possessive adjective in the following sentences.

1. I go to school with (he/him) every day.
2. I see (she/her/herself) at the Union every Friday.
3. She speaks to (we/us/ourselves) every morning.
4. Isn't (she/her) a nice person?
5. (He/Him) is going to New York on vacation.
6. (She/Her) and John gave the money to the boy.
7. (Yours/Your) record is scratched and (my/mine) is too.
8. I hurt (my/mine/the) leg.
9. John bought (himself/herself/hisself) a new coat.
10. (We/Us) girls are going camping over the weekend.
11. Mr. Jones cut (hisself/himself) shaving.
12. We like (our/ours) new car very much.
13. The dog bit (she/her) on the leg.
14. John (he/himself) went to the meeting.
15. You'll stick (you/your/yourself) with the pins if you are not careful.
16. Mary and (I/me) would rather go to the movies.
17. Everyone has to do (their/his) own research.
18. Just between you and (I/me), I don't like this food.
19. Monday is a holiday for (we/us) teachers.
20. (Her/Hers) car does not go as fast as (our/ours).

8. Verbs as Complements

● *Verbs that are always followed by the infinitive:* Some verbs can take another verb as the complement instead of a noun. Sometimes the verb functioning as the complement must be in the infinitive (*to* + verb) and sometimes it must be in the gerund (verb + *ing*) form. The following verbs are always followed by the infinitive if the complement is a verb.

agree	attempt	claim	decide	demand
desire	fail	forget	hesitate	hope
intend	learn	need	offer	plan
prepare	pretend	refuse	seem	strive
tend	try	want	wish	

John expects to begin studying law next semester.
Mary learned to swim when she was very young.
The budget committee decided to postpone this meeting.
The president will attempt to reduce inflation in the next four years.
The soldiers are preparing to attack the village.
Cynthia has agreed to act as a liason between the two countries.

● *Verbs that are always followed by the gerund:* Other verbs must always be followed by the gerund. These verbs include:

admit	appreciate	avoid	can't help	consider
delay	deny	enjoy	finish	mind
miss	postpone	practice	quit	recall
regret	report	resent	resist	resume
risk	suggest			

John admitted stealing the jewels.
We enjoyed seeing them again after so many years.
You shouldn't risk entering that building in its present condition.
Michael was considering buying a new car until the prices went up.
The Coast Guard has reported seeing another ship in the Florida Straits.
Would you mind not smoking in this office?

NOTE: These sentences are made negative by adding the negative particle *not* before the infinitive or gerund.

John decided not to buy the car.
We regretted not going to the party last night.

The following verbs can be followed by either the infinitive or the gerund with no change in meaning.

begin	can't stand	continue	dread	hate
like	love	prefer	start	

He started to study after dinner.   OR   He started studying after dinner.
Joan hates to ride her bicycle to school.   OR   Joan hates riding her bicycle to school.

• *Verbs + prepositions followed by the gerund:* If a verb + preposition, adjective + preposition, noun + preposition, or preposition alone is followed directly by a verb, the verb will always be in the gerund form. The following list consists of verbs + prepositions.

approve of	be better off	count on	depend on
give up	insist on	keep on	put off
rely on	succeed in	think about	think of
worry about			

The following expressions contain the preposition *to*. The word *to* in these expressions must not be confused with the *to* in the infinitive. These verb + preposition expressions must also be followed by the gerund.

| object to | look forward to | confess to |

TO verb + ing

John gave up smoking because of his doctor's advice.
Mary insisted on taking the bus instead of the plane.
Fred confessed to stealing the jewels.
We are not looking forward to going back to school.
Henry is thinking of going to France in August.
You would be better off leaving now instead of tomorrow.

• *Adjectives + prepositions followed by the gerund:* The following adjectives + prepositions are also followed by the gerund.

| accustomed to | afraid of | capable of | fond of |
| intent on | interested in | successful in | tired of |

verb + ing

Mitch is afraid of getting married now.
We are accustomed to sleeping late on weekends.
Jean is not capable of understanding the predicament.
Alvaro is intent on finishing school next year.
Craig is fond of dancing.
We are interested in seeing this film.

• *Nouns + prepositions followed by the gerund:* The following nouns + prepositions are also followed by the gerund.

| choice of | excuse for | intention of | method for |
| possibility of | | reason for | (method of) |

verb + ing

George has no excuse for dropping out of school.
There is a possibility of acquiring this property at a good price.
There is no reason for leaving this early.
Connie has developed a method for evaluating this problem.

Any time a preposition is followed directly by a verb, the verb will be in the gerund form. (ing)

After leaving the party, Ali drove home.
He should have stayed in New York instead of moving to Maine.

• *Adjectives followed by the infinitive:* The following adjectives are always followed by the infinitive form of the verb and never by the gerund.

anxious	boring	dangerous	hard
eager	easy	good	strange
pleased	prepared	ready	able*
usual	common	difficult	

Able means the same as *capable* in many instances, but the grammar is very different. While *able* is followed by the infinitive, *capable* is followed by *of* + [verb + *ing*].

These students are not yet able to handle such difficult problems.
These students are not yet capable of handling such difficult problems.

Examples of adjectives followed by infinitives:

Mohammad is anxious to see his family.
It is dangerous to drive in this weather.
We are ready to leave now.
It is difficult to pass this test.
It is uncommon to find such good crops in this section of the country.
Ritsuko was pleased to be admitted to the college.

Some verbs can be followed by either the infinitive or the gerund, but the meaning changes.

stop	remember	forget

John stopped studying.   (John is not going to study anymore.)
John stopped to study   (John stopped doing something in order to study.)

Exercise 13: Verbs as Complements

Choose the correct form of the verb in parentheses in the following sentences.

1. The teacher decided (accepting/to accept) the paper.
2. They appreciate (to have/having) this information.
3. His father doesn't approve of his (going/to go) to Europe.
4. We found it very difficult (reaching/to reach) a decision.
5. Donna is interested in (to open/opening) a bar.
6. George has no intention of (to leave/leaving) the city now.
7. We are eager (to return/returning) to school in the fall.
8. You would be better off (to buy/buying) this car.
9. She refused (to accept/accepting) the gift.
10. Mary regrets (to be/being) the one to have to tell him.
11. George pretended (to be/being) sick yesterday.
12. Carlos hopes (to finish/finishing) his thesis this year.
13. They agreed (to leave/leaving) early.
14. Helen was anxious (to tell/telling) her family about her promotion.
15. We are not ready (to stop/stopping) this research at this time.
16. Henry shouldn't risk (to drive/driving) so fast.
17. He demands (to know/knowing) what is going on.
18. She is looking forward to (return/returning) to her country.
19. There is no excuse for (to leave/leaving) the room in this condition.
20. Gerald returned to his home after (to leave/leaving) the game.

● *Pronouns before the gerund or infinitive:* In cases where the infinitive is used as a complement, any noun or pronoun directly preceding it will be in the *complement form.* Some common verbs which are followed by the infinitive and which often require an indirect object are listed here.

allow	ask	beg	convince	expect	instruct
invite	order	permit	persuade	prepare	promise
remind	urge	want			

$$\text{subject + verb + complement form} \begin{Bmatrix} \text{pronoun} \\ \text{noun} \end{Bmatrix} + [to + \text{verb}] \ldots$$

Joe asked Mary to call him when she woke up.
We ordered him to appear in court.
I urge you to reconsider your decision.
They were trying to persuade him to change his mind.
The teacher permitted them to turn their assignments in late.
You should prepare your son to take this examination.

However, before the gerund, a noun or pronoun must appear in the *possessive form.*

$$\text{subject} + \text{verb} + \text{possessive form} \begin{Bmatrix} \text{noun} \\ \text{pronoun} \end{Bmatrix} + [\text{verb} + ing] \ldots$$

We understand your not being able to stay longer.
He regrets her leaving.
We are looking forward to their coming next year.
We don't approve of John's buying this house.
We resent the teacher's not announcing the test sooner.
We object to their calling at this hour.

Exercise 14: Pronouns with Verbs as Complements

Choose the correct form of the pronoun in each of the following sentences.

1. Richard is expecting (us/our) to go to class tomorrow.
2. You shouldn't rely on (him/his) calling you in the morning.
3. They don't approve of (us/our) leaving early.
4. George asked (me/my) to call him last night.
5. We understand (him/his) having to leave early.
6. John resented (George/George's) losing the paper.
7. We object to (the defense attorney/the defense attorney's) calling the extra witness.
8. We are expecting (Henry/Henry's) to call us.
9. They are looking forward to (us/our) visiting them.
10. Susan regrets (John/John's) being in trouble.

9. The Verb Need

The verb *need* is followed by the infinitive only if a living thing is the subject. If a thing (an inanimate object) is the subject of this verb, the verb is followed by a gerund or the verb *be* plus the past participle.

$$\text{living thing as subject} + [\text{verb in infinitive}] \ldots$$

John and his brother need to paint the house.
My friend needs to learn Spanish.
He will need to drive alone tonight.

$$
\text{thing as subject} + \begin{cases} \text{[verb + } ing\text{]} \\ to\ be + \text{[verb in past participle]} \end{cases} \cdots
$$

The grass <u>needs</u> <u>cutting</u>.   OR   The grass <u>needs to be cut</u>.
The television <u>needs</u> <u>repairing</u>.   OR   The television <u>needs</u> to be repaired.
The composition <u>needs</u> rewriting.   OR   The composition <u>needs</u> <u>to be</u> rewritten.

● *In need of:* It is also possible to use the expression *in need of* in some cases instead of using *need* as a verb. Because *need* is not a verb in this case, it must be preceded by the verb *be*. Study the following rule.

$$
\boxed{\text{subject} + be + in\ need\ of + \text{noun} \ldots}
$$

Jill <u>is</u> <u>in need of</u> <u>money</u>.   (Jill needs money.)
The <u>roof</u> <u>is</u> <u>in need of</u> <u>repair</u>.   (The roof needs to be repaired.)
The <u>organization</u> <u>is</u> <u>in need of</u> <u>volunteers</u>. (The organization needs volunteers.)

Exercise 15: Need

Supply the correct form of the verb after *need* in each of the following sentences.

1. It's too hot and my hair needs _____ (cut).
2. The flowers need to be _____ (water).
3. James needs _____ (see) a doctor soon.
4. Mary will need _____ (make) a new dress for the party.
5. His car needs _____ (tune).
6. You will need _____ (be) here at eight.
7. The squeaky door needs to be _____ (oil).
8. I need _____ (go) shopping this afternoon.
9. They need _____ (study) harder for that test.
10. The house needs to be _____ (paint) soon.

10. Questions

Remember that, when forming a question, one must place the auxiliary or the verb *be* before the subject. If there is no auxiliary or *be*, one must use the correct form of *do, does,* or *did*. After *do, does,* or *did,* the simple form of the verb must be used. The tense and person are only shown by this auxiliary, not by the main verb.

- Yes/no *questions:* These are questions for which the answer is *yes* or *no.*

$$\begin{Bmatrix} \text{auxiliary} \\ be \\ do, does, did \end{Bmatrix} + \text{subject} + \text{verb} \ldots$$

<u>Is</u> Mary <u>going</u> to school today?
<u>Was</u> Mark sick yesterday?
<u>Have</u> you <u>seen</u> this movie before?
<u>Will</u> the committee <u>decide</u> on the proposal today?
<u>Do</u> you <u>want</u> to use the telephone?
<u>Does</u> George <u>like</u> peanut butter?
<u>Did</u> you <u>go</u> to class yesterday?

- *Information questions:* These are questions for which the answer is more than *yes* or *no;* there must be some information in the answer. There are three different rules in this part:

(1) *Who* or *what* in subject questions: A subject question is one in which the *subject is unknown.*

$$\begin{Bmatrix} who \\ what \end{Bmatrix} + \text{verb} + \text{(complement)} + \text{(modifier)}$$

<u>Someone</u> <u>opened</u> the door.   (*Who* opened the door?)
<u>Something</u> <u>happened</u> last night.   (*What* happened last night?)

Note: It is NOT CORRECT to say: <u>Who</u> did open the door?
<u>What</u> did happen last night?

(2) *Whom* and *what* in complement questions: A complement question is one in which the *complement is unknown.*

$$\begin{Bmatrix} whom \\ what \end{Bmatrix} + \begin{Bmatrix} \text{auxiliary} \\ do, does, did \end{Bmatrix} + \text{subject} + \text{verb} + \text{(modifier)}$$

NOTE: Although in speech, most people use *who* rather than *whom* in these questions, in correct written English, you should use *whom* to indicate that the question word comes from the complement position.

Ahmad <u>knows</u> <u>someone</u> from Venezuela. <u>Whom</u> <u>does</u> Ahmad <u>know</u> from Venezuela?
George <u>bought</u> <u>something</u> at the store. <u>What</u> <u>did</u> George <u>buy</u> at the store?

(3) *When, where, how,* and *why* questions: These questions are formed the same as complement questions.

$$\left.\begin{cases} when \\ where \\ how \\ why \end{cases}\right\} + \text{auxiliary} + \text{subject} + \text{verb} + \text{(complement)} + \text{(modifier)} \ldots$$

When did John move to Jacksonville?
Where does Mohammad live?
Why did George leave so early?
How did Maria get to school today?
Where has Henry gone?
When will Bertha go back to Mexico?

• *Embedded questions:* An embedded question is one which is included in a sentence or another question. The word order is *not* that of typical questions except for subject questions. Study the following rule.

subject + verb (phrase) + question word + subject + verb

NOTE: There *must not* be an auxiliary between the question word and the subject in an embedded question.

Question: Where will the meeting take place?
Embedded question: We haven't ascertained where the meeting
           Q word *subject*
       will take place.
       verb phrase

Question: Why did the plane land at the wrong airport?
Embedded question: The authorities cannot figure out why the plane
              Q word *subject*
       landed at the wrong airport.
       verb

The following rule applies if the embedded question is embedded in another question.

auxiliary + subject + verb + question word + subject + verb

Do you know where he went?
Could you tell me what time it is?

NOTE: Question words can be single words or phrases. Phrases include: *whose* + noun, *how many, how much, how long, how often, what time,* and *what kind.*

The professor didn't know <u>how many students</u> would be in her afternoon class.

I have no idea <u>how long</u> the interview will take.

Do they know <u>how often</u> the bus runs at night?

Can you tell me <u>how far</u> the museum is from the college?

I'll tell you <u>what kind</u> of ice cream tastes best.

The teacher asked us <u>whose book</u> was on his desk.

NOTE: There is no change in the order of subject position questions because the question word is functioning as the subject.

<u>Who will paint</u> that picture?

They can't decide <u>who will paint</u> that picture?

<u>Whose car is parked</u> in the lot?

The police can't determine <u>whose car is parked</u> in the lot.

Exercise 16: Embedded Questions

Complete the following sentences making embedded questions from the questions given before each one. Example: Where did he go? I know <u>where he went.</u>

1. Who will be elected president? I'm not sure _____.

2. Whose book is it? They haven't discovered _____.

3. How much will it cost to repair the car? The mechanic told me _____.

4. How was the murder committed? The police are still trying to decide _____.

5. How tall is John? Do you know _____?

6. How well does she play the guitar? You can't imagine _____ _____.

7. When will the next exam take place? Do you know _____ _____?

8. Where did they spend their vacation? Angela told me _____ .

9. Why are they buying a new house? I don't know _____ _____.

10. How long does the class last? The catalog doesn't say _____ _____.

• *Tag questions:* In a tag question, the speaker makes a statement, but is not completely certain of the truth, so he or she uses a tag question to verify the previous statement. Sentences using tag questions should have the main clause separated from the tag by a comma. The sentence will always end with a question mark. Observe the following rules.

1. Use the same auxiliary verb as in the main clause. If there is no auxiliary, use *do, does,* or *did.*
2. If the main clause is negative, the tag is affirmative; if the main clause is affirmative, the tag is negative.
3. Don't change the tense.
4. Use the same subject in the main clause and the tag. The tag must always contain the subject form of the pronoun.
5. Negative forms are usually contracted (*n't*). (If they are not, they follow the order auxiliary + subject + *not:* He saw this yesterday, <u>did he not?</u>)
6. *There is, there are,* and *it is* forms contain a pseudo-subject so the tag will also contain *there* or *it* as if it were a subject pronoun.
7. The verb *have* may be used as a main verb (I *have* a new car) or it may be used as an auxiliary (John *has gone* to class already). When it functions as a main verb in American English, the auxiliary forms *do, does,* or *did* must be used in the tag.

<u>There are</u> only twenty-eight days in February, <u>aren't there?</u>
<u>It's</u> raining now, <u>isn't it?</u> <u>It isn't</u> raining now, <u>is it?</u>
<u>The boys don't</u> have class tomorrow, <u>do they?</u>
<u>You and I talked</u> with the professor yesterday, <u>didn't we?</u>
<u>You won't</u> be leaving for another hour, <u>will you?</u>
<u>Jill and Joe have</u> been to Mexico, <u>haven't they?</u>
<u>You have</u> two children, <u>don't you?</u>

In *British English,* you would be correct to say:
<u>You have</u> two children, <u>haven't you?</u>

On TOEFL, which tests standard *American English,* you must use a form of *do* if *have* is the main verb in the sentence.

<u>She has</u> an exam tomorrow, <u>doesn't she?</u>

Exercise 17: Tag Questions

Finish these sentences by adding a tag question with the correct form of the verb and the subject pronoun.

1. You're going to school tomorrow, _____ ?
2. Gary signed the petition, _____ ?
3. There's an exam tomorrow, _____ ?

4. Beverly will be attending the university in September, _____ ?
5. She's been studying English for two years, _____ ?
6. It sure is sunny today, _____ ?
7. He should stay in bed, _____ ?
8. You can't play tennis today, _____ ?
9. There aren't any peaches left, _____ ?
10. We've seen that movie, _____ ?

11. Affirmative Agreement

When indicating that one person or thing does something and then adding that another does the same, use the word *so* or *too*. To avoid needless repetition of words from the affirmative statement, use the conjunction *and*, followed by a simple statement using *so* or *too*. The order of this statement will depend on whether *so* or *too* is used.

(1) When a form of the verb *be* is used in the main clause, the same tense of the verb *be* is used in the simple statement that follows.

$$\text{affirmative statement } (be) + and + \begin{cases} \text{subject} + \text{verb } (be) + too \\ so + \text{verb } (be) + \text{subject} \end{cases}$$

I am happy, and you are too.
I am happy, and so are you.

(2) When a compound verb (auxiliary + verb), for example, *will go, should do, has done, have written, must examine,* etc., occurs in the main clause, the auxiliary of the main verb is used in the simple statement, and the subject and verb must agree.

$$\begin{array}{l} \text{affirmative statement} + and + \begin{cases} \text{subject} + \text{auxiliary only} + too \\ so + \text{auxiliary only} + \text{subject} \end{cases} \\ \text{(compound verb)} \end{array}$$

They will work in the lab tomorrow, and you will too.
They will work in the lab tomorrow, and so will you.

(3) When any verb except *be* appears without any auxiliaries in the main clause, the auxiliary *do, does,* or *did* is used in the simple statement. The subject and verb must agree and the tense must be the same.

$$\begin{array}{l} \text{affirmative statement} + and + \begin{cases} \text{subject} + do, \text{ does, or } did + too \\ so + do, \text{ does, or } did + \text{subject} \end{cases} \\ \text{(single verb except } be) \end{array}$$

Jane goes to that school, and <u>my sister</u> does too.
Jane goes to that school, and <u>so does</u> <u>my sister</u>.

Additional examples:

John went to the mountains on his vacation, and <u>we did</u> too.
John went to the mountains on his vacation, and <u>so did</u> <u>we</u>.

I will be in New Mexico in August, and <u>they will</u> too.
I will be in New Mexico in August, and <u>so will</u> <u>they</u>.

He has seen her plays, and <u>the girls have</u> too.
He has seen her plays, and <u>so have</u> <u>the girls</u>.

We are going to the movies tonight, and <u>Suzy is</u> too.
We are going to the movies tonight, and <u>so is</u> <u>Suzy</u>.

She will wear a costume to the party, and <u>we will</u> too.
She will wear a costume to the party, and <u>so will</u> <u>we</u>.

Velázquez was a famous painter, and <u>Rubens was</u> too.
Velázquez was a famous painter, and <u>so was</u> <u>Rubens</u>.

Exercise 18: Affirmative Agreement

Supply the correct form of the verb for the simple statement in each of the following sentences.

1. Rose likes to fly, and her brother _____ Does _____ too.
2. They will leave at noon, and I _____ will _____ too.
3. He has an early appointment, and so _____ do _____ I.
4. She has already written her composition, and so _____ her friends.
5. Their plane is arriving at nine o'clock, and so _____ mine.
6. I should go grocery shopping this afternoon, and so _____ my neighbor.
7. We like to swim in the pool, and they _____ too.
8. Our Spanish teacher loves to travel, and so _____ we.
9. He has lived in Mexico for five years, and you _____ too.
10. I must write them a letter, and she _____ too.

12. Negative Agreement

Either and *neither* function in simple statements much like *so* and *too* in affirmative sentences. However, *either* and *neither* are used to indicate negative agreement. The same rules for auxiliaries, *be* and *do, does,* or *did* apply.

---

negative statement + *and* $\begin{cases} \text{subject + negative auxiliary or } be + either \\ neither + \text{positive auxiliary or } be + \text{subject} \end{cases}$

I didn't see Mary this morning.   John didn't see Mary this morning.

I didn't see Mary this morning, and John didn't either.

I didn't see Mary this morning, and neither did John.

She won't be going to the conference.   Her colleagues won't be going to the conference.

She won't be going to the conference, and her colleagues won't either.

She won't be going to the conference, and neither will her colleagues.

John hasn't seen the new movie yet.   I haven't seen the new movie yet.

John hasn't seen the new movie yet, and I haven't either.

John hasn't seen the new movie yet, and neither have I.

Exercise 19: Negative Agreement

Fill in the blanks with the correct form of *either* or *neither*.

1. The children shouldn't take that medicine, and _____ should she.
2. We don't plan to attend the concert, and _____ do they.
3. I don't like tennis, and he doesn't _____ .
4. She didn't see anyone she knew, and _____ did Tim.
5. The Yankees couldn't play due to the bad weather, and _____ could the Angels.
6. Mary can't type well, and her sister can't _____ .
7. I'm not interested in reading that book, and _____ is she.
8. They won't have to work on weekends, and we won't _____ .
9. I can't stand listening to that music, and she can't _____ .
10. Michael doesn't speak English, and his family doesn't _____ .

Exercise 20: Negative Agreement

In the following sentences, supply the correct form of the missing verb.

1. That scientist isn't too happy with the project, and neither _____ her supervisors.
2. We can't study in the library, and they _____ either.
3. I haven't worked there long, and neither _____ you.
4. You didn't pay the rent, and she _____ either.
5. They didn't want anything to drink, and neither _____ we.
6. John shouldn't run so fast, and neither _____ you.
7. The students won't accept the dean's decision, and the faculty _____ either.
8. Your class hasn't begun yet, and neither _____ mine.
9. She couldn't attend the lecture, and her sister _____ either.
10. He didn't know the answer, and neither _____ I.

13. Negation

To make a sentence negative, add the negative particle *not* after the auxiliary or verb *be*. If there is no auxiliary or *be*, add the appropriate form of *do, does,* or *did* and place the word *not* after that.

John is rich.	John is not rich.
Sandra is going to Hawaii.	Sandra is not going to Hawaii.
Mark has seen Bill.	Mark has not seen Bill.
Mary can leave now.	Mary can not leave now.

The following examples contain no auxiliary, and thus use *do, does,* or *did*.

Marvin likes spinach.	Marvin does not like spinach.
Isaac went to class.	Isaac did not go to class.
They want to leave now.	They do not want to leave now.

● *Some/any:* If there is a noun in the complement of a negative sentence, one should add the particle *any* before the noun. NOTE: the following rule applies to the use of *some* and *any*.

> *some*–affirmative sentences
> *any*–negative sentences and questions

John has some money.   John doesn't have any money.

It is also possible to make sentences such as this negative by adding the negative particle *no* before the noun. In this case, the verb CANNOT be negative.

John has no money.

● *Hardly, barely, rarely, seldom, etc.:* Remember that in an English sentence it is usually incorrect to have two negatives together. This is called a double negative and is not acceptable in standard English. The following words have a negative meaning and, thus, *must be used with a positive verb.*

hardly barely scarcely	mean	almost nothing or almost not at all	rarely seldom hardly ever	mean	almost never

John rarely comes to class on time.   (John usually does not come to class on time.)

Jerry hardly studied last night.   (Jerry studied very little last night.)

She scarcely remembers the accident.   (She almost doesn't remember the accident.)

We seldom see photos of these animals.   (We almost never see photos of
these animals.)

Jane barely arrived on time.   (Jane almost didn't arrive on time.)

I hardly ever go to sleep before midnight. (I usually don't go to sleep
before midnight.)

14. Commands

A command is an imperative statement. One person orders another to do
something. It can be preceded by *please*. The understood subject is *you*. Use
the simple form of the verb.

Close the door.	Leave the room.
Please turn off the light.	Open your book.
Open the window.	Be quiet.

● *Negative commands:* A negative command is formed by adding the word
don't before the verb.

Don't close the door.
Please don't turn off the light.
Don't open the window.

● *Indirect commands:* Usually the verbs *order, ask, tell,* or *say* are used to
indicate an indirect command. They are followed by the infinitive
[*to* + verb].

John told Mary to close the door.
Jack asked Jill to turn off the light.
The teacher told Christopher to open the window.
Please tell Jaime to leave the room.
John ordered Bill to open his book.
The policeman ordered the suspect to be quiet.

● *Negative indirect commands:* To make an indirect command negative,
add the particle *not* before the infinitive.

subject + verb + complement + *not* + [verb in infinitive]

John told Mary not to close the door.
Jack asked Jill not to turn off the light.
The teacher told Christopher not to open the window.
Please tell Jaime not to leave the room.
John ordered Bill not to open his book.

MINI-TEST 1 FOR GRAMMAR ITEMS 3 THROUGH 14

Following is a mini-test containing questions on all the material up to this point in Section II, items 3 through 14. This mini-test is similar to Section II, Part B, of the TOEFL. You should review everything up to this point before attempting the mini-test. After you take the test, check your answers, and if you do not understand why a given answer is incorrect, study that section again.

DIRECTIONS

Each question on this mini-test consists of a sentence in which four words or phrases are underlined. The four underlined parts of the sentence are marked, A, B, C, D. You are to identify the *one* underlined word or phrase that *would not be acceptable in standard written English*. Circle the letter of the underlined portion which is not correct. *Example:*

The study of <u>these</u> animals <u>are</u> truly fascinating, and
          A   B

many books <u>have</u> been <u>written about them</u>.
       C   D

In this sentence, the verb *are* in answer B is incorrect because the subject is *study,* which is singular. Thus B is the correct answer. Remember that if a prepositional phrase separates a subject and verb, it has no effect on the verb.

The study [of these animals] is . . .
singular subject   *singular verb*

1. Buying clothes <u>are</u> often <u>a very time-consuming</u> practice <u>because those</u>
          A   B   C
clothes that a person likes <u>are rarely the ones</u> that fit him or her.
                          D

2. <u>Because</u> they had spent <u>too many</u> time <u>considering</u> the new contract,
     A   B   C
the students <u>lost the opportunity to lease</u> the apartment.
               D

3. <u>These</u> televisions are <u>all too expensive</u> for <u>we to buy</u> at <u>this time</u>,
  A   B   C   D
but perhaps we will return later.

4. After she <u>had bought</u> <u>himself</u> a new automobile, <u>she sold</u> <u>her</u> bicycle.
          A   B   C   D

5. The next <u>important</u> question we <u>have to decide</u> is when <u>do we have to</u>
            A   B   C
   <u>submit</u> the proposal.
     D

6. George <u>has not</u> completed <u>the assignment</u> <u>yet</u>, and Maria
            A   B   C
   <u>hasn't neither</u>.
      D

7. John decided <u>to buy</u> <u>in the morning a new car</u>, but <u>in the afternoon</u>
              A   B   C
   <u>he changed his mind</u>.
       D

8. <u>Some of the plants</u> in this store require very <u>little care</u>, but this
        A   B
   one needs <u>much more sunlight</u> than the <u>others ones</u>.
               C   D

9. After George <u>had returned</u> <u>to his house</u>, <u>he</u> <u>was reading</u> a book.
               A   B   C   D

10. <u>Many</u> theories on conserving the purity of water <u>has been</u> proposed,
    A   B
   but <u>not one has</u> been <u>as widely accepted</u> as this one.
        C   D

11. <u>The food</u> that Mark <u>is cooking</u> in the kitchen is <u>smelling</u> <u>delicious</u>.
     A   B   C   D

12. After John <u>eaten</u> dinner, he wrote <u>several letters</u> and <u>went to bed</u>.
         A   B   C   D

13. The manager <u>has finished</u> <u>working</u> on <u>the report</u> last night, and now
             A   B   C
   she will begin <u>to write</u> the other proposal.
             D

14. <u>Because</u> Sam and Michelle <u>had done</u> all of the work <u>theirselves</u>, they
    A   B   C
   were <u>unwilling to give</u> the results to Joan.
         D

15. Daniel said that if he <u>had to do</u> <u>another</u> homework tonight, he
                  A   B
   <u>would not be able</u> <u>to attend</u> the concert.
      C   D

16. After to take the medication, the patient became drowsy and more
        A   B   C
manageable.
    D

17. We insist on you leaving the meeting before any further outbursts
            A B   C   D
take place.

18. It has been a long time since we have talked to John, isn't it?
      A   B   C   D

19. Henry objects to our buying this house without the approval
               A   B
of our attorney, and John does so.
     C   D

20. Rita enjoyed to be able to meet several Congress members during
            A   B   C
her vacation.
   D

21. After being indicted for his part in a bank robbery, the reputed
      A   B   C
mobster decided find another attorney.
            D

22. Harry's advisor persuaded his taking several courses which did
                     A   B
not involve much knowledge of mathematics.
   C   D

23. The only teachers who were required to attend the meeting were
     A   B   C
George, Betty, Jill, and me.
              D

24. The work performed by these officers are not worth our paying
            A   B   C
them any longer.
   D

25. The president went fishing after he has finished with the conferences.
    A   B C   D

26. Peter and Tom plays tennis every afternoon with Mary and me.
             A   B   C   D

27. There were a time that I used to swim five laps every day, but now
      A   B   C
I do not have enough time.
        D

28. He was drink a cup of coffee when the telephone rang.
      A   B   C   D

29. We called yesterday our friends in Boston to tell them about
          A   B   C   D
the reunion that we are planning.

30. The children were playing last night outdoors when it began
              A   B   C
to rain very hard.
   D

31. Those homework that your teacher assigned is due on Tuesday unless
    A   B   C
you have made prior arrangements to turn it in late.
        D

32. Please give me a few coffee and some donuts if you have any left.
         A   B   C   D

33. There are ten childs playing in the yard near her house, but
        A   B
your child is not among them.
    C   D

34. People respected George Washington because he was a honest man,
    A   B   C
and he turned out to be one of our greatest military leaders.
                        D

35. He isn't driving to the convention in March, and neither they are.
        A   B   C   D

36. Catherine is studying law at the university, and so does John.
          A   B   C   D

37. The company has so little money that it can't hardly operate anymore.
         A   B   C   D

38. My cousin attends an university in the Midwest which specializes
    A   B   C
in astronomy.
   D

39. The students were interested in take a field trip to The National
          A   B   C
History Museum, but they were not able to raise enough money.
                      D

40. Because they have moved away, they hardly never go to the beach
    A   B   C   D
anymore.

41. Us students would rather not attend night classes in the summer,
       A   B
    but we often have to.
        C   D

42. The policeman ordered the suspect to don't remove his hands
                       A   B   C
    from the hood of the car.
      D

43. It was him who came running into the classroom with the news.
        A B   C   D

44. My brother doesn't care how much does the car cost because
       A   B   C
    he is going to buy it anyway.
        D

45. Mary and her sister studied biology last year, and so does Jean.
        A   B   C   D

46. Pete had already saw that musical before he read the reviews about it.
           A   B   C   D

47. There's a new Oriental restaurant in town, isn't it?
       A B   C   D

48. The government has decided voting on the resolution now rather than
            A   B   C   D
    next month.

49. The professor is thinking to go to the conference on aerodynamics
             A   B   C
    next month.
      D

50. His father does not approve of him to go to the banquet
         A   B
    without dressing formally.
        C   D

15. Modal Auxiliaries

The modal auxiliaries have a number of different meanings. They are generally used to indicate something which is potential or uncertain. Remember that a modal is an auxiliary, and thus is NEVER used with *do, does,* or *did.* The modals include:

PRESENT TENSE	PAST TENSE
will	would (used to)
can	could
may	might
shall	should (ought to) (had better)
must (have to)	(had to)

NOTE: Words in parentheses (   ) indicate semi-modals. These have similar meanings to the modals, but are not grammatically the same.

● *Negation of modals:* To make a modal negative, add the particle *not* after the modal.

John <u>would like</u> to leave.   John <u>would not like</u> to leave.

● *Questions with modals:* To make a question, one places the modal at the beginning of the sentence.

<u>Would</u> John <u>like</u> to leave?

NOTE: A modal is always directly followed by the simple form (verb word). This is the infinitive without *to*.

INFINITIVE	SIMPLE FORM
to be	be
to go	go
to have	have

This means that after a modal there can NEVER be: [verb + *ing*], [verb + *s*], past tense, or infinitive.

There are two ways that a modal can occur:

(1) modal + simple form of the verb

would be   could go   will have

(2) modal + *have* + [verb in past participle]

would have been   could have gone   will have had

NOTE: The word *have,* of course, must always be in the simple form after a modal; it can never be *has* or *had*.

● *Meanings of the modals:* Each of the modals has a different meaning. It is necessary to know the meaning of each.

- *Will:* Will indicates future certainty.

  John <u>will begin</u> the job tomorrow.
  Maria <u>will leave</u> in January.

- *Conditional sentences:* The modals *will, would, can,* and *could* often appear in conditional sentences. Usually conditional sentences contain the word *if.* There are two types of conditionals: the real (factual and habitual) and the unreal (contrary to fact or hypothetical). The real, or "future possible" as it is sometimes called, is used when the speaker expresses an action or situation which usually occurs, or will occur if the circumstances in the main clause are met.

  > Hypothetical situation: If I am not planning anything for this evening, when someone asks me if I want to go to the movies, I say:

  > <u>If</u> I <u>have</u> the time, I <u>will</u> go.
  >   X   Y

  > (I will go unless I don't have time.)
  > (If X is true, then Y is true.)

  > <u>If</u> my headache <u>disappears</u>, we <u>can</u> play tennis.
  > (I will play tennis unless I have a headache.)

However, the unreal condition expresses a situation (past, present, or future) that would take place or would have taken place if the circumstances expressed were or had been different now or in the past.

  > Hypothetical situation: If I don't have time to go to the movies, but I actually want to go, I say:

  > <u>If</u> I <u>had</u> the time, I <u>would</u> go.
  > (I know I don't have time, and therefore, I can't go to the movies.)

  > This sentence is contrary to fact because I can *not* go.

  > <u>If</u> today <u>were</u> Saturday, we <u>could</u> go to the beach.
  > (Today is not Saturday, so we can't go to the beach.)

The *if* clause can come first or last in the sentence with no change in meaning.

  > <u>If</u> we <u>didn't have</u> to study, we <u>could</u> go out tonight.

  OR

  > We <u>could</u> go out tonight <u>if</u> we <u>didn't have</u> to study.
  > (Both sentences mean: we can't go out tonight because we have to study.)

NOTE: The word *if* is generally not followed directly by the modal; the modal appears in the other part of the sentence unless there are two modals in one sentence.

> *if* + subject + conjugated verb . . . + modal . . .

OR

> subject + modal . . . + *if* . . . + conjugated verb . . .

NOTE: In the unreal condition, the past tense form of *be* is always *were* in a conditional sentence; it can NEVER be *was* in correct English.

If I were . . .	If we were . . .
If you were . . .	If you were . . .
If he were . . .	
If she were . . .	If they were . . .
If it were . . .	

Unreal conditional sentences are difficult for foreign students to understand because it seems that the truth value of a sentence is the opposite of the way the sentence appears. If a verb in an unreal conditional sentence is negative, the meaning is actually positive; if a verb is positive, the meaning is actually negative.

If I were rich, I would travel around the world.
(I am *not* rich.)   (I'm *not* going to travel around the world.)

If he were sick, he would stay home today.
(He's *not* sick.)   (He's *not* going to stay home today.)

BUT

If I hadn't been in a hurry, I wouldn't have spilled the milk.
(I *was* in a hurry.)   (I *spilled* the milk.)

If the firemen hadn't arrived when they did, they couldn't have saved the house.
(The firemen *arrived* on time.)   (They *saved* the house.)

We would have left yesterday if it hadn't snowed.
(We *didn't leave* yesterday.)   (It *snowed*.)

The following rules will guide you in deciding which tense to use in conditional sentences. Remember:

past perfect = *had* + [verb in past participle]
modal + perfect = modal + *have* + [verb in past participle]

Remember that the following rules can be reversed. The *if* clause can go either at the beginning or in the middle of the sentence.

- *Real conditions:* (possibly true)

FUTURE TIME

$$if + \text{subject} + \text{simple present tense} \ldots + \begin{Bmatrix} will \\ can \\ may \\ must \end{Bmatrix} + [\text{verb in simple form}]$$

If I have the money, I will buy a new car.
We will have plenty of time to finish the project before dinner if it is only ten o'clock now.

HABITUAL

$$if + \text{subject} + \text{simple present tense} \ldots + \text{simple present tense} \ldots$$

If the doctor has morning office hours, he visits his patients in the hospital in the afternoon. (no modal)
John usually walks to school if he has enough time.

COMMAND

$$if + \text{subject} + \text{simple present tense} \ldots + \text{command form*} \ldots$$

*Remember that the command form consists of the simple form of the verb.

If you go to the Post Office, please mail this letter for me.
Please call me if you hear from Jane.

- *Unreal conditions:* (not true)

PRESENT OR FUTURE TIME

$$if + \text{subject} + \text{simple past tense} \ldots + \begin{Bmatrix} would \\ could \\ might \end{Bmatrix} + [\text{verb in simple form}]$$

If I had the time, I would go to the beach with you this weekend.
(I *don't have* the time.)   (I'm *not going* to the beach with you.)

He would tell you about it if he were here.
(He *won't tell* you about it.)   (He's *not here.*)

If he didn't speak so quickly, you could understand him.
(He *speaks* very quickly.)   (You *can't understand* him.)

PAST TIME

if + subject + past perfect . . . + $\begin{Bmatrix} would \\ could \\ might \end{Bmatrix}$ + *have* + [verb in past participle]

If we <u>had known</u> that you were there, we <u>would have written</u> you a letter.
(We *didn't know* that you were there.)   (We *didn't write* you a letter.)

She <u>would have sold</u> the house if she <u>had found</u> the right buyer.
(She *didn't sell* the house.)   (She *didn't find* the right buyer.)

If we <u>hadn't lost</u> our way, we <u>would have arrived</u> sooner.
(We *lost* our way.)   (We *didn't arrive* early.)

NOTE: It is also possible to indicate a past unreal condition without using the word *if*. In this case, the auxiliary *had* is placed before, rather than after, the subject. This clause will usually come first in the sentence.

had + subject + [verb in past participle] . . .

<u>Had we known</u> that you were there, we <u>would have written</u> you a letter.
<u>Had she found</u> the right buyer, she <u>would have sold</u> the house.

The above rules indicate the most common methods of using tenses in conditional sentences. However, if the two actions clearly happened at quite different times, the verbs should show that difference.

Less common: If she <u>had seen</u> the movie, she <u>would tell</u> you.
                  past   *future*
More common: If she <u>had seen</u> the movie, she <u>would have told</u> you.
                  past   *past*

● *As if/as though:* These conjunctions indicate something unreal or contrary to fact and thus are very similar in form to conditional sentences. The verb which follows these conjunctions must be in the past tense or past perfect. Remember that the past tense of *be* in a contrary to fact statement must be *were* and NEVER *was*.

subject + verb (present) + $\begin{Bmatrix} as\ if \\ as\ though \end{Bmatrix}$ + subject + verb (past) . . .

The old lady <u>dresses</u> <u>as if</u> it <u>were</u> winter even in the summer.
(It is *not* winter.)

Angelique walks as though she studied modeling.
(She *didn't* study modeling.)

He acts as though he were rich.
(He is *not* rich.)

---

subject + verb (past) + $\begin{Bmatrix} as\ if \\ as\ though \end{Bmatrix}$ + subject + verb (past perfect) . . .

Betty talked about the contest as if she had won the grand prize.
(She *didn't win* the grand prize.)

Jeff looked as if he had seen a ghost.
(He *didn't see* a ghost.)

He looked as though he had run ten miles.
(He *didn't run* ten miles.)

NOTE: The two preceding rules apply only when *as if* or *as though* indicates a contrary to fact meaning. At times, they do not have that meaning and then would not be followed by these tenses.

He looks as if he has finished the test.
(*Perhaps* he has finished.)
He looked as though he was leaving.
(*Perhaps* he was leaving.)

• *Hope/wish:* These two verbs, while they are similar in meaning, are not at all the same grammatically. The verb *hope* is used to indicate something that possibly happened or will possibly happen. The verb *wish* is used to indicate something that definitely did not happen or definitely will not happen. The verb *hope* can be followed by any tense. The verb *wish* must NOT be followed by *any present tense verb or present tense auxiliary.* Be sure that you understand the difference in the following sentences with *wish* and *hope.*

We hope that they will come.   (We *don't know* if they are coming.)
We wish that they could come.   (They are *not* coming.)
We hope that they came yesterday.   (We *don't know* if they came.)
We wish that they had come yesterday.   (They *didn't* come.)

Remember that *wish* is very similar to a contrary to fact or unreal condition.

Present unreal condition: If I were rich, I would be very happy.
Present wish: I wish I were rich.
Past unreal condition: If you had been here last night, we would have enjoyed it.
Past wish: We wish that you had been here last night.

NOTE: In the following rules, notice that the word *that* is optional.

FUTURE WISH

subject* + *wish* + (*that*) + subject + $\begin{cases} could + \text{verb} \\ would + \text{verb} \\ were + [\text{verb} + ing] \end{cases}$ ...

*Subjects can be the same or different.

We wish that you could come to the party tonight.   (You *can't come*.)
I wish that you would stop saying that.   (You *probably won't stop*.)
She wishes that she were coming with us.   (She is *not coming* with us.)

PRESENT WISH

subject + *wish* + (*that*) + subject + simple past tense ...

I wish that I had enough time to finish my homework.   (I *don't have* enough time.)
We wish that you were old enough to come with us.   (You *are not* old enough.)
They wish that they didn't have to go to class today.   (They *have to* go to class.)

PAST WISH

subject + *wish* + (*that*) + subject + $\begin{cases} \text{past perfect} \\ could\ have + [\text{verb in past participle}] \end{cases}$

I wish that I had washed the clothes yesterday.   (I *didn't wash* the clothes.)
She wishes that she could have been there.   (She *couldn't be* there.)
We wish that we had had more time last night.   (We *didn't have* more time.)

Exercise 21: Conditional Sentences

Supply the correct form of the verb in parentheses for each of the following sentences. Review the formulas if you have trouble.

1. Henry talks to his dog as if it _____ (understand) him.
2. If they had left the house earlier, they _____ (be; negative) so late getting to the airport that they could not check their baggage.
3. If I finish the dress before Saturday, I _____ (give) it to my sister for her birthday.
4. If I had seen the movie, I _____ (tell) you about it last night.

5. Had Bob not interfered in his sister's marital problems, there _____ (be) peace between them.
6. He would give you the money if he _____ (have) it.
7. I wish they _____ (stop) making so much noise so that I could concentrate.
8. She would call you immediately if she _____ (need) help.
9. Had they arrived at the sale early, they _____ (find) a better selection.
10. We hope that you _____ (enjoy) the party last night.
11. If you have enough time, please _____ (paint) the chair before you leave.
12. We could go for a drive if today _____ (be) Saturday.
13. If she wins the prize, it will be because she _____ (write) very well.
14. Mike wished that the editors _____ (permit) him to copy some of their material.
15. Joel wishes that he _____ (spend) his vacation on the Gulf Coast next year.
16. I _____ (accept) if they invite me to the party.
17. If your mother _____ (buy) that car for you, will you be happy?
18. If he _____ (decide) earlier, he could have left on the afternoon flight.
19. Had we known your address, we _____ (write) you a letter.
20. If the roofer doesn't come soon, the rain _____ (leak) inside.
21. Because Rose did so poorly on the exam, she wishes that she _____ (study) harder last night.
22. My dog always wakes me up if he _____ (hear) strange noises.
23. If you _____ (see) Mary today, please ask her to call me.
24. If he _____ (get) the raise, it will be because he does a good job.
25. The teacher will not accept our work if we _____ (turn) it in late.
26. Mrs. Wood always talks to her tenth-grade students as though they _____ (be) adults.
27. If he had left already, he _____ (call) us.
28. If they had known him, they _____ (talk) to him.
29. He would understand it if you _____ (explain) it to him more slowly.
30. I could understand the French teacher if she _____ (speak) more slowly.

• *Would:* Besides its use in conditional sentences, *would* can also mean a past time habit.

When David was young, he <u>would swim</u> once a day.

• *Used to:* In this usage, the expression *used to* means the same as *would*.

Used to is always in this form; it can NEVER be *use to*. Also, there are two grammar rules for *used to*. Notice the difference in meaning as well as in grammar.

> subject + *used to* + [verb in simple form] . . .

When David was young, he used to swim once a day.   (past time habit)

> subject + $\begin{Bmatrix} be \\ get \end{Bmatrix}$ + *used to* + [verb + *ing*] . . .

John is used to swimming every day.   (He is accustomed to swimming every day.

John got used to swimming every day.   (He became accustomed to swimming every day.)

NOTE: *Be used to* means to *be accustomed to,* and *get used to* means to *become accustomed to.*

The program director used to write his own letters.   (past time habit)

George is used to eating at 7:00 P.M.   (is accustomed to)

We got used to cooking our own food when we had to live alone.   (became accustomed to)

Mary was used to driving to school.   (was accustomed to)

The government used to restrict these pills.   (past time habit)

The man is used to reading his newspaper in the morning.   (is accustomed to)

Exercise 22: Used To

Supply the simple form or [verb + *ing*] as required in the following sentences.

1. I was used to _____ (eat) at noon when I started school.
2. He used to _____ (eat) dinner at five o'clock.
3. When I was young, I used to _____ (swim) every day.
4. He used to _____ (like) her, but he doesn't anymore.
5. Don't worry. Some day you will get used to _____ (speak) English.
6. Alvaro can't get used to _____ (study).
7. He used to _____ (dance) every night, but now he studies.
8. Adam is used to _____ (sleep) late on weekends.
9. Chieko is used to _____ (eat) American food now.
10. She finally got used to _____ (eat) our food.

• *Would rather:* *Would rather* means the same as *prefer*, except that the grammar is different. *Would rather* must be followed by a verb, but *prefer* may or may not be followed by a verb.

John would rather drink Coca-Cola than orange juice.
John prefers drinking Coca-Cola to drinking orange juice.

OR

John prefers Coca-Cola to orange juice.

NOTE: *Would rather* is followed by *than* when two things are mentioned, but *prefer* is followed by *to*.

There are different rules for *would rather* depending on the number of subjects and the meaning of the sentence.

PRESENT

> subject + *would rather* + [verb in simple form] . . .

Jim would rather go to class tomorrow than today.

PAST

> subject + *would rather* + *have* + [verb in past participle]

John would rather have gone to class yesterday than today.

Would rather that, when used with two subjects in the present, can be followed by either the simple form of the verb or the past tense. It will be followed by the simple form when it has a subjunctive meaning (as explained in Grammar item 25). It will be followed by the past tense when the meaning of the sentence is "contrary to fact" just as that rule affects conditional sentences and the verb *wish*.

PRESENT SUBJUNCTIVE

> subject$_1$ + *would rather that* + subject$_2$ + [verb in simple form]

I would rather that you call me tomorrow.
We would rather that he take this train.

PRESENT CONTRARY TO FACT

> subject$_1$ + *would rather that* + subject$_2$ + [verb in simple past tense] . . .

Henry would rather that his girlfriend worked in the same department as he does.
(His girlfriend does *not* work in the same department.)

Jane would rather that it were winter now.
  (It is *not* winter now.)

The following rule applies to *would rather* when there are two subjects and the time is past. In this case, the meaning must always be contrary to fact.

PAST CONTRARY TO FACT

subject$_1$ + *would rather that* + subject$_2$ + past perfect . . .

Jim would rather that Jill had gone to class yesterday.
  (Jill did *not* go to class yesterday.)

Notice how each of the following sentences becomes negative. When there is only one subject and when you have a present subjunctive, simply place *not* before the verb.

John would rather not go to class tomorrow.
John would rather not have gone to class yesterday.
John would rather that you not call me tomorrow.

For the present and past contrary to fact sentences, use *didn't* + [verb in simple form] and *hadn't* + [verb in past participle] respectively.

Henry would rather that his girlfriend didn't work in the same department as he does.
  (She *does* work in the same department.)

John would rather that Jill had not gone to class yesterday.
  (Jill *went* to class yesterday.)

Examples of *would rather:*

Jorge would rather stay home tonight.
We would rather that you call tonight.
Mayra would rather drink coffee than Coke.
Ricardo would rather not be here.
Ritsuko would rather that we didn't leave now, but we must go to work.
Roberto would rather that we hadn't left yesterday.

Exercise 23: Would Rather

Fill in the blanks with the correct form of the verb in the following sentences.

1. We would rather _____ (stay) home tonight.
2. Mr. Jones would rather _____ (stay) home last night.
3. The policeman would rather _____ (work) on Saturday than on Sunday.
4. Maria would rather that we _____ (study) more than we do.

5. George would rather _____ (study; negative) tonight.
6. The photographer would rather _____ (have) more light.
7. The photographer would rather that we _____ (stand) closer together than we are standing.
8. Carmen would rather _____ (cook; negative) for the entire family.
9. She would rather that you _____ (arrive; negative) last night.
10. John would rather _____ (sleep) than worked last night.

• *Would like:* This expression is often used in invitations; it can also mean *want*. NOTE: It is NOT CORRECT to say: "Do you like . . .?" to invite somebody to do something.

> subject + *would like* + [*to* + verb] . . .

Would you like to dance with me?
I would like to visit Japan.
We would like to order now please.
The president would like to be re-elected.
They would like to study at the university.
Would you like to see a movie tonight?

• *Could/may/might:* Although *could* is used in conditionals, it can also be used to mean possibility. In this case, *could, may,* or *might* mean the same. The speaker is not sure of the statement made when using these modals.

It might rain tomorrow.   It will *possibly* rain tomorrow.
It may rain tomorrow.   =   OR
It could rain tomorrow.   *Maybe* it will rain tomorrow.

NOTE: *Maybe* is a combination of *may* and *be*, but it is one word and is not an auxiliary. It means the same as *perhaps*.

Examples of *could, may,* and *might:*

The president said that there might be a strike next week.
I don't know what I'm doing tomorrow. I may go to the beach or I may stay home.
It might be warmer tomorrow.
I may not be able to go with you tonight.
I don't know where Jaime is. He could be at home.

• *Should:* This modal is used to indicate:

(1) A recommendation, advice, or obligation (see *must* for further explanation).

Henry should study tonight.
One should exercise daily.
Maria should go on a diet.
You should see a doctor about this problem.

(2) Expectation; used to indicate something that the speaker expects to happen.

It should rain tomorrow.   (I expect it to rain tomorrow.)
My check should arrive next week.   (I expect it to arrive next week.)

NOTE: The expressions *had better, ought to,* and *be supposed to* generally mean the same as *should* in either of the two definitions.

$$\text{subject} + \left\{ \begin{array}{l} \textit{had better} \\ \textit{should} \\ \textit{ought to} \\ \textit{be supposed to} \end{array} \right\} + \text{[verb in simple form]} \ldots$$

John should study tonight.
John had better study tonight.
John ought to study tonight.
John is supposed to study tonight.

● *Must:* This modal is used to indicate:

(1) Complete obligation; this is stronger than *should*. With *should* the person has some choice on whether or not to act, but with *must* the person has no choice.

One must endorse a check before one cashes it.
George must call his insurance agent today.
A pharmacist must keep a record of the prescriptions that are filled.
An automobile must have gasoline to run.
An attorney must pass an examination before practicing law.
This freezer must be kept at $-20°$.

(2) Logical conclusion; *must* is used to indicate that the speaker assumes something to be true from the facts that are available but is not absolutely certain of the truth.

John's lights are out.   He must be asleep.
   (We assume that John is asleep because the lights are out.)
The grass is wet.   It must be raining.
   (We assume that it is raining because the grass is wet.)

• *Have to:* This pseudo-modal means the same as *must* (meaning complete obligation).

George has to call his insurance agent today.
A pharmacist has to keep a record of the prescriptions that are filled.

For a past time obligation, it is necessary to use *had to.*
Must CANNOT be used to mean a past obligation.

George had to call his insurance agent yesterday.
Mrs. Kinsey had to pass an examination before she could practice law.

• *Modals + perfective:* You have already seen these in the section on conditionals; however, it is also possible to use other modals in this form. The modal + perfective is *usually used* to indicate past time.

> modal + *have* + [verb in past participle] . . .

NOTE: Remember that a modal is *always* followed by the simple form of the verb. Thus, *have* can *never* be *has* or *had*.

• Could/may/might + *perfective:* Use any of these modals + perfective to indicate a past possibility. Remember that these modals also mean possibility in the present.

It may have rained last night, but I'm not sure.
The cause of death could have been bacteria.
John might have gone to the movies yesterday.

• Should + *perfective:* This is used to indicate an obligation that was supposed to occur in the past, but for some reason it did not occur.

John should have gone to the post office this morning.
(He *did not go* to the post office.)

Maria shouldn't have called John last night.
(She *did call* him.)

The policeman should have made a report about the burglary.
(He *did not make* a report.)

NOTE: The expression *was/were supposed to* + [verb in simple form] means much the same as *should* + perfective.

John was supposed to go to the post office this morning.
(He *didn't go.*)

The policeman was supposed to make a report about the burglary.
(He *didn't make* a report.)

● Must + *perfective:* This is NOT *used to indicate a past obligation.*
Remember to use only *had to, should* + perfective, or *be supposed to* to
indicate a past obligation. *Must* + perfective can *only* mean a logical
conclusion in the past.

The grass is wet.   It must have rained last night.
                     (It *probably rained* last night.)

Tony's lights are out.   He must have gone to sleep.
                          (He *probably went* to sleep.)

Jane did very well on the exam.   She must have studied.
                                   (She *probably studied.*)

Sandra failed the test.   She must not have studied.
                           (She *probably did not study.*)

Exercise 24: Must/Should + *Perfective.*

Choose between *must* + perfective and *should* + perfective in the
following sentences.

1. Henri was deported for having an expired visa. He _____ (have)
   his visa renewed.
2. Julietta was absent for the first time yesterday. She _____ (be)
   sick.
3. The photos are black. The X rays at the airport _____ (damage)
   them.
4. Blanca got a parking ticket. She _____ (park; negative) in a
   reserved spot, since she had no permit.
5. Carmencita did very well on the exam. She _____ (study) very
   hard.
6. Jeanette did very badly on the exam. She _____ (study) harder.
7. German called us as soon as his wife had her baby. He _____ (be)
   very proud.
8. Eve had to pay $5.00 because she wrote a bad check. She _____
   (deposit) her money before she wrote a check.
9. John isn't here yet. He _____ (forget) about our meeting.
10. Alexis failed the exam. He _____ (study; negative) enough.

Exercise 25: Modals + *Perfective*

Choose the correct answer in each of the following sentences according to
meaning and tense.

1. If I had a bicycle, (I would/I will) ride it every day.
2. George (would have gone/would go) on a trip to Chicago if he had had
   time.

3. Marcela didn't come to class yesterday. She (will have had/may have had) an accident.

4. John didn't do his homework, so the teacher became very angry. John (must have done/should have done) his homework.

5. Sharon was supposed to be here at nine o'clock. She (must forget/must have forgotten) about our meeting.

6. Where do you think Juan is today? I have no idea. He (should have slept/may have slept) late.

7. George missed class today. He (might have had/might had had) an accident.

8. Robert arrived without his book. He (could have lost/would have lost) it.

9. Thomas received a warning for speeding. He (should have driven/ shouldn't have driven) so fast.

10. Henry's car stopped on the highway. It (may run/may have run) out of gas.

16. Adjectives and Adverbs

● *Adjectives:* Adjectives fall into two categories: descriptive and limiting. Descriptive adjectives are those which describe the color, size, or quality of a person or thing (noun or pronoun). Limiting adjectives place restrictions on the words they modify (quantity, distance, possession, etc.). NOTE: Only *these* and *those* are plural forms. All others remain the same whether the noun is singular or plural.

DESCRIPTIVE	LIMITING	
beautiful	cardinal numbers	(one, two)
large	ordinal numbers	(first, second)
red	possessives	(my, your, his)
interesting	demonstratives	(this, that, these, those)
important	quantity	(few, many, much)
colorful	articles	(a, an, the)

When descriptive adjectives modify a singular countable noun, they are usually preceded by *a, an,* or *the.*

 a pretty girl   an interesting story   the red dress

Adjectives normally precede the nouns they modify, or follow linking verbs. Adjectives modify only nouns, pronouns, and linking verbs. (See next section for an explanation of linking verbs.) NOTE: An adjective answers the question: What kind . . . ?

• *Adverbs:* Adverbs modify verbs (except linking verbs), adjectives, or other adverbs. Many descriptive adjectives can be changed to adverbs by adding *-ly* to the adjective base.

ADJECTIVES	ADVERBS
bright	brightly
careful	carefully
quiet	quietly

NOTE: The following words are also adverbs: *so, very, almost, soon, often, fast, rather, well, there, too.* An adverb answers the question: How . . . ?

John is reading carefully.	(*How* is John reading?)
Maria Elena speaks Spanish fluently.	(*How* does she speak?)
Rita drank too much coffee?	(*How much* coffee did she drink?)
I don't play tennis very well.	(*How well* do I play?)
He was driving fast.	(*How* was he driving?)
She reviewed her notes carefully.	(*How* did she review her notes?)

Exercise 26: Adjectives and Adverbs

Circle the correct form in parentheses.

1. Rita plays the violin (good/well).
2. That is an (intense/intensely) novel.
3. The sun is shining (bright/brightly).
4. The girls speak (fluent/fluently) French.
5. The boys speak Spanish (fluent/fluently).
6. The table has a (smooth/smoothly) surface.
7. We must figure our income tax returns (accurate/accurately).
8. We don't like to drink (bitter/bitterly) tea.
9. The plane will arrive (soon/soonly).
10. He had an accident because he was driving too (fast/fastly).

• *Adjectives with linking (copulative) verbs:* A special category of verbs connects or links the subject with the subject complement (predicate adjective). Unlike most verbs, these do not show action. They must be modified by adjectives, not adverbs.

be	appear	feel
become	seem	look
remain	sound	smell
stay		taste

Mary feels bad about her test grade.
Children become tired quite easily.
Lucy will look radiant in her new dress.
They were sorry to see us leave.
The flowers smell sweet.
The soup tastes good.

Be, become, and *remain* can be followed by noun phrases as well as adjectives.

They remained sad even though I tried to cheer them up.
          adjective

Doug remained chairman of the board despite the opposition.
          noun phrase

Children often become bored at meetings.
          adjective

Christine became class president after a long, hard campaign.
          noun phrase

Sally will be happy when she hears the good news.
          adjective

Ted will be prom king this year.
          noun phrase

Feel, look, smell, and *taste* may also be transitive verbs and take a direct object. When they function in this way, they become active and are modified by adverbs. Notice the following pairs of sentences. Those which take objects are active, and those which do not are linking.

The doctor felt the leg carefully to see if there were any
        object   *adverb*
   broken bones.

Mike felt ecstatic after passing his law school exam.
      adjective

Professor Ingells looked at the exams happily.
          object   *adverb*

Joey does not look happy today.
       adjective

The lady is smelling the flowers gingerly.
         object   *adverb*

After being closed up for so long, the house smells musty.
              adjective

The chef tasted the meat cautiously before presenting it
        object   *adverb*
   to the king.

Your chocolate cake tastes delicious.
         adjective

Exercise 27: Linking (Copulative) Verbs

Circle the correct form in parentheses.

1. Your cold sounds (terrible/terribly).
2. The pianist plays very (good/well).
3. The food in the restaurant always tastes (good/well).
4. The campers remained (calm/calmly) despite the thunderstorm.
5. They became (sick/sickly) after eating the contaminated food.
6. Professor Calandra looked (quick/quickly) at the students' sketches.
7. Paco was working (diligent/diligently) on the project.
8. Paul protested (vehement, vehemently) about the new proposals.
9. Our neighbors appeared (relaxed/relaxedly) after their vacation.
10. The music sounded too (noisy/noisily) to be classical.

17. Comparisons

Comparisons indicate degrees of difference with adjectives and adverbs, and may be equal or unequal.

● *Equal comparisons:* An equal comparison indicates that the two entities are (or are not if negative) exactly the same. The following rule generally applies to this type of comparison.

$$\text{subject} + \text{verb} + as + \begin{Bmatrix} \text{adjective} \\ \text{adverb} \end{Bmatrix} + as + \begin{Bmatrix} \text{noun} \\ \text{pronoun} \end{Bmatrix}$$

NOTE: Sometimes you may see *so* instead of *as* before the adjective or adverb in negative comparisons.

He is <u>not</u> <u>as</u> <u>tall</u> <u>as</u> his father.

OR

He is <u>not</u> <u>so</u> <u>tall</u> <u>as</u> his father.

NOTE: Remember that the subject form of the pronoun will always be used after *as* in correct English.

Peter is as tall as <u>I</u>.   You are as old as <u>she</u>.

Examples of equal comparisons:

My book is <u>as interesting</u> as yours.	(adjective)
His car runs <u>as fast</u> as a race car.	(adverb)
John sings <u>as well</u> as his sister.	(adverb)
Their house is <u>as big</u> as that one.	(adjective)

His job is not as difficult as mine.
            OR   (adjective)
His job is not so difficult as mine.
They are as lucky as we.   (adjective)

The same idea can also be conveyed in another way.

$$\text{subject} + \text{verb} + \textit{the same} + (\text{noun}) + \textit{as} + \left\{ \begin{array}{l} \text{noun} \\ \text{pronoun} \end{array} \right\}$$

NOTE: *As high as* means the same as *the same height as*.

My house is as high as his.
My house is the same height as his.

Be sure that you know the following adjectives and their corresponding nouns.

ADJECTIVES	NOUNS
heavy, light	weight
wide, narrow	width
deep, shallow	depth
long, short	length
big, small	size

NOTE: Remember that the opposite of *the same as* is *different from*. NEVER use *different than*.

My nationality is different from hers.
Our climate is different from Canada's.

Examples of *the same as* and *different from:*

These trees are the same as those.
He speaks the same language as she.
Her address is the same as Rita's.
Their teacher is different from ours.
My typewriter types the same as yours.
She takes the same courses as her husband.

• *Unequal comparisons:* This type of comparative implies that the entities are comparable in a greater or lesser degree. The following rules generally apply to this type of comparative.

1. Add -er to the adjective base of most one- and two-syllable adjectives. (thick–thicker; cold–colder; quiet–quieter)
2. Use the form *more* + adjective for most three-syllable adjectives. (*more* beautiful, *more* important, *more* believable)
3. Use the form *more* + adjective for adjectives ending in the following suffixes: -ed, -ful, -ing, -ish, and -ous. (*more* useful, *more* boring, *more* cautious)
4. Double the final consonant of one-syllable adjectives which end in a single consonant (except w, x, and z) and are preceded by a single vowel. (big–bigger, red–redder, hot–hotter)
5. When an adjective ends in a consonant + y, change the y to i and add -er. (happy–happier, dry–drier)

NOTE: The -er suffix means exactly the same as *more*. Therefore, they can NEVER be used together. It is NOT CORRECT to say:

more prettier, more faster, more better

$$\text{subject} + \text{verb} + \begin{cases} \text{adjective} + er \\ \text{adverb} + er* \\ more + \text{adjective/adverb} \\ less + \text{adjective/adverb} \end{cases} + than + \begin{cases} \text{noun} \\ \text{pronoun} \end{cases}$$

*One can add -er to only a few adverbs: *faster, quicker, sooner,* and *later.*
NOTE: Remember always to use the subject form of the pronoun after *than.*

Examples:

John's grades are higher than his sister's.	(adjective)
Today is hotter than yesterday.	(adjective)
This chair is more comfortable than the other.	(adjective)
He speaks Spanish more fluently than I.	(adverb)
He visits his family less frequently than she does.	(adverb)
This year's exhibit is less impressive than last year's.	(adjective)

Unequal comparisons can be further intensified by adding *much* or *far* before the comparative form.

$$\text{subject} + \text{verb} + \begin{cases} far \\ much \end{cases} + \text{adjective} + er + than + \begin{cases} \text{noun} \\ \text{pronoun} \end{cases}$$

$$\text{subject} + \text{verb} + \begin{Bmatrix} far \\ much \end{Bmatrix} + more + \begin{Bmatrix} \text{adjective} \\ \text{adverb} \end{Bmatrix} + than + \begin{Bmatrix} \text{noun} \\ \text{pronoun} \end{Bmatrix}$$

Harry's watch is far more expensive than mine.
That movie we saw last night was much more interesting than the one on television.
A watermelon is much sweeter than a lemon.
She dances much more artistically than her predecessor.
He speaks English much more rapidly than he does Spanish.
His car is far better than yours.

Nouns can also be used in comparisons. Be sure to use the determiners correctly depending on whether the adjectives are countable or noncountable.

$$\text{subject} + \text{verb} + as + \begin{Bmatrix} many \\ much \\ little \\ few \end{Bmatrix} + \text{noun} + as + \begin{Bmatrix} \text{noun} \\ \text{pronoun} \end{Bmatrix}$$

OR

$$\text{subject} + \text{verb} + \begin{Bmatrix} more \\ fewer \\ less \end{Bmatrix} + \text{noun} + than + \begin{Bmatrix} \text{noun} \\ \text{pronoun} \end{Bmatrix}$$

I have more books than she.
February has fewer days than March.
He earns as much money as his brother.
They have as few classes as we.
Their job allows them less freedom than ours does.
Before payday, I have as little money as my brother.

• *Illogical comparisons:* An illogical comparison is one in which unlike entities have been compared. Be sure that the items being compared are the same. These forms can be divided into three categories: possessives, *that of,* and *those of.*

Incorrect: His drawings are as perfect as his instructor.
              (This sentence compares *drawings* with *instructor.*)
Correct: His drawings are as perfect as his instructor's.
              (*instructor's* = instructor's drawings)

Incorrect: The salary of a professor is higher than a secretary.
(This sentence compares *salary* with *secretary*.)

Correct: The salary of a professor is higher than <u>that of</u>
a secretary.
(*that of* = the salary of)

Incorrect: The duties of a policeman are more dangerous than
a teacher.
(This sentence compares *duties* with *teacher*.)

Correct: The duties of a policeman are more dangerous than <u>those</u>
of a teacher.
(*those of* = the duties of)

Examples of logical comparisons:

John's car runs <u>better than</u> <u>Mary's</u>.
(*Mary's* = Mary's car)

The climate in Florida is <u>as mild as</u> <u>that of</u> California.
(*that of* = the climate of)

Classes in the university are <u>more difficult than</u> <u>those in</u> the college.
(*those in* = the classes in)

The basketball games at the university are <u>better than</u> <u>those of</u> the high
school.
(*those of* = the games of)

Your accent is not <u>as strong as</u> <u>my mother's</u>.
(*my mother's* = my mother's accent)

My sewing machine is <u>better than</u> <u>Jane's</u>.
(*Jane's* = Jane's sewing machine)

• *Irregular comparatives and superlatives:* A few adjectives and adverbs
have irregular forms for the comparative and superlative. Study them.

ADJECTIVE OR ADVERB	COMPARATIVE	SUPERLATIVE
far	farther / further	farthest / furthest
little	less	least
much / many	more	most
good / well	better	best
bad / badly	worse	worst

I feel <u>much better</u> today <u>than</u> I did last week.
The university is <u>farther</u> <u>than</u> the mall.
He has <u>less time</u> now <u>than</u> he had before.
Marjorie has <u>more books</u> <u>than</u> Sue.
This magazine is <u>better</u> <u>than</u> that one.
He acts <u>worse</u> now <u>than</u> ever before.

Exercise 28: Comparisons

Supply the correct form of the adjectives and adverbs in parentheses. Let *as* and *than* be your clues. Add any other words that may be necessary.

1. John and his friends left _____ (soon) as the professor had finished his lecture.
2. His job is _____ (important) than his friend's.
3. He plays the guitar _____ (well) as Andrés Segovia.
4. A new house is much _____ (expensive) than an older one.
5. Last week was _____ (hot) as this week.
6. Martha is _____ (talented) than her cousin.
7. Bill's descriptions are _____ (colorful) than his wife's.
8. Nobody is _____ (happy) than María Elena.
9. The boys felt _____ (bad) than the girls about losing the game.
10. A greyhound runs _____ (fast) than a Chihuahua.

Exercise 29: Comparisons

Supply *than*, *as*, or *from* in each of the following sentences.
1. The Empire State Building is taller _____ the Statue of Liberty.
2. California is farther from New York _____ Pennsylvania.
3. His assignment is different _____ mine.
4. Louie reads more quickly _____ his sisters.
5. No animal is so big _____ King Kong.
6. That report is less impressive _____ the government's.
7. Sam wears the same shirt _____ his teammates.
8. Dave paints much more realistically _____ his professor.
9. The twins have less money at the end of the month _____ they have at the beginning.
10. Her sports car is different _____ Nancy's.

• *Multiple number comparatives:* Number multiples can include: *half, twice, three times, four times,* etc. Study the following rule.

$$\text{subject} + \text{verb} + \text{number multiple} + as + \begin{Bmatrix} much \\ many \end{Bmatrix} + (\text{noun}) + as + \begin{Bmatrix} \text{noun} \\ \text{pronoun} \end{Bmatrix}$$

NOTE: It is *incorrect* to say: "twice more than," etc.

This encyclopedia costs twice as much as the other one.

At the clambake last week, Fred ate three times as many oysters as Barney.

Jerome has half as many records now as I had last year.

● *Double comparatives:* These sentences begin with a comparative construction, and thus the second clause must also begin with a comparative.

> *the* + comparative + subject + verb + *the* + comparative + subject + verb

The hotter it is, the more miserable I feel.

The higher we flew, the worse Edna felt.

The bigger they are, the harder they fall.

The sooner you take your medicine, the better you will feel.

The sooner you leave, the earlier you will arrive at your destination.

> *the more* + subject + verb + *the* + comparative + subject + verb

The more you study, the smarter you will become.

The more he rowed the boat, the farther away he got.

The more he slept, the more irritable he became.

● *No sooner:* If the expression *no sooner* appears at the beginning of a sentence, the word *than* must introduce the second clause. Note also that the auxiliary precedes the subject.

> *no sooner* + auxiliary + subject + verb + *than* + subject + verb

No sooner had we started out for California, than it started to rain.

No sooner will he arrive, than he will want to leave.

No sooner had she entered the building, than she felt the presence of somebody else.

NOTE: *No longer* means *not anymore.* NEVER use *not longer* in a sentence that has this meaning.

John no longer studies at the university.

(John *does not* study at the university *anymore.*)

Cynthia may no longer use the library because her card has expired.

(Cynthia *may not* use the library *anymore.*)

• *Positives, comparatives, and superlatives:* Most descriptive adjectives have three forms: the positive (*happy*), the comparative (*happier*), and the superlative (*happiest*).

POSITIVE	COMPARATIVE	SUPERLATIVE
hot	hotter	hottest
interesting	more interesting	most interesting
sick	sicker	sickest
colorful	more colorful	most colorful

The *positive* shows no comparison. It describes only the simple quality of a person, thing, or group.

The house is big.   The flowers are fragrant.

The *comparative* involves *two* entities and shows a greater or lesser degree of difference between them.

My dog is smarter than yours.
Bob is more athletic than Richard.
Spinach is less appealing than carrots.

It is also possible to compare two entities without using *than*. In this case the expression *of the two* will usually appear someplace in the sentence.

---

subject + verb + *the* + comparative + *of the two* + (noun)

OR

---

of the two + (noun) + subject + verb + *the* + comparative

Harvey is the smarter of the two boys.
Of the two shirts, this one is the prettier.
Please give me the smaller of the two pieces of cake.
Of the two landscapes that you have shown me, this one is the more picturesque.
Of the two books, this one is the more interesting.

Remember:

> 2 entities–comparative
> 3 or more–superlative

In the *superlative* degree, three or more entities are compared, one of which is superior or inferior to the others. The following rule applies.

$$\text{subject} + \text{verb} + the + \begin{Bmatrix} \text{adjective} + est \\ most + \text{adjective} \\ least + \text{adjective} \end{Bmatrix} + \begin{Bmatrix} in + \text{singular count noun} \\ of + \text{plural count noun} \end{Bmatrix}$$

John is the tallest boy in the family.
Deana is the shortest of the three sisters.
These shoes are the least expensive of all.
Of the three shirts, this one is the prettiest.

NOTE: After the expression *one of the* + superlative, be sure that the noun is plural and the verb is singular.

One of the greatest tennis players in the world is Bjorn Borg.
Kuwait is one of the biggest oil producers in the world.

Adverbs usually are not followed by *-er* or *-est*. Instead, they are compared by adding *more* or *less* for the comparative degree, and by adding *most* or *least* to form the superlative.

POSITIVE	COMPARATIVE	SUPERLATIVE
carefully	more carefully	most carefully
	less carefully	least carefully
cautiously	more cautiously	most cautiously
	less cautiously	least cautiously

Sal drove more cautiously than Bob.   (comparative)
Joe dances more gracefully than his partner.   (comparative)
That child behaves the most carelessly of all.   (superlative)
Irene plays the most recklessly of all.   (superlative)

Exercise 30: Comparisons

Select the correct form in parentheses in the following sentences.

1. Of the four dresses, I like the red one (better/best).
2. Phil is the (happier/happiest) person that we know.
3. Pat's car is (faster/fastest) than Dan's.
4. This is the (creamier/creamiest) ice cream I have had in a long time.
5. This poster is (colorfuler/more colorful) than the one in the hall.
6. Does Fred feel (weller/better) today than he did yesterday?
7. This vegetable soup tastes very (good/well).
8. While trying to balance the baskets on her head, the woman walked (awkwarder/more awkwardly) than her daughter.
9. Jane is the (less/least) athletic of all the women.
10. My cat is the (prettier/prettiest) of the two.

11. This summary is (the better/the best) of the pair.
12. Your heritage is different (from/than) mine.
13. This painting is (less impressive/least impressive) than the one in the other gallery.
14. The colder the weather gets, (sicker/the sicker) I feel.
15. No sooner had he received the letter (when/than) he called Maria.
16. A mink coat costs (twice more than/twice as much as) a sable coat.
17. Jim has as (little/few) opportunities to play tennis as I.
18. That recipe calls for (many/much) more sugar than mine does.
19. The museum is the (farther/farthest) away of the three buildings.
20. George Washington is (famouser/more famous) than John Jay.

18. Nouns Functioning as Adjectives

In English, many nouns can function as adjectives when they appear before other nouns (a wool coat, a gold watch, a history teacher). The first noun of the combination functions as an adjective, describing the second one, which functions as a noun. The nouns which function as adjectives are always in the singular even though they may modify a plural noun. Number-noun combinations always appear hyphenated.

We took a tour that lasted five weeks.

(*Weeks* functions as a noun in this sentence.)

We took a five-week tour.
      adjective noun

His subscription to that magazine is for two years.

(*Years* functions as a noun in this sentence.)

He has a two-year subscription to that magazine.
      adjective   noun

That student wrote a report that was ten pages long.

(*Pages* functions as a noun in this sentence.)

That student wrote a ten-page report.
      adjective noun

These shoes cost twenty dollars.

(*Dollars* functions as a noun in this sentence.)

These are twenty-dollar shoes.
      adjective   noun

Exercise 31: Nouns Functioning as Adjectives

In each of the following sets, choose the appropriate form for the blank in the second sentence.

Example: Her call to California lasted ten minutes.
                She made a ten-minute call to California.

1. Sam's new apartment is in a building which has twelve stories.
   Sam's new apartment is in a _____ building.
2. We teach languages.
   We are _____ teachers.
3. My parents saw a play in three acts last night.
   My parents saw a _____ play last night.
4. The manager said that the sale would last for two days.
   The manager said that it would be a _____ sale.
5. Hal bought a tool set containing 79 pieces.
   Hal bought a _____ tool set.
6. Margie has a bookcase with five shelves.
   Margie has a _____ bookcase.
7. I need two cans of tomatoes that weigh 16 ounces each.
   I need two _____ cans of tomatoes.
8. I'm looking for a pressure cooker that holds six quarts.
   I'm looking for a _____ pressure cooker.
9. He is a specialist at building houses made of bricks.
   He is a specialist at building _____ houses.
10. Mrs. Jansen just bought her daughter a bicycle with ten speeds.
    Mrs. Jansen just bought her daughter a _____ bicycle.

19. Enough *with Adjectives, Adverbs, and Nouns*

Enough changes positions depending on whether it is modifying a noun, an adjective, or an adverb. When modifying an adjective or an adverb, *enough* follows.

$$\left\{ \begin{array}{c} \text{adjective} \\ \text{adverb} \end{array} \right\} + enough$$

Are those french fries <u>crisp enough</u> for you?
            adjective

She speaks Spanish <u>well enough</u> to be an interpreter.
                   adverb

It is not <u>cold enough</u> to wear a heavy jacket.
          adjective

When modifying a noun, *enough* precedes the noun.

$$enough + \text{noun}$$

Do you have <u>enough sugar</u> for the cake?
                   noun

Jake bought <u>enough</u> <u>red paint</u> to finish the barn.
noun phrase

He does not have <u>enough</u> <u>money</u> to attend the concert.
noun

NOTE: The noun that is modified by *enough* may sometimes be deleted with no change in meaning.

I forgot my money. Do you have <u>enough</u>?
(We understand that the speaker means "enough money.")

Exercise 32: Enough

In the following sentences, choose the correct form in parentheses.

1. There were not (enough people/people enough) to have the meeting.
2. Allen has learned (enough French/French enough) to study in France next year.
3. Do you have (enough time/time enough) to talk now?
4. She drove (enough fast/fast enough) to win the race.
5. Mike will graduate from law school (enough soon/soon enough) to join his father's firm.
6. We arrived (enough early/early enough) to have some coffee before class began.
7. It has rained (enough hard/hard enough) to flood the low-lying areas.
8. You should type (enough slowly/slowly enough) that you will not make an error.
9. He has just (enough flour/flour enough) to bake that loaf of bread.
10. There are (enough books/books enough) for each student to have one.

20. *Cause Connectors*

This section demonstrates the usage of several grammatical devices which show cause.

● *Because/because of: Because* must always be followed by a complete sentence. (There must be a verb.) *Because of* is followed *only* by a noun or noun phrase. (There must NOT be a conjugated verb.)

. . . *because* + subject + verb

. . . *because of* + noun (phrase)

NOTE *Because of* is often interchangeable with the expression *due to.*

Jan was worried because <u>it</u> <u>had started</u> to rain.
 *subject* *verb*

Jan was worried <u>because of</u> <u>the rain</u>.
 *noun phrase*

The students arrived late <u>because</u> <u>there was</u> a traffic jam.
 *subject* *verb*

The students arrived late <u>because of</u> <u>the traffic jam</u>.
 *noun phrase*

We have to cut down on our driving <u>because</u> <u>there is</u> an oil shortage.
 *subject* *verb*

We have to cut down on our driving <u>because of</u> <u>the oil shortage</u>.
 *noun phrase*

NOTE: It is also possible for the cause clause to begin the sentence.

<u>Because of the rain</u>, we have cancelled the party.

Exercise 33: Because/Because Of

Supply either *because* or *because of* as appropriate.

1. It was difficult to deliver the letter _____ the sender had written the wrong address on the envelope.
2. We decided to leave early _____ the party was boring.
3. Rescue attempts were temporarily halted _____ the bad weather.
4. They visited their friends often _____ they enjoyed their company.
5. Paul cannot go to the football game _____ his grades.
6. Marcella was awarded a scholarship _____ her superior scholastic ability.
7. Nobody ventured outdoors _____ the hurricane warnings.
8. We plan to spend our vacation in the mountains _____ the air is purer there.
9. We have to drive around the bay _____ the bridge was destroyed in the storm.
10. The chickens have died _____ the intense heat.

● *Purpose and result* (so that): Clauses showing purpose are followed by the conjunction *so that*. After *so that* is a result clause with both a subject and a verb. The time of the result clause must be future in relation to the time of the purpose clause.

> subject + verb + *so that* + subject + verb

NOTE: It is NOT correct in formal written English to eliminate *that* in these sentences, although it is possible in spoken English.

He studied very hard so that he could pass the test.

She is sending the package early so that it will arrive in time for her sister's birthday.

Damien is practicing the guitar so that he can play for the dance.

I am learning German so that I will be able to speak it when I go to Austria next summer.

Susan drove to Miami instead of flying so that she could save money.

Will you let me know about the party so that I can make plans to attend?

● *Cause and effect* (so, such): The following constructions are used to indicate a cause and effect (result) relationship.

(1)

$$\text{subject} + \text{verb} + so + \begin{Bmatrix} \text{adjective} \\ \text{adverb} \end{Bmatrix} + that + \text{subject} + \text{verb}$$

NOTE: Do NOT use a noun after *so*. See rule (3).

The soprano sang so well that she received a standing ovation.

Terry ran so fast that he broke the previous speed record.

Judy worked so diligently that she received an increase in salary.

The soup tastes so good that everyone will ask for more.

The little boy looks so unhappy that we all feel sorry for him.

The student had behaved so badly that he was dismissed from the class.

The rules for clauses including the intensive modifiers are:

(2)

$$\text{subject} + \text{verb} + so + \begin{Bmatrix} \text{many} \\ \text{few} \end{Bmatrix} + \text{plural count noun} + that + \text{subject} + \text{verb}$$

The Smiths had so many children that they formed their own baseball team.

I had so few job offers that it wasn't difficult to select one.

$$\text{subject} + \text{verb} + so + \begin{Bmatrix} \text{much} \\ \text{little} \end{Bmatrix} + \text{non-count noun} + that + \text{subject} + \text{verb}$$

He has invested so much money in the project that he cannot abandon it now.

The grass received so little water that it turned brown in the heat.

(3)

> subject + verb + *such* + *a* + adjective + singular count noun + *that* . . .

OR

> subject + verb + *so* + adjective + *a* + singular count noun + *that* . . .

NOTE: *Such* + *a* + adjective is the more common of the two.

It was such a hot day that we decided to stay indoors.

OR

It was so hot a day that we decided to stay indoors.

It was such an interesting book that he couldn't put it down.

OR

It was so interesting a book that he couldn't put it down.

> subject + verb + *such* + adjective + $\begin{Bmatrix} \text{plural count noun} \\ \text{non-count noun} \end{Bmatrix}$ + *that* + subject + verb

She has such exceptional abilities that everyone is jealous of her.
plural count noun

They are such beautiful pictures that everybody will want one.
plural count noun

Perry has had such bad luck that he's decided not to gamble.
non-count noun

This is such difficult homework that I will never finish it.
non-count noun

NOTE: It is NOT possible to use *so* in the above rule.

Meanings:

It has been such a long time since I've seen him that I'm not sure if I will remember him.
(I'm not sure if I will remember him *because* it has been a long time.)
Cause: It has been a long time.
Effect: I'm not sure if I will remember him.

He has so heavy a work load that it is difficult for him to travel.
(It is difficult for him to travel *because* he has a heavy work load.)
Cause: He has a very heavy work load.
Effect: It is difficult for him to travel.

Peter has <u>such long fingers that</u> he should play the piano.

(Peter should play the piano *because* he has very long fingers.)

Cause: Peter has very long fingers.

Effect: He should play the piano.

Professor Sands gives <u>such interesting lectures that</u> his classes are never boring.

(Professor Sands's classes are never boring *because* he gives very interesting lectures.)

Cause: Professor Sands gives very interesting lectures.

Effect: His classes are never boring.

This is <u>such tasty ice cream that</u> I'll have another helping.

(I'll have another helping of ice cream *because* it is very tasty.)

Cause: The ice cream is very tasty.

Effect: I'll have another helping.

Exercise 34: So/Such

Following the formulas, use either *so* or *such* in these sentences as appropriate.

1. The sun shone _____ brightly that Maria had to put on her sunglasses.

2. Dean was _____ a powerful swimmer that he always won the races.

3. There were _____ few students registered that the class was cancelled.

4. We had _____ wonderful memories of that place that we decided to return.

5. We had _____ good a time at the party that we hated to leave.

6. The benefit was _____ great a success that the promoters decided to repeat it.

7. It was _____ a nice day that we decided to go to the beach.

8. Jane looked _____ sick that the nurse told her to go home.

9. Those were _____ difficult assignments that we spent two weeks finishing them.

10. Ray called at _____ an early hour that we weren't awake yet.

11. The book looked _____ interesting that he decided to read it.

12. He worked _____ carefully that it took him a long time to complete the project.

13. We stayed in the sun for _____ a long time that we became sunburned.

14. There were _____ many people on the bus that we decided to walk.

15. The program was _____ entertaining that nobody wanted to miss it.

MINI-TEST 2 FOR GRAMMAR ITEMS 15 THROUGH 20

DIRECTIONS

Each question on this mini-test consists of a sentence in which four words or phrases are underlined. The four underlined parts of the sentence are marked A, B, C, D. You are to identify the *one* underlined word or phrase that *would not be acceptable in standard written English*. Circle the letter of the underlined portion which is not correct.

1. Children enjoy telling and listening to ghosts stories, especially
                      A   B   C
   on Halloween night.
        D

2. At the rate the clerks were processing the applications, Harry
                                  A
   figured that it will take four hours for his to be reviewed.
                    B   C   D

3. No one would have attended the lecture if you told the truth about
                     A   B   C
   the guest speaker.
        D

4. We had better to review this chapter carefully because we will
                  A   B
   have some questions on it on our test tomorrow.
        C   D

5. The little boy's mother bought him a five-speeds racing bicycle
      A   B   C
   for his birthday.
       D

6. Despite the time of the year, yesterday's temperature was enough hot
      A   B   C
   to turn on the air conditioning.
      D

7. The Andersons just had an enclosed bricks patio built
         A   B   C
   after fighting off the insects for two months.
         D

8. Danny spent such enjoyable vacation in Europe this summer that he
                   A   B
   plans to return as soon as he saves enough money.
            C   D

9. Although the quantity was small, we had supplies enough to finish
      A   B   C
   the experiment.
   D

10. Kurt had so interesting and creative plans that everyone wanted to
            A   B   C
    work on his committee.
        D

11. If Rudy would have studied German in college, he would not
            A   B
    have found the scientific terminology so difficult to understand.
            C   D

12. I have to depositing this money in my checking account or else the
           A   B
    check I just wrote will bounce.
          C   D

13. We wish today was sunny so that we could spend the day in the country
          A   B   C   D
    communing with nature.

14. Paul did so well in his speech today that he should have rehearsed
        A   B   C
    it many times this past week.
            D

15. Bess is used to fly after having crossed the continent many times
          A   B   C
    during the past decade.
         D

16. Our Spanish professor would like us spending more time in the
                    A B   C
    laboratory practicing our pronunciation.
         D

17. Sam used to living in Oklahoma, but his company had him transferred
          A   B   C
    to a better position in Georgia.
      D

18. The bolder the matador's display in the arena became, louder the
          A   B   C
    audience expressed its approval of his presentation.
            D

19. Hal's new sports car costs much more than his friend Joel.
            A   B   C   D

20. Max would rather to be fishing from his boat in the lake than
                  A   B   C

    sitting at his desk in the office.
         D

21. Sally must have called her sister last night, but she arrived
          A   B

    home too late to call her.
        C   D

22. If a crisis would occur, those unfamiliar with the procedures would
            A   B   C

    not know how to handle the situation.
           D

23. Standing among so many strangers, the frightened child began to sob
         A   B   C

    uncontrollable.
        D

24. The teacher tried to make the classes enjoyable experiences for the
              A

    students so they would take a greater interest in the subject.
        B   C   D

25. Whenever students asked for help or guidance, the counselor
                 A

    would advise them or refer them to someone who will.
      B   C   D

26. Anybody who plans to attend the meeting ought send a short note
           A   B   C

    to the chairperson.
      D

27. The teachers and the administrators are having such difficult time
                                A

    agreeing on a contract for the forthcoming year that the teachers
      B   C

    may go on strike.
       D

28. Mary usually arrives at the office at nine o'clock, but because the
        A   B   C

    storm, she was two hours late.
                   D

29. Our new television <u>came</u> with a <u>ninety-days warranty</u> <u>on all</u>
                   A   B   C

    electrical <u>components</u>.
              D

30. It is <u>difficult</u> to get used <u>to sleep</u> in a tent after <u>having</u> a soft,
           A   B   C

    comfortable bed <u>to lie on</u>.
                  D

31. The director felt <u>badly</u> about <u>not giving</u> Mary the position <u>that</u>
                    A   B   C

    she <u>had sought</u> with his company.
          D

32. Tom and Mark hope <u>go skiing</u> <u>in the mountains</u> this weekend <u>if the</u>
                     A   B   C

    weather <u>permits</u>.
          D

33. <u>The</u> political candidate talked as if she <u>has</u> already <u>been elected</u>
     A   B   C

    <u>to the</u> presidency.
     D

34. The salad tasted <u>so well</u> that my brother <u>returned to the</u>
                   A   B

    <u>salad bar for</u> <u>another helping</u>.
         C   D

35. <u>Even though</u> she <u>looks</u> very young, she is twice <u>older than</u> my
       A   B   C

    <u>twenty-year-old</u> sister.
        D

36. <u>Despite</u> his <u>smiling</u> face, the <u>second-place contestant</u> is
      A   B   C

    <u>more sadder</u> than the winner.
        D

37. I do not believe that I <u>have ever seen</u> as many expensive cars <u>than</u> <u>were</u>
                      A   B C

    in <u>that shopping center</u>.
        D

38. The members of the orchestra <u>had to arrived</u> an hour
     A   B

    <u>prior to the performance</u> <u>for a short</u> rehearsal.
           C   D

39. We thought our cameras were the same, but his is different than the
    A   B   C
    one that I bought.
              D

40. If Monique had not attended the conference, she never would meet
                                A   B
    her old friend Dan, whom she had not seen in years.
                        C   D

41. Having lived here for seven years, my friend is used to speak
        A   B   C
    English with all her classmates.
                   D

42. No one in our office wants to drive to work any more because of
                        A   B
    there are always traffic jams at rush hour.
          C   D

43. That novel is definitely a dense-packed narrative, but
                   A   B
    one which requires a vast knowledge of cultural background or an
        C   D
    excellent encyclopedia.

44. Louise is the more capable of the three girls who have tried out
                A   B   C
    for the part in the play.
                 D

45. They played so good game of tennis last night that they surprised
            A   B   C
    their audience.
    D

46. I would rather that they do not travel during the bad weather,
                    A   B   C
    but they insist that they must return home today.
                              D

47. Among us students are many foreigners who attend languages classes
        A   B   C   D
    at the south campus.

48. My book is different than yours because mine has a vocabulary
                        A   B
    section at the bottom of each page, and yours has one in the back.
            C   D

49. That product that you <u>bought</u> at the lower price is <u>the more inferior</u>
$$\text{A}\text{B}$$
   to the <u>one</u> that we sell at a <u>slightly</u> higher price.
$$\text{C}\text{D}$$

50. After a <u>carefully</u> investigation, we <u>soon discovered</u> that the house
$$\text{A}\text{B}$$
   <u>was</u> <u>infested with</u> termites.
$$\text{C}\text{D}$$

21. Passive Voice

A sentence can be either in the active or passive voice. In an "active" sentence, the subject performs the action. In a "passive" sentence, the subject receives the action. To make an active sentence into a passive sentence, follow these steps.

---

(1) Place the complement of the active sentence at the beginning of the passive sentence.

(2) If there are any auxiliaries in the active sentence, place them immediately after the new subject agreeing in number with the subject.

(3) Insert the verb *be* after the auxiliary or auxiliaries in the same form as the main verb in the active sentence.

(4) Place the main verb from the active sentence after the auxiliaries and *be* in the past participle.

(5) Place the subject of the active sentence after the verb in the passive sentence preceded by the preposition *by*. (This can be eliminated completely if it is not important or is understood.)

Study the following possible word orders for passive voice.

SIMPLE PRESENT OR SIMPLE PAST

$$\left.\begin{array}{l} am \\ is \\ are \\ was \\ were \end{array}\right\} + \text{[verb in past participle]}$$

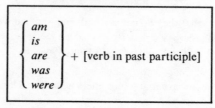

Active: Hurricanes destroy a great deal of property each year.
                  subject   *present*   *complement*

Passive: A great deal of property is destroyed by hurricanes
                  singular subject   *be*   *past*
                                              participle

each year.

Active: The tornado destroyed thirty houses.
<u>subject</u>   <u>past</u>   <u>complement</u>

Passive: Thirty houses were destroyed by the tornado.
<u>plural subject</u>   <u>be</u>   <u>past participle</u>

PRESENT PROGRESSIVE OR PAST PROGRESSIVE

$$\left\{ \begin{array}{l} am \\ is \\ are \\ was \\ were \end{array} \right\} + being + \text{[verb in past participle]}$$

Active: The committee is considering several new proposals.
<u>subject</u>   <u>present progressive</u>   <u>complement</u>

Passive: Several new proposals are being considered
<u>plural subject</u>   <u>auxil- iary</u>   <u>be</u>   <u>past participle</u>
by the committee.

Active: The committee was considering several new proposals.
<u>subject</u>   <u>past progressive</u>   <u>complement</u>

Passive: Several new proposals were being considered by the
<u>plural subject</u>   <u>auxil- iary</u>   <u>be</u>   <u>past participle</u>
committee.

PRESENT PERFECT OR PAST PERFECT

$$\left\{ \begin{array}{l} has \\ have \\ had \end{array} \right\} + been + \text{[verb in past participle]}$$

Active: The company has ordered some new equipment.
<u>subject</u>   <u>present perfect</u>   <u>complement</u>

Passive: Some new equipment has been ordered by the company.
<u>singular subject</u>   <u>auxil- iary</u>   <u>be</u>   <u>past participle</u>

Active: The company had ordered some new equipment before
<u>subject</u>   <u>past perfect</u>   <u>complement</u>
the strike began.

Passive: Some new equipment had been ordered by the company
<u>subject</u>   <u>auxil- iary</u>   <u>be</u>   <u>past participle</u>
before the strike began.

MODALS

> modal + *be* + [verb in past participle]

Active: The manager should sign these contracts today.
                 subject   *modal + verb*   *complement*

Passive: These contracts should be signed by the manager today.
                  subject   *modal* *be* *past*
                                                                     participle

MODALS + PERFECT

> modal + *have* + *been* + [verb in past participle]

Active: Somebody should have called the president this morning.
                 subject   *modal + perfect*   *complement*

Passive: The president should have been called this morning.
                  subject   *modal* *have* *be* *past*
                                                                          participle

Exercise 35: Passive Voice

Change the following sentences from active to passive voice.

1. Somebody calls the president every day.
2. John is calling the other members.
3. Martha was delivering the documents to the department.
4. The other members have repealed the amendment.
5. The delegates had received the information before the recess.
6. The teacher should buy the supplies for this class.
7. Somebody will call Mr. Watson tonight.
8. The fire has caused considerable damage.
9. The company was developing a new procedure before the bankruptcy hearings began.
10. John will have received the papers by tomorrow.

22. *Causative Verbs*

The causative verbs are used to indicate that one person causes a second person to do something for the first person. One can cause somebody to do something for him or her by paying, asking, or forcing the person. The causative verbs are: *have, get, make.*

● *Have/get:* The clause following *have* or *get* may be active or passive. Study the following rules.

(1) ACTIVE

> subject + *have* + complement + [verb in simple form] . . .
> *(any tense)* *(usually person)*

(2) ACTIVE

> subject + *get* + complement + [verb in infinitive] . . .
> *(any tense)* *(usually person)*

(3) PASSIVE

> subject + $\left\{ \begin{array}{l} have \\ get \end{array} \right\}$ + complement + [verb in past participle] . . .
> *(usually thing)*

(1) Mary had John wash the car. (John washed the car.) active
(2) Mary got John to wash the car. (John washed the car.) active
(3) Mary got the car washed.
     Mary had the car washed. (The car was washed by somebody.) passive

Examples of active clauses in causative sentences:

   The president had his advisors arrange a press conference.
   George is getting his teachers to give him a make-up exam.
   Mary has had a friend type all of her papers.
   John is having his father contact the officials.
   The editor had the contributors attend a composition workshop.
   Morris got his dog to bring him the newspaper.

Examples of passive clauses in causative sentences:

   James has his shirts cleaned at the drycleaners.
   Pat is having her car repaired this week.
   Anna got her paper typed by a friend.
   The president is having a press conference arranged by his advisors.
   Mary got her husband arrested. (Exception: a person is the complement,
      but the second clause is passive.)
   Rick was having his hair cut when John called.

• *Make:* Make can be followed only by a clause in the active voice.
It is stronger than *have* or *get*. It means *force*.

> subject + *make* + complement + [verb in simple form] . . .
> *(any tense)*

The robber <u>made</u> the teller <u>give</u> him the money.
(The robber *forced* the teller *to give* him the money.)

NOTE: *force* + [verb in infinitive]

Examples of *make:*

The manager <u>made</u> the salesmen <u>attend</u> the conference.
The teacher always <u>makes</u> the children <u>stay</u> in their seats.
George <u>made</u> his son <u>be</u> quiet in the theater.
The president <u>is making</u> his cabinet members <u>sign</u> this document.
The teacher <u>had made</u> the students' parents <u>sign</u> release forms before he let the students jump on the trampoline.

● *Let: Let* is usually added to the list of causatives in grammar textbooks. It is not actually causative. It means *allow* or *permit*. Notice the difference in grammar.

---

subject + *let* + complement + [verb in simple form] . . .

---

subject + $\begin{Bmatrix} permit \\ allow \end{Bmatrix}$ + complement + [verb in infinitive] . . .

NOTE: *Let* is NOT INTERCHANGEABLE WITH *leave*, which means *to go away.*

Examples:

John <u>let</u> his daughter <u>swim</u> with her friends.
(John <u>allowed</u> his daughter <u>to swim</u> with her friends.)
(John <u>permitted</u> his daughter <u>to swim</u> with her friends.)

The teacher <u>let</u> the students <u>leave</u> class early.
The policeman <u>let</u> the suspect <u>make</u> one phone call.
Dr. Jones <u>is letting</u> the students <u>hand</u> in the papers on Monday.
Mrs. Binion <u>let</u> her son <u>spend</u> the night with a friend.
We <u>are going to let</u> her <u>write</u> the letter.
Mr. Brown always <u>lets</u> his children <u>watch</u> cartoons on Saturday mornings.

● *Help: Help* is not actually a causative verb either, but is generally considered with causative verbs in grammar textbooks. It is usually followed by the simple form, but can be followed by the infinitive in some cases. It means *assist.*

---

subject + *help* + complement + $\begin{Bmatrix} \text{[verb in simple form]} \\ \text{[verb in infinitive]} \end{Bmatrix}$

John helped Mary wash the dishes.

Jorge helped the old woman with the packages (to) find a taxi.

The teacher helped Carolina find the research materials.

Exercise 36: Causative Verbs

Use the correct form of the verb in parentheses in each of the following sentences.

1. The teacher made Juan _____ (leave) the room.
2. Toshiko had her car _____ (repair) by a mechanic.
3. Ellen got Marvin _____ (type) her paper.
4. I made Jane _____ (call) her friend on the telephone.
5. We got our house _____ (paint) last week.
6. Dr. Byrd is having the students _____ (write) a composition.
7. The policemen made the suspect _____ (lie) on the ground.
8. Mark got his transcripts _____ (send) to the university.
9. Maria is getting her hair _____ (cut) tomorrow.
10. We will have to get the Dean _____ (sign) this form.
11. The teacher let Al _____ (leave) the classroom.
12. Maria got Ed _____ (wash) the pipettes.
13. She always has her car _____ (fix) by the same mechanic.
14. Gene got his book _____ (publish) by a subsidy publisher.
15. We have to help Janet _____ (find) her keys.

23. Relative Clauses

● *The relative pronoun:* A relative clause is used to form one sentence from two separate sentences. The relative pronoun replaces one of two identical noun phrases and relates the clauses to each other. The relative pronouns and their uses are listed here.

PRONOUN	USE IN FORMAL ENGLISH
that	things
which	things
who	people
whom	people
whose	usually people

NOTE: In speaking, *that* can be used for people, but NOT in formal written English.

The relative pronoun completely replaces a duplicate noun phrase. *There can be no regular pronoun along with the relative pronoun.*

Incorrect: This is the book that I bought it at the bookstore.

Correct: This is the book that I bought at the bookstore.

Remember that a sentence with a relative clause can always be reduced to two separate sentences, so each clause *must contain a verb.*

We bought the stereo. The stereo had been advertised at a reduced price.

duplicate noun phrase

We bought the stereo that had been advertised at a reduced price.

John bought a boat. The boat cost thirty thousand dollars.
John bought a boat that cost thirty thousand dollars.

George is going to buy the house. We have been thinking of
  buying the house.
George is going to buy the house that we have been thinking of buying.

John is the man. We are going to recommend John for the job.

John is the man whom we are going to recommend for the job.

• *Who/whom: Who* is used when the noun phrase being replaced is in the subject position of the sentence. *Whom* is used when it is from the complement position. NOTE: In speech, *whom* is rarely used, but it should be used when appropriate in formal written English. If you have difficulty deciding whether *who* or *whom* should be used, remember the following rule.

> *. . . who* + verb . . .
> *. . . whom* + noun . . .

Consider the following sentences.

The men are angry. The men are in this room.

These sentences can also be considered as:

The men [the men are in this room] are angry.

subject

The men who are in this room are angry.

The men are angry. I don't like the men.
The men [I don't like the men] are angry.

complement

The men whom I don't like are angry.

We also use the form *whom* after a preposition. In this case, the preposition should also be moved to the position before *whom* in formal written English.

The men are angry. The woman is talking to the men.
The men [the woman is talking to the men] are angry.

complement of
preposition

The men to whom the woman is talking are angry.

However, if the preposition is part of a combination such as a two-word verb, meaning that the preposition cannot reasonably be moved away from the verb, it will remain with the verb.

● *Restrictive and nonrestrictive clauses:* A relative clause can be either restrictive or nonrestrictive. A restrictive clause is one that cannot be omitted from a sentence if the sentence is to keep its original meaning. A nonrestrictive clause contains additional information which is not required to give the meaning of the sentence. A nonrestrictive clause is set off from the other clause by commas and a restrictive clause is not. *Who, whom,* and *which* can be used in restrictive or nonrestrictive clauses. *That* can be used *only in restrictive clauses.* Normally, *that* is the preferred word to use in a restrictive clause, although *which* is acceptable. TOEFL does not test the use of *which* and *that* in restrictive clauses.

Examples of restrictive and nonrestrictive clauses:

Restrictive: Weeds that float to the surface should be removed before they decay.
(We are not speaking of all weeds, only those that float to the surface. Thus, the sentence is restrictive; if "that float to the surface" were omitted, the sentence would have a different meaning.)

Nonrestrictive: My car, which is very large, uses too much gasoline.
(The fact that my car is very large is additional information and not important to the rest of the sentence. Notice that it is not possible to use the pronoun *that* in place of *which* in this sentence.)

Examples of relative clauses:

Dr. Jones is the only doctor whom I have seen about this problem.
Hurricanes that are born off the coast of Africa often prove to be the most deadly.
Teachers who do not spend enough time on class preparation often have difficulty explaining new lessons.
This rum, which I bought in the Virgin Islands, is very smooth.
Film that has been exposed to X rays often produces poor photographs.
The woman to whom we gave the check has left.

● *Whose:* This relative pronoun indicates possession.

The board was composed of citizens. The citizens' dedication was evident.
The board was composed of citizens whose dedication was evident.

James [James's father is the president of the company] has received a promotion.
James, whose father is the president of the company, has received a promotion.

John found a cat. The cat's leg was broken.
John found a cat whose leg was broken.

Harold [Harold's car was stolen last night] is at the police station.
Harold, whose car was stolen last night, is at the police station.

The company [the company's employees are on strike] is closing down for two weeks.
The company, whose employees are on strike, is closing down for two weeks.

The dentist is with a child. The child's teeth are causing some problems.
The dentist is with a child whose teeth are causing some problems.

The president [the president's advisors have quit] is giving a press conference.
The president, whose advisors have quit, is giving a press conference.

Exercise 37: Relative Clauses

Combine the following individual sentences into single sentences with relative clauses.

1. The last record [the record was produced by this company] became a gold record.
2. Checking accounts [the checking accounts require a minimum balance] are very common now.
3. The professor [you spoke to the professor yesterday] is not here today.
4. John [John's grades are the highest in the school] has received a scholarship.
5. Felipe bought a camera. The camera has three lenses.
6. Frank is the man. We are going to nominate Frank for the office of treasurer.
7. The doctor is with a patient. The patient's leg was broken in an accident.
8. Jane is the woman. Jane is going to China next year.
9. Janet wants a typewriter. The typewriter self-corrects.
10. This book [I found the book last week] contains some useful information.
11. Mr. Bryant [Mr. Bryant's team has lost the game] looks very sad.
12. James wrote an article. The article indicated that he disliked the president.
13. The director of the program [the director graduated from Harvard University] is planning to retire next year.
14. This is the book. I have been looking for this book all year.
15. William [William's brother is a lawyer] wants to become a judge.

● *Optional relative clause reduction:* In restrictive relative clauses, it is possible to omit the relative pronoun and the verb *be* (along with any other auxiliaries) in the following cases.

(1) Before relative clauses in the passive voice:

This is the Z value <u>which was obtained</u> from the table
areas under the normal curve.

OR

This is the Z value <u>obtained</u> from the table areas under the
normal curve.

(2) Before prepositional phrases:

The beaker <u>that is on the counter</u> contains a solution.

OR

The beaker <u>on the counter</u> contains a solution.

(3) Before progressive (continuous) verb structures:

The girl <u>who is running</u> down the street might be in trouble.

OR

The girl <u>running</u> down the street might be in trouble.

It is also possible to omit the relative pronoun and the verb *be* in nonrestrictive clauses before noun phrases.

Mr. Jackson, <u>who is a professor</u>, is traveling in the Mideast this year.
Mr. Jackson, <u>a professor</u>, is traveling in the Mideast this year.

Exercise 38: Relative Clause Reduction

Reduce the relative clauses in the following sentences.

1. George is the man who was chosen to represent the committee at the convention.
2. All of the money that was accepted has already been released.
3. The papers that are on the table belong to Patricia.
4. The man who was brought to the police station confessed to the crime.
5. The girl who is drinking coffee is Mary Allen.
6. John's wife, who is a professor, has written several papers on this subject.
7. The man who is talking to the policeman is my uncle.
8. The book that is on the top shelf is the one that I need.
9. The number of students who have been counted is quite high.
10. Leo Evans, who is a doctor, eats in this restaurant every day.

24. That—*other uses*

● *Optional:* The word *that* has several uses besides its use in relative clauses.
One such use is as a conjunction. Sometimes when *that* is used as a
conjunction it is optional, and sometimes it is obligatory. *That* is usually
optional after the following verbs.

say	tell	think	believe

John said that he was leaving next week.

OR

John said he was leaving next week.

Henry told me that he had a lot of work to do.

OR

Henry told me he had a lot of work to do.

● *Obligatory: That* is usually *obligatory* after the following verbs when introducing another clause.

mention	declare	report	state

The mayor declared that on June the first he would announce the results of the search.

George mentioned that he was going to France next year.

The article stated that this solution was flammable.

● That *clauses:* Some clauses, generally introduced by noun phrases, also contain *that*. These clauses are reversible.

It is well known that many residents of third world countries are dying.

OR

That many residents of third world countries are dying is well known.

NOTE: If a sentence begins with a *that* clause, be sure that both clauses contain a verb.

It surprises me that John would do such a thing.

OR

That John would do such a thing surprises me.

It wasn't believed until the fifteenth century that the earth revolves around the sun.

OR

That the earth revolves around the sun wasn't believed until the fifteenth century.

It is obvious that the Williams boy is abusing drugs.

OR

That the Williams boy is abusing drugs is obvious.

25. Subjunctive

The subjunctive in English is the simple form of the verb when used after certain verbs indicating that one person wants another person to do something. The word *that* must always appear in subjunctive sentences. If it is omitted, most of the verbs are followed by the infinitive.

We urge that you leave now.
We urge you to leave now.

Study the following list of verbs.

advise	decree	move	prefer	request	suggest
ask	demand	order	propose	require	urge
command	insist		recommend	stipulate	

NOTE: The verb *want* itself is not one of these verbs.

In the following rule, *verb* indicates one of the above verbs.

subject +   verb   + *that* + subject + [verb in simple form] . . .
            (any tense)

The judge insisted that the jury return a verdict immediately.
The university requires that all its students take this course.
The doctor suggested that his patient stop smoking.
Congress has decreed that the gasoline tax be abolished.
We proposed that he take a vacation.
I move that we adjourn until this afternoon.

The simple form of the verb is also used after impersonal expressions with the same meaning as the above verbs. The adjectives that fit into this formula include the following.

advised	necessary	recommended	urgent
important	obligatory	required	imperative
mandatory	proposed	suggested	

In the following rule, *adjective* indicates one of the above adjectives.

it +   *be*   + adjective + *that* + subject + [verb in simple form] . . .
         (any tense)

It is necessary that he find the books.
It was urgent that she leave at once.
It has been proposed that we change the topic.
It is important that you remember this question.
It has been suggested that he forget the election.
It was recommended that we wait for the authorities.

Exercise 39: Subjunctive

Correct the errors in the following sentences; if there are no errors, write *correct*.

1. The teacher demanded that the student left the room.
2. It was urgent that he called her immediately.
3. It was very important that we delay discussion.
4. She intends to move that the committee suspends discussion on this issue.
5. The king decreed that the new laws took effect the following month.
6. I propose that you should stop this rally.
7. I advise you take the prerequisites before registering for this course.
8. His father prefers that he attends a different university.
9. The faculty stipulated that the rule be abolished.
10. She urged that we found another alternative.

26. Inclusives

The expressions *not only . . . but also, both . . . and,* and *as well as* mean *in addition to.* Like entities must be used together (noun with noun, adjective with adjective, etc.).

• *Not only . . . but also:* The correlative conjunctions *not only . . . but also* must be used as a pair in joining like entities.

subject + verb + *not only* + { noun / adjective / adverb / propositional phrase } + *but (also)* + { noun / adjective / adverb / prepositional phrase }

OR

subject + *not only* + verb + *but (also)* + verb

Robert is <u>not only</u> <u>talented</u> but also <u>handsome</u>.
               adjective   *adjective*
Beth plays <u>not only</u> <u>the guitar</u> but also <u>the violin</u>.
            noun   *noun*
He writes <u>not only</u> <u>correctly</u> but also <u>neatly</u>.
            adverb   *adverb*
Marta excels <u>not only</u> <u>in mathematics</u> but also <u>in science</u>.
            prepositional phrase   *prepositional phrase*
Paul Anka <u>not only</u> <u>plays</u> the piano <u>but also</u> <u>composes</u> music.
          verb   *verb*

Make sure that the *not only* clause immediately precedes the phrase to which it refers. Notice the following examples.

Incorrect: He is <u>not only famous</u> in Italy <u>but also</u> in Switzerland.
Correct: He is <u>famous not only</u> in Italy <u>but also</u> in Switzerland.

NOTE: If there is only one adjective, it usually precedes the *not only* clause. In the above sentence, the adjective *famous* refers both to Italy and to Switzerland.

● *As well as:* The following rules apply to this conjunction.

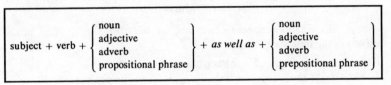

OR

subject + verb + *as well as* + verb . . .

Robert is <u>talented</u> as well as <u>handsome</u>.
       adjective   *adjective*
Beth plays <u>the guitar</u> as well as <u>the violin</u>.
       noun   *noun*
He writes <u>correctly</u> as well as <u>neatly</u>.
      adverb   *adverb*
Marta excels <u>in mathematics</u> as well as <u>in science</u>.
       prepositional   *prepositional*
        phrase   *phrase*
Paul Anka <u>plays</u> the piano as well as <u>composes</u> music.
    verb   *verb*

NOTE: When using *as well as* to indicate a compound subject, the phrase should be set off by commas. The verb will agree with the principal subject, NOT with the noun closest to it.

The <u>teacher</u>, as well as her students, <u>is going</u> to the concert.
<u>My cousins</u>, as well as Tim, <u>have</u> a test tomorrow.

● *Both . . . and:* These correlative conjunctions appear as a pair in a sentence. They follow the same rule as the one given for *not only . . . but also*.

Robert is <u>both talented and handsome</u>.
         adjective   *adjective*

Beth plays <u>both</u> <u>the guitar</u> <u>and</u> <u>the violin</u>.
                 noun   *noun*

He writes <u>both</u> <u>correctly</u> <u>and</u> <u>neatly</u>.
               adverb   *adverb*

Marta excels <u>both</u> <u>in mathematics</u> <u>and</u> <u>in science</u>.
                prepositional   *prepositional*
                  phrase   *phrase*

Paul Anka <u>both</u> <u>plays</u> the piano <u>and</u> <u>composes</u> music.
               verb   *verb*

NOTE: It is NOT CORRECT to use *both* and *as well as* in the same sentence.

Exercise 40: Inclusives

Supply the missing connectors (*not only . . . but also, both . . . and*, or *as well as*) in the following sentences.

1. Julia speaks _____ Spanish but also French.
2. She bought the yellow sweater _____ the beige skirt.
3. They have houses _____ in the country and in the city.
4. He is not only industrious _____ ingenious.
5. Her children have American cousins _____ Spanish ones.
6. Their European tour includes _____ Germany and Austria but also Switzerland.
7. He bandaged the arm both tightly _____ quickly.
8. Clark not only practices law _____ teaches it.
9. Tom Tryon is a playwright _____ an actor.
10. The bride's bouquet included roses _____ orchids.

27. Know/Know How

Study the following rules concerning the use of the verb *know*. *Know how* is usually used to indicate that one has the skill or ability to do something. Thus, it is *usually* followed by a verb, and when it is, the verb must be in the infinitive.

$$\boxed{\text{subject} + know\ how + \text{[verb in infinitive]} \ldots}$$

Know by itself, on the other hand, is usually followed by a noun, a prepositional phrase, or a sentence.

$$\boxed{\text{subject} + know + \left\{ \begin{array}{l} \text{noun} \\ \text{prepositional phrase} \\ \text{sentence} \end{array} \right\}}$$

Bill <u>knows how</u> <u>to play</u> tennis well.

Maggie and her sister <u>know how to prepare</u> Chinese food.
Do you <u>know how to get</u> to Jerry's house from here?
Jason <u>knew the answer</u> to the teacher's question.
No one <u>knows about</u> Roy's accepting the new position.
I didn't <u>know</u> that <u>you were going to France</u>.

Exercise 41: Know/Know How

Choose the correct form of *know* or *know how* in these sentences.

1. The fourth graders _____ to multiply.
2. How many people here _____ to ski?
3. We _____ about Mary's engagement to James.
4. The chemistry students _____ the formula for salt.
5. Although he has been driving for fifteen years, he doesn't _____ to change a tire properly.
6. Leon _____ that his friends would react to his proposition.
7. Nobody _____ to get to the turnpike yesterday.
8. The owner of the store was away, but she _____ about the robbery.
9. We _____ to type before we entered the university.
10. He doesn't _____ to dance, but he tries.

28. Clauses of Concession

Clauses of concession (yielding) show a contrast between two ideas. They are introduced by *although, even though, though, despite,* or *in spite of.*

• *Despite/in spite of:* These are prepositions which can be used interchangeably. They mean the same as *although,* etc.; however, the grammar is different. They can go at the beginning or in the middle of a sentence.

$$\left\{ \begin{array}{l} despite \\ in\ spite\ of \end{array} \right\} + \text{noun phrase}$$

<u>Despite</u> his physical handicap, he has become a successful businessman.
<u>In spite of</u> his physical handicap, he has become a successful businessman.
Jane will be admitted to the university <u>despite</u> her bad grades.
Jane will be admitted to the university <u>in spite of</u> her bad grades.

• *Although/even though/though:* These are subordinate conjunctions used to connect two clauses. Notice how the grammar is different from that of *despite* and *in spite of.*

$$\left\{\begin{array}{l} \textit{although} \\ \textit{even though} \\ \textit{though} \end{array}\right\} + \text{subject} + \text{verb} + \text{(complement)} \ldots$$

<u>Although</u> he has a physical handicap, he has become a successful businessman.

Jane will be admitted to the university <u>even though she has bad grades</u>.

Additional examples of clauses of concession:

<u>In spite of</u> the bad weather, we are going to have a picnic.
noun phrase

The child ate the cookie <u>even though</u> his mother had told him not to.
subject + verb

<u>Although</u> the weather was very bad, we had a picnic.
subject + verb

The committee voted to ratify the amendment <u>despite the objections</u>.
noun phrase

<u>Though</u> he had not finished the paper , he went to sleep.
subject + verb

She attended the class <u>although she did not feel alert</u>.
subject + verb

Exercise 42: Clauses of Concession

Change these sentences to incorporate the expressions in parentheses.

1. Despite her dislike for coffee, she drank it to keep herself warm. (although)
2. Mary will take a plane, even though she dislikes flying. (in spite of)
3. In spite of Marcy's sadness at losing the contest, she managed to smile. (although)
4. We took many pictures though the sky was cloudy. (despite)
5. Despite her poor memory, the old woman told interesting stories to the children. (even though)
6. Though he has been absent frequently, he has managed to pass the test. (in spite of)
7. Nancy told me the secret, despite having promised not to do so. (though)
8. We plan to buy a ticket for the drawing although we know we will not win a prize. (even though)
9. In spite of the high prices, my daughters insist on going to the movies every Saturday. (even though)
10. He ate the chocolate cake even though he is on a diet. (in spite of)

29. Problem Verbs

The verbs *lie/lay, rise/raise,* and *sit/set* cause problems even for native English speakers. The solution to the problem is to remember which verbs are transitive (verbs that take a complement) and which are intransitive (verbs that do not take a complement).

INTRANSITIVE

rise	rose	risen	rising
lie	lay	lain	lying
sit	sat	sat	sitting

TRANSITIVE

raise	raised	raised	raising
lay	laid	laid	laying
set	set	set	setting

● *Rise:* This verb means to *get up, move up under one's own power* (without the help of someone else), *increase.* Notice that there is *no* complement.

The sun <u>rises</u> early in the summer.
When the bell rings, the students <u>rise</u> from their seats.
When oil and water mix, oil <u>rises</u> to the top.
Jim <u>rose</u> early so that he could play golf before the others.
It must be late; the moon <u>has risen</u>.
Prices <u>have risen</u> more than ten percent in a very short time.

● *Raise:* This verb means to *lift* or *elevate an object;* or to *increase something.*

The students <u>raise their hands</u> in class.
               complement
The weightlifter <u>raises the barbells</u> over his head.
                 complement
The crane <u>raised the car</u> out of the lake.
             complement
After studying very hard, John <u>raised his grades</u> substantially.
                     complement
Mr. Daniels <u>has raised his tenants' rent</u> another fifteen dollars.
               complement
The OPEC countries <u>have raised the price</u> of oil.
                complement

● *Lie:* This verb means to *rest, repose,* or to *be situated in a place.* It is often used with the preposition *down.* NOTE: This verb should not be confused with the verb *lie, lied, lied,* which means to *say something that is not true.*

The university <u>lies</u> in the western section of town.
If the children are tired, they should <u>lie down</u> for a nap.
María Elena <u>lay</u> on the beach for three hours yesterday sunbathing.
The old dog just <u>lay</u> on the grass watching the children at play.

Don't disturb Mary; she has lain down for a rest.

That old rug had lain in the corner for many years before it was put in the garage.

- *Lay:* This verb means to *put somebody or something on a surface.*

Don't lay your clothes on the bed.
    complement

The boy lays his books on the table every day.
    complement

The enemy soldiers laid down their weapons and surrendered.
            complement

The children laid their toys on the floor when they had
        complement

finished using them.

The students had laid their compositions on the teacher's desk
        complement

before the bell rang.

The nurse laid the baby in the crib.
    complement

- *Sit:* This verb means to *take a seat.* It is also often used with the preposition *down.*

We are going to sit in the fifth row at the opera.

Bullfight fans sit in the shade because it is cool.

Because the weather was nice, we sat on the patio.

After swimming, Bob sat on the beach to dry off.

Nobody has sat through as many boring lectures as Pete has.

They have sat in the same position for two hours.

- *Set:* This verb means to *put somebody or something on a surface or in a place.* It is often interchangeable with *lay* or *put* except in certain idiomatic expressions like *set the table.*

The little girl helps her father set the table every night.
                complement

The carpenters set their tools in the box at noon and go to lunch.
            complement

The botanist set her plants in the sun so that they would grow.
        complement

After carrying her son from the car, the mother set   him   in his crib.
                    complement

Don't set the chocolate near the oven or it will melt.
    complement

No sooner had they set the roast in the oven, than the electricity went out.
            complement

● *Idiomatic expressions with* set, lay, *and* raise:

The company had to lay off twenty-five employees because of a production slowdown.

Dr. Jacobs has set many broken bones in plaster casts.

John set his alarm for six o'clock.

The chef is hoping that the Jell-O will set quickly.

While playing with matches, the children set fire to the sofa.

That farmer raises chickens for a living.

Exercise 43: Problem Verbs

Circle the correct form of the verb in parentheses and underline the complement if there is one. Remember that complements do *not* begin with prepositions.

1. You will see on the map that the Public Auditorium (lies/lays) north of the lake.
2. My dog loves to (sit/set) in the sun.
3. The delivery boy (lay/laid) the groceries on the table.
4. After the heavy rain, the water in the lake (raised/rose) another two feet.
5. The paper hangers decided to (raise/rise) the picture a few more inches.
6. He was exhausted so he decided to (lie/lay) down for a little while.
7. The workers were (lying/laying) cement for the patio when it began to rain.
8. The soldier (rose/raised) the flag when he heard the bugle blow.
9. In chemistry class, we learned that hot air (rises/raises).
10. They tried to (set/sit) the explosives carefully on the floor.

MINI-TEST 3 FOR GRAMMAR ITEMS 21 THROUGH 29

DIRECTIONS

Each question on this mini-test consists of a sentence in which four words or phrases are underlined. The four underlined parts of the sentence are marked A, B, C, D. You are to identify the *one* underlined word or phrase that *would not be acceptable in standard written English.* Circle the letter of the underlined portion which is not correct.

1. Writers like William Shakespeare and Edgar Allan Poe are
      A   B   C

   not only prolific but too interesting .
                 D

2. James's counselor recommended that <u>he should take</u> a foreign language
                                          A
in <u>his</u> freshman year instead <u>of waiting</u> until <u>the following year</u>.
   B   C   D

3. Although Mark <u>has been cooking</u> for many years, he <u>still</u> doesn't
                       A   B
<u>know</u> to prepare French foods <u>in the traditional manner</u>.
   C   D

4. It is most important that <u>he</u> <u>speaks</u> to <u>the</u> dean before <u>leaving</u> for
                             A   B   C   D
his vacation.

5. <u>Visitors</u> were not permitted <u>entering</u> the park after dark <u>because of</u>
   A   B   C
the lack <u>of</u> security and lighting.
         D

6. I need <u>both</u> <u>fine</u> brown sugar as well <u>as</u> powdered sugar <u>to bake</u> a
          A   B   C   D
Hawaiian cake.

7. <u>In spite</u> Nellie's fear of heights, she decided <u>to fly</u> with a group
   A   B
of her classmates <u>to the Bahamas</u> during <u>the</u> spring recess.
                   C   D

8. Let Nancy and <u>her</u> <u>to make</u> all the plans for the party, and you and
                 A   B
<u>I will provide</u> <u>the refreshments</u> and entertainment.
   C   D

9. After <u>rising</u> the flag <u>to commemorate</u> <u>the holiday</u>, the mayor gave
         A   B   C
<u>a long speech</u>.
   D

10. The general commanded <u>the Officers' Club</u> be <u>off limits</u> to <u>the new</u>
    A   B   C   D
recruits.

11. Louie got his sister <u>read</u> his class assignment, and then asked her
                         A
<u>to write</u> the report <u>for him</u> because he did not have <u>enough time</u>.
   B   C   D

12. Marcy said that she knew how the procedures for doing
                              ‾‾‾‾‾‾‾‾
                                 A

    the experiment, but when we began to work in the laboratory,
                                      ‾‾‾‾‾‾‾
                                         B

    she found that she was mistaken.
                  ‾‾‾‾   ‾‾‾‾‾‾‾‾
                   C   D

13. News of Charles Lindbergh's famous transatlantic flight in 1927 spread
    ‾‾‾‾   ‾‾‾‾‾‾
     A   B

    rapidly despite of the lack of an international communication system.
            ‾‾‾‾‾‾‾‾‾   ‾‾
                C   D

14. It was suggested that Pedro studies the material more thoroughly
       ‾‾‾   ‾‾‾‾‾‾‾   ‾‾‾‾‾‾‾‾‾‾‾‾‾‾‾
        A   B   C

    before attempting to pass the exam.
           ‾‾‾‾‾‾‾‾‾‾‾‾‾‾‾‾
                  D

15. The piano teacher requires that her student practices at least
                               ‾‾‾‾   ‾‾‾‾‾‾‾‾‾
                                 A   B

    forty-five minutes every day in preparation for next week's recital.
    ‾‾‾‾‾‾‾‾‾‾‾‾‾‾‾‾‾‾   ‾‾‾‾‾‾‾‾‾‾‾‾‾‾‾‾‾
            C   D

16. Marie's cousin is studied law at one of the ivy-league universities
                      ‾‾‾‾‾‾‾   ‾‾ ‾‾‾‾‾‾
                         A   B   C

    in the East.
    ‾‾‾‾‾‾‾‾‾‾
        D

17. If you set in that position for too long, you may get a cramp in your leg.
           ‾‾‾ ‾‾‾‾‾‾‾‾‾‾‾   ‾‾‾‾‾‾‾‾   ‾‾‾‾‾‾‾‾‾‾
            A   B   C   D

18. The president mentioned to the cabinet members he was going
                            ‾‾   ‾‾
                            A   B

    to negotiate a new treaty with the foreign minister.
    ‾‾‾‾‾‾‾‾‾‾‾   ‾‾‾‾‾‾‾‾‾‾‾‾‾‾‾‾‾‾‾
         C   D

19. The conquerors stole not only the gold and silver that were needed to
                               ‾‾‾   ‾‾‾‾‾‾‾‾‾‾‾‾‾‾‾‾
                                A   B

    replenish the badly depleted treasury but also the supplies that were
                  ‾‾‾‾‾
                    C

    vital to the colonists as well.
                           ‾‾‾‾‾‾
                             D

20. Despite the roadblock, the police allowed us enter the restricted
    ‾‾‾‾‾‾‾   ‾‾‾‾‾‾‾
       A   B

    area to search for our friends.
         ‾‾‾‾‾‾‾‾‾ ‾‾‾‾‾‾‾‾‾‾‾
             C   D

21. Did you <u>know how</u> that the actors' strike <u>will delay</u> the beginning
    A   B
    <u>of the new</u> television season and <u>cause the cancellation of</u>
    C   D
    many contracts?

22. We should <u>have been informed</u> Janis <u>about</u> the change in plans
    A   B
    <u>regarding</u> our <u>weekend trip</u> to the mountains.
    C   D

23. When we arrived <u>at the</u> store <u>to purchase</u> the dishwasher <u>advertise</u>
    A   B   C
    in the newspaper, we learned that all the dishwasers had <u>been sold</u>.
    D

24. That manufacturer is not only <u>raising</u> his prices <u>but also</u> <u>decreasing</u>
    A   B   C
    the production of his product <u>as well</u>.
    D

25. The director encouraged them <u>work</u> in committees <u>to plan</u>
    A   B
    <u>a more effective</u> advertising campaign <u>for the new</u> product.
    C   D

26. Jason's professor had him <u>to rewrite</u> his thesis <u>many times</u>
    A   B
    before <u>allowing him</u> to present it to the <u>committee</u>.
    C   D

27. Mr. Harris will <u>be divided</u> <u>the</u> biology class <u>into two sections</u> to
    A   B   C
    prevent <u>overcrowding</u> in his classroom.
    D

28. <u>Hundreds of</u> houses and <u>other</u> buildings <u>were destroying</u> by the <u>raging</u>
    A   B   C   D
    tropical storm which later developed into a hurricane.

29. Maribel <u>has registered</u> for both the afternoon anthropology class
    A
    <u>as well as</u> the <u>evening</u> sociology <u>lecture</u>.
    B   C   D

30. Food prices have <u>raised</u> <u>so rapidly</u> in the past few months <u>that</u> some
    A   B   C
    families have been <u>forced to alter their eating habits</u>.
    D

31. The man, of whom the red car is parked in front of our house, is a
            A   B   C   D
    prominent physician in this town.

32. Although her severe pain, Pat decided to come to the meeting so that
        A   B   C
    there would be a quorum.
            D

33. The proposal has repealed after a thirty-minute discussion and
                    A   B
    a number of objections to its failure to include our district.
        C   D

34. He is the only candidate who the faculty members voted not to retain
                A   B   C
    on the list of eligible replacements for Professor Kotey.
        D

35. In spite of the tenants' objections, the apartment manager decided
        A   B
    to rise the rent by forty dollars per month.
        C   D

36. This class, that is a prerequisite for microbiology, is so difficult
                A   B   C
    that I would rather drop it.
                D

37. The doctor told Mr. Anderson that, because of his severe cramps,
                A   B
    he should lay in bed for a few days.
                C   D

38. If you had sat the plant in a cooler location, the leaves would not
                A   B   C
    have burned.
        D

39. Dr. Harder, which is the professor for this class, will be absent
                A   B
    this week because of illness.
        C   D

40. Despite of a language barrier, humans have managed to communicate
        A   B
    with others through sign language, in which certain motions stand for
        C   D
    letters, words, or ideas.

41. This class <u>has cancelled</u> <u>because</u> <u>too few</u> students <u>had registered</u>
             A   B   C   D
before registration closed.

42. After Allan <u>had searched</u> <u>for</u> twenty minutes, he realized that his
             A   B
jacket had been <u>laying</u> on the table <u>the entire time</u>.
           C   D

43. The problems that <u>discovered</u> <u>since</u> the initial research
                   A   B
<u>had been completed</u> caused the committee members <u>to table the</u>
      C   D
proposal temporarily.

44. The doctor suggested that he <u>lay</u> <u>in bed</u> for <u>several</u> days as a
                           A   B   C
precaution against <u>further damage</u> to the tendons.
                  D

45. Dr. Alvarez was <u>displeased</u> because the student <u>had turned in an</u>
                A   B
<u>unacceptable</u> report, <u>so</u> he made him <u>to rewrite</u> it.
  (B)   C   D

46. The project director <u>stated he</u> believed <u>it was necessary</u> <u>to study the</u>
                   A   B   C
proposals for several more months <u>before making a decision</u>.
                                  D

47. <u>Although</u> the danger that he might <u>be injured</u>, Boris
  A   B
<u>bravely entered</u> the burning house in order to save the <u>youngster</u>.
      C   D

48. <u>That</u> these students <u>have improved</u> their grades <u>because of their</u>
  A   B   C
<u>participation in</u> the test review class.
      D

49. <u>Despite Martha's attempts</u> <u>to rise</u> her test score, she did not receive
  A   B
<u>a high enough</u> score <u>to be accepted</u> by the law school.
     C   D

50. <u>That</u> Mr. Jones is not prepared to teach this course is not <u>doubted</u>;
  A   B
however, at this late date <u>it is not likely that</u> we will be
                            C
<u>able finding</u> a replacement.
  D

STYLE IN WRITTEN ENGLISH

Written English is not always the same as spoken English. In spoken English, many people are not careful about the way they word sentences. As mentioned previously, the grammar section of the TOEFL tests your knowledge of *formal written English*. Many questions involve simple grammatical rules such as those that you've just studied. However, many questions, especially those in Part A, involve more than simple grammar. They are concerned with style; you must choose the clearest, most concise, best-stated answer. In some of these questions, several possible answers may contain acceptable grammar, but one choice is better than the others because it is stylistically acceptable.

Following are some stylistic problems that often appear in grammar questions and some methods for eliminating incorrect answers.

1. Common Stylistic Problems That Appear in Grammar Questions

● *Sequence of tenses:* When two clauses make up a sentence, they show a time relationship based on certain time words and verb tenses. This relationship is called "sequence of tenses." The verb tense of the main clause will determine that of the dependent clause.

If the *main clause* is	then the *dependent clause* will be
present tense	(1) present progressive
	(2) *will, can,* or *may* + verb
	(3) past tense
	(4) present perfect

(1) By using a present progressive with a present tense, we show two *simultaneous* actions.

I see that Harriet is writing her composition.
Do you know who is riding the bicycle?

(2) These modals in the dependent clause indicate that the action takes place *after* that of the main verb. (*be going to* is also used in this pattern.)

He says that he will look for a job next week.
I know that she is going to win that prize.
Mary says that she can play the piano.

155

(3) Past tenses in the dependent clause show that this action took place *before* that of the main clause.

I <u>hope</u> he <u>arrived</u> safely.
They <u>think</u> he <u>was</u> here last night.

(4) Use of the present perfect in the dependent clause indicates that the action took place at *an indefinite time before* that of the main clause.

He <u>tells</u> us that he <u>has been</u> to the mountains before.
We <u>know</u> that you <u>have spoken</u> with Mike about the party.

If the *main clause* is	then the *dependent clause* will be
past tense	(1) past progressive or simple past (2) *would*, *could*, or *might* + verb (3) past perfect

---

NOTE: NO PRESENT FORM can come after the past tense.

(1) Simple past or present progressive in the dependent clause indicates a *simultaneous* action with the main clause.

I <u>gave</u> the package to my sister when she <u>visited</u> us last week.
Mike <u>visited</u> the Prado Art Museum while he <u>was studying</u> in Madrid.

(2) These modals in the dependent clause indicate that the action takes place *after* that of the main verb.

He <u>said</u> that he <u>would look</u> for a job next week.
Mary <u>said</u> that she <u>could play</u> piano.

(3) Past perfect in the dependent clause shows that the action occurred *before* that of the main clause.

I <u>hoped</u> he <u>had arrived</u> safely.
They <u>thought</u> he <u>had been</u> here last night.

Exercise 44: Sequence of Tenses

The following contain sentences with present tense verbs in the main clause. Change the main clause to past and adjust the dependent clause as necessary. *Example:*

We <u>hope</u> that he <u>will be</u> able to attend.
We <u>hoped</u> that he <u>would be</u> able to attend.

1. He says that he will finish the project by May.
2. Mark thinks he is going to win the award.

3. I hear that Kate has accepted a new position at the East Side Clinic.
4. Steve says that he will make the dessert for the party.
5. Lou tells his friends that they are good tennis players.
6. I realize that they are older than they look.
7. Mary Ellen says that she eats three well-balanced meals every day.
8. The student is asking the professor when the class will do the next experiment.
9. We hope that you can play tennis later.
10. We know that you may move to France next year.

● *Say/tell:* These verbs have the same meaning; however, the grammar is different. If there is an indirect object (if we mention the person to whom the words are spoken), we use *tell*. If there is no indirect object, we use *say*. Study the following rules.

> subject + *say* + (*that*) + subject + verb . . .

> subject + *tell* + indirect object + (*that*) + subject + verb . . .

Tell can also be followed occasionally by a direct object. Always use *tell* before the following nouns whether there is an indirect object or not.

> tell {
> a story
> a joke
> a secret
> a lie
> the truth
> the time
> }

John told a story last night.

OR

John told us a story last night.

The little boy was punished because he told a lie.

OR

The little boy was punished because he told his mother a lie.

NOTE: Remember to use the appropriate sequence of tense with *say* and *tell*.

Present: He says that he is busy today.
            He says that he will be busy today.
Past: He said that he was busy today.
           He said that he would be busy today.

Exercise 45: Say/Tell

Write the correct form of *say* or *tell* in the following sentences. Be careful to observe sequence of tenses.

1. Harvey _____ he would take us on a picnic today.
2. Pete _____ the children some funny stories now.
3. Who _____ you that he was going to New York?
4. When did you _____ Mary that the party would be?
5. My sister _____ us that it had snowed in her town last week.
6. No one in the second grade class could _____ time.
7. The comedian always _____ his friends funny jokes when he is at a party.
8. What time did you _____ that the lecture had begun?
9. Who _____ that we are having an exam tomorrow?
10. The judge instructed the witness to _____ the whole truth about the accident.
11. The little boy _____ a lie about not eating the cookies before lunch.
12. Hamlet _____, "To be or not to be, that is the question."
13. Our teacher _____ that we would not have any homework during the vacation.
14. Because he could not _____ time, the boy arrived home very late one evening.
15. I saw my friend in the library and _____ that I had wanted to talk to him.
16. Shaun _____ that he had already seen the movie.
17. Larry _____ that his friends would be going camping next week.
18. James _____ that he has already done his homework.
19. I wonder who _____ that blondes had more fun.
20. Never _____ a secret to a person who spreads gossip.

● *Antecedents of pronouns:* If a pronoun is used in a sentence, there must be a noun before it of the same person and number. There must be one, and only one, antecedent to which the pronoun refers.

Examples of pronouns without antecedents:

Incorrect: Henry was denied admission to graduate school because they did not believe that he could handle the work load.
(The pronoun *they* does not have an antecedent in the sentence. The *graduate school* is a singular unit, and the members of its faculty are not mentioned.)

Correct: The members of the admissions committee denied Henry admission to graduate school because they did not believe that he could handle the work load.
(In this sentence, *they* refers to *members.*)

OR

Henry was denied admission to graduate school because the <u>members</u> of the admissions committee did not believe that he could handle the work load.

(Here the noun is given instead of the pronoun.)

Incorrect: George dislikes politics because he believes that <u>they</u> are corrupt.

(The pronoun *they* does not have an antecedent in this sentence. The word *politics* is singular, so *they* cannot refer to it.)

Correct: George dislikes politics because he believes that <u>politicians</u> are corrupt.

OR

George dislikes <u>politicians</u> because he believes that <u>they</u> are corrupt.

Examples of pronouns with unclear antecedents:

Incorrect: Mr. Brown told Mr. Adams that <u>he</u> would have to work all night in order to finish the report.

(It is not clear whether the pronoun *he* refers to Mr. Brown or Mr. Adams.)

Correct: According to Mr. Brown, <u>Mr. Adams</u> will have to work all night in order to finish the report.

OR

Mr. Brown said that, in order to finish the report, <u>Mr. Adams</u> would have to work all night.

Incorrect: Janet visited her friend every day while <u>she</u> was on vacation.

(The pronoun *she* could refer to either Janet or her friend.)

Correct: While <u>Janet</u> was on vacation, <u>she</u> visited her friend every day.

Exercise 46: Antecedents of Pronouns

Rewrite the following sentences so that each pronoun has a clear antecedent. If you have to supply a noun, use any noun that will make the sentence correct.

1. The dispute between the faculty and the administration was not resolved until they got better working conditions.
2. Ellen spotted her friend as she walked towards the Student Union.
3. Foreigners are easily impressed by the bullfighters as they march into the arena.
4. In their spare time, many great books have been written about the famous Greek and Roman heroes.
5. Dr. Byrd's book was accepted for publication because they thought it would be beneficial to students.

6. Bob and Helen hate flying because they make too much noise.
7. Casey was not admitted to the country club because they thought he was not socially acceptable.
8. Mary loves touring the country by train because it is so interesting.
9. The colonel was decorated for bravery, having fought them off.
10. The children were frightened because they made such eerie sounds.

● *The pronouns* one *and* you: If *one* (meaning a person in general) is used in a sentence, a subsequent pronoun referring to the same person must also be *one* or *he*. If *you* is used, the subsequent pronoun must also be *you*. *He* or *you* can be in the possessive, complement, or reflexive case.

$$one + verb \ldots \begin{cases} one \\ one's + noun \\ he^* \\ his + noun \end{cases} + (verb) \ldots$$

*NOTE: Many times it is considered more appropriate to use *he or she* and similar expressions so that the masculine pronoun is not used exclusively. On the TOEFL, however, you need not worry about this problem. If a sentence begins with *one*, be sure that *you* or *they* DOES NOT follow.

If one takes this exam without studying, one is likely to fail.
If one takes this exam without studying, he is likely to fail.

One should always do one's homework.
One should always do his homework.

$$you + verb \ldots + \begin{cases} you \\ your \end{cases} + (verb) \ldots$$

If you take this exam without studying, you are likely to fail.
You should always do your homework.

NOTE: It is NEVER CORRECT to say:

If __one__ takes this exam without studying, __you__ are likely to fail.
   3rd person   *2nd person*

If __one__ takes this exam without studying, they are likely to fail.
   singular   *plural*

Additional examples for both forms:

One should never tell his secrets to a gossip if he wishes them to remain secret.
You should always look both ways before you cross the street.
If one wants to make a lot of money, he needs to work hard.

If one's knowledge of English is complete, he will be able to pass TOEFL.

If you do not want your test scores reported, you must request that they be cancelled.

One should always remember his family.

● *Illogical participial modifiers (dangling participles):* A participial phrase (one containing a [verb + *ing*] without auxiliaries) can be used to join two sentences with a common subject. When the two phrases do not share a common subject, we call the participial phrase an illogical participial modifier. Actually, the subject of the participial phrase is understood rather than explicit. Consider the following sentence.

Incorrect: After jumping out of a boat, the shark bit the man.
(We understand that the actual subject of the verb *jumping* is *the man;* therefore, immediately after the comma, we must mention *the man.*)

Correct: After jumping out of the boat, the man was bitten by a shark.

For clarity, introductory participial phrases must be followed immediately by the noun which is logically responsible for the action of the participle. There is no written subject in the participial phrase; thus no change of subject is possible. Sometimes the participial phrase is preceded by a preposition. The following prepositions commonly precede participial phrases.

by	upon	before	after	while

After preparing the dinner, Michelle will read a book.

By working a ten-hour day for four days, we can have a long weekend.

While reviewing for the test, Marcia realized that she had forgotten to study the use of participial phrases.

If only the [verb + *ing*] appears in the participial phrase, the time of the sentence is determined by the tense of the verb in the main clause; the two actions generally occur simultaneously.

(preposition) + (*not*) + [verb + *ing*] . . . + noun + verb . . .

Present: Practicing her swing every day, Tricia hopes to get a job as a golf instructor.

Past: Having a terrible toothache, Felipe called the dentist for an appointment.

Future: Finishing the letter later tonight, Sally will mail it tomorrow morning.

The perfect form (*having* + [verb in past participle]) is used to indicate that the action of the participial phrase took place before that of the main verb.

(*not*) + *having* + [verb in past participle] ... + noun + verb ...

Having finished their supper, the boys went out to play.
(After the *boys* had finished ...)

Having written his composition, Louie handed it to his teacher.
(After *Louie* had written ...)

Not having read the book, she could not answer the question.
(Because *she* had not read ...)

The participial phrase can also be used to express an idea in the passive voice, one in which the subject was not responsible for the action.

(*not*) + *having been* + [verb in past participle] ... + noun + verb ...

Having been notified by the court, Melissa reported for jury duty.
(After *Melissa* had been notified ...)

Having been delayed by the snowstorm, Jason and I missed our connecting flight.
(After *we* had been delayed ...)

Not having been notified of the change in meeting times, George arrived late.
(Because *he* had not been notified ...)

Observe the corrected form of the following illogical participial modifiers. Remember that the noun appearing after the comma must be the logical subject of the [verb + *ing*].

Illogical: Having apprehended the hijackers, they were whisked off to FBI headquarters by the security guards.

Correct: Having apprehended the hijackers, the security guards whisked them off to FBI headquarters.
(After *the guards* had apprehended the hijackers, the guards whisked ...)

OR

Having been apprehended, the hijackers were whisked off to FBI headquarters by the security guards.
(After *the hijackers* had been apprehended, they were whisked ...)

Illogical: Before singing the school song, a poem was recited.

Correct: Before singing the school song, the students recited a poem.
(Before *the students* sang ...)

Illogical: Guiding us through the museum, a special explanation was given by the director.

Correct: Guiding us through the museum, the director gave us a special explanation.

(While *the director* was guiding us . . .)

Exercise 47: Illogical Participial Modifiers

Following the examples given above, correct these illogical participial modifiers. You may have to reword the main clause and add a subject.

1. Being thoroughly dissatisfied with the picture, it was hidden in the closet.
2. Seeing the advancing army, all valuables were hidden under the stairwell.
3. Plunging into the water, the drowning child was rescued.
4. Criticizing the defendant for his cruel behavior, the sentence was handed down by the judge.
5. After painting the car, it was given to the man's wife by the man.
6. Being an early riser, it was easy for Edna to adjust to her company's new summer schedule.
7. After winning the tennis match, the victory made Nancy jump for joy.
8. Having wandered through the mountain passes for days, an abandoned shack where they could take shelter was discovered by the hikers.
9. Being very protective of its young, all those who approach the nest are attacked by the mother eagle.
10. Before playing ball, a two-minute period of silence was observed by the baseball players for their recently deceased teammate.

● *Participles as adjectives:* Very often, when there is no regular adjective form for a verb, the present or past participle of the verb can be used as an adjective. It is sometimes difficult for foreign students to decide whether to use the present [verb + *ing*] or past [verb + *ed*] or [verb + *en*] participle as an adjective.

The present participle [verb + *ing*] is used as an adjective when the noun it modifies performs or is responsible for an action. The verb is usually intransitive (it doesn't take an object) and the verb form of the sentence is the progressive (continous) aspect.

The crying baby woke Mr. Binion.
    (The baby *was crying.*)
The purring kitten snuggled close to the fireplace.
    (The kitten *was purring.*)
The blooming flowers in the meadow created a rainbow of colors.
    (The flowers *were blooming.*)

The past participle is used as an adjective when the noun it modifies is the receiver of the action. The sentence from which this adjective comes is generally in the passive aspect.

The sorted mail was delivered to the offices before noon.
(The mail *had been sorted.*)
Frozen food is often easier to prepare than fresh food.
(The food *had been frozen.*)
The imprisoned men were unhappy with their living conditions.
(The men *had been imprisoned.*)

Other verbs such as *interest, bore, excite,* and *frighten* are even more difficult. The rule is basically the same as that given above. The [verb + *ing*] form is used when the noun causes the action and the [verb + *ed*] form is used when it receives the action. Compare the following groups of sentences.

The boring professor put the students to sleep.
The boring lecture put the students to sleep.
The bored students went to sleep during the boring lecture.

The child saw a frightening movie.
The frightened child began to cry.

Exercise 48: Participles as Adjectives

Choose the correct form of the participles used as adjectives in the following sentences.

1. The (breaking/broken) dishes lay on the floor.
2. The (trembling/trembled) children were given a blanket for warmth.
3. Compassionate friends tried to console the (crying/cried) victims of the accident.
4. The (interesting/interested) tennis match caused a great deal of excitement.
5. When James noticed the (burning/burnt) building, he notified the fire department immediately.
6. The (exciting/excited) passengers jumped into the lifeboats when notified that the ship was sinking.
7. The (smiling/smiled) *Mona Lisa* is on display in the Louvre in Paris.
8. The wind made such (frightening/frightened) noises that the children ran to their parents' room.
9. The (frightening/frightened) hostages only wanted to be left alone.
10. We saw the (advancing/advanced) army from across town.
11. Mrs. Harris's (approving/approved) smile let us know that our speeches were well done.
12. Our representative presented the (approving/approved) plan to the public.
13. The (blowing/blown) wind of the hurricane damaged the waterfront property.

14. We were going to see the movie at the Center Theater, but our friends told us it was a (boring/bored) movie.
15. Mary's (cleaning/cleaned) service comes every Wednesday.
16. The (cleaning/cleaned) shoes were placed in the sun to dry.
17. We found it difficult to get through the (closing/closed) door without a key.
18. As we entered the (crowding/crowded) room, I noticed my cousins.
19. Dr. Jameson told my brother to elevate his (aching/ached) foot.
20. The police towed away the (parking/parked) cars because they were blocking the entrance.

● *Redundancy:* A sentence in which some information is unnecessarily repeated is called redundant. Given here are some word combinations that are *always redundant,* and thus should NEVER be used.

advance forward *proceed forward* *progress forward*	*advance, proceed,* and *progress* all mean "to move in a forward direction"; thus, the word *forward* is not necessary
return back *revert back*	*return* and *revert* mean "to go back or to send back" so *back* is not necessary
sufficient enough	these words are identical; one or the other should be used
compete together	*compete* means "to take part in a contest against others"
reason . . . because	these words indicate the same thing; the correct pattern is *reason . . . that*
join together	*join* means "to bring together," "to put together" or "to become a part or member of," "to take place among"
repeat again	*repeat* means "to say again" (*re-* usually means "again")
new innovations	*innovation* means "a new idea"
matinee performance	*matinee* means "a performance in the afternoon"
same identical	these words are identical
two twins	*twins* means "two brothers or sisters"
the time when	*the time* and *when* indicate the same thing; one or the other should be used
the place where	*the place* and *where* indicate the same thing; one or the other should be used

Examples of correct sentences:

The army <u>advanced</u> after the big battle.

OR

The army <u>moved forward</u> after the big battle.

The peace talks <u>advanced</u>.

OR

The peace talks <u>progressed</u>.

We have <u>sufficient</u> money to buy the new dress.

They have <u>enough</u> time to eat a sandwich before going to work.

The teacher <u>proceeded</u> to explain the lesson.

John and his brother are <u>competing</u> in the running games.

The teacher asked us to <u>join</u> the students who were cleaning the room.

Mary <u>repeated</u> the question slowly so that Jim would understand.

Besides the two evening showings, there will also be a <u>matinee</u>.

The <u>reason</u> I want to take that class is <u>that</u> the professor is supposed to be very eloquent.

This is <u>where</u> I left him.

That was <u>the time</u> I hit a home run.

Exercise 49: Redundancy

Cross out the redundant word in each of the following sentences. *Example:*

The carpenter joined the two beams ~~together~~ with long nails.
(*Together* is the redundant word.)

1. After Jill had shown Tim how to insert the paper once, she repeated the operation again.
2. The twins have the same identical birthmarks on their backs.
3. I think we have sufficient enough information to write the report.
4. When the roads became too slippery, we decided to return back to the cabin and wait for the storm to subside.
5. Nobody could get out of work early enough to attend the matinee performance.
6. The mountain climbers proceeded forward on their long trek up the side of the mountain.
7. Rita and her sister competed together in the musical talent show.
8. I think that we should come up with a new innovation for doing this job.
9. The minister joined the bride and groom together in holy wedlock.
10. My cousins love to play with the two twins from across the street.

● *Parallel structure:* When information in a sentence is given in the form of a list or series, all components must be grammatically parallel or equal. There may be only two components or there may be many components in a list; however, if the first is, for example, an infinitive, the rest must also be infinitives. Consider the following correct and incorrect sentences.

Not parallel: Peter is rich, handsome, and many people like him.
                          adjec-   *adjective*   *sentence*
                          tive

Parallel: Peter is rich, handsome, and popular.
                          adjec-   *adjective*   *adjective*
                          tive

Not parallel: Mr. Henry is a lawyer, a politician, and he teaches.
                          noun   *noun*   *sentence*

Parallel: Mr. Henry is a lawyer, a politician, and a teacher.
                          noun   *noun*   *noun*

Not parallel: The soldiers approached the enemy camp slowly and
                                                      adverb
             silent.
             adjective

Parallel: The soldiers approached the enemy camp slowly
                                                     adverb
             and silently.
                 adverb

Not parallel: She likes to fish, swim, and surfing
                          infini- *simple* *[verb + ing]*
                          tive   *form*

Parallel: She likes to fish, to swim, and to surf.
                        infinitive *infinitive*   *infinitive*
                         OR
             She likes fishing, swimming, and surfing.
                   [verb + ing] *[verb + ing]*   *[verb + ing]*

Not parallel: When teenagers finish high school, they have several choices: going to college, getting a job, or the army.
                          verb + noun   *verb + noun*   *noun*

Parallel: When teenagers finish high school, they have several choices: going to college, getting a job,
                            verb + noun   *verb + noun*
             or joining the army.
                 verb + noun

Not parallel: Enrique entered the room, sat down, and is opening
                      past   *past*   *present*
                                                  progressive
             his book.

Parallel: Enrique entered the room, sat down, and opened
                      past   *past*   *past*
             his book.

NOTE: If the sentence indicates that the different clauses definitely happened or will happen at different times, then this rule does not need to be followed. *For example:*

She is a senior, studies every day, and will graduate a semester early.
    present   *present*   *future*

Exercise 50: Parallel Structure

Change the following sentences so that they are parallel.

1. The puppy stood up slowly, wagged its tail, blinking its eyes, and barked.
2. Ecologists are trying to preserve our environment for future generations by protecting the ozone layer, purifying the air, and have replanted the trees that have been cut down.
3. The chief of police demanded from his assistants an orderly investigation, a well-written report, and that they work hard.
4. Marcia is a scholar, an athlete, and artistic.
5. Slowly and with care, the museum director removed the Ming vase from the shelf and placed it on the display pedestal.
6. The farmer plows the fields, plants the seeds, and will harvest the crop.
7. Abraham Lincoln was a good president and was self-educated, hard-working, and always told the truth.
8. Children love playing in the mud, running through puddles, and they get very dirty.
9. Collecting stamps, playing chess, and to mount beautiful butterflies are Derrick's hobbies.
10. Despite America's affluence, many people are without jobs, on welfare, and have a lot of debts.

• *Transformation of direct and indirect objects:* There are two ways of writing the objects of many verbs without changing the meaning of the sentence. The indirect object may occur after the direct object, preceded by a preposition, or it may occur before the direct object without being preceded by a preposition. The prepositions that are generally used in this structure are *for* and *to.*

NOTE: The indirect object is an animate object or objects to whom or for whom something is done. The direct object can be a person or a thing and is the first receiver of the action.

I gave the book to Dan.
        direct   *indirect*
        object   *object*

(*The book* is the direct object because the first action was that of taking the book in my hand, and the second action, the indirect one, was to give it to Dan.)

Not all verbs allow for this object transformation. Here are some that do.

bring	find	make	promise	tell
build	get	offer	read	write
buy	give	owe	sell	
cut	hand	paint	send	
draw	leave	pass	show	
feed	lend	pay	teach	

Some of these verbs can be followed by either the preposition *for* or *to*, while others must be followed by one or the other. The transformation means exactly the same as the sentence with the original preposition. Study the following rules.

subject + verb + direct object + $\begin{Bmatrix} for \\ to \end{Bmatrix}$ + indirect object

subject + verb + indirect object + direct object

NOTE: In the second rule, where the indirect object precedes the direct object, NO preposition exists.

Correct: The director's secretary sent the manuscript to them last night.
Correct: The director's secretary sent them the manuscript last night.
Incorrect: The director's secretary sent to them the manuscript last night.

NOTE: If the direct object and the indirect object are both pronouns, the first rule is generally used.

Correct: They gave it to us.
Incorrect: They gave us it.

Additional examples:

John gave the essay to his teacher.
John gave his teacher the essay.

The little boy brought some flowers for his grandmother.
The little boy brought his grandmother some flowers.

I fixed a drink for Maria.
I fixed Maria a drink.

He drew a picture for his mother.
He drew his mother a picture.

He lent his car to his brother.
He lent his brother his car.

We owe several thousand dollars to the bank.
We owe the bank several thousand dollars.

NOTE: The verbs *introduce* and *mention* must use the preposition *to*. The transformation is NOT POSSIBLE.

I introduced John to Dr. Jackson.
I introduced Dr. Jackson to John.
He mentioned the party to me.

Exercise 51: Transformation of Direct and Indirect Object

Rewrite these sentences placing the indirect object immediately after the verb and eliminating the preposition.

1. Mary showed the photographs to me.
2. I'll send the books to you next week.
3. My sister sent a game to my daughter for her birthday.
4. He brought the telegram to her this morning.
5. The author gave an autographed copy of his book to his friend.
6. They wrote a letter to us.
7. Louie drew a lovely picture for his mother.
8. She made a bookcase for her cousin.
9. That teacher taught grammar to us last year.
10. Mary handed the tray to her brother.

Exercise 52: Transformation of Direct and Indirect Object

Rewrite these sentences placing the direct object immediately after the verb and supplying the correct preposition.

1. John owes his friend the money.
2. My friends sent me a bouquet of flowers while I was in the hospital.
3. The clerk sold us the records.
4. They found him a good, inexpensive car.
5. Picasso painted his wife a beautiful portrait.
6. My father read us the newspaper article.
7. Pass me the salt please.
8. She bought him a red jacket.
9. The girls couldn't wait to show us the bicycles.
10. The construction crew built them a house in four weeks.

● *Adverbials at the beginning of a sentence:* It is sometimes possible to place adverbials at the beginning of a sentence. This indicates a stronger emphasis on the action than when the adverbial is in its normal position. If the adverbial appears at the beginning of a sentence, the grammar of the sentence is somewhat different.

Juan <u>hardly remembers</u> the accident that took his sister's life.
<u>Hardly does Juan remember</u> the accident that took his sister's life.

$$\left.\begin{array}{l} hardly \\ rarely \\ seldom \\ never \\ only \ldots \end{array}\right\} + \text{auxiliary} + \text{subject} + \text{verb} \ldots$$

<u>Never</u> <u>have so many people</u> <u>been</u> unemployed as today.
adverb auxiliary   subject   verb

  (So many people <u>have never been</u> unemployed as today.)

<u>Hardly</u> <u>had</u> <u>he</u> <u>fallen</u> asleep when he began to dream of far-away lands.
adverb auxiliary subject verb

  (He <u>had hardly fallen</u> asleep when he began to dream . . .)

<u>Rarely</u> <u>have</u> <u>we</u> <u>seen</u> such an effective actor as he has proven
adverb auxiliary subject verb

himself to be.

  (We <u>have rarely seen</u> such an effective actor . . .)

<u>Seldom</u> <u>does class</u> <u>let</u> out early.
adverb auxiliary subject verb

  (Class <u>seldom lets</u> out early.)

<u>Only by hard work</u> <u>will we</u> <u>be</u> able to accomplish this great task.
      adverb   auxiliary subject verb

  (We <u>will be able</u> to accomplish this great task <u>only by hard work</u>.)

Exercise 53: Adverbials at the Beginning of a Sentence

Change each of the following sentences so that the adverbial is at the beginning of the sentence.

1. Jorge rarely forgets to do his homework.
2. Jane can finish this work only by staying up all night.
3. Henry had hardly started working when he realized that he needed to go to the library.

4. We have never heard so moving a rendition as this one.
5. Maria seldom missed a football game when she was in the United States.
6. We will be able to buy the car only with a bank loan.
7. We rarely watch television during the week.
8. He has never played a better game than he has today.
9. This professor seldom lets his students leave class early.
10. Jennifer had hardly entered the room when she felt the presence of another person.

2. Elimination of Incorrect Answers in Style Questions

Very often in the Structure and Written Expression section of the TOEFL, especially in Part A, Structure, you will find that the questions cannot be solved simply by applying a single grammatical rule. In order to solve these questions, you should eliminate any possible answer choices which are incorrect until you arrive at the correct choice. Follow these steps in eliminating incorrect answers.

(1) Check each answer for faulty grammar. Look for:

    (a) subject/verb agreement
    (b) adjective/adverb usage
    (c) placement of modifiers
    (d) sequence of tenses
    (e) logical pronoun reference
    (f) parallel structure

(2) Eliminate answers that are verbose (wordy). The sentence should convey its meaning in the most concise way.

    (a) Avoid answers containing expressions like:
        John read the letter in a thoughtful manner.   (4 words)
        There is usually a less wordy adverb such as:
        John read the letter thoughtfully.   (1 word)
    (b) Avoid answers containing two words that have the same meaning.

(3) Eliminate answers which contain improper vocabulary.

    (a) Be sure that all words show the meaning of the sentence.
    (b) Be sure that two-word verbs are connected with the proper preposition. (These are covered in the next section, Problem Vocabulary and Prepositions.)

(4) Eliminate answer choices containing slang expressions. Slang is nonstandard vocabulary that is sometimes used in speech, but not considered correct in formal English. Some examples are:

really when it is used to mean "very"
bunch when it is used to mean "many"
any noun + *wise* when it is used to mean "in relation to _____"

● Examples of style questions:

1. Before we can decide on the future uses of this drug, _____.
   (A) many more informations must be reviewed
   (B) is necessary to review more information
   (C) we must review much more information
   (D) another information must to be reviewed

Analysis:
   (A) 2 errors in grammar: *many* + non-count noun is not possible; a non-count noun *cannot* be plural (*information*).
   (B) 1 grammar error: no subject.
   (C) Correct.
   (D) 2 grammar errors: *another* + non-count noun is not possible; a modal must be followed by the simple form (*must be reviewed*)

2. In this country, a growing concern about the possible hazardous effects of chemical wastes _____.
   (A) have resulted in a bunch of new laws
   (B) has resulted in several new laws
   (C) is causing the results of numerous new laws
   (D) result in news laws

Analysis:
   (A) 1 grammar error and 1 improper use of vocabulary (slang): The subject is *concern,* which is singular, so *have* should be *has.* The word *bunch* is not acceptable in formal English.
   (B) Correct.
   (C) Verbose; has too many unnecessary words.
   (D) 2 grammar errors: *result* is plural and the subject is singular; it is not possible to have a plural adjective (*new laws*).

MINI-TEST 4: STYLISTIC PROBLEMS

Part A: Structure

DIRECTIONS

Each sentence in Part A is an incomplete sentence. Four words or phrases, marked (A), (B), (C), (D) are given beneath each sentence. You are to choose the *one* word or phrase that best completes the sentence. Remember to eliminate answers that are incorrect and to choose the one that would be correct in formal written English.

1. The defendant refused to answer the prosecutor's questions _____.
   (A) because he was afraid it would incriminate him
   (B) for fear that they will incriminate him
   (C) because he was afraid that his answers would incriminate him
   (D) fearing that he will be incriminated by it

2. _____ will Mr. Forbes be able to regain control of the company.
   (A) With hard work
   (B) In spite of his hard work
   (C) Only if he works hardly
   (D) Only with hard work

3. Mrs. Walker has returned _____.
   (A) a wallet back to its original owner
   (B) to its original owner the wallet
   (C) the wallet to its originally owner
   (D) the wallet to its original owner

4. The hospital owes _____ for the construction of the new wing.
   (A) the government twenty million dollars
   (B) for the government twenty millions dollars
   (C) to the government twenty million dollars
   (D) twenty millions of dollars to the government

5. Maria _____ that she could not attend classes next week.
   (A) told to her professors
   (B) said her professors
   (C) told her professors
   (D) is telling her professors

6. Having been asked to speak at the convention, _____.
   (A) some notes were prepared for Dr. Casagrande
   (B) Dr. Casagrande prepared some notes
   (C) the convention members were pleased to hear Dr. Casagrande
   (D) some notes were prepared by Dr. Casagrande

7. _____ so many people been out of work as today.
   (A) More than ever before
   (B) Never before have
   (C) In the past, there never have
   (D) Formerly, there never were

8. The artist was asked to show some paintings at the contest because
_____.
   (A) he painted very good
   (B) they believed he painted well
   (C) of their belief that he was an good artist
   (D) the judges had been told of his talents

9. Having finished lunch, _____.
   (A) the detectives began to discuss the case
   (B) the case was discussed again by the detectives
   (C) they discussed the case
   (D) a bunch of detectives discussed the case

10. Ms. Sierra offered _____because she had faith in his capabilities.
    (A) to Mr. Armstrong the position
    (B) Mr. Armstrong the position
    (C) the position for Mr. Armstrong
    (D) Mr. Armstrong to the position

11. _____did Jerome accept the job.
    (A) Only because it was interesting work
    (B) Because it was interesting work
    (C) Only because it was interested work
    (D) The work was interesting

12. _____were slowly lowered to the ground for medical attention.
    (A) The victims who were screaming and who were burning
    (B) The screaming burn victims
    (C) The screamed burnt victims
    (D) The victims who were burning screamed

13. This car has many features including _____.
    (A) stereo, safety devices, air condition, and it saves gas
    (B) good music, safe devices, air conditioning, and gas
    (C) stereo, safety devices, air conditioned, and good gas
    (D) stereo, safety devices, air conditioning, and low gas mileage

14. The proposal was tabled _____that it would be helpful.
    (A) temporarily because there was not sufficient evidence
    (B) because for the time being there were not sufficient evidence
    (C) because at the present time there was not sufficient evidence
    (D) temporarily because there was not sufficient enough evidence

15. Adams was dismissed from his position _____.
    (A) because his financial records were improperly
    (B) because financewise he kept poor records
    (C) for keeping improper financial records
    (D) for keep financial records that were improper

Part B: Written Expression

DIRECTIONS

Each question on this mini-test consists of a sentence in which four words or phrases are underlined. The four underlined parts of the sentence are marked A, B, C, D. You are to identify the *one* underlined word or phrase that would not be acceptable *in standard written English*. Circle the letter of the underlined portion which is not correct.

16. <u>Some</u> Italian scholars <u>stressed</u> <u>the study of</u> grammar, rhetoric,
      A   B   C

    <u>learning about history</u>, and poetry.
           D

17. When the tank car <u>carried</u> the <u>toxic</u> gas derailed, the firemen <u>tried</u>
                 A   B   C

    to isolate the village <u>from</u> all traffic.
           D

18. While the boys were <u>ice skating</u>, they <u>slip</u> on the thin ice and <u>fell</u>
                A   B   C

    <u>into</u> the deep water.
      D

19. If motorists do <u>not observe</u> <u>the</u> traffic regulations, <u>they</u> will be
                A   B   C

    stopped, ticketed, and <u>have to pay a fine</u>.
                D

20. Fred, who usually conducts <u>the choir rehearsals</u>, did not <u>show up</u>
                     A   B

    last night because he <u>had</u> an accident <u>on his way to the practice</u>.
              C   D

21. A <u>short time</u> before her operation <u>last</u> month, Mrs. Carlyle <u>dreams</u>
       A   B   C

    of her daughter who <u>lives overseas</u>.
            D

22. The atmosphere of friendliness <u>in Andalucia</u> is open, warm and
                     A

    <u>gives a welcome feeling</u> to all <u>who have</u> <u>the good</u> fortune to visit there.
           B   C   D

23. <u>Now that</u> they have <u>successfully</u> passed the TOEFL, the students
       A   B

    <u>were ready</u> <u>to begin</u> their classes at the university.
       C   D

24. <u>Being that he was</u> a good swimmer, John jumped <u>into</u> the water and
             A   B

    rescued the <u>drowning</u> child.
      C   D

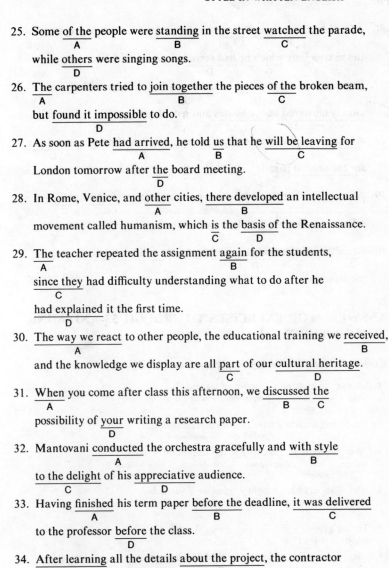

25. Some of the people were standing in the street watched the parade,
         A   B   C
    while others were singing songs.
        D

26. The carpenters tried to join together the pieces of the broken beam,
     A   B   C
    but found it impossible to do.
       D

27. As soon as Pete had arrived, he told us that he will be leaving for
             A   B   C
    London tomorrow after the board meeting.
           D

28. In Rome, Venice, and other cities, there developed an intellectual
              A   B
    movement called humanism, which is the basis of the Renaissance.
                C   D

29. The teacher repeated the assignment again for the students,
     A   B
    since they had difficulty understanding what to do after he
      C
    had explained it the first time.
       D

30. The way we react to other people, the educational training we received,
         A   B
    and the knowledge we display are all part of our cultural heritage.
                    C   D

31. When you come after class this afternoon, we discussed the
     A   B   C
    possibility of your writing a research paper.
           D

32. Mantovani conducted the orchestra gracefully and with style
           A   B
    to the delight of his appreciative audience.
       C   D

33. Having finished his term paper before the deadline, it was delivered
        A   B   C
    to the professor before the class.
          D

34. After learning all the details about the project, the contractor
       A   B
    told us them at the planning meeting.
      C   D

35. The new student's progress advanced forward with such speed that all
                 A   B   C
    his teachers were amazed.
       D

36. After Mr. Peabody <u>had died</u>, the money from his estate reverted <u>back</u>
    　　　　　　　　　A　　　　　　　　　　　　　　　　　　　　　　　　　　B

    to the company <u>which</u> he <u>had served</u> as president for ten years.
    　　　　　　　　　C　　　　　　D

37. In the distance <u>could be seen</u> the <u>sleepy</u> little village with <u>their</u>
    　　　　　　　　　　　A　　　　　　　　B　　　　　　　　　　　　C

    <u>closely clustered adobe houses</u> and red, clay-tile roofs.
    　　　　　　　　D

38. <u>Although</u> the weather was not perfect, <u>a bunch of</u> people <u>turned out</u>
    　　　A　　　　　　　　　　　　　　　　　　　B　　　　　　　C

    for the annual parade.
    <u>　　　　D　　　</u>

39. After she had dressed and <u>ate</u> breakfast, Lucy <u>rushed off</u> <u>to her</u>
    　　　　　　　　　　　　　　A　　　　　　　　　　　B　　　　　C

    office for a meeting <u>with</u> her accountant.
    　　　　　　　　　　　D

40. <u>After</u> the rain had <u>let out</u>, the Mitchells <u>continued</u> <u>their</u> hike up
    　A　　　　　　　　B　　　　　　　　　　　　　　C　　　　　D

    the mountain.

ANSWERS FOR EXERCISES 1 THROUGH 53 AND MINI-TESTS 1 THROUGH 4

Exercise 1: Subject, Verb, Complement, and Modifier

1. George / is cooking / dinner / tonight.
   　subject　　verb　　complement　　modifier
   　　　　　phrase　　　　　　　　　of time

2. Henry and Marcia / have visited / the president.
   　　　subject　　　　verb phrase　　complement

3. We / can eat / lunch / in this restaurant / today.
   subject　verb　complement　　modifier of　　modifier of
   　　　phrase　　　　　　　　place　　　　time

4. Pat / should have bought / gasoline / yesterday.
   subject　　verb phrase　　complement　　modifier of
   　　　　　　　　　　　　　　　　time

5. Trees / grow.
   subject　verb

6. It / was raining / at seven o'clock this morning.
   subject　verb　　　　modifer of time
   　　　phrase

7. She / opened / a checking account / at the bank / last week.
   subject　verb　　complement　　modifier of　　modifier of
   　　　　　　　　　　　　place　　　　time

8. Harry / is washing / dishes / right now.
   subject　verb phrase　complement　modifier of
   　　　　　　　　　　　　time

9. She / opened / her book.
   subject   verb   complement

10. Paul, William, and Mary / were watching / television / a few minutes ago.
   subject   verb phrase   complement   modifier of time

Exercise 2: Count and Non-Count Nouns

television (count)   water (non-count)   cup (count)
car (count)   pencil (count)   money (non-count)
news (non-count)   food (non-count)   hydrogen (non-count)
geography (non-count)   tooth (count)   minute (count)
atmosphere (non-count)   soap (non-count)
person (count)   soup (non-count)

Exercise 3: Determiners

1. much 2. a little 3. those 4. fewer 5. too much 6. this
7. too much 8. few 9. less 10. too much

Exercise 4: Articles

∅ = nothing

1. the	11. ∅, the	21. the, a
2. the, ∅, the	12. ∅, the, ∅	22. the, ∅
3. ∅, ∅	13. ∅, the	23. the *or* a, a, the, the
4. the, the, the	14. ∅, a *or* the, ∅	24. ∅, the, ∅
5. a, ∅, ∅, ∅	15. ∅	25. the
6. the, the	16. ∅, ∅, the	26. an, ∅, the
7. the *or* ∅, the, ∅	17. the *or* ∅, the *or* ∅	27. a
8. ∅	18. ∅, an	28. the
9. the, a, ∅, a	19. the, an	29. the, the
10. a, ∅, the	20. ∅	30. ∅, the

Exercise 5: Other

1. another *or* the other *or* another one *or* the other one
2. another
3. the other
4. the others
5. the others, other
6. another, another, the others
7. the other
8. another, another, another *or* the other
9. others, the others, other
10. the other

Exercise 6: Simple Present and Present Progressive

1. smells 4. are driving 7. is swimming 10. is mowing
2. are eating 5. believe 8. hates
3. practices 6. has 9. gets

Exercise 7: Simple Past Tense and Past Progressive

1. was eating
2. was sleeping (preferred) *or* slept
3. was studying
4. were having
5. went
6. entered
7. was looking (preferred) *or* looked
8. saw
9. owned
10. was writing, broke

Exercise 8: Present Perfect and Simple Past

1. wrote
2. has seen
3. has read
4. has worked
5. have not begun (haven't begun)
6. went
7. has traveled
8. wrote
9. called
10. have not seen (haven't seen)

Exercise 9: Past Perfect and Simple Past

1. had arrested
2. had washed
3. had waited
4. entered
5. washed
6. had received
7. sat
8. had flipped
9. had taken
10. had lived

Exercise 10: Subject-Verb Agreement

1. is
2. brings
3. is
4. aren't
5. have
6. has
7. are
8. are
9. has
10. vary

Exercise 11: Subject-Verb Agreement

1. is
2. is
3. is
4. were
5. has
6. were
7. were
8. has
9. was
10. has
11. makes
12. was
13. was
14. has
15. is
16. has
17. is
18. have
19. has
20. have

Exercise 12: Pronouns

1. him
2. her
3. us
4. she
5. he
6. she
7. your, mine
8. my
9. himself
10. we
11. himself
12. our
13. her
14. himself
15. yourself
16. I
17. his
18. me
19. us
20. her, ours

Exercise 13: Verbs as Complements

1. to accept	6. leaving	11. to be	16. driving
2. having	7. to return	12. to finish	17. to know
3. going	8. buying	13. to leave	18. returning
4. to reach	9. to accept	14. to tell	19. leaving
5. opening	10. being	15. to stop	20. leaving

Exercise 14: Pronouns with Verbs as Complements

1. us   2. his   3. our   4. me   5. his   6. George's
7. the defense attorney's   8. Henry   9. our   10. John's

Exercise 15: Need

1. cutting *or* to be cut	5. tuning *or* to be tuned	9. to study
2. watered	6. to be	10. painted
3. to see	7. oiled	
4. to make	8. to go	

Exercise 16: Embedded Questions

1. who will be elected president
2. whose book it is
3. how much it would cost to repair the car
4. how the murder was committed
5. how tall John is
6. how well she plays the guitar
7. when the next exam will take place
8. where they spent their vacation
9. why they are buying a new house
10. how long the class lasts

Exericse 17: Tag Questions

1. aren't you   2. didn't he   3. isn't there   4. won't she   5. hasn't she
6. isn't it   7. shouldn't he   8. can you   9. are there   10. haven't we

Exercise 18: Affirmative Agreement

1. does   2. will   3. do   4. have   5. is   6. should   7. do
8. do   9. have   10. must

Exercise 19: Negative Agreement

1. neither   2. neither   3. either   4. neither   5. neither   6. either
7. neither   8. either   9. either   10. either

Exercise 20: Negative Agreement

1. are   2. can't   3. have   4. didn't   5. did   6. should   7. won't
8. has   9. couldn't   10. did

Mini-Test Test 1 for Grammar Items 3 through 14

1. (A) should be *is*. Use a singular verb when a [verb + *ing*] is the subject.

2. (B) should be *too much*. As used in this sentence, *time* is a non-count noun.

3. (C) should be *us*. It is the object of the preposition *for*.

4. (B) should be *herself*. The subject is *she;* the reflexive pronoun must agree with the subject.

5. (C) should be *when we have to*. This is an embedded question; question word + subject + verb.

6. (D) should be *hasn't either*. Subject + auxiliary (negative) + *either*.

7. (B) should be *a new car in the morning*. Subject/verb/complement/ modifier.

8. (D) should be *the others* or *the other ones*. *Other* is an adjective when it appears before a noun and cannot be plural.

9. (D) should be *read*. Use the simple past with the past perfect.

10. (B) should be *have been*. *Have been* agrees with the plural subject *many theories*.

11. (C) should be *smells*. Use the simple present tense for present time with stative (linking) verbs.

12. (A) should be *had eaten*. Use the past perfect for the past action that happened first.

13. (A) should be *finished*. Use the simple past because *last night* is a specific time in the past.

14. (C) should be *themselves*. *Theirselves* is NEVER correct.

15. (B) should be *any more*. *Another* cannot be used with non-count nouns such as *homework*.

16. (A) should be *taking*. Use the gerund [verb + *ing*] after a preposition.

17. (A) should be *your*. Use the possessive adjective before the gerund.

18. (D) should be *hasn't it*. The auxiliary in the main sentence is *has*.

19. (D) should be *John does too* or *so does John*. See the affirmative agreement rule.

20. (A) should be *being*. *Enjoy* + gerund.

21. (D) should be *to find*. *Decide* + infinitive.

22. (A) should be *him to take*. *Persuade* + complement pronoun + infinitive.

23. (D) should be *I*. Use subject pronouns after the verb *be*.

24. (B) should be *is*. *Is* agrees with the singular subject *the work*.

25. **(D)** should be *had finished*. There were two actions in the past. First he finished the conference, then he went fishing.
26. **(A)** should be *play*. *Play* (the plural form of the verb) agrees with the plural subject *Peter and Tom*.
27. **(A)** should be *was*. The singular *was* agrees with the singular subject *a time*.
28. **(A)** should be *was drinking*. This is the past progressive:

$$\begin{Bmatrix} was \\ were \end{Bmatrix} + [\text{verb} + ing]$$

29. **(B)** should be *our friends in Boston yesterday*. Subject/verb/complement/modifier.
30. **(B)** should be *outdoors last night*. Modifier of place + modifier of time.
31. **(A)** should be *that*. *Homework* is a non-count noun and cannot be used with the plural *those*.
32. **(B)** should be *a little*. *Coffee* is a non-count noun and cannot be used with *few*.
33. **(B)** should be *children*. The plural of *child* is *children*.
34. **(C)** should be *an honest man*. Use the article *an* before words beginning with a vowel sound.
35. **(D)** should be *neither are they* or *they aren't either*. See the rule for negative agreement.
36. **(D)** should be *so is John*. *Is* agrees with the auxiliary *is* in the main sentence.
37. **(D)** should be *can hardly*. *Hardly* is negative and is always used with a positive verb.
38. **(B)** should be *a university*. The article *a* is used before words that begin with a consonant sound.
39. **(C)** should be *in taking*. Use the gerund after a preposition.
40. **(C)** should be *hardly ever*. *Hardly* is a negative word and cannot be used with another negative.
41. **(A)** should be *we*. *We students* is the subject of the sentence.
42. **(B)** should be *not to remove*. See the rule for negative indirect commands.
43. **(A)** should be *he*. Use subject pronouns after the verb *be*.
44. **(B)** should be *the car costs*. This is an embedded question; question word + subject + verb.
45. **(D)** should be *so did Jean*. *Did* agrees in tense (past) with the main sentence verb *studied*.
46. **(A)** should be *seen*. This is past perfect. *Had* + [verb in past participle].
47. **(D)** should be *isn't there*. When *there* appears in the subject position of a sentence, it is also used in the tag question.

48. **(B)** should be *to vote. Decide* + infinitive.
49. **(B)** should be *of going. Think of* or *think about* + [verb + *ing*]; NEVER use *think* + infinitive.
50. **(B)** should be *his going.* Use a possessive adjective and gerund after a preposition.

Exercise 21: *Conditional Sentences*

1. understood *or* could understand	11. paint	21. had studied
2. would not have been	12. were	22. hears
3. will give	13. writes	23. see
4. would have told	14. would permit *or* had permitted	24. gets
5. would have been	15. could spend	25. turn
6. had	16. will accept	26. were
7. would stop	17. buys	27. would have called
8. needed	18. had decided	28. would have talked
9. would have found	19. would have written	29. explained
10. enjoyed	20. will leak *or* may leak	30. spoke

Exercise 22: **Used To**

1. eating 2. eat 3. swim 4. like 5. speaking 6. studying
7. dance 8. sleeping 9. eating 10. eating

Exercise 23: **Would Rather**

1. stay 2. have stayed 3. work 4. studied 5. not study 6. have
7. stood 8. not cook 9. had not arrived 10. have slept

Exercise 24: **Must/Should** + *Perfective*

1. should have had	6. should have studied
2. must have been	7. must have been
3. must have damaged	8. should have deposited
4. should not have parked	9. must have forgotten
5. must have studied	10. must not have studied

Exercise 25: *Modals* + *Perfective*

1. I would	6. may have slept
2. would have gone	7. might have had
3. may have had	8. could have lost
4. should have done	9. shouldn't have driven
5. must have forgotten	10. may have run

Exercise 26: *Adjectives and Adverbs*

1. well   2. intense   3. brightly   4. fluent   5. fluently   6. smooth
7. accurately   8. bitter   9. soon   10. fast

Exercise 27: *Linking (Copulative) Verbs*

1. terrible   2. well   3. good   4. calm   5. sick   6. quickly
7. diligently   8. vehemently   9. relaxed   10. noisy

Exercise 28: *Comparisons*

1. as soon   2. more important   3. as well   4. more expensive
5. as hot   6. more talented   7. more colorful   8. happier
9. worse   10. faster

Exercise 29: *Comparisons*

1. than   2. than   3. from   4. than   5. as   6. than   7. as
8. than   9. than   10. from

Exercise 30: *Comparisons*

1. best	6. better	11. the better	16. twice as
2. happiest	7. good	12. from	much as
3. faster	8. more	13. less	17. few
4. creamiest	awkwardly	impressive	18. much
5. more	9. least	14. the sicker	19. farthest
colorful	10. prettier	15. than	20. famous

Exercise 31: *Nouns Functioning as Adjectives*

1. twelve-story   2. language   3. three-act   4. two-day   5. 79-piece
6. five-shelf   7. 16-ounce   8. six-quart   9. brick   10. ten-speed

Exercise 32: **Enough**

1. enough people   5. soon enough   9. enough flour
2. enough French   6. early enough   10. enough books
3. enough time   7. hard enough
4. fast enough   8. slowly enough

Exercise 33: **Because/Because Of**

1. because   2. because   3. because of   4. because   5. because of
6. because of   7. because of   8. because   9. because   10. because of

Exercise 34: So/Such

1. so 2. such 3. so 4. such 5. so 6. so 7. such 8. so
9. such 10. such 11. so 12. so 13. such 14. so 15. so

Mini-Test 2 for Grammar Items 15 through 20

1. (B) should be *ghost*. *Ghost* is an adjective in this sentence modifying the noun *stories* and thus cannot be in the plural form.
2. (B) should be *would take*. The correct sequence of tenses is *were . . . would take*.
3. (B) should be *had told*. This is a past unreal condition. *Would have attended . . . had told*.
4. (A) should be *review*. *Had better* + [verb in simple form].
5. (C) should be *five-speed*. *Five-speed* is an adjective modifying the noun *bicycle*.
6. (C) should be *hot enough*. Adjective + *enough*.
7. (C) should be *brick*. *Brick* is an adjective in this sentence modifying the noun *patio*.
8. (A) should be *such an enjoyable*. *Such* + (*a*) + adjective + singular count noun.
9. (C) should be *enough supplies*. *Enough* + noun.
10. (A) should be *such*. *Such* + adjective + noun (noun = *plans*).
11. (A) should be *had studied*. NEVER use *would* immediately after *if*.
12. (A) should be *deposit*. *Have to* + [verb in simple form].
13. (A) should be *were*. NEVER use *was* after the verb *wish*.
14. (C) should be *must have rehearsed*. This is a logical conclusion in the past (meaning "probably rehearsed").
15. (A) should be *flying*. *Be used to* + [verb + *ing*].
16. (B) should be *to spend*. *Would like* + (complement) + infinitive.
17. (A) should be *live*. *Used to* + [verb in simple form].
18. (C) should be *the louder*. This is a double comparative ("the bolder the . . . display, the louder . . . its approval").
19. (D) should be *his friend Joel's*. The original sentence makes an illogical comparison (comparing the *car* with *Joel*). What should be compared are *Hal's sports car* with *Joel's sports car*. NOTE: *Sports car* is an exception to the rule calling for a singular adjective before a noun.
20. (A) should be *be fishing*. *Would rather* + [verb in simple form].
21. (A) should be *should have talked*. This is an unfulfilled past obligation (meaning "she did not call").
22. (A) should be *occurred*. NEVER use *would* immediately after *if*.
23. (D) should be *uncontrollably*. An adverb must modify the verb *sob*, not an adjective. (*How* did the child sob?)

24. (B) should be *so that*. Use *so that* + result clause.
25. (D) should be *would*. The sequence of tense should be *would advise . . . would*.
26. (C) should be *ought to send*. *Ought to* + [verb in simple form].
27. (A) should be *such a difficult time*. *Such* + (*a*) + adjective + singular count noun.
28. (C) should be *because of*. *Because of* + noun (phrase).
29. (B) should be *ninety-day warranty*. *Ninety-day* is functioning as an adjective of the noun *warranty*.
30. (B) should be *to sleeping*. *Get used to* + [verb + *ing*].
31. (A) should be *bad*. *Feel* is a stative (linking) verb and is modified by an adjective, not an adverb.
32. (A) should be *to go*. *Hope* + infinitive.
33. (B) should be *had*. *As if* indicates an unreal (contrary-to-fact) idea. Use the same rule as for a past unreal condition.
34. (A) should be *so good*. *Taste* is a stative (linking) verb and is modified by an adjective, not an adverb.
35. (C) should be *as old as*. This is a multiple number comparative.
36. (D) should be *sadder than*. It is not correct to use *more* + adjective + *er* at the same time.
37. (B) should be *as*. *As many* + adjective + noun + *as*.
38. (B) should be *had to arrive*. *Have to* + [verb in simple form].
39. (C) should be *from*. The correct idiom is *different from*.
40. (B) should be *never would have met* or *would never have met*. This is a past unreal condition.
41. (C) should be *speaking*. *Be used to* + [verb + *ing*].
42. (B) should be *because*. *Because* + sentence.
43. (B) should be *densely packed*. Use an adverb (*densely*) to modify an adjective (*packed*). (*How* is it packed?)
44. (A) should be *the most*. Use the superlative with more than two.
45. (B) should be *so good a game* or *such a good game*. Cause/effect.
46. (B) should be *did not*. Subject$_1$ + *would rather that* + subject$_2$ + [verb in past tense]. The sentence is contrary to fact. They *are* traveling during the bad weather.
47. (D) should be *language*. *Language* is functioning as an adjective modifying the noun *classes* and cannot be plural.
48. (A) should be *from*. The correct idiom is *different from*.
49. (B) should be *inferior*. This adjective can be used in only the positive form, not the comparative or superlative.
50. (A) should be *careful*. This should be an adjective because it is modifying the noun *investigation*. (*What kind* of investigation was it?)

Exercise 35: Passive Voice

1. The president is called (by somebody) every day.
2. The other members are being called by John.
3. The documents were being delivered to the department by Martha.
4. The amendment has been repealed by the other members.
5. The information had been received by the delegates before the recess.
6. The supplies for this class should be bought by the teacher.
7. Mr. Watson will be called (by somebody) tonight.
8. Considerable damage has been caused by the fire.
9. A new procedure was being developed by the company before the bankruptcy hearings began.
10. The papers will have been received by John by tomorrow.

Exercise 36: Causative Verbs

1. leave	4. call	7. lie	10. to sign	13. fixed
2. repaired	5. painted	8. sent	11. leave	14. published
3. to type	6. write	9. cut	12. to wash	15. find

Exercise 37: Relative Clauses

The word *which* shown in parentheses in these answers indicates optional acceptable answers. In each such case, *that* is the preferred choice, but *which* is not incorrect.

1. The last record that (which) was produced by this company became a gold record.
2. Checking accounts that (which) require a minimum balance are very common now.
3. The professor to whom you spoke yesterday is not here today.
4. John, whose grades are the highest in the school, has received a scholarship.
5. Felipe bought a camera that (which) has three lenses.
6. Frank is the man whom we are going to nominate for the office of treasurer.
7. The doctor is with a patient whose leg was broken in an accident.
8. Jane is the woman who is going to China next year.
9. Janet wants a typewriter that (which) self-corrects.
10. This book, which I found last week, contains some useful information.
11. Mr. Bryant, whose team has lost the game, looks very sad.
12. James wrote an article that (which) indicated that he disliked the president.
13. The director of the program, who graduated from Harvard University, is planning to retire next year.
14. This is the book that (which) I have been looking for all year.
15. William, whose brother is a lawyer, wants to become a judge.

Exercise 38: Relative Clause Reduction

1. George is the man chosen to represent the committee at the convention.
2. All the money accepted has already been released.
3. The papers on the table belong to Patricia.
4. The man brought to the police station confessed to the crime.
5. The girl drinking coffee is Mary Allen.
6. John's wife, a professor, has written several papers on this subject.
7. The man talking to the policeman is my uncle.
8. The book on the top shelf is the one I need.
9. The number of students counted is quite high.
10. Leo Evans, a doctor, eats in this restaurant every day.

Exercise 39: Subjunctive

1. The teacher demanded that the student *leave* the room.
2. It was urgent that he *call* her immediately.
3. Correct.
4. She intends to move that the committee *suspend* discussion on this issue.
5. The king decreed that the new laws *take* effect the following month.
6. I propose that you *stop* this rally.
7. I advise *that* you take the prerequisites before registering for this course. *or* I advise you *to take* the prerequisites before registering for this course.
8. His father prefers that he *attend* a different university.
9. Correct.
10. She urged that we *find* another alternative.

Exercise 40: Inclusives

1. not only   2. as well as   3. both   4. but also   5. as well as
6. not only   7. and   8. but also   9. as well as   10. as well as

Exercise 41: Know/Know How

1. know how   2. know how   3. know   4. know   5. know how
6. knew   7. knew how   8. knew   9. knew how   10. know how

Exercise 42: Clauses of Concession

1. Although she disliked coffee, she drank it to keep herself warm.
2. Mary will take a plane in spite of her dislike of flying.
3. Although Marcy was sad after losing the contest, she managed to smile.
4. We took many pictures despite the cloudy sky.

5. Even though she had a poor memory, the old woman told interesting stories to the children.
6. In spite of his frequent absences, he has managed to pass the test.
7. Nancy told me the secret though she had promised not to do so.
8. We plan to buy a ticket for the drawing even though we know we will not win a prize.
9. Even though the prices are high, my daughters insist on going to the movies every Saturday.
10. He ate the chocolate cake in spite of his diet.

Exercise 43: Problem Verbs

1. lies
2. sit
3. laid
   (complement = *the groceries*)
4. rose
5. raise
   (complement = *the picture*)
6. lie
7. laying
   (complement = *cement*)
8. raised
   (complement = *the flag*)
9. rises
10. set
    (complement = *the explosives*)

Mini-Test 3 for Grammar Items 21 through 29

∅ = nothing

1. (D) should be *but also interesting. Not only . . . but also.*
2. (A) should be *he take. Recommend that* + [verb in simple form].
3. (C) should be *know how. Know how* + [verb in infinitive].
4. (B) should be *speak. It is important that* + [verb in simple form].
5. (B) should be *to enter. Permit* + infinitive.
6. (A) should be ∅. It is redundant to say *both . . . as well as.*
7. (A) should be *in spite of* or *despite.*
8. (B) should be *make. Let* + [verb in simple form].
9. (A) should be *raising. Raise* + complement (complement = *the flag*).
10. (B) should be *that the Officers' Club. Command that* + [verb in simple form].
11. (A) should be *to read. Get* + infinitive.
12. (A) should be *knew. Know* + noun; *know how* + verb.
13. (C) should be *despite* or *in spite of.*
14. (B) should be *study. It was suggested that* + [verb in simple form].
15. (B) should be *practice. Require that* + [verb in simple form].
16. (A) should be *studying.* The present progressive is *be* + [verb + *ing*].
17. (A) should be *sit.* There is no complement in the sentence.
18. (B) should be *that he.* After the verb *mention* one must use *that.*
19. (D) should be ∅. It is redundant to use *as well* after *not only . . . but also.*

20. **(B)** should be *us to enter. Allow* + infinitive.
21. **(A)** should be *know. Know* + sentence.
22. **(A)** should be *have informed.* The sentence is in the active voice and *should have been informed* is the passive form.
23. **(C)** should be *advertised* or *that had been advertised.* This is a relative clause in passive voice and can be reduced.
24. **(D)** should be ∅. It is redundant to use *as well* after *not only ... but also.*
25. **(A)** should be *to work. Encourage* + infinitive.
26. **(A)** should be *rewrite. Have* + person complement + [verb in simple form]; causative.
27. **(A)** should be *divide.* The sentence is in the active voice, and *will be divided* is in the passive form.
28. **(C)** should be *were destroyed.* Passive voice.
29. **(B)** should be *and. Both ... and.*
30. **(A)** should be *risen.* There is no complement.
31. **(A)** should be *whose.* Use the possessive relative pronoun.
32. **(A)** should be *in spite of* or *despite. Although* + sentence:

$$\begin{Bmatrix} in\ spite\ of \\ despite \end{Bmatrix} + noun\ phrase.$$

33. **(A)** should be *has been repealed.* Passive voice.
34. **(B)** should be *whom.* Use the complement relative pronoun (... they voted not to retain *him*).
35. **(C)** should be *to raise.* Complement = *the rent.*
36. **(A)** should be *which.* This is a nonrestrictive relative clause and must use *which,* not *that.*
37. **(C)** should be *lie.* There is no complement in this sentence.
38. **(A)** should be *set.* Complement = *the plant.*
39. **(A)** should be *who. Which* is used with things, *who* with people.
40. **(A)** should be *despite* or *in spite of.*
41. **(A)** should be *has been cancelled.* Passive voice.
42. **(C)** should be *lying.* There is no complement in this sentence.
43. **(A)** should be *were discovered.* If a relative clause is reduced, the pronoun *that* must also be omitted.
44. **(A)** should be *lie.* There is no complement in this sentence.
45. **(D)** should be *rewrite. Make* + [verb in simple form].
46. **(A)** should be *stated that he. State that.*
47. **(A)** should be *in spite of* or *despite. The danger* is a noun phrase, and *although* must be followed by a sentence. *That he might be injured* is a relative clause.
48. **(A)** should be ∅. If a sentence begins with *that,* it must contain two clauses and thus two verbs.
49. **(B)** should be *to raise.* Complement = *her test score.*
50. **(D)** should be *able to find. Able* + infinitive.

Exercise 44: Sequence of Tenses

1. He *said* that he *would finish* the project by May.
2. Mark *thought* he *was going* to win the award.
3. I *heard* that Kate *had accepted* a new position at the East Side Clinic.
4. Steve *said* that he *would make* the dessert for the party.
5. Lou *told* his friends that they *were* good tennis players.
6. I *realized* that they *were* older than they *looked*.
7. Mary Ellen *said* that she *ate* three well-balanced meals every day.
8. The student *was asking* the professor when the class *would do* the next experiment.
9. We *hoped* that you *could play* tennis later.
10. We *knew* that you *might move* to France next year.

Exercise 45: Say/Tell

1. said	6. tell	11. told	16. said
2. is telling	7. tells	12. said	17. said
3. told	8. say	13. said	18. says
4. tell	9. says	14. tell	19. said
5. told	10. tell	15. said	20. tell

Exercise 46: Antecedents of Pronouns

Note that other choices are possible.

1. The dispute between the faculty and the administration was not resolved until the faculty (members) got better working conditions.
2. As Ellen walked towards the Student Union, she spotted her friend.
3. When the bullfighters march into the arena, foreigners are easily impressed.
4. In their spare time, authors have written many great books about the famous Greek and Roman heroes.
5. Dr. Byrd's book was accepted for publication because the publishers thought it would be beneficial to students.
6. Bob and Helen hate flying because planes make too much noise.
7. Casey was not admitted to the country club because the members thought he was not socially acceptable.
8. Mary loves touring the country by train because the countryside is so interesting.
9. The colonel was decorated for bravery, having fought off the enemy (soldiers).
10. The children were frightened because the animals (or any noun) made such eerie sounds.

Exercise 47: Illogical Participial Modifiers

Note that other choices are possible.

1. Being thoroughly dissatisfied with the picture, *Mary* (or any animate noun) hid it in the closet.
2. Seeing the advancing army, *the family* (or any animate noun) hid the valuables under the stairwell.
3. Plunging into the water, *the lifeguard* (or any animate noun) rescued the drowning child.
4. Criticizing the defendant for his cruel behavior, the judge handed down the sentence.
5. After painting the car, the man gave it to his wife.
6. Being an early riser, Edna adjusted easily to her company's new summer schedule.
7. After winning the match, Nancy jumped for joy.
8. Having wandered through the mountain passes for days, the hikers discovered an abandoned shack where they could take shelter.
9. Being very protective of its young, the mother eagle attacks all those who approach the nest.
10. Before playing ball, the baseball players observed a two-minute silence for their recently deceased teammate.

Exercise 48: Participles as Adjectives

1. broken	6. excited	11. approving	16. cleaned
2. trembling	7. smiling	12. approved	17. closed
3. crying	8. frightening	13. blowing	18. crowded
4. interesting	9. frightened	14. boring	19. aching
5. burning	10. advancing	15. cleaning	20. parked

Exercise 49: Redundancy

The redundant word is listed here.

1. again   2. identical *or* the same   3. enough *or* sufficient   4. back
5. performance   6. forward   7. together   8. new
9. together   10. two

Exercise 50: Parallel Structure

1. The puppy stood up slowly, wagged its tail, *blinked* its eyes, and barked. (past tense verbs)
2. Ecologists are trying to preserve our environment for future generations by protecting the ozone layer, purifying the air, and *replanting the trees* that have been cut down. (verbs + *ing*)

3. The chief of police demanded from his assistants an orderly investigation, a well-written report, and *hard work*. (adjective + noun)
4. Marcia is a scholar, an athlete, and *an artist*. (nouns)
5. Slowly and *carefully,* the museum director removed the Ming vase from the shelf and placed it on the display pedestal. (adverbs)
6. The farmer plows the fields, plants the seeds, and *harvests* the crop. (present tense verbs)
7. Abraham Lincoln was a good president—self-educated, hard working, and *honest*. (adjectives)
8. Children love playing in the mud, running through puddles, and *getting* very dirty. (verbs + *ing*)
9. Collecting stamps, playing chess, and *mounting* beautiful butterflies are Derrick's hobbies. (verbs + *ing* + nouns)
10. Despite America's affluence, many people are without jobs, on welfare, and *in debt*. (prepositional phrases)

Exercise 51: Transformation of Direct and Indirect Object

1. Mary showed *me* the photographs.
2. I'll send *you* the books next week.
3. My sister sent *my daughter* a game for her birthday.
4. He brought *her* the telegram this morning.
5. The author gave *his friend* an autographed copy of his book.
6. They wrote *us* a letter.
7. Louie drew *his mother* a lovely picture.
8. She made *her cousin* a bookcase.
9. That teacher taught *us* grammar last year.
10. Mary handed *her brother* the tray.

Exercise 52: Transformation of Direct and Indirect Object

1. John owes the money *to his friend*.
2. My friends sent a bouquet of flowers *to me* while I was in the hospital.
3. The clerk sold the records *to us*.
4. They found a good, inexpensive car *for him*.
5. Picasso painted a beautiful portrait *for his wife*.
6. My father read the newspaper article *to us*.
7. Pass the salt *to me* please.
8. She bought a red jacket *for him*.
9. The girls couldn't wait to show the bicycles *to us*.
10. The construction crew built a house *for them* in four weeks.

Exercise 53: Adverbials at the Beginning of a Sentence

1. Rarely does Jorge forget to do his homework.
2. Only by staying up all night can Jane finish this work.
3. Hardly had Henry started working when he realized that he needed to go to the library.
4. Never have we heard so moving a rendition as this one.
5. Seldom did Maria miss a football game when she was in the United States.
6. Only with a bank loan will we be able to buy the car.
7. Rarely do we watch television during the week.
8. Never has he played a better game than he has today.
9. Seldom does this professor let his students leave class early.
10. Hardly had Jennifer entered the room when she felt the presence of another person.

Mini-Test 4: Stylistic Problems

For Part A of this mini-test, the answer key analyzes why each incorrect answer choice is incorrect.

PART A

1. (A) Style error. There is no antecedent for the pronoun *it*.
   (B) 2 style errors. *Refused . . . will* is an incorrect sequence of tense; there is no antecedent for the pronoun *they*.
   (C) Correct.
   (D) 2 style errors. There is an incorrect sequence of tense; there is no antecedent for the pronoun *it*.

2. (A) and (B) Style error. Because the structure of the sentence is auxiliary + subject + verb, the sentence must begin with an adverbial.
   (C) Vocabulary error. *Hardly* means "almost."
   (D) Correct

3. (A) Style error. It is redundant to say *return . . . back.*
   (B) Grammar error. When the indirect object precedes the direct object, no preposition is possible.
   (C) Grammar error. *Originally* is an adverb and is not correct because it modifies the noun *owner*.
   (D) Correct.

4. (A) Correct.
   (B) 2 grammar errors. It is not correct to use a preposition when the indirect object precedes the direct object; when *million* is preceded by a number, it cannot be plural (one million, two million).

(C) Grammar error. It is not correct to use a preposition when the indirect object precedes the direct object.

(D) 2 grammar errors. When *million* is preceded by a number, it cannot be plural, and when *million* is preceded by a number and followed by a noun, the preposition *of* is incorrect.

5. (A) Grammar error. *Tell* must be followed directly by the indirect object; there can be no preposition.

(B) Grammar error. It is not correct to follow the verb *say* with the name of a person or people.

(C) Correct.

(D) Grammar error. *Is telling . . . could* is an incorrect sequence of tense.

6. (A), (C), and (D) Style errors. These choices contain dangling participles. *Dr. Casagrande* is the subject of *having been asked,* and thus his name must follow the comma.

(B) Correct.

7. (A) Grammar error. The only verb in the sentence is a past participle, *been,* and choice (A) contains no auxiliary verb.

(B) Correct. Adverbial + auxiliary + subject + verb.

(C) Grammar error. The choice uses incorrect word order.

(D) Grammar error. The choice uses incorrect word order; *were* cannot be followed by the participle *been.*

8. (A) Grammar error. *Good* is an adjective and modifies the verb *painted;* it should always be *well.*

(B) Style error. The pronoun *they* has no antecedent.

(C) Style error. The pronoun *their* has no antecedent; *an* cannot precede a word beginning with a consonant sound.

(D) Correct.

9. (A) Correct

(B) Style error. This choice contains a dangling participle. *The detectives* is the subject of *having finished* and must immediately follow the comma.

(C) Style error. The pronoun *they* has no antecedent.

(D) Style error. *A bunch of* is slang and not appropriate in formal English.

10. (A) Grammar error. It is not correct to use a preposition when the indirect object precedes the direct object.

(B) Correct.

(C) Grammar error. *For* is the wrong preposition (*offer* something *to* somebody).

(D) Grammar error. This choice uses incorrect word order.

11. (A) Correct.
    (B) Style error. Because the construction is auxiliary + subject + verb, the sentence must begin with an adverbial.
    (C) Grammar error. *Interested* should be *interesting*.
    (D) Style error. This choice uses incorrect word order.

12. (A) Style error. The choice is verbose, using too many unnecessary words (repeating *who were*).
    (B) Correct.
    (C) Grammar error. *Screamed* should be *screaming*.
    (D) Grammar error. The conjugated verb *screamed* immediately before the verb *were* is not possible.

13. (A) Improper word choice. It should read *air conditioning; and it saves gas* is not parallel.
    (B) Improper word choice. *Good music* does not mean the same as *stereo;* a *safe device* is a device that is safe, but a *safety device* is a device that makes something else safe; *gas* is not a "feature."
    (C) *Air conditioned* is improper word choice; *good gas* does not mean the same as *low gas mileage.*
    (D) Correct.

14. (A) Correct.
    (B) Grammar error. *Were* is plural and *evidence* is non-count.
    (C) Style error. *At the present time* is not correct because the sentence is in the past.
    (D) Style error. *Sufficient* and *enough* have the same meaning and when used together are redundant.

15. (A) Grammar error. *Improperly* is an adverb. An adverb cannot modify the noun *records.*
    (B) Style error. *Financewise* is not correct.
    (C) Correct.
    (D) Grammar error and style error. *For keeping* is correct, not *for keep* (preposition + [verb + *ing*]); *financial records that were improper* should be *improper financial records* because it is the more concise way of conveying the idea.

PART B

16. (D) should be *history*. *History* is parallel structure; noun, noun, noun.
17. (A) should be *carrying*. Use the present participle because the subject (*the tank car*) was involved in the action.
18. (B) should be *slipped*. The correct sequence of tenses is *were ... slipped.*
19. (D) should be *fined*. For parallel structure, all past participles are required.

20. (C) should be *had had*. The past perfect should be used; the accident happened first.

21. (C) should be *dreamed*. Use past time because it happened last month.

22. (B) should be *welcoming*. For parallel structure, all adjectives are required.

23. (C) should be *are*. *Now* indicates present time.

24. (A) should be ∅. The wording is verbose. The sentence should read: *Being a good swimmer* . . .

25. (C) should be *watching*. *Were standing . . . watching* is correct parallel structure.

26. (B) should be *join*. It is redundant to say *join together*.

27. (C) should be *would be leaving*. The correct sequence of tense is *told . . . would be*.

28. (C) should be *was*. *Was* (past) is the correct sequence of tense because the sentence is in the past.

29. (B) should be ∅. It is redundant to say *repeat again*.

30. (B) should be *receive*. For parallel structure, *react . . . receive . . . display* (all present tense) is required.

31. (B) should be *will discuss*. The correct sequence of tense is *come . . . will discuss*.

32. (B) should be *stylishly*. Parallel structure requires *gracefully* (adverb) . . . *stylishly* (adverb).

33. (C) should be *he delivered it*. A person is the subject of the verb *having finished*, and thus that person's name must appear immediately after the comma.

34. (C) should be *them to us*. Two pronouns cannot take the order of indirect object + direct object.

35. (A) should be *advanced*. It is redundant to say *advance forward*.

36. (B) should be ∅. It is redundant to say *revert back*.

37. (C) should be *its*. *Village* is singular, so the possessive pronoun must also be singular.

38. (B) should be *many*. *A bunch of* is slang.

39. (A) should be *eaten*. Parallel structure requires *had dressed and eaten*.

40. (B) should be *let up*. *Let up* means "to diminish"; *let out* means "to dismiss."

PROBLEM VOCABULARY AND PREPOSITIONS

This section contains information and exercises on commonly misused words, confusingly related words, use of prepositions, and two-word verbs. With each section are example sentences and exercises. The answers to the exercises will be found at the end of this section.

It should be noted that the material presented here may appear not only in the vocabulary section of TOEFL but also in the grammar section and even in the listening comprehension section. Some exercises are adapted to the use of these items in both the vocabulary section and the grammar section.

Memorizing long lists of words may result in frustration and is actually not very useful. There is no way to know which of the words you memorize will appear on TOEFL. Therefore, you should try to improve your vocabulary as you improve your English in general. The following suggestions will be useful in helping you improve your vocabulary.

1. Read well-written books, magazines, and newspapers. Magazines such as *Time* and *Newsweek,* for example, and major newspapers contain sophisticated vocabulary and grammatical constructions. Reading such materials is very useful.
2. Look up every word that is unfamiliar to you in the practice tests in this book and in other reading material. Keep a notebook of unfamiliar words. After looking up the word, write the word, the definition, and an original sentence in your notebook and study it often.
3. Study the problem vocabulary items and two-word verbs (verbal idioms) in this book.

COMMONLY MISUSED WORDS

The following words are often misused by native English speakers as well as nonnative speakers. Sometimes the spellings are so similar that people fail to distinguish between them. Others are pronounced exactly the same, but they are spelled differently and have different meanings. Words in the latter category are called homonyms. Study the words, parts of speech (noun, verb, etc.), definitions, and sample sentences in this list.

ANGEL (noun) a spiritual or heavenly being. The Christmas card portrayed a choir of *angels* hovering over the shepherds.

ANGLE (noun) a figure formed by two lines meeting at a common point. The carpenters placed the planks at right *angles*.

CITE (verb) quote as an example. In her term paper, Janis had to *cite* many references.

199

SITE (noun) location. The corner of North Main and Mimosa Streets will be the *site* of the new shopping center.

SIGHT (a) (noun) aim (of a gun or telescope). Through the *sight* of the rifle, the soldier spotted the enemy. (b) (noun) view. Watching the landing of the space capsule was a pleasant *sight*. (c) (verb) see. We *sighted* a ship in the bay.

COSTUME (noun) clothing, typical style of dress. We all decided to wear colonial *costumes* to the Fourth of July celebration.

CUSTOM (noun) a practice that is traditionally followed by a particular group of people. It is a *custom* in Western Europe for little boys to wear short pants to school.

DECENT (adjective) respectable or suitable. When one appears in court, one must wear *decent* clothing.

DESCENT (noun) (a) downward motion. The mountain climbers found their *descent* more hazardous than their ascent. (b) lineage. Vladimir is of Russian *descent*.

DESSERT (noun) the final course of a meal, usually something sweet. We had apple pie for *dessert* last night.

DESERT (noun) (désert) a hot, dry place. It is difficult to survive in the *desert* without water.

DESERT (verb) (desért) abandon. After *deserting* his post, the soldier ran away from the camp.

LATER (adverb) a time in the future or following a previous action. We went to the movies and *later* had ice cream at Dairy Isle.

LATTER (adjective) last of two things mentioned. Germany and England both developed dirigibles for use during World War II, the *latter* primarily for coastal reconnaissance. (*latter = England*)

LOOSE (adjective) opposite of *tight*. After dieting, Marcy found that her clothes had become so *loose* that she had to buy a new wardrobe.

LOSE (verb) (a) to be unable to find something. Mary *lost* her glasses last week. (b) opposite of win. If Harry doesn't practice his tennis more, he may *lose* the match.

PASSED (verb) past tense of *pass* (a) elapse. Five hours *passed* before the jury reached its verdict. (b) go by or beyond. While we were sitting in the park, several of our friends *passed* us. (c) succeed. The students are happy that they *passed* their exams.

PAST (a) (adjective) a time or event before the present. This *past* week has been very hectic for the students returning to the university. (b) (noun) time before the present. In the *past*, he had been a cook, a teacher, and a historian.

PEACE (noun) harmony or freedom from war. *Peace* was restored to the community after a week of rioting.

PIECE (noun) part of a whole. Heidi ate a *piece* of chocolate cake for dessert.

PRINCIPAL (a) (noun) director of an elementary or secondary school. The *principal* called a faculty meeting. (b) (adjective) main or most important. An anthropologist, who had worked with the indigenous tribes in Australia, was the *principal* speaker at Friday's luncheon.

PRINCIPLE (noun) fundamental rule or adherence to such a rule. Mr. Connors is a man who believes that truthfulness is the best *principle*.

QUIET (adjective) serene, without noise. The night was so *quiet* that you could hear the breeze blowing.

QUITE (adverb) (a) completely. Louise is *quite* capable of taking over the household chores while her mother is away. (b) somewhat or rather. He was *quite* tired after his first day of classes.

QUIT (verb) stop. Herman *quit* smoking on his doctor's advice.

STATIONARY (adjective) nonmovable, having a fixed location. The weatherman said that the warm front would be *stationary* for several days.

STATIONERY (noun) special writing paper. Lucille used only monogrammed *stationery* for correspondence.

THAN (conjunction) used in unequal comparisons. Today's weather is better *than* yesterday's.

THEN (adverb) a time following a previously mentioned time. First, Julie filled out her schedule; *then,* she paid her fees.

THEIR (adjective) plural possessive adjective. *Their* team scored the most points during the game.

THERE (adverb) (a) location away from here. Look over *there* between the trees. (b) used with the verb *be* to indicate existence. *There* is a book on the teacher's desk.

THEY'RE (pronoun + verb) contraction of *they* + *are*. *They're* leaving on the noon flight to Zurich.

TO (preposition) toward, until, as far as. Go *to* the blackboard and write out the equation.

TWO (noun or adjective) number following *one*. *Two* theories have been proposed to explain that incident.

TOO (adverb) (a) excessively. This morning was *too* cold for the children to go swimming. (b) also. Jane went to the movie, and we did *too*.

WEATHER (noun) atmospheric conditions. Our flight was delayed because of bad *weather*.

WHETHER (conjunction) if, indicates a choice. Because of the gas shortage, we do not know *whether* we will go away for our vacation or stay home.

WHOSE (pronoun) possessive relative pronoun. The person *whose* name is drawn first will win the grand prize.

WHO'S (relative pronoun + verb) contraction of *who + is. Who's* your new biology professor?

YOUR (adjective) possessive of *you.* We are all happy about *your* accepting the position with the company in Baltimore.

YOU'RE (pronoun + verb) contraction of *you + are. You're* going to enjoy the panorama from the top of the hill.

Exercise 54: Commonly Misused Words

Select the correct word in parentheses to complete the meaning of the sentence.

1. A beautiful (angle/angel) adorned their Christmas tree.
2. I have (your/ you're) notes here, but I cannot find mine.
3. The rescuers were a welcome (cite/sight/site) for those trapped on the snow-covered mountain.
4. (Who's/Whose) supposed to supply the refreshments for tonight's meeting?
5. It is a (costume/custom) in the United States to eat turkey on Thanksgiving.
6. (Weather/Whether) we drive or fly depends on the length of our vacation.
7. Pasquale is of French (decent/descent), but his cousin is English.
8. Dr. Hipple will not be coming (to/two/too) the meeting because he has (to/two/too) many papers to grade.
9. Although my mother never eats (desert/dessert), I prefer something sweet.
10. I guess (their/there/they're) not interested because we have not heard from them.
11. Doris and Marge teach kindergarten; the (latter/later) works in Putnam.
12. Isaac Asimov's science books are more easily understood (than/then) most scientists'.
13. The fender on Sean's bike came (loose/lose) and had to be tightened.
14. Nobody had any (stationary/stationery), so we had to use notebook paper to write the letter.
15. The hikers had (passed/past) many hours waiting to be rescued.
16. Lisa had to (quiet/quit/quite) eating apples after the orthodontist put braces on her teeth.

17. After any war, the world desires a lasting (peace/piece).
18. Albert Einstein expressed his (principal/principle) of relativity.
19. Marcia was (quit/quiet/quite) tired after the long walk to class.
20. You must remember to (cite/site/sight) your references when you write a paper.

CONFUSINGLY RELATED WORDS

These are words that cause problems when the speaker is not able to distinguish between them. They are similar in meaning or pronunciation but CANNOT be used interchangeably. Learn the definition of each and its use before employing it in conversation.

ACCEPT (verb) to take what is given. Professor Perez will *accept* the chairmanship of the humanities department.

EXCEPT (preposition) excluding or omitting a thing or person. Everyone is going to the convention *except* Bob, who has to work.

ACCESS (noun) availability, way of gaining entrance. The teachers had no *access* to the students' files, which were locked in the principal's office.

EXCESS (a) (adjective) abundant, superfluous. We paid a surcharge on our *excess* baggage. (b) (noun) extra amount. The demand for funds was in *excess* of the actual need.

ADVICE (noun) opinion given to someone, counseling. If you heed the teacher's *advice,* you will do well in your studies.

ADVISE (verb) act of giving an opinion or counsel. The Congress *advised* the president against signing the treaty at that time.

AFFECT (verb) to produce a change in. The doctors wanted to see how the medication would *affect* the patient.

EFFECT (a) (noun) end result or consequence. The children suffered no ill *effects* from their long plane ride. (b) (verb) to produce as a result. To *effect* a change in city government we must all vote on Tuesday.

AGAIN (adverb) repetition of an action, one more time. Mike wrote to the publishers *again,* inquiring about his manuscript.

AGAINST (preposition) (a) in opposition to someone or something. The athletic director was *against* our dancing in the new gym. (b) next to, adjacent. The boy standing *against* the piano is my cousin Bill.

ALREADY (adverb) an action that happened at an indefinite time before the present. Jan's plane had *already* landed before we got to the airport.

ALL READY (noun + adjective) prepared to do something. We are *all ready* to go boating.

AMONG (preposition) shows a relationship or selection involving three or more entities. It was difficult to select a winner from *among* so many contestants.

BETWEEN (preposition) shows a relationship or selection involving only two entities. *Between* writing her book *and* teaching, Mary Ellen had little time for anything else. NOTE: When *between* is followed by two nouns or noun phrases, the two nouns or noun phrases must be separated by *and* and never by *or*.

BESIDE (preposition) next to. There is a small table *beside* the bed.

BESIDES (preposition or adverb) in addition to, also, moreover. I have five history books here *besides* the four that I left at home.

ASIDE (adverb) to one side. Harry sets money *aside* every payday for his daughter's education.

COMPARE (verb) show similarities. Sue *compared* her new school with the last one she had attended.

CONTRAST (verb) show differences. In her composition, Marta chose to *contrast* life in a big city with that of a small town.

CONSECUTIVE (adjective) indicates an uninterrupted sequence. Today is the tenth *consecutive* day of this unbearable heat wave.

SUCCESSIVE (adjective) indicates a series of separate events. The United States won gold medals in two *successive* Olympic Games.

CONSIDERABLE (adjective) rather large amount or degree. Even though Marge had *considerable* experience in the field, she was not hired for the job.

CONSIDERATE (adjective) thoughtful, polite. It was very *considerate* of Harry to send his hostess a bouquet of flowers.

CREDIBLE (adjective) believable. His explanation of the rescue at sea seemed *credible*.

CREDITABLE (adjective) worthy of praise. The fireman's daring rescue of those trapped in the burning building was a *creditable* deed.

CREDULOUS (adjective) gullible. Rita is so *credulous* that she will accept any excuse you offer.

DETRACT (verb) take away or lessen the value of a person or thing. Molly's nervousness *detracted* from her singing.

DISTRACT (verb) cause a lack of mental concentration on what one is doing or the goals one has set. Please don't *distract* your father while he is writing his checks or else his checkbook won't balance.

DEVICE (noun) an invention or plan. This is a clever *device* for cleaning fish without getting pinched by the scales.

DEVISE (verb) invent, create, contrive. The general *devised* a plan for attacking the enemy camp at night while the soldiers were celebrating.

ELICIT (verb) draw out, evoke. The prosecutor's barrage of questions finally *elicited* the truth from the witness.

ILLICIT (adjective) unlawful. The politician's *illicit* dealings with organized crime caused him to lose his government position.

EMIGRANT (noun) one who leaves one's own country to live in another. After World War II many *emigrants* left Europe to go to the United States.

IMMIGRANT (noun) one who comes to a new country to settle. The United States is a country composed of *immigrants*. NOTE: The verbs are *emigrate* and *immigrate*. It is possible to be both an emigrant and an immigrant at the same time as one leaves one's own country (emigrant) and comes to another country (immigrant) to settle.

EXAMPLE (noun) anything used to prove a point. Picasso's *Guernica* is an excellent *example* of expressionism in art.

SAMPLE (noun) a representative part of a whole. My niece loves to go to the supermarket because the dairy lady always gives her a *sample* of cheese.

FORMERLY (adverb) previously. He *formerly* worked as a professor, but now he is a physicist.

FORMALLY (adverb) (a) an elegant way of dressing, usually a tuxedo for men and a long gown for women. At the resort we were required to dress *formally* for dinner every night. (b) properly, officially. She has *formally* requested a name change.

HARD (adjective) (a) difficult. Yesterday's test was so *hard* that nobody passed. (b) opposite of *soft*. The stadium seats were *hard,* so we rented a cushion.

HARDLY (adverb) barely, scarcely. He had so much work to do after the vacation that he *hardly* knew where to begin.

HELPLESS (adjective) unable to remedy (an animate thing is helpless). Because I could not speak their language, I felt *helpless* trying to understand the tourists' plight.

USELESS (adjective) worthless, unserviceable. An umbrella is *useless* in a hurricane.

HOUSE (noun) and **HOME** (noun) are many times used interchangeably, but there exists a difference in meaning. (a) *House* refers to the building or structure. The Chapmans are building a new *house* in Buckingham Estates. (b) *Home* refers to the atmosphere or feeling of domestic tranquility found in a house. *Home* is where the heart is.

IMAGINARY (adjective) something not real that exists in one's imagination. Since Ralph has no brothers or sisters, he has created an *imaginary* playmate.

IMAGINATIVE (adjective) showing signs of great imagination. *Star Wars* was created by a highly *imaginative* writer.

IMMORTAL (adjective) incapable of dying. The *immortal* works of Shakespeare are still being read and enjoyed three centuries after their writing.

IMMORAL (adjective) against the moral law, bad, evil. Their *immoral* behavior in front of the students cost the teachers their jobs.

IMPLICIT (adjective) understood, but not specifically stated. Our supervisor has *implicit* faith in our ability to finish this project on time.

EXPLICIT (adjective) expressed in a clear and precise manner. The professor gave *explicit* instructions for carrying out the research project.

INDUSTRIAL (adjective) pertaining to industry. Paul had an *industrial* accident and was in the hospital for three months.

INDUSTRIOUS (adjective) diligent, hard working. Mark was such an *industrious* student that he received a four-year scholarship to the university.

INFLICT (verb) impose something unwelcome. Because the prisoners had created a riot and had assaulted several guards, the warden *inflicted* severe punishments on all the participants.

AFFLICT (verb) cause physical or mental pain. During the Middle Ages, millions of people were *afflicted* by the plague.

INSPIRATION (noun) stimulation to learn or discover. Thomas A. Edison, inventor of the phonograph, said that an idea was ninety-nine percent perspiration and one percent *inspiration.*

ASPIRATION (noun) (a) ambition, desire, goal. Gail's lifelong *aspiration* has been that of becoming a doctor. (b) expulsion of breath. To pronounce certain words, proper *aspiration* is necessary.

INTELLIGENT (adjective) possessing a great deal of mental ability. Dan was so *intelligent* that he received good grades without ever having to study.

INTELLIGIBLE (adjective) clear, easily understood. The science teacher's explanations were so *intelligible* that students had no problems doing their assignments.

INTELLECTUAL (a) (noun) any person who possesses a great deal of knowledge. Because Fabian is an *intellectual,* he finds it difficult to associate with his classmates who are less intelligent. (b) (adjective) wise. John was involved in an *intellectual* conversation with his old professor.

INTENSE (adjective) extreme. Last winter's *intense* cold almost depleted the natural gas supply.

INTENSIVE (adjective) concentrated. Before going to Mexico, Phil took an *intensive* course in Spanish.

LATE (a) (adjective or adverb) not punctual. Professor Carmichael hates to see his students arrive *late*. (b) (adjective) no longer living. Her *late* husband was the author of that book.

LATELY (adverb) recently. I haven't seen Burt *lately*. He must be extremely busy with his research.

LEARN (verb) obtain knowledge. The new cashier had to *learn* how to operate the computerized cash register.

TEACH (verb) impart knowledge. The instructor is *teaching* us how to program computers.

LEND (verb) and **LOAN** (verb) give something for temporary use with the promise of returning it. (*Lend* and *loan* as verbs may be used interchangeably.) Jill *loaned* (*lent*) me her red dress to wear to the dance.

BORROW (verb) receive something for temporary use with the promise of returning it. I *borrowed* Jill's red dress to wear to the dance.

LIQUEFY (verb) change to a watery or liquid state. The ice cream began to *liquefy* in the intense heat.

LIQUIDATE (verb) eliminate, get rid of, change to cash. The foreign agents tried to *liquidate* the traitor before he passed the information to his contacts.

LONELY (adjective) depressed feeling as a result of abandonment or being alone. After her husband's death, Debbie was very *lonely* and withdrawn.

ALONE (adjective) physical state of solitude, unaccompanied. After losing in the Olympic tryouts, Phil asked to be left *alone*.

NEAR (preposition or adverb) used to indicate a place not too far distant. My biology class meets *near* the Student Union.

NEARLY (adverb) almost. We were *nearly* hit by the speeding car on the turnpike.

OBSERVATION (noun) act of paying attention to or being paid attention. The ancient Egyptians' *observation* of the heavenly bodies helped them know when to plant and harvest.

OBSERVANCE (noun) act of following custom or ceremony. There will be numerous parades and displays of fireworks in *observance* of Independence Day.

PERSECUTE (verb) torture, harass. Throughout history many people have been *persecuted* for their religious beliefs.

PROSECUTE (verb) in legal terms, to bring suit against or enforce a law through a legal process. Shoplifters will be *prosecuted* to the fullest extent of the law.

PRECEDE (verb) to come before. Weather Service warnings *preceded* the hurricane.

PROCEED (verb) continue an action after a rest period or interruption. After the fire drill, the teacher *proceeded* to explain the experiment to the physics class.

QUANTITY (noun) used with non-count nouns to indicate amount, bulk. A large *quantity* of sand was removed before the archeologists found the prehistoric animal bones.

NUMBER (noun) used with count nouns to designate individual amount. A *number* of artifacts were found at the excavation site.

REMEMBER (verb) to recall or think of again. I do not *remember* what time he asked me to call. You don't *remember* me, do you?

REMIND (verb) to cause (someone) to remember, to bring into (someone's) mind. Please *remind* me to call Henry at 7 o'clock tonight. Henry *reminds* me of my uncle.

SENSIBLE (adjective) having good judgment. When it is raining hard, *sensible* people stay indoors.

SENSITIVE (adjective) excitable, touchy, easily affected by outside influences. Stephen cannot be out in the sun very long because he has very *sensitive* skin and burns easily.

SPECIAL (adjective) that which receives a lot of attention because of a distinct characteristic. Meyer's Department Store will have a *special* sale for their charge customers.

ESPECIALLY (adverb) particularly. Rita is *especially* talented in the fine arts. She has a *special* talent for playing music by ear.

USE (noun) act of putting into practice or service, application. The salesman said that regular *use* of fertilizer would ensure a greener, healthier lawn.

USAGE (noun) way in which something is used. Norm Crosby's *usage* of English vocabulary in his comedy routine is hilarious.

Exercise 55: Confusingly Related Words

Select the word in parentheses that completes the meaning in each sentence.

1. Betty's insulting remark greatly (effected/affected) Kurt, who is a very sensitive person.

2. Detroit manufacturers hope to develop an easily attachable (device/ devise) for the carburetor to improve gas mileage.
3. While doing the experiment, we asked the lab technician's (advice/ advise).
4. After declaring bankruptcy, the company was forced to (liquefy/ liquidate) its assets.
5. Keith's company's headquarters were (formerly/formally) located in Philadelphia.
6. (Especially/Special) attention must be given to the questions at the end of each chapter.
7. George was (among/between) those students selected to participate in the debate.
8. They were (already/all ready) to leave when a telegram arrived.
9. By asking many questions, the instructor tried to (elicit/illicit) information from the students.
10. You should not say things that might make a highly (sensitive/sensible) person upset.
11. The United States is a "melting pot," a land of (emigrants/ immigrants).
12. A large (number/quantity) of whales beached and died last year because of ear problems.
13. When Louise set the table, she placed the silverware (besides/beside) the plates.
14. Mark is (sensible/sensitive) enough to swim close to shore.
15. In 1969 the astronauts who landed on the moon collected (examples/ samples) of rocks and soil.
16. Maria has been working very (hardly/hard) on her thesis.
17. The government will (persecute/prosecute) the guilty parties for polluting the waters.
18. Every time Mariela travels with her children, she carries (access/ excess) baggage.
19. Dante's (immoral/immortal) literary masterpieces are read in universities across the country.
20. An explanation will (precede/proceed) each section of the test.
21. Eric's courageous rescue of the drowning child was a (credulous/ creditable) deed.
22. Perry's spare flashlight was (helpless/useless) the night of the storm because the batteries were corroded.
23. The gaudy decorations in the hall (detracted/distracted) from the beauty of the celebration.
24. Everything (accept/except) our swimwear is packed and ready to go.
25. "Your essay is very (imaginary/imaginative) and worthy of an 'A' grade," said Mrs. Jameson to her student.

USE OF PREPOSITIONS

Prepositions are difficult because almost every definition for a preposition has exceptions. The best way to learn them is to picture how they function in comparison with other prepositions and to study certain common uses and expressions using the various prepositions.

The following diagram will give you a general idea of how prepositions work. Often, however, the diagram will not help you to understand certain expressions containing prepositions. For the following expressions which are not self-explanatory, a definition is given in parentheses. Study the example sentences to understand the meaning of each expression. These prepositions and expressions are important in ALL sections of the TOEFL.

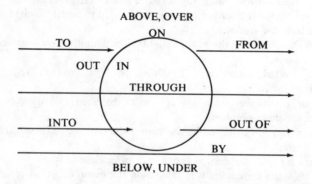

DURING: This preposition should be distinguished from *since* and *for*. *During* is usually followed by a noun indicating time. It indicates *duration* of time. *During our vacation,* we visited many relatives across the country. *During the summer,* we do not have to study.

FROM: This preposition generally means the opposite of *to* (see diagram). He came *from* Miami last night. (opposite of: He went *to* Miami.)

1. Common usage of *from: from* $\begin{Bmatrix} \text{a time} \\ \text{a place} \end{Bmatrix}$ *to* $\begin{Bmatrix} \text{a time} \\ \text{a place} \end{Bmatrix}$. He lived in Germany *from* 1972 *to* 1978. We drove *from* Atlanta *to* New York in one day.

2. Common expressions with *from:* from time to time (occasionally). We visit the art museum *from time to time.*

OUT OF: This preposition generally means the opposite of *into* (see diagram). He walked *out of* the room angrily when John admonished him.

1. Common usage of *out of: out of* + noun (to lack, to be without). Maria went to the store because she was *out of* milk.

2. Common expressions with *out of:*

   a. out of town (away). Mr. Adams cannot see you this week because he is *out of town.*

   b. out of date (old). Don't use that dictionary. It is *out of date.* Find one that is up to date.

   c. out of work (jobless, unemployed). Henry has been very unhappy since he has been *out of work.*

   d. out of the question (impossible). Your request for an extension of credit is *out of the question.*

   e. out of order (not functioning). We had to use our neighbor's telephone because ours was *out of order.*

BY: This preposition generally means to *go past a place* or to *be situated near a place.* We walked *by* the library on the way home. Your books are *by* the window.

1. Common usage of *by:*

   a. to indicate the agent in passive sentences. *Romeo and Juliet* was written *by* William Shakespeare.

   b. *by* + specific time (before). We usually eat supper *by* six o'clock in the evening.

   c. by bus/plane/train/ship/car/bike (indicates mode of travel) (see *on,* 1. b.). We traveled to Boston *by* train.

2. Common expressions with *by:*

   a. by then (before a time in the past or future). I will graduate from the university in 1983. *By then,* I hope to have found a job.

   b. by way of (via). We are driving to Atlanta *by way of* Baton Rouge.

   c. by the way (incidentally). *By the way,* I've got two tickets for Saturday's game. Would you like to go with me?

   d. by far (considerably). This book is *by far* the best on the subject.

   e. by accident/by mistake (not intentionally, opposite of *on purpose*). Nobody will receive a check on Friday because the wrong cards were put into the computer *by accident.*

IN: This preposition generally means *inside of a place or enclosure.* It is the opposite of *out* (see diagram). Dr. Jones is *in* his office.

1. Common usage of *in:*

   a. in a room/building/drawer/closet (inside). Your socks are *in the drawer.*

b. *in* + month/year (see *on*, 1. a.). His birthday is *in January*. Peter will begin class *in 1981*.

c. in time (not late, early enough) (see *on time*, 2. a.). We arrived at the airport *in time* to eat before the plane left.

d. in the street (see *on*, 1. c.). The children were warned not to play *in the street*.

e. in the morning/afternoon/evening (see *at night*, 2. b.). I have a dental appointment *in the morning*, but I will be free *in the afternoon*.

f. in the past/future. *In the past*, attendance at school was not compulsory, but it is today.

g. in the beginning/end. Everyone seemed unfriendly *in the beginning*, but *in the end* everyone made friends.

h. in the way (obstructing) (see *on the way*, 2. d.). He could not park his car in the driveway because another car was *in the way*.

i. once in a while (occasionally). *Once in a while*, we eat dinner in a Chinese restaurant.

j. in no time at all (in a very short time). George finished his assignment *in no time at all*.

k. in the meantime (at the same time, meanwhile). We start school in several weeks, but *in the meantime*, we can take a trip.

l. in the middle. Grace stood *in the middle* of the room looking for her friend.

m. in the army/air force/navy. My brother was *in the army* for ten years.

n. in a row. We are going to sit *in the tenth row* of the auditorium.

o. in the event that (if). *In the event that* you win the prize, you will be notified by mail.

p. in case (if). I will give you the key to the house so you'll have it *in case* I arrive a little late.

q. (get) in touch with, (get) in contact with. It's very difficult to *get in touch with* Jenny because she works all day.

ON: This preposition generally means *a position above, but in contact with an object*. The records are *on* the table.

1. Common usage of *on:*

a. on a day/date (see *in*, 1. b.). I will call you *on Thursday*. His birthday is *on January 28*.

b. on $\begin{Bmatrix} a \\ the \end{Bmatrix}$ bus/plane/train/ship/bike (see *by*, 1. c.). It's too late to see Jane; she's already *on the plane*. I came to school this morning *on the bus*.

c . on a street (situation of a building) (see *in,* 2. d. and *at,* 1. a.).
George lives *on 16th Avenue.*

d . on the floor of a building. Henri lives *on the fifteenth floor* of that
building.

2. Common expressions with *on:*

a . on time (punctual, used for a scheduled event or appointment, more
specific than *in time*) (see *in,* 2. c.). Despite the bad weather, our
plane left *on time.*

b . on the corner (of two streets) (see *in,* 2. b.). Norman Hall is *on the
corner* of 13th Street and 5th Avenue.

c . on the sidewalk. Don't walk in the street. Walk *on the sidewalk.*

d . on the way (enroute) (see *in,* 2. h.). We can stop at the grocery
store *on the way* to their house.

e . on the right/left. Paul sits *on the left* side of the room and Dave sits
on the right.

f . on television/(the) radio. The president's "State of the Union
Address" will be *on television* and *on the radio* tonight.

g . on the telephone. Janet will be here soon; she is *on the telephone.*

h . on the whole (in general, all things considered). *On the whole,* the
rescue mission was well executed.

i . on the other hand (however, nevertheless). The present perfect
aspect is never used to indicate a specific time; *on the other hand,*
the simple past tense is.

k . on sale (offered for sale). The house will go *on sale* this weekend.
(offered at a lower than normal price) The regular price of the
radio is $39.95, but today it's *on sale* for $25.

l . on foot (walking). My car would not start so I came *on foot.*

AT: This preposition generally is used to indicate a general location. It is not
as specific as *in.* Jane is *at* the bank.

1. Common usage of *at:*

a . *at* + an address (see *on,* 1. c.). George lives *at 712 16th Avenue.*

b . *at* + a specific time. The class begins *at 3:10.*

2. Common expressions with *at:*

a . at home/school/work. From nine to five, Charles is *at work* and his
roommate is *at school.* At night, they are usually *at home.*

b . at night (see *in,* 2. e.). We never go out *at night* because we live too
far from town.

c . at least (at the minimum). We will have to spend *at least* two
weeks doing the experiments.

d . at once (immediately.) Please come home *at once.*

e . at present/the moment (now). She is studying *at the moment.*

f . at times (occasionally). *At times,* it is difficult to understand him because he speaks too fast.

g . at first (initially). Jane was nervous *at first,* but later she felt more relaxed.

Miscellaneous Expressions with Prepositions

1. on the beach. We walked *on the beach* for several hours last night.
2. in place of (instead of). Sam is going to the meeting *in place of* his brother, who has to work.
3. for the most part (mainly). The article discusses, *for the most part,* the possibility of life on other planets.
4. in hopes of (hoping to). John called his brother *in hopes of* finding somebody to watch his children.
5. of course (certainly). *Of course,* if you study the material very thoroughly, you will have no trouble on the examination.
6. off and on (intermittently). It rained *off and on* all day yesterday.
7. all of a sudden (suddenly). We were walking through the woods when, *all of a sudden,* we heard a strange sound.
8. for good (forever). Helen is leaving Chicago *for good.*

Exercise 56: Use of Prepositions

Write the correct preposition in the following sentences. There may be several possible answers for some blanks.

___(1)___ the summer, we went ___(2)___ the beach every day. We stayed ___(3)___ a lovely motel right ___(4)___ the beach. ___(5)___ the morning we would get up ___(6)___ 9:30, have breakfast, and then spend four hours ___(7)___ the pool ___(8)___ all the other guests. ___(9)___ 1:00 we would have lunch ___(10)___ our room. ___(11)___ lunch we would eat something light like sandwiches and fruit. ___(12)___ the afternoon we would return ___(13)___ the pool area and sit ___(14)___ the sun ___(15)___ a while. ___(16)___ night we would take long walks ___(17)___ the beach or visit some friends who lived ___(18)___ 520 Volusia Avenue ___(19)___ Daytona Beach.

Many people from ___(20)___ ___(21)___ town stayed ___(22)___ that motel. Like us, they had been coming ___(23)___ that same motel ___(24)___ 1975. Most ___(25)___ them were ___(26)___ Ohio. ___(27)___ time ___(28)___ time we would eat out ___(29)___ a nice restaurant, where we did not have to wait long ___(30)___ the waitress to serve us. ___(31)___ July it is usually very crowded, but this year ___(32)___ least, it was not as crowded as ___(33)___ the past. Once ___(34)___ a while we went ___(35)___ the movies ___(36)___ the theater ___(37)___ the corner ___(38)___ Las Olas Boulevard and Castillo Avenue. We arrived there ___(39)___ no time ___(40)___ all ___(41)___ car. We sat __(42)__ the middle __(43)__ the theater, __(44)__ the twelfth row. The movie started __(45)__ 7:00 sharp, so we got there just __(46)__ time to buy some popcorn and find our seat __(47)__ it started. __(48)__ first, I thought I would not enjoy it, but __(49)__ the end, it turned __(50)__ to be a very interesting movie. __(51)__ the whole, it was an enjoyable evening.

We decided to get a Coke __(52)__ __(53)__ the machine, but unfortunately it was __(54)__ __(55)__ order. So __(56)__ place __(57)__ the Coke, we decided to get some ice cream __(58)__ the Dairy Isle which was located __(59)__ the corner __(60)__ Harper Ave. and Washington St.

__(61)__ returning __(62)__ our motel, I decided to finish reading my novel. It is __(63)__ far the most exciting book that Victoria Holt has ever written. __(64)__ the most part, her book deals __(65)__ a group __(66)__ archeologists who go __(67)__ Egypt __(68)__ hopes __(69)__ discovering some pharaoh's tomb. __(70)__ accident they uncover a plot to smuggle the treasures __(71)__ __(72)__ Egypt. __(73)__ course the archeologists got __(74)__ touch __(75)__ the authorities, who had heard some rumors about smuggling off and __(76)__. All __(77)__ a sudden, one day the police showed up and caught them __(78)__ the act and arrested them.

VERBAL IDIOMS

A verbal idiom is a group of words, containing a verb, that has a meaning different from the meaning of any individual word within it. The following list of two- and three-word verbal idioms should be learned. Because they are idiomatic, you are less likely to find them in the grammar section of the TOEFL. Many of them, however, may appear in the listening comprehension section.

BREAK OFF: end. As a result of the recent, unprovoked attack, the two countries *broke off* their diplomatic relations.

BRING UP: raise, initiate. The county commissioner *brought up* the heated issue of restricting on-street parking.

CALL ON: (a) ask. The teacher *called on* James to write the equation on the blackboard. (b) visit. The new minister *called on* each of the families of his church in order to become better acquainted with them.

CARE FOR: (a) like. Because Marita doesn't *care for* dark colors, she buys only brightly colored clothes. (b) look after. My neighbors asked me to *care for* their children after school.

CHECK OUT: (a) borrow books, etc., from a library. I went to the library and *checked out* thirty books last night for my research paper. (b) investigate. This photocopy machine is not working properly. Could you *check out* the problem?

CHECK OUT OF: leave. We were told that we had to *check out of* the hotel before one o'clock, or else we would have to pay for another day.

CHECK (UP) ON: investigate. The insurance company decided to *check up on* his driving record before insuring him.

CLOSE IN ON: draw nearer, approach. In his hallucinatory state, the addict felt that the walls were *closing in on* him.

COME ALONG WITH: accompany. June *came along with* her supervisor to the budget meeting.

COME DOWN WITH: become ill with. During the summer, many people *come down with* intestinal disorders.

COUNT ON: depend on, rely on. Maria was *counting on* the grant money to pay her way through graduate school.

DO AWAY WITH: eliminate, get rid of. Because of the increasing number of problems created after the football games, the director has decided to *do away with* all sports activities.

DRAW UP: write, draft (such as plans or contracts). A new advertising contract was *drawn up* after the terms had been decided.

DROP OUT OF: quit, withdraw from. This organization has done a great deal to prevent young people from *dropping out of* school.

FIGURE OUT: solve, decipher, interpret, understand. After failing to *figure out* his income tax return, Hal decided to see an accountant.

FIND OUT: discover. Erin just *found out* that her ancestors had come from Scotland, not Ireland.

GET BY: manage to survive. Despite the high cost of living, we will *get by* on my salary.

GET THROUGH: (a) finish. Jerry called for an earlier appointment because he *got through* with his project sooner than he had expected. (b) manage to communicate. It is difficult to *get through* to someone who doesn't understand your language.

GET UP: (a) arise. Pete usually *gets up* early in the morning, but this morning he overslept. (b) organize. Paul is trying to *get up* a group of square dancers to go to Switzerland.

GIVE UP: stop, cease. Helen *gave up* working for the company because she felt that the employees were not treated fairly.

GO ALONG WITH: agree. Mr. Robbins always *goes along with* anything his employer wants to do.

HOLD ON TO: grasp, maintain. Despite moving to the Western world, Mariko *held on to* her Oriental ways.

HOLD UP: (a) rob at gunpoint. The convenience store was *held up* last night. (b) endure or withstand pressure or use. Mrs. Jones *held up* very well after her husband's death. (c) stop. Last night's freeway traffic *held up* rush hour traffic for two hours.

KEEP ON: continue. I *keep on* urging Rita to practice the violin, but she doesn't heed my advice.

LOOK AFTER: care for. After my aunt had died, her lawyer *looked after* my uncle's financial affairs.

LOOK INTO: investigate. Lynnette is *looking into* the possibility of opening a drugstore in Dallas as well as in Fort Worth.

PASS OUT/HAND OUT: distribute. The political candidate *passed out* campaign literature to her coworkers.

PASS OUT: faint. The intense heat in the garden caused Maria to *pass out*.

PICK OUT: select, choose, The judges were asked to *pick out* the essays that showed the most originality.

POINT OUT: indicate. Being a professional writer, Janos helped us by *pointing out* problems in our style.

PUT OFF: postpone. Because Brian was a poor correspondent, he *put off* answering his letters.

RUN ACROSS: discover. While rummaging through some old boxes in the attic, I *ran across* my grandmother's wedding dress.

RUN INTO: meet by accident. When Jack was in New York, he *ran into* an old friend at the theater.

SEE ABOUT: consider, attend to. My neighbor is going to *see about* getting tickets for next Saturday's football game.

TAKE OFF: leave the ground to fly. Our flight to Toronto *took off* on schedule.

TAKE OVER FOR: substitute for. Marie had a class this afternoon, so Janet *took over for* her.

TALK OVER: discuss. The committee is *talking over* the plans for the homecoming dance and banquet.

TRY OUT: (a) test. General Mills asked us to *try out* their new product. (b) audition for a play. Marguerite plans to *try out* for the lead in the new musical.

TURN IN: (a) submit. The students *turned in* their term papers on Monday. (b) go to bed. After a long hard day, we decided to *turn in* early.

WATCH OUT FOR: be cautious or alert. While driving through that development, we had to *watch out for* the little children playing in the street.

Exercise 57: Verbal Idioms

Change the underlined words to incorporate two-word verbs. Make all necessary tense changes. Example:

> The senator raised the question of the treaty negotiations.
> The senator brought up the question of the treaty negotiations.

1. Louis doesn't like peas unless they're mixed in with something else.
2. Because of the shortage of funds, we will have to eliminate all extracurricular activities.

3. Many teenagers quit school before graduation and regret it later.

4. Mike and Mary Ellen will be very happy when they finish writing their book.

5. Marsha was so upset by her fiancé's disloyalty that she ended their engagement.

6. The local convenience store was robbed last night and $225 was taken.

7. Thomas Jefferson was one of the men responsible for writing the Declaration of Independence.

8. I am trying to interpret this writing, but it is not easy.

9. Continue driving at 55 miles per hour if you want to save gasoline and prevent accidents.

10. Mrs. Davis asked me to serve as chairman of the entertainment committee.

11. Pete promised to stop smoking immediately.

12. The police are approaching the robbers' hideout.

13. María Elena will take care of the neighbors' children while they attend the school meeting.

14. Joey became ill with the measles just before his scout troop went to camp.

15. Mrs. Lastinger will substitute for the history teacher who is out of town.

16. The mountain climbers grasped the rope tightly to avoid falling.

17. We plan to investigate the possibility of spending a week at the seashore.

18. My mother distributed candy to the children last Halloween.

19. The manager said we had to leave the motel no later than noon.

20. Mike just discovered that his passport had expired three months previously.

21. When buying apples, remember to select only the firm, red ones.

22. We were counting on a raise in pay, but we'll have to manage without it.

23. Rita will accompany her sister to the Skating Palace on Saturday night.

24. The tour guide indicated the historical monuments of the city.

25. I knew I could rely on them to get the job done.

26. The dance had to be postponed because of the bad weather.

27. I accidently met an old friend in the shopping center last week.

28. The manager said he would consider hiring another secretary to take care of the backlog of work.

29. Last night Mr. Robbins raised the issue of student parking on city streets.

30. Henry was so upset at the sight of his injured daughter that he fainted.

31. Before making a decision on the project, the board of directors decided to discuss the matter.

32. Procter and Gamble is <u>testing</u> a new product and has sent everyone a sample.
33. All budget proposals had to be <u>submitted</u> by last Friday.
34. What time did you <u>awaken</u> this morning.
35. <u>Be careful of</u> speeding cars when you cross the street.

COMMON COMBINATIONS WITH PREPOSITIONS

Many nouns, verbs, and adjectives are generally followed by specific prepositions. However, there are many exceptions to any rule listing certain words which must appear with certain prepositions. This is something that one must learn from constant contact with and attention to the elements of a new language. Listed here are some nouns, verbs, and adjectives that USUALLY appear with the accompanying prepositions

Nouns + Prepositions

equivalent of	number of	example of
quality of	reason for	exception to
pair of	sample of	possibility of

These nouns can be followed by either *of* or *for*.

fear	method	hatred	need	means

The <u>quality of</u> this photograph is not noticeably different from that one.
I saw a <u>sample of</u> her work and was quite impressed.
They have yet to discover a new <u>method of/method for</u> analyzing this data.

Verbs + Prepositions

decide on	plan on	depend on
detract from	engage in	approve of
emerge from	pay for	succeed in
participate in	escape from	mingle with
confide in	remove from	rely on

NOTE: Do not confuse the *to* of an infinitive with *to* as a preposition. Some of these verbs can be followed either by an infinitive or by a preposition + gerund. We have decided *to stay* in the United States for several more weeks. We have decided *on staying* in the United States for several more weeks.

Three dangerous criminals <u>escaped from</u> prison yesterday.
You can <u>depend on</u> Harry if you want the job done correctly.

He is going to <u>participate in</u> the demonstration next week.

Adjectives + Prepositions

satisfied with	fond of	amenable to
divorced from	isolated from	inferior to
guilty of	afraid of	similar to
interested in	accustomed to	different from

William is quite <u>fond of</u> cooking Oriental food.
My employer says she is not <u>satisfied with</u> my performance.
Margaret is <u>afraid of</u> large dogs.

Keep in mind that other prepositions MAY be used with the above words in different contexts. Watch for prepositions when you read so that you can develop a "feel" for their use.

Some of the following exercises contain prepositions that have not been included in this list. See if you have acquired a native speaker's feel for them yet.

MINI-TEST 5: PROBLEM VOCABULARY AND PREPOSITIONS

DIRECTIONS

Select the correct word to complete each sentence

1. Scientists are trying to (device/devise) an inexpensive substitute for gasoline.
2. On Halloween night, most children dress in (costumes/customs) and go from house to house asking for treats.
3. Mr. Miller's prejudice (of/towards) his neighbors caused him to be ostracized.
4. (Besides/Beside) geology, Herman is studying math, French, and literature.
5. Melanie said that she would arrive (later/latter) than the rest of us.
6. Despite his sore muscle, Paul planned on participating (with/in) the Olympic skating.
7. A fear (at/of) closed-in areas is called claustrophobia.
8. After being apprehended, all hijackers are (persecuted/prosecuted).
9. Mitzi didn't (loose/lose) any time in applying for the teaching position in math.
10. The letters were (already/all ready) for mailing when we realized that we had written the wrong addresses on the envelopes.
11. This report is (quite/quiet) complete and needs no revision.
12. Professor Baker teaches the same number of hours per week as Professor Jones, but the (later/latter) always looks more tired.

13. Ms. Davis asked us to help pass (out/up) some free (samples/examples).
14. Julie's skirt will be (to/too) (lose/loose) for her sister to wear.
15. Even though Marlon Brando had won an Oscar, he refused to (except/accept) it at the presentation ceremonies.

DIRECTIONS

In the following sentences, choose the form in parentheses that means the same as the underlined word or words.

16. Louis was depending on the Pittsburgh Steelers to win the championship. (picking out/counting on)
17. Dr. Clements distributed the materials at the deans' conference. (passed out/brought up)
18. Archeologists continue searching for buried Egyptian treasures. (keep on/do away with)
19. Four armed men robbed the bank last week and escaped with an undetermined amount of cash. (held up/pointed out)
20. We had to postpone the meeting because too many people had the flu. (drop out of/put off)
21. When Karen became ill, her colleagues had to manage without her. (get along/take off)
22. The Department Chairman asked his staff to help with the registration. (called on/counted on)
23. If we terminate our relations with that country, we'll have to find another supplier of raw materials. (break off/draw up)
24. After arriving at the check-in counter, Dennis discovered that he was in the wrong airport. (found out/pointed out)
25. Kevin quit the engineering program because he found it too difficult. (checked out of/dropped out of)
26. The gasoline fumes caused Mike to faint. (pass out/break off)
27. The baseball game had to be postponed because of the inclement weather. (put off/put on)
28. All bids for the project had to be submitted by November 1. (turned in/drawn up)
29. Because she is so tall, Sandy doesn't like high-heeled shoes. (care for/pick out)
30. My adviser indicated numerous errors in my proposal and told me to rewrite it. (figured out/pointed out)

MINI-TEST 6: PROBLEM VOCABULARY AND PREPOSITIONS

DIRECTIONS

Each question on this mini-test consists of a sentence in which four words or phrases are underlined. The four underlined parts of the sentence are marked A,B,C,D. You are to identify the *one* underlined word or phrase that *would not be acceptable in standard written English*. Circle the letter of the underlined portion which is not correct.

1. Even though the girls have all ready visited St. Augustine,
   A   B

   they want to return to the Castillo de San Marcos.
   C   D

2. As a result of his inconsistency in represent his constituents,
   A   B

   the senator was not reelected to the state legislature.
                        C   D

3. Knowing that it would be helpless to continue working for
   A   B   C

   a nearly bankrupt company, Louise decided to go away
   and find another type of employment.
                 D

4. Excepting for the graduate students, everyone will have
   A   B   C

   to take the tests on the same day.
   D

5. John always arrives lately for his chemistry class even
        A   B

   though he leaves his dormitory in plenty of time.
             C   D

6. Soon after Mel has finished his thesis, he will leave
                    A   B

   for Boston, where he has a job waiting on him.
               C   D

7. The Nelsons asked us to look over their plants for them
                    A   B

   while they were away on vacation.
                   C   D

8. The refugees are very much upset because they have been
   A   B   C

   deprived to their homeland and their families.
   D

9. <u>According</u> the weatherman, <u>there is</u> a fifty percent chance of
      A   B
   rain <u>forecast</u> for today and a greater chance for <u>over the weekend</u>.
         C   D

10. The athlete was disqualified <u>from</u> the tournament <u>for</u>
    A   B   C
    participating <u>at</u> an illegal demonstration.
                  D

11. My English teacher said we <u>should write</u> another composition
                                    A
    for tomorrow <u>related for</u> our experience <u>at</u> last <u>week's</u> workshop.
                     B   C   D

12. If it <u>had not been</u> for the computerized register tape
          A
    from <u>the grocery store</u>, I <u>never</u> would have been able to
             B   C
    <u>figure on</u> my expenditures.
        D

13. Eric and his sister <u>won first prize</u> for the <u>most</u>
                            A   B
    elaborate <u>customs</u> they had worn to <u>the Halloween</u> party.
                  C   D

14. Our new office building <u>will be located</u> downtown <u>in the corner</u>
                                A   B
    of <u>Euclid Avenue</u> and <u>East</u> Ninth Street.
       C   D

15. <u>After checking out</u> the motor and the carburetor <u>for problems,</u>
        A   B
    Jesse found that the noise <u>was caused</u> by a <u>lose</u> fan belt.
                                   C   D

16. The customer was interested <u>to see</u> one of <u>those</u> new
    A   B   C
    pocket cameras with <u>the built-in</u> flash.
                            D

17. Because the committee was <u>anxious</u> to attend the celebration,
                                  A
    the president <u>dispensed</u> to <u>reading</u> the <u>minutes</u>.
        B   C   D

18. Scientists were <u>interested about</u> the radioactivity
    A   B
    <u>emanating</u> <u>from</u> the nuclear power plant.
        C   D

19. The coach was <u>depending for</u> his team <u>to win</u> the game <u>so that</u>
                        A   B   C
they would have a chance to play <u>in the Super Bowl</u>.
                                      D

20. <u>Because it was faster,</u> John <u>insisted in</u> my <u>taking</u> the
           A   B   C
plane to Miami <u>instead of the train</u>.
                       D

21. His <u>highly</u> <u>imaginary</u> composition won <u>the</u> judges' approval
        A   B   C
and <u>the first prize</u> in the high school essay contest.
          D

22. The spring conference <u>will be held</u> <u>in</u> Milwaukee on three
                           A   B
<u>successive</u> days, <u>namely</u> May 15, 16, and 17.
   C   D

23. Although Clyde is <u>formally</u> from Pennsylvania, he finds it
                     A
<u>difficult</u> to <u>get used to</u> the cold winters we <u>are having</u>.
  B   C   D

24. <u>Admittance for</u> the inauguration <u>ceremonies</u> was only <u>by</u>
      A   B   C
special invitation <u>of the</u> committee.
                 D

25. Paris <u>has been</u> well <u>known about</u> its famous monuments,
        A   B   C
beautiful music, and wonderful restaurants <u>for over</u>
                                            D
one hundred years.

Exercise 58: Vocabulary

Each of the following sentences has a word or phrase underlined. Below each sentence are four other words or phrases. You are to choose the *one* word or phrase which would *best keep the meaning* of the original sentence if it were substituted for the underlined word.

1. A democratic leader <u>delegates</u> authority and responsibility to others.
   (A) disputes   (C) directs
   (B) concentrates   (D) disseminates

2. During the Inquisition, heretics were <u>persecuted</u> for their religious beliefs.
   - (A) prosecuted
   - (B) tortured
   - (C) investigated
   - (D) admired

3. The campus library was able to build a new wing because it had a rich <u>benefactor</u>.
   - (A) bank account
   - (B) patron
   - (C) campaign manager
   - (D) heir

4. Imagine the advertiser's <u>chagrin</u> when he realized that he had put the wrong date in the ad.
   - (A) humiliation
   - (B) indifference
   - (C) surprise
   - (D) anger

5. The elegant decorations <u>transformed</u> the gym into a starlit ballroom.
   - (A) reverted
   - (B) changed
   - (C) sustained
   - (D) interrupted

6. Every effort was made to reduce the budget <u>substantially</u>.
   - (A) proportionately
   - (B) effectively
   - (C) greatly
   - (D) purposely

7. His <u>fidelity</u> to the ill-fated project was commendable.
   - (A) dedication
   - (B) treachery
   - (C) fiendishness
   - (D) fierceness

8. <u>Intermittent</u> showers were forecast for the day.
   - (A) all-day
   - (B) instantaneous
   - (C) heavy
   - (D) recurrent

9. The captor told the hostages to assume a <u>prone</u> position on the floor.
   - (A) face-down
   - (B) sitting
   - (C) standing
   - (D) quiet

10. The plant manager was promoted to an <u>executive</u> position.
    - (A) better-paying
    - (B) administrative
    - (C) better
    - (D) experienced

11. Peter was an <u>agile</u> and athletic youth.
    - (A) awkward
    - (B) active
    - (C) ponderous
    - (D) inept

12. John felt <u>confident</u> about his grade on the test he had just taken.
    - (A) depressed
    - (B) sure
    - (C) ecstatic
    - (D) uncertain

13. The uproarious reaction to the proposal convinced the union leaders to abandon it.
    - (A) jubilant
    - (B) clamorous
    - (C) unprecedented
    - (D) uncivilized

14. The Romans subdued the Celts during the reign of Julius Caesar.
    - (A) surrendered
    - (B) attacked
    - (C) befriended
    - (D) vanquished

15. A hush fell over the guests who had gathered for the wedding celebration.
    - (A) witnessed
    - (B) gaped
    - (C) participated
    - (D) assembled

16. The once beautiful flowers in the vase had withered.
    - (A) wilted
    - (B) wandered
    - (C) wavered
    - (D) writhed

17. Volunteer firefighters valiantly tried to extinguish the raging forest fire.
    - (A) wretched
    - (B) sluggish
    - (C) intense
    - (D) riling

18. Ponce de León believed that the waters of the Fountain of Youth had the power to make one young.
    - (A) stupefy
    - (B) rejuvenate
    - (C) ponder
    - (D) submerse

19. When it comes to buying clothes, Herman is impetuous.
    - (A) illustrious
    - (B) immune
    - (C) impolite
    - (D) impulsive

20. Waking up in that immense room made Jane's head swim.
    - (A) frightening
    - (B) huge
    - (C) bleak
    - (D) colorful

21. Mathematics is a compulsory subject in American high schools.
    - (A) difficult
    - (B) easy
    - (C) required
    - (D) despised

22. The gymnast's exercises made her feel exhilarated.
    - (A) tired
    - (B) exhausted
    - (C) stimulated
    - (D) exigent

23. The splendor of the spring morning was breathtaking.
    - (A) serenity
    - (B) sight
    - (C) dismalness
    - (D) magnificence

24. The soldiers were told to <u>commence</u> firing.
   (A) stop   (C) begin
   (B) cease   (D) evoke

25. Many millionaires become <u>eccentric</u> in their old age.
   (A) miserly   (C) peculiar
   (B) dull   (D) irritable

Exercise 59: Vocabulary

Each of the following sentences has a word or phrase underlined. Below each sentence are four other words or phrases. You are to choose the *one* word or phrase which would *best keep the meaning* of the original sentence if it were substituted for the underlined word.

1. After discussing the matter with the bank manager, John <u>instantly</u> received his loan.
   (A) casually   (C) soon
   (B) finally   (D) immediately

2. There is a campaign against those hunters who mercilessly <u>slaughter</u> baby seals.
   (A) net   (C) kill
   (B) capture   (D) skin

3. He made an obscene <u>gesture</u> before leaving the counselor's office.
   (A) remark   (C) statement
   (B) motion   (D) retribution

4. Striding <u>briskly</u> down the cobblestone road, she caught her shoe between the bricks.
   (A) carelessly   (C) quickly
   (B) unpretentiously   (D) quietly

5. The nurse was dismissed because she was found to be <u>negligent</u>.
   (A) scrupulous   (C) contagious
   (B) remiss   (D) vigilant

6. The speaker walked <u>confidently</u> and quickly to the podium.
   (A) assuredly   (C) clumsily
   (B) carefully   (D) thoughtfully

7. The <u>proprietor</u> of the inn was a corpulent man.
   (A) guest   (C) waiter
   (B) cook   (D) owner

8. That matter was totally <u>irrelevant</u> to the discussion at hand.
   - (A) suitable
   - (B) alien
   - (C) uninvited
   - (D) disappointing

9. The snow was so heavy that it <u>obliterated</u> the highway.
   - (A) froze
   - (B) blocked
   - (C) endangered
   - (D) effaced

10. The new teacher was appalled at the <u>chaotic</u> condition of her classroom.
    - (A) disorderly
    - (B) noisy
    - (C) chronic
    - (D) refined

11. The fugitive <u>eluded</u> capture for more than seven years.
    - (A) elucidated
    - (B) evaded
    - (C) effected
    - (D) elevated

12. The young man <u>winced</u> in pain as the doctor stitched up the gash in his arm.
    - (A) howled
    - (B) shrieked
    - (C) flinched
    - (D) cried

13. That new soap made her face feel <u>taut</u>.
    - (A) soft
    - (B) smooth
    - (C) tight
    - (D) awful

14. Having fasted for five days, the woman was <u>starved</u>.
    - (A) famished
    - (B) prudent
    - (D) circumspect
    - (D) heedless

15. The policeman's <u>alert</u> mind caught the suspect's lies.
    - (A) professional
    - (B) vigilant
    - (C) sluggish
    - (D) oblivious

16. The groom's hand <u>caressed</u> the soft mane of the horse.
    - (A) provoked
    - (B) combed
    - (C) struck
    - (D) fondled

17. As we approached the pyramids, a <u>massive</u> stone sphinx greeted us at the entrance.
    - (A) terrifying
    - (B) inspiring
    - (C) immense
    - (D) magnificent

18. Beethoven, having composed symphonies at three, was considered <u>precocious</u>.
    - (A) gifted
    - (B) musical
    - (C) obtuse
    - (D) preliminary

19. The teacher picked up the student's book and <u>scrutinized</u> it.
    (A) examined   (C) read
    (B) corrected   (D) graded

20. Despite the raging storm outside, the speaker did not <u>deviate</u> from his lecture.
    (A) delay   (C) divulge
    (B) disappear   (D) depart

21. The interviewer promised not to <u>divulge</u> the source of his information.
    (A) recall   (C) retain
    (B) reveal   (D) redirect

22. The toxic material on the derailed train <u>contaminated</u> the atmosphere.
    (A) polluted   (C) congested
    (B) intoxicated   (D) cremated

23. The warranty guaranteed that all <u>defective</u> parts would be replaced without charge.
    (A) lost   (C) unused
    (B) imperfect   (D) dorsal

24. The gas company <u>detected</u> a leak in the main line and evacuated all the tenants of the building.
    (A) discovered   (C) expected
    (B) smelled   (D) predicted

25. It was difficult to find the missing papers on Gary's <u>cluttered</u> desk.
    (A) refurbished   (C) tarnished
    (B) well-organized   (D) littered

ANSWERS FOR EXERCISES 54 THROUGH 59 AND MINI-TESTS 5 AND 6

Exercise 54: Commonly Misused Words

1. angel	6. Whether	11. latter	16. quit
2. your	7. descent	12. than	17. peace
3. sight	8. to, too	13. loose	18. principle
4. Who's	9. dessert	14. stationery	19. quite
5. custom	10. they're	15. passed	20. cite

Exercise 55: Confusingly Related Words

1. affected	8. all ready	14. sensible	20. precede
2. device	9. elicit	15. samples	21. creditable
3. advice	10. sensitive	16. hard	22. useless
4. liquidate	11. immigrants	17. prosecute	23. detracted
5. formerly	12. number	18. excess	24. except
6. Special	13. beside	19. immortal	25. imaginative
7. among			

Exercise 56: Use of Prepositions

1. during   2. to   3. at   4. on   5. in   6. at   7. in (at, around, near)
8. with   9. at   10. in   11. for   12. in (during)   13. to   14. in
15. for 16. at   17. on (along)   18. at   19. in   20. out   21. of   22. at
23. to   24. since   25. of   26. from   27. from   28. to   29. at
30. for   31. in (during)   32. at   33. in   34. in   35. to   36. at
37. on   38. of   39. in   40. at   41. by   42. in   43. of   44. in
45. at   46. in   47. before   48. at   49. in   50. out   51. on   52. out
53. of   54. out   55. of   56. in   57. of   58. at   59. on (at)   60. of
61. after (upon)   62. to   63. by   64. for   65. with   66. of   67. to
68. in   69. of   70. by   71. out   72. of   73. of   74. in   75. with
76. on   77. of   78. in

Exercise 57: Verbal Idioms

1. care for	13. look after	25. count on
2. do away with	14. came down with	26. put off
3. drop out of	15. fill in	27. ran into
4. get through	16. held on to	28. see about
5. broke off	17. look into	29. brought up
6. held up	18. passed out (handed out)	30. passed out
7. drawing up	19. check out of	31. talk over
8. figure out	20. found out	32. trying out
9. keep on	21. pick out	33. turned in
10. called on	22. get by (get along)	34. get up (wake up)
11. give up	23. come along with	35. watch out for
12. closing in on	24. pointed out	

Mini-Test 5: Problem Vocabulary and Prepositions

1. devise	6. in	11. quite
2. costumes	7. of	12. latter
3. towards	8. prosecuted	13. out, samples
4. Besides	9. lose	14. too, loose
5. later	10. all ready	15. accept

16. counting on	21. get along	26. pass out
17. passed out	22. called on	27. put off
18. keep on	23. break off	28. turned in
19. held up	24. found out	29. care for
20. put off	25. dropped out of	30. pointed out

Mini-Test 6: Problem Vocabulary and Prepositions

1. (B) already	9. (A) according to	18. (B) interested in
2. (B) in representing	10. (D) in	19. (A) depending on
3. (B) useless	11. (B) related to	20. (B) insisted on
4. (A) except for	12. (D) figure out	21. (B) imaginative
5. (B) late	13. (C) costumes	22. (C) consecutive
6. (D) for him	14. (B) on the corner	23. (A) formerly
7. (B) look after	15. (D) loose	24. (A) admittance to
(take care of)	16. (B) in seeing	25. (B) known for
8. (D) deprived of	17. (C) with reading	

Exercise 58: Vocabulary

1. (D)	6. (C)	11. (B)	16. (A)	21. (C)
2. (B)	7. (A)	12. (B)	17. (C)	22. (C)
3. (B)	8. (D)	13. (B)	18. (B)	23. (D)
4. (A)	9. (A)	14. (D)	19. (D)	24. (C)
5. (B)	10. (B)	15. (D)	20. (B)	25. (C)

Exercise 59: Vocabulary

1. (D)	6. (A)	11. (B)	16. (D)	21. (B)
2. (C)	7. (D)	12. (C)	17. (C)	22. (A)
3. (B)	8. (B)	13. (C)	18. (A)	23. (B)
4. (C)	9. (D)	14. (A)	19. (A)	24. (A)
5. (B)	10. (A)	15. (B)	20. (D)	25. (D)

PART IV: Practice-Review-Analyze-Practice
Six Full-Length Practice Tests

These practice tests are very similar to actual TOEFL examinations. The format, levels of difficulty, question structure, and number of questions are similar to those on the actual TOEFL. The actual TOEFL is copyrighted and may not be duplicated, and these questions are not taken directly from the actual tests.

You should take these tests under the same conditions you will face when you take the TOEFL. Find a quiet place where you can take the test in its entirety without being disturbed. Be sure to use the answer sheets provided for each test. Follow the time limits exactly. Remember that when the time for one section is over, you must go on to the next section of the test, and you may not return to any previous section. Remember not to leave any answers blank, as you are not penalized for guessing. The time limits for each section are:

Section I: Listening Comprehension—approximately 30 minutes
Section II: Structure and Written Expression—25 minutes
Section III: Reading Comprehension and Vocabulary—45 minutes

After you take each test, turn to Part V of this guide and follow the instructions for scoring your exam. Use the answers, the explanations, and the review cross-references to guide your study.

ANSWER SHEET FOR PRACTICE TEST 1
(Remove This Sheet and Use it to Mark Your Answers)

SECTION I	SECTION II
LISTENING COMPREHENSION	STRUCTURE AND WRITTEN EXPRESSION

SECTION I — LISTENING COMPREHENSION

1 Ⓐ Ⓑ Ⓒ Ⓓ   26 Ⓐ Ⓑ Ⓒ Ⓓ
2 Ⓐ Ⓑ Ⓒ Ⓓ   27 Ⓐ Ⓑ Ⓒ Ⓓ
3 Ⓐ Ⓑ Ⓒ Ⓓ   28 Ⓐ Ⓑ Ⓒ Ⓓ
4 Ⓐ Ⓑ Ⓒ Ⓓ   29 Ⓐ Ⓑ Ⓒ Ⓓ
5 Ⓐ Ⓑ Ⓒ Ⓓ   30 Ⓐ Ⓑ Ⓒ Ⓓ

6 Ⓐ Ⓑ Ⓒ Ⓓ   31 Ⓐ Ⓑ Ⓒ Ⓓ
7 Ⓐ Ⓑ Ⓒ Ⓓ   32 Ⓐ Ⓑ Ⓒ Ⓓ
8 Ⓐ Ⓑ Ⓒ Ⓓ   33 Ⓐ Ⓑ Ⓒ Ⓓ
9 Ⓐ Ⓑ Ⓒ Ⓓ   34 Ⓐ Ⓑ Ⓒ Ⓓ
10 Ⓐ Ⓑ Ⓒ Ⓓ   35 Ⓐ Ⓑ Ⓒ Ⓓ

11 Ⓐ Ⓑ Ⓒ Ⓓ   36 Ⓐ Ⓑ Ⓒ Ⓓ
12 Ⓐ Ⓑ Ⓒ Ⓓ   37 Ⓐ Ⓑ Ⓒ Ⓓ
13 Ⓐ Ⓑ Ⓒ Ⓓ   38 Ⓐ Ⓑ Ⓒ Ⓓ
14 Ⓐ Ⓑ Ⓒ Ⓓ   39 Ⓐ Ⓑ Ⓒ Ⓓ
15 Ⓐ Ⓑ Ⓒ Ⓓ   40 Ⓐ Ⓑ Ⓒ Ⓓ

16 Ⓐ Ⓑ Ⓒ Ⓓ   41 Ⓐ Ⓑ Ⓒ Ⓓ
17 Ⓐ Ⓑ Ⓒ Ⓓ   42 Ⓐ Ⓑ Ⓒ Ⓓ
18 Ⓐ Ⓑ Ⓒ Ⓓ   43 Ⓐ Ⓑ Ⓒ Ⓓ
19 Ⓐ Ⓑ Ⓒ Ⓓ   44 Ⓐ Ⓑ Ⓒ Ⓓ
20 Ⓐ Ⓑ Ⓒ Ⓓ   45 Ⓐ Ⓑ Ⓒ Ⓓ

21 Ⓐ Ⓑ Ⓒ Ⓓ   46 Ⓐ Ⓑ Ⓒ Ⓓ
22 Ⓐ Ⓑ Ⓒ Ⓓ   47 Ⓐ Ⓑ Ⓒ Ⓓ
23 Ⓐ Ⓑ Ⓒ Ⓓ   48 Ⓐ Ⓑ Ⓒ Ⓓ
24 Ⓐ Ⓑ Ⓒ Ⓓ   49 Ⓐ Ⓑ Ⓒ Ⓓ
25 Ⓐ Ⓑ Ⓒ Ⓓ   50 Ⓐ Ⓑ Ⓒ Ⓓ

SECTION II — STRUCTURE AND WRITTEN EXPRESSION

1 Ⓐ Ⓑ Ⓒ Ⓓ   26 Ⓐ Ⓑ Ⓒ Ⓓ
2 Ⓐ Ⓑ Ⓒ Ⓓ   27 Ⓐ Ⓑ Ⓒ Ⓓ
3 Ⓐ Ⓑ Ⓒ Ⓓ   28 Ⓐ Ⓑ Ⓒ Ⓓ
4 Ⓐ Ⓑ Ⓒ Ⓓ   29 Ⓐ Ⓑ Ⓒ Ⓓ
5 Ⓐ Ⓑ Ⓒ Ⓓ   30 Ⓐ Ⓑ Ⓒ Ⓓ

6 Ⓐ Ⓑ Ⓒ Ⓓ   31 Ⓐ Ⓑ Ⓒ Ⓓ
7 Ⓐ Ⓑ Ⓒ Ⓓ   32 Ⓐ Ⓑ Ⓒ Ⓓ
8 Ⓐ Ⓑ Ⓒ Ⓓ   33 Ⓐ Ⓑ Ⓒ Ⓓ
9 Ⓐ Ⓑ Ⓒ Ⓓ   34 Ⓐ Ⓑ Ⓒ Ⓓ
10 Ⓐ Ⓑ Ⓒ Ⓓ   35 Ⓐ Ⓑ Ⓒ Ⓓ

11 Ⓐ Ⓑ Ⓒ Ⓓ   36 Ⓐ Ⓑ Ⓒ Ⓓ
12 Ⓐ Ⓑ Ⓒ Ⓓ   37 Ⓐ Ⓑ Ⓒ Ⓓ
13 Ⓐ Ⓑ Ⓒ Ⓓ   38 Ⓐ Ⓑ Ⓒ Ⓓ
14 Ⓐ Ⓑ Ⓒ Ⓓ   39 Ⓐ Ⓑ Ⓒ Ⓓ
15 Ⓐ Ⓑ Ⓒ Ⓓ   40 Ⓐ Ⓑ Ⓒ Ⓓ

16 Ⓐ Ⓑ Ⓒ Ⓓ
17 Ⓐ Ⓑ Ⓒ Ⓓ
18 Ⓐ Ⓑ Ⓒ Ⓓ
19 Ⓐ Ⓑ Ⓒ Ⓓ
20 Ⓐ Ⓑ Ⓒ Ⓓ

21 Ⓐ Ⓑ Ⓒ Ⓓ
22 Ⓐ Ⓑ Ⓒ Ⓓ
23 Ⓐ Ⓑ Ⓒ Ⓓ
24 Ⓐ Ⓑ Ⓒ Ⓓ
25 Ⓐ Ⓑ Ⓒ Ⓓ

SECTION III

READING COMPREHENSION AND VOCABULARY

1 Ⓐ Ⓑ Ⓒ Ⓓ	26 Ⓐ Ⓑ Ⓒ Ⓓ	51 Ⓐ Ⓑ Ⓒ Ⓓ
2 Ⓐ Ⓑ Ⓒ Ⓓ	27 Ⓐ Ⓑ Ⓒ Ⓓ	52 Ⓐ Ⓑ Ⓒ Ⓓ
3 Ⓐ Ⓑ Ⓒ Ⓓ	28 Ⓐ Ⓑ Ⓒ Ⓓ	53 Ⓐ Ⓑ Ⓒ Ⓓ
4 Ⓐ Ⓑ Ⓒ Ⓓ	29 Ⓐ Ⓑ Ⓒ Ⓓ	54 Ⓐ Ⓑ Ⓒ Ⓓ
5 Ⓐ Ⓑ Ⓒ Ⓓ	30 Ⓐ Ⓑ Ⓒ Ⓓ	55 Ⓐ Ⓑ Ⓒ Ⓓ
6 Ⓐ Ⓑ Ⓒ Ⓓ	31 Ⓐ Ⓑ Ⓒ Ⓓ	56 Ⓐ Ⓑ Ⓒ Ⓓ
7 Ⓐ Ⓑ Ⓒ Ⓓ	32 Ⓐ Ⓑ Ⓒ Ⓓ	57 Ⓐ Ⓑ Ⓒ Ⓓ
8 Ⓐ Ⓑ Ⓒ Ⓓ	33 Ⓐ Ⓑ Ⓒ Ⓓ	58 Ⓐ Ⓑ Ⓒ Ⓓ
9 Ⓐ Ⓑ Ⓒ Ⓓ	34 Ⓐ Ⓑ Ⓒ Ⓓ	59 Ⓐ Ⓑ Ⓒ Ⓓ
10 Ⓐ Ⓑ Ⓒ Ⓓ	35 Ⓐ Ⓑ Ⓒ Ⓓ	60 Ⓐ Ⓑ Ⓒ Ⓓ
11 Ⓐ Ⓑ Ⓒ Ⓓ	36 Ⓐ Ⓑ Ⓒ Ⓓ	
12 Ⓐ Ⓑ Ⓒ Ⓓ	37 Ⓐ Ⓑ Ⓒ Ⓓ	
13 Ⓐ Ⓑ Ⓒ Ⓓ	38 Ⓐ Ⓑ Ⓒ Ⓓ	
14 Ⓐ Ⓑ Ⓒ Ⓓ	39 Ⓐ Ⓑ Ⓒ Ⓓ	
15 Ⓐ Ⓑ Ⓒ Ⓓ	40 Ⓐ Ⓑ Ⓒ Ⓓ	
16 Ⓐ Ⓑ Ⓒ Ⓓ	41 Ⓐ Ⓑ Ⓒ Ⓓ	
17 Ⓐ Ⓑ Ⓒ Ⓓ	42 Ⓐ Ⓑ Ⓒ Ⓓ	
18 Ⓐ Ⓑ Ⓒ Ⓓ	43 Ⓐ Ⓑ Ⓒ Ⓓ	
19 Ⓐ Ⓑ Ⓒ Ⓓ	44 Ⓐ Ⓑ Ⓒ Ⓓ	
20 Ⓐ Ⓑ Ⓒ Ⓓ	45 Ⓐ Ⓑ Ⓒ Ⓓ	
21 Ⓐ Ⓑ Ⓒ Ⓓ	46 Ⓐ Ⓑ Ⓒ Ⓓ	
22 Ⓐ Ⓑ Ⓒ Ⓓ	47 Ⓐ Ⓑ Ⓒ Ⓓ	
23 Ⓐ Ⓑ Ⓒ Ⓓ	48 Ⓐ Ⓑ Ⓒ Ⓓ	
24 Ⓐ Ⓑ Ⓒ Ⓓ	49 Ⓐ Ⓑ Ⓒ Ⓓ	
25 Ⓐ Ⓑ Ⓒ Ⓓ	50 Ⓐ Ⓑ Ⓒ Ⓓ	

CUT HERE

ANSWER SHEET FOR PRACTICE TEST 2
(Remove This Sheet and Use it to Mark Your Answers)

SECTION I	SECTION II
LISTENING COMPREHENSION	STRUCTURE AND WRITTEN EXPRESSION

SECTION I — LISTENING COMPREHENSION

1 Ⓐ Ⓑ Ⓒ Ⓓ	26 Ⓐ Ⓑ Ⓒ Ⓓ
2 Ⓐ Ⓑ Ⓒ Ⓓ	27 Ⓐ Ⓑ Ⓒ Ⓓ
3 Ⓐ Ⓑ Ⓒ Ⓓ	28 Ⓐ Ⓑ Ⓒ Ⓓ
4 Ⓐ Ⓑ Ⓒ Ⓓ	29 Ⓐ Ⓑ Ⓒ Ⓓ
5 Ⓐ Ⓑ Ⓒ Ⓓ	30 Ⓐ Ⓑ Ⓒ Ⓓ
6 Ⓐ Ⓑ Ⓒ Ⓓ	31 Ⓐ Ⓑ Ⓒ Ⓓ
7 Ⓐ Ⓑ Ⓒ Ⓓ	32 Ⓐ Ⓑ Ⓒ Ⓓ
8 Ⓐ Ⓑ Ⓒ Ⓓ	33 Ⓐ Ⓑ Ⓒ Ⓓ
9 Ⓐ Ⓑ Ⓒ Ⓓ	34 Ⓐ Ⓑ Ⓒ Ⓓ
10 Ⓐ Ⓑ Ⓒ Ⓓ	35 Ⓐ Ⓑ Ⓒ Ⓓ
11 Ⓐ Ⓑ Ⓒ Ⓓ	36 Ⓐ Ⓑ Ⓒ Ⓓ
12 Ⓐ Ⓑ Ⓒ Ⓓ	37 Ⓐ Ⓑ Ⓒ Ⓓ
13 Ⓐ Ⓑ Ⓒ Ⓓ	38 Ⓐ Ⓑ Ⓒ Ⓓ
14 Ⓐ Ⓑ Ⓒ Ⓓ	39 Ⓐ Ⓑ Ⓒ Ⓓ
15 Ⓐ Ⓑ Ⓒ Ⓓ	40 Ⓐ Ⓑ Ⓒ Ⓓ
16 Ⓐ Ⓑ Ⓒ Ⓓ	41 Ⓐ Ⓑ Ⓒ Ⓓ
17 Ⓐ Ⓑ Ⓒ Ⓓ	42 Ⓐ Ⓑ Ⓒ Ⓓ
18 Ⓐ Ⓑ Ⓒ Ⓓ	43 Ⓐ Ⓑ Ⓒ Ⓓ
19 Ⓐ Ⓑ Ⓒ Ⓓ	44 Ⓐ Ⓑ Ⓒ Ⓓ
20 Ⓐ Ⓑ Ⓒ Ⓓ	45 Ⓐ Ⓑ Ⓒ Ⓓ
21 Ⓐ Ⓑ Ⓒ Ⓓ	46 Ⓐ Ⓑ Ⓒ Ⓓ
22 Ⓐ Ⓑ Ⓒ Ⓓ	47 Ⓐ Ⓑ Ⓒ Ⓓ
23 Ⓐ Ⓑ Ⓒ Ⓓ	48 Ⓐ Ⓑ Ⓒ Ⓓ
24 Ⓐ Ⓑ Ⓒ Ⓓ	49 Ⓐ Ⓑ Ⓒ Ⓓ
25 Ⓐ Ⓑ Ⓒ Ⓓ	50 Ⓐ Ⓑ Ⓒ Ⓓ

SECTION II — STRUCTURE AND WRITTEN EXPRESSION

1 Ⓐ Ⓑ Ⓒ Ⓓ	26 Ⓐ Ⓑ Ⓒ Ⓓ
2 Ⓐ Ⓑ Ⓒ Ⓓ	27 Ⓐ Ⓑ Ⓒ Ⓓ
3 Ⓐ Ⓑ Ⓒ Ⓓ	28 Ⓐ Ⓑ Ⓒ Ⓓ
4 Ⓐ Ⓑ Ⓒ Ⓓ	29 Ⓐ Ⓑ Ⓒ Ⓓ
5 Ⓐ Ⓑ Ⓒ Ⓓ	30 Ⓐ Ⓑ Ⓒ Ⓓ
6 Ⓐ Ⓑ Ⓒ Ⓓ	31 Ⓐ Ⓑ Ⓒ Ⓓ
7 Ⓐ Ⓑ Ⓒ Ⓓ	32 Ⓐ Ⓑ Ⓒ Ⓓ
8 Ⓐ Ⓑ Ⓒ Ⓓ	33 Ⓐ Ⓑ Ⓒ Ⓓ
9 Ⓐ Ⓑ Ⓒ Ⓓ	34 Ⓐ Ⓑ Ⓒ Ⓓ
10 Ⓐ Ⓑ Ⓒ Ⓓ	35 Ⓐ Ⓑ Ⓒ Ⓓ
11 Ⓐ Ⓑ Ⓒ Ⓓ	36 Ⓐ Ⓑ Ⓒ Ⓓ
12 Ⓐ Ⓑ Ⓒ Ⓓ	37 Ⓐ Ⓑ Ⓒ Ⓓ
13 Ⓐ Ⓑ Ⓒ Ⓓ	38 Ⓐ Ⓑ Ⓒ Ⓓ
14 Ⓐ Ⓑ Ⓒ Ⓓ	39 Ⓐ Ⓑ Ⓒ Ⓓ
15 Ⓐ Ⓑ Ⓒ Ⓓ	40 Ⓐ Ⓑ Ⓒ Ⓓ
16 Ⓐ Ⓑ Ⓒ Ⓓ	
17 Ⓐ Ⓑ Ⓒ Ⓓ	
18 Ⓐ Ⓑ Ⓒ Ⓓ	
19 Ⓐ Ⓑ Ⓒ Ⓓ	
20 Ⓐ Ⓑ Ⓒ Ⓓ	
21 Ⓐ Ⓑ Ⓒ Ⓓ	
22 Ⓐ Ⓑ Ⓒ Ⓓ	
23 Ⓐ Ⓑ Ⓒ Ⓓ	
24 Ⓐ Ⓑ Ⓒ Ⓓ	
25 Ⓐ Ⓑ Ⓒ Ⓓ	

-- CUT HERE --

ANSWER SHEET FOR PRACTICE TEST 2
(Remove This Sheet and Use it to Mark Your Answers)

SECTION III
READING COMPREHENSION AND VOCABULARY

1 Ⓐ Ⓑ Ⓒ Ⓓ	26 Ⓐ Ⓑ Ⓒ Ⓓ	51 Ⓐ Ⓑ Ⓒ Ⓓ
2 Ⓐ Ⓑ Ⓒ Ⓓ	27 Ⓐ Ⓑ Ⓒ Ⓓ	52 Ⓐ Ⓑ Ⓒ Ⓓ
3 Ⓐ Ⓑ Ⓒ Ⓓ	28 Ⓐ Ⓑ Ⓒ Ⓓ	53 Ⓐ Ⓑ Ⓒ Ⓓ
4 Ⓐ Ⓑ Ⓒ Ⓓ	29 Ⓐ Ⓑ Ⓒ Ⓓ	54 Ⓐ Ⓑ Ⓒ Ⓓ
5 Ⓐ Ⓑ Ⓒ Ⓓ	30 Ⓐ Ⓑ Ⓒ Ⓓ	55 Ⓐ Ⓑ Ⓒ Ⓓ
6 Ⓐ Ⓑ Ⓒ Ⓓ	31 Ⓐ Ⓑ Ⓒ Ⓓ	56 Ⓐ Ⓑ Ⓒ Ⓓ
7 Ⓐ Ⓑ Ⓒ Ⓓ	32 Ⓐ Ⓑ Ⓒ Ⓓ	57 Ⓐ Ⓑ Ⓒ Ⓓ
8 Ⓐ Ⓑ Ⓒ Ⓓ	33 Ⓐ Ⓑ Ⓒ Ⓓ	58 Ⓐ Ⓑ Ⓒ Ⓓ
9 Ⓐ Ⓑ Ⓒ Ⓓ	34 Ⓐ Ⓑ Ⓒ Ⓓ	59 Ⓐ Ⓑ Ⓒ Ⓓ
10 Ⓐ Ⓑ Ⓒ Ⓓ	35 Ⓐ Ⓑ Ⓒ Ⓓ	60 Ⓐ Ⓑ Ⓒ Ⓓ
11 Ⓐ Ⓑ Ⓒ Ⓓ	36 Ⓐ Ⓑ Ⓒ Ⓓ	
12 Ⓐ Ⓑ Ⓒ Ⓓ	37 Ⓐ Ⓑ Ⓒ Ⓓ	
13 Ⓐ Ⓑ Ⓒ Ⓓ	38 Ⓐ Ⓑ Ⓒ Ⓓ	
14 Ⓐ Ⓑ Ⓒ Ⓓ	39 Ⓐ Ⓑ Ⓒ Ⓓ	
15 Ⓐ Ⓑ Ⓒ Ⓓ	40 Ⓐ Ⓑ Ⓒ Ⓓ	
16 Ⓐ Ⓑ Ⓒ Ⓓ	41 Ⓐ Ⓑ Ⓒ Ⓓ	
17 Ⓐ Ⓑ Ⓒ Ⓓ	42 Ⓐ Ⓑ Ⓒ Ⓓ	
18 Ⓐ Ⓑ Ⓒ Ⓓ	43 Ⓐ Ⓑ Ⓒ Ⓓ	
19 Ⓐ Ⓑ Ⓒ Ⓓ	44 Ⓐ Ⓑ Ⓒ Ⓓ	
20 Ⓐ Ⓑ Ⓒ Ⓓ	45 Ⓐ Ⓑ Ⓒ Ⓓ	
21 Ⓐ Ⓑ Ⓒ Ⓓ	46 Ⓐ Ⓑ Ⓒ Ⓓ	
22 Ⓐ Ⓑ Ⓒ Ⓓ	47 Ⓐ Ⓑ Ⓒ Ⓓ	
23 Ⓐ Ⓑ Ⓒ Ⓓ	48 Ⓐ Ⓑ Ⓒ Ⓓ	
24 Ⓐ Ⓑ Ⓒ Ⓓ	49 Ⓐ Ⓑ Ⓒ Ⓓ	
25 Ⓐ Ⓑ Ⓒ Ⓓ	50 Ⓐ Ⓑ Ⓒ Ⓓ	

CUT HERE

ANSWER SHEET FOR PRACTICE TEST 3
(Remove This Sheet and Use it to Mark Your Answers)

SECTION I
LISTENING COMPREHENSION

1	Ⓐ Ⓑ Ⓒ Ⓓ		26	Ⓐ Ⓑ Ⓒ Ⓓ
2	Ⓐ Ⓑ Ⓒ Ⓓ		27	Ⓐ Ⓑ Ⓒ Ⓓ
3	Ⓐ Ⓑ Ⓒ Ⓓ		28	Ⓐ Ⓑ Ⓒ Ⓓ
4	Ⓐ Ⓑ Ⓒ Ⓓ		29	Ⓐ Ⓑ Ⓒ Ⓓ
5	Ⓐ Ⓑ Ⓒ Ⓓ		30	Ⓐ Ⓑ Ⓒ Ⓓ
6	Ⓐ Ⓑ Ⓒ Ⓓ		31	Ⓐ Ⓑ Ⓒ Ⓓ
7	Ⓐ Ⓑ Ⓒ Ⓓ		32	Ⓐ Ⓑ Ⓒ Ⓓ
8	Ⓐ Ⓑ Ⓒ Ⓓ		33	Ⓐ Ⓑ Ⓒ Ⓓ
9	Ⓐ Ⓑ Ⓒ Ⓓ		34	Ⓐ Ⓑ Ⓒ Ⓓ
10	Ⓐ Ⓑ Ⓒ Ⓓ		35	Ⓐ Ⓑ Ⓒ Ⓓ
11	Ⓐ Ⓑ Ⓒ Ⓓ		36	Ⓐ Ⓑ Ⓒ Ⓓ
12	Ⓐ Ⓑ Ⓒ Ⓓ		37	Ⓐ Ⓑ Ⓒ Ⓓ
13	Ⓐ Ⓑ Ⓒ Ⓓ		38	Ⓐ Ⓑ Ⓒ Ⓓ
14	Ⓐ Ⓑ Ⓒ Ⓓ		39	Ⓐ Ⓑ Ⓒ Ⓓ
15	Ⓐ Ⓑ Ⓒ Ⓓ		40	Ⓐ Ⓑ Ⓒ Ⓓ
16	Ⓐ Ⓑ Ⓒ Ⓓ		41	Ⓐ Ⓑ Ⓒ Ⓓ
17	Ⓐ Ⓑ Ⓒ Ⓓ		42	Ⓐ Ⓑ Ⓒ Ⓓ
18	Ⓐ Ⓑ Ⓒ Ⓓ		43	Ⓐ Ⓑ Ⓒ Ⓓ
19	Ⓐ Ⓑ Ⓒ Ⓓ		44	Ⓐ Ⓑ Ⓒ Ⓓ
20	Ⓐ Ⓑ Ⓒ Ⓓ		45	Ⓐ Ⓑ Ⓒ Ⓓ
21	Ⓐ Ⓑ Ⓒ Ⓓ		46	Ⓐ Ⓑ Ⓒ Ⓓ
22	Ⓐ Ⓑ Ⓒ Ⓓ		47	Ⓐ Ⓑ Ⓒ Ⓓ
23	Ⓐ Ⓑ Ⓒ Ⓓ		48	Ⓐ Ⓑ Ⓒ Ⓓ
24	Ⓐ Ⓑ Ⓒ Ⓓ		49	Ⓐ Ⓑ Ⓒ Ⓓ
25	Ⓐ Ⓑ Ⓒ Ⓓ		50	Ⓐ Ⓑ Ⓒ Ⓓ

SECTION II
STRUCTURE AND WRITTEN EXPRESSION

1	Ⓐ Ⓑ Ⓒ Ⓓ		26	Ⓐ Ⓑ Ⓒ Ⓓ
2	Ⓐ Ⓑ Ⓒ Ⓓ		27	Ⓐ Ⓑ Ⓒ Ⓓ
3	Ⓐ Ⓑ Ⓒ Ⓓ		28	Ⓐ Ⓑ Ⓒ Ⓓ
4	Ⓐ Ⓑ Ⓒ Ⓓ		29	Ⓐ Ⓑ Ⓒ Ⓓ
5	Ⓐ Ⓑ Ⓒ Ⓓ		30	Ⓐ Ⓑ Ⓒ Ⓓ
6	Ⓐ Ⓑ Ⓒ Ⓓ		31	Ⓐ Ⓑ Ⓒ Ⓓ
7	Ⓐ Ⓑ Ⓒ Ⓓ		32	Ⓐ Ⓑ Ⓒ Ⓓ
8	Ⓐ Ⓑ Ⓒ Ⓓ		33	Ⓐ Ⓑ Ⓒ Ⓓ
9	Ⓐ Ⓑ Ⓒ Ⓓ		34	Ⓐ Ⓑ Ⓒ Ⓓ
10	Ⓐ Ⓑ Ⓒ Ⓓ		35	Ⓐ Ⓑ Ⓒ Ⓓ
11	Ⓐ Ⓑ Ⓒ Ⓓ		36	Ⓐ Ⓑ Ⓒ Ⓓ
12	Ⓐ Ⓑ Ⓒ Ⓓ		37	Ⓐ Ⓑ Ⓒ Ⓓ
13	Ⓐ Ⓑ Ⓒ Ⓓ		38	Ⓐ Ⓑ Ⓒ Ⓓ
14	Ⓐ Ⓑ Ⓒ Ⓓ		39	Ⓐ Ⓑ Ⓒ Ⓓ
15	Ⓐ Ⓑ Ⓒ Ⓓ		40	Ⓐ Ⓑ Ⓒ Ⓓ
16	Ⓐ Ⓑ Ⓒ Ⓓ		
17	Ⓐ Ⓑ Ⓒ Ⓓ		
18	Ⓐ Ⓑ Ⓒ Ⓓ		
19	Ⓐ Ⓑ Ⓒ Ⓓ		
20	Ⓐ Ⓑ Ⓒ Ⓓ		
21	Ⓐ Ⓑ Ⓒ Ⓓ		
22	Ⓐ Ⓑ Ⓒ Ⓓ		
23	Ⓐ Ⓑ Ⓒ Ⓓ		
24	Ⓐ Ⓑ Ⓒ Ⓓ		
25	Ⓐ Ⓑ Ⓒ Ⓓ		

CUT HERE

239

ANSWER SHEET FOR PRACTICE TEST 3
(Remove This Sheet and Use it to Mark Your Answers)

SECTION III
READING COMPREHENSION AND VOCABULARY

1 Ⓐ Ⓑ Ⓒ Ⓓ	26 Ⓐ Ⓑ Ⓒ Ⓓ	51 Ⓐ Ⓑ Ⓒ Ⓓ
2 Ⓐ Ⓑ Ⓒ Ⓓ	27 Ⓐ Ⓑ Ⓒ Ⓓ	52 Ⓐ Ⓑ Ⓒ Ⓓ
3 Ⓐ Ⓑ Ⓒ Ⓓ	28 Ⓐ Ⓑ Ⓒ Ⓓ	53 Ⓐ Ⓑ Ⓒ Ⓓ
4 Ⓐ Ⓑ Ⓒ Ⓓ	29 Ⓐ Ⓑ Ⓒ Ⓓ	54 Ⓐ Ⓑ Ⓒ Ⓓ
5 Ⓐ Ⓑ Ⓒ Ⓓ	30 Ⓐ Ⓑ Ⓒ Ⓓ	55 Ⓐ Ⓑ Ⓒ Ⓓ
6 Ⓐ Ⓑ Ⓒ Ⓓ	31 Ⓐ Ⓑ Ⓒ Ⓓ	56 Ⓐ Ⓑ Ⓒ Ⓓ
7 Ⓐ Ⓑ Ⓒ Ⓓ	32 Ⓐ Ⓑ Ⓒ Ⓓ	57 Ⓐ Ⓑ Ⓒ Ⓓ
8 Ⓐ Ⓑ Ⓒ Ⓓ	33 Ⓐ Ⓑ Ⓒ Ⓓ	58 Ⓐ Ⓑ Ⓒ Ⓓ
9 Ⓐ Ⓑ Ⓒ Ⓓ	34 Ⓐ Ⓑ Ⓒ Ⓓ	59 Ⓐ Ⓑ Ⓒ Ⓓ
10 Ⓐ Ⓑ Ⓒ Ⓓ	35 Ⓐ Ⓑ Ⓒ Ⓓ	60 Ⓐ Ⓑ Ⓒ Ⓓ
11 Ⓐ Ⓑ Ⓒ Ⓓ	36 Ⓐ Ⓑ Ⓒ Ⓓ	
12 Ⓐ Ⓑ Ⓒ Ⓓ	37 Ⓐ Ⓑ Ⓒ Ⓓ	
13 Ⓐ Ⓑ Ⓒ Ⓓ	38 Ⓐ Ⓑ Ⓒ Ⓓ	
14 Ⓐ Ⓑ Ⓒ Ⓓ	39 Ⓐ Ⓑ Ⓒ Ⓓ	
15 Ⓐ Ⓑ Ⓒ Ⓓ	40 Ⓐ Ⓑ Ⓒ Ⓓ	
16 Ⓐ Ⓑ Ⓒ Ⓓ	41 Ⓐ Ⓑ Ⓒ Ⓓ	
17 Ⓐ Ⓑ Ⓒ Ⓓ	42 Ⓐ Ⓑ Ⓒ Ⓓ	
18 Ⓐ Ⓑ Ⓒ Ⓓ	43 Ⓐ Ⓑ Ⓒ Ⓓ	
19 Ⓐ Ⓑ Ⓒ Ⓓ	44 Ⓐ Ⓑ Ⓒ Ⓓ	
20 Ⓐ Ⓑ Ⓒ Ⓓ	45 Ⓐ Ⓑ Ⓒ Ⓓ	
21 Ⓐ Ⓑ Ⓒ Ⓓ	46 Ⓐ Ⓑ Ⓒ Ⓓ	
22 Ⓐ Ⓑ Ⓒ Ⓓ	47 Ⓐ Ⓑ Ⓒ Ⓓ	
23 Ⓐ Ⓑ Ⓒ Ⓓ	48 Ⓐ Ⓑ Ⓒ Ⓓ	
24 Ⓐ Ⓑ Ⓒ Ⓓ	49 Ⓐ Ⓑ Ⓒ Ⓓ	
25 Ⓐ Ⓑ Ⓒ Ⓓ	50 Ⓐ Ⓑ Ⓒ Ⓓ	

CUT HERE

ANSWER SHEET FOR PRACTICE TEST 4
(Remove This Sheet and Use it to Mark Your Answers)

SECTION I	SECTION II
LISTENING COMPREHENSION	STRUCTURE AND WRITTEN EXPRESSION

CUT HERE

SECTION I

1 Ⓐ Ⓑ Ⓒ Ⓓ	26 Ⓐ Ⓑ Ⓒ Ⓓ
2 Ⓐ Ⓑ Ⓒ Ⓓ	27 Ⓐ Ⓑ Ⓒ Ⓓ
3 Ⓐ Ⓑ Ⓒ Ⓓ	28 Ⓐ Ⓑ Ⓒ Ⓓ
4 Ⓐ Ⓑ Ⓒ Ⓓ	29 Ⓐ Ⓑ Ⓒ Ⓓ
5 Ⓐ Ⓑ Ⓒ Ⓓ	30 Ⓐ Ⓑ Ⓒ Ⓓ
6 Ⓐ Ⓑ Ⓒ Ⓓ	31 Ⓐ Ⓑ Ⓒ Ⓓ
7 Ⓐ Ⓑ Ⓒ Ⓓ	32 Ⓐ Ⓑ Ⓒ Ⓓ
8 Ⓐ Ⓑ Ⓒ Ⓓ	33 Ⓐ Ⓑ Ⓒ Ⓓ
9 Ⓐ Ⓑ Ⓒ Ⓓ	34 Ⓐ Ⓑ Ⓒ Ⓓ
10 Ⓐ Ⓑ Ⓒ Ⓓ	35 Ⓐ Ⓑ Ⓒ Ⓓ
11 Ⓐ Ⓑ Ⓒ Ⓓ	36 Ⓐ Ⓑ Ⓒ Ⓓ
12 Ⓐ Ⓑ Ⓒ Ⓓ	37 Ⓐ Ⓑ Ⓒ Ⓓ
13 Ⓐ Ⓑ Ⓒ Ⓓ	38 Ⓐ Ⓑ Ⓒ Ⓓ
14 Ⓐ Ⓑ Ⓒ Ⓓ	39 Ⓐ Ⓑ Ⓒ Ⓓ
15 Ⓐ Ⓑ Ⓒ Ⓓ	40 Ⓐ Ⓑ Ⓒ Ⓓ
16 Ⓐ Ⓑ Ⓒ Ⓓ	41 Ⓐ Ⓑ Ⓒ Ⓓ
17 Ⓐ Ⓑ Ⓒ Ⓓ	42 Ⓐ Ⓑ Ⓒ Ⓓ
18 Ⓐ Ⓑ Ⓒ Ⓓ	43 Ⓐ Ⓑ Ⓒ Ⓓ
19 Ⓐ Ⓑ Ⓒ Ⓓ	44 Ⓐ Ⓑ Ⓒ Ⓓ
20 Ⓐ Ⓑ Ⓒ Ⓓ	45 Ⓐ Ⓑ Ⓒ Ⓓ
21 Ⓐ Ⓑ Ⓒ Ⓓ	46 Ⓐ Ⓑ Ⓒ Ⓓ
22 Ⓐ Ⓑ Ⓒ Ⓓ	47 Ⓐ Ⓑ Ⓒ Ⓓ
23 Ⓐ Ⓑ Ⓒ Ⓓ	48 Ⓐ Ⓑ Ⓒ Ⓓ
24 Ⓐ Ⓑ Ⓒ Ⓓ	49 Ⓐ Ⓑ Ⓒ Ⓓ
25 Ⓐ Ⓑ Ⓒ Ⓓ	50 Ⓐ Ⓑ Ⓒ Ⓓ

SECTION II

1 Ⓐ Ⓑ Ⓒ Ⓓ	26 Ⓐ Ⓑ Ⓒ Ⓓ
2 Ⓐ Ⓑ Ⓒ Ⓓ	27 Ⓐ Ⓑ Ⓒ Ⓓ
3 Ⓐ Ⓑ Ⓒ Ⓓ	28 Ⓐ Ⓑ Ⓒ Ⓓ
4 Ⓐ Ⓑ Ⓒ Ⓓ	29 Ⓐ Ⓑ Ⓒ Ⓓ
5 Ⓐ Ⓑ Ⓒ Ⓓ	30 Ⓐ Ⓑ Ⓒ Ⓓ
6 Ⓐ Ⓑ Ⓒ Ⓓ	31 Ⓐ Ⓑ Ⓒ Ⓓ
7 Ⓐ Ⓑ Ⓒ Ⓓ	32 Ⓐ Ⓑ Ⓒ Ⓓ
8 Ⓐ Ⓑ Ⓒ Ⓓ	33 Ⓐ Ⓑ Ⓒ Ⓓ
9 Ⓐ Ⓑ Ⓒ Ⓓ	34 Ⓐ Ⓑ Ⓒ Ⓓ
10 Ⓐ Ⓑ Ⓒ Ⓓ	35 Ⓐ Ⓑ Ⓒ Ⓓ
11 Ⓐ Ⓑ Ⓒ Ⓓ	36 Ⓐ Ⓑ Ⓒ Ⓓ
12 Ⓐ Ⓑ Ⓒ Ⓓ	37 Ⓐ Ⓑ Ⓒ Ⓓ
13 Ⓐ Ⓑ Ⓒ Ⓓ	38 Ⓐ Ⓑ Ⓒ Ⓓ
14 Ⓐ Ⓑ Ⓒ Ⓓ	39 Ⓐ Ⓑ Ⓒ Ⓓ
15 Ⓐ Ⓑ Ⓒ Ⓓ	40 Ⓐ Ⓑ Ⓒ Ⓓ
16 Ⓐ Ⓑ Ⓒ Ⓓ	
17 Ⓐ Ⓑ Ⓒ Ⓓ	
18 Ⓐ Ⓑ Ⓒ Ⓓ	
19 Ⓐ Ⓑ Ⓒ Ⓓ	
20 Ⓐ Ⓑ Ⓒ Ⓓ	
21 Ⓐ Ⓑ Ⓒ Ⓓ	
22 Ⓐ Ⓑ Ⓒ Ⓓ	
23 Ⓐ Ⓑ Ⓒ Ⓓ	
24 Ⓐ Ⓑ Ⓒ Ⓓ	
25 Ⓐ Ⓑ Ⓒ Ⓓ	

ANSWER SHEET FOR PRACTICE TEST 4
(Remove This Sheet and Use it to Mark Your Answers)

SECTION III

READING COMPREHENSION AND VOCABULARY

1 Ⓐ Ⓑ Ⓒ Ⓓ	26 Ⓐ Ⓑ Ⓒ Ⓓ	51 Ⓐ Ⓑ Ⓒ Ⓓ
2 Ⓐ Ⓑ Ⓒ Ⓓ	27 Ⓐ Ⓑ Ⓒ Ⓓ	52 Ⓐ Ⓑ Ⓒ Ⓓ
3 Ⓐ Ⓑ Ⓒ Ⓓ	28 Ⓐ Ⓑ Ⓒ Ⓓ	53 Ⓐ Ⓑ Ⓒ Ⓓ
4 Ⓐ Ⓑ Ⓒ Ⓓ	29 Ⓐ Ⓑ Ⓒ Ⓓ	54 Ⓐ Ⓑ Ⓒ Ⓓ
5 Ⓐ Ⓑ Ⓒ Ⓓ	30 Ⓐ Ⓑ Ⓒ Ⓓ	55 Ⓐ Ⓑ Ⓒ Ⓓ
6 Ⓐ Ⓑ Ⓒ Ⓓ	31 Ⓐ Ⓑ Ⓒ Ⓓ	56 Ⓐ Ⓑ Ⓒ Ⓓ
7 Ⓐ Ⓑ Ⓒ Ⓓ	32 Ⓐ Ⓑ Ⓒ Ⓓ	57 Ⓐ Ⓑ Ⓒ Ⓓ
8 Ⓐ Ⓑ Ⓒ Ⓓ	33 Ⓐ Ⓑ Ⓒ Ⓓ	58 Ⓐ Ⓑ Ⓒ Ⓓ
9 Ⓐ Ⓑ Ⓒ Ⓓ	34 Ⓐ Ⓑ Ⓒ Ⓓ	59 Ⓐ Ⓑ Ⓒ Ⓓ
10 Ⓐ Ⓑ Ⓒ Ⓓ	35 Ⓐ Ⓑ Ⓒ Ⓓ	60 Ⓐ Ⓑ Ⓒ Ⓓ
11 Ⓐ Ⓑ Ⓒ Ⓓ	36 Ⓐ Ⓑ Ⓒ Ⓓ	
12 Ⓐ Ⓑ Ⓒ Ⓓ	37 Ⓐ Ⓑ Ⓒ Ⓓ	
13 Ⓐ Ⓑ Ⓒ Ⓓ	38 Ⓐ Ⓑ Ⓒ Ⓓ	
14 Ⓐ Ⓑ Ⓒ Ⓓ	39 Ⓐ Ⓑ Ⓒ Ⓓ	
15 Ⓐ Ⓑ Ⓒ Ⓓ	40 Ⓐ Ⓑ Ⓒ Ⓓ	
16 Ⓐ Ⓑ Ⓒ Ⓓ	41 Ⓐ Ⓑ Ⓒ Ⓓ	
17 Ⓐ Ⓑ Ⓒ Ⓓ	42 Ⓐ Ⓑ Ⓒ Ⓓ	
18 Ⓐ Ⓑ Ⓒ Ⓓ	43 Ⓐ Ⓑ Ⓒ Ⓓ	
19 Ⓐ Ⓑ Ⓒ Ⓓ	44 Ⓐ Ⓑ Ⓒ Ⓓ	
20 Ⓐ Ⓑ Ⓒ Ⓓ	45 Ⓐ Ⓑ Ⓒ Ⓓ	
21 Ⓐ Ⓑ Ⓒ Ⓓ	46 Ⓐ Ⓑ Ⓒ Ⓓ	
22 Ⓐ Ⓑ Ⓒ Ⓓ	47 Ⓐ Ⓑ Ⓒ Ⓓ	
23 Ⓐ Ⓑ Ⓒ Ⓓ	48 Ⓐ Ⓑ Ⓒ Ⓓ	
24 Ⓐ Ⓑ Ⓒ Ⓓ	49 Ⓐ Ⓑ Ⓒ Ⓓ	
25 Ⓐ Ⓑ Ⓒ Ⓓ	50 Ⓐ Ⓑ Ⓒ Ⓓ	

--CUT HERE--

ANSWER SHEET FOR PRACTICE TEST 5
(Remove This Sheet and Use it to Mark Your Answers)

SECTION I	**SECTION II**
LISTENING COMPREHENSION	STRUCTURE AND WRITTEN EXPRESSION

SECTION I — LISTENING COMPREHENSION

1 Ⓐ Ⓑ Ⓒ Ⓓ	26 Ⓐ Ⓑ Ⓒ Ⓓ		
2 Ⓐ Ⓑ Ⓒ Ⓓ	27 Ⓐ Ⓑ Ⓒ Ⓓ		
3 Ⓐ Ⓑ Ⓒ Ⓓ	28 Ⓐ Ⓑ Ⓒ Ⓓ		
4 Ⓐ Ⓑ Ⓒ Ⓓ	29 Ⓐ Ⓑ Ⓒ Ⓓ		
5 Ⓐ Ⓑ Ⓒ Ⓓ	30 Ⓐ Ⓑ Ⓒ Ⓓ		
6 Ⓐ Ⓑ Ⓒ Ⓓ	31 Ⓐ Ⓑ Ⓒ Ⓓ		
7 Ⓐ Ⓑ Ⓒ Ⓓ	32 Ⓐ Ⓑ Ⓒ Ⓓ		
8 Ⓐ Ⓑ Ⓒ Ⓓ	33 Ⓐ Ⓑ Ⓒ Ⓓ		
9 Ⓐ Ⓑ Ⓒ Ⓓ	34 Ⓐ Ⓑ Ⓒ Ⓓ		
10 Ⓐ Ⓑ Ⓒ Ⓓ	35 Ⓐ Ⓑ Ⓒ Ⓓ		
11 Ⓐ Ⓑ Ⓒ Ⓓ	36 Ⓐ Ⓑ Ⓒ Ⓓ		
12 Ⓐ Ⓑ Ⓒ Ⓓ	37 Ⓐ Ⓑ Ⓒ Ⓓ		
13 Ⓐ Ⓑ Ⓒ Ⓓ	38 Ⓐ Ⓑ Ⓒ Ⓓ		
14 Ⓐ Ⓑ Ⓒ Ⓓ	39 Ⓐ Ⓑ Ⓒ Ⓓ		
15 Ⓐ Ⓑ Ⓒ Ⓓ	40 Ⓐ Ⓑ Ⓒ Ⓓ		
16 Ⓐ Ⓑ Ⓒ Ⓓ	41 Ⓐ Ⓑ Ⓒ Ⓓ		
17 Ⓐ Ⓑ Ⓒ Ⓓ	42 Ⓐ Ⓑ Ⓒ Ⓓ		
18 Ⓐ Ⓑ Ⓒ Ⓓ	43 Ⓐ Ⓑ Ⓒ Ⓓ		
19 Ⓐ Ⓑ Ⓒ Ⓓ	44 Ⓐ Ⓑ Ⓒ Ⓓ		
20 Ⓐ Ⓑ Ⓒ Ⓓ	45 Ⓐ Ⓑ Ⓒ Ⓓ		
21 Ⓐ Ⓑ Ⓒ Ⓓ	46 Ⓐ Ⓑ Ⓒ Ⓓ		
22 Ⓐ Ⓑ Ⓒ Ⓓ	47 Ⓐ Ⓑ Ⓒ Ⓓ		
23 Ⓐ Ⓑ Ⓒ Ⓓ	48 Ⓐ Ⓑ Ⓒ Ⓓ		
24 Ⓐ Ⓑ Ⓒ Ⓓ	49 Ⓐ Ⓑ Ⓒ Ⓓ		
25 Ⓐ Ⓑ Ⓒ Ⓓ	50 Ⓐ Ⓑ Ⓒ Ⓓ		

SECTION II — STRUCTURE AND WRITTEN EXPRESSION

1 Ⓐ Ⓑ Ⓒ Ⓓ	26 Ⓐ Ⓑ Ⓒ Ⓓ
2 Ⓐ Ⓑ Ⓒ Ⓓ	27 Ⓐ Ⓑ Ⓒ Ⓓ
3 Ⓐ Ⓑ Ⓒ Ⓓ	28 Ⓐ Ⓑ Ⓒ Ⓓ
4 Ⓐ Ⓑ Ⓒ Ⓓ	29 Ⓐ Ⓑ Ⓒ Ⓓ
5 Ⓐ Ⓑ Ⓒ Ⓓ	30 Ⓐ Ⓑ Ⓒ Ⓓ
6 Ⓐ Ⓑ Ⓒ Ⓓ	31 Ⓐ Ⓑ Ⓒ Ⓓ
7 Ⓐ Ⓑ Ⓒ Ⓓ	32 Ⓐ Ⓑ Ⓒ Ⓓ
8 Ⓐ Ⓑ Ⓒ Ⓓ	33 Ⓐ Ⓑ Ⓒ Ⓓ
9 Ⓐ Ⓑ Ⓒ Ⓓ	34 Ⓐ Ⓑ Ⓒ Ⓓ
10 Ⓐ Ⓑ Ⓒ Ⓓ	35 Ⓐ Ⓑ Ⓒ Ⓓ
11 Ⓐ Ⓑ Ⓒ Ⓓ	36 Ⓐ Ⓑ Ⓒ Ⓓ
12 Ⓐ Ⓑ Ⓒ Ⓓ	37 Ⓐ Ⓑ Ⓒ Ⓓ
13 Ⓐ Ⓑ Ⓒ Ⓓ	38 Ⓐ Ⓑ Ⓒ Ⓓ
14 Ⓐ Ⓑ Ⓒ Ⓓ	39 Ⓐ Ⓑ Ⓒ Ⓓ
15 Ⓐ Ⓑ Ⓒ Ⓓ	40 Ⓐ Ⓑ Ⓒ Ⓓ
16 Ⓐ Ⓑ Ⓒ Ⓓ	
17 Ⓐ Ⓑ Ⓒ Ⓓ	
18 Ⓐ Ⓑ Ⓒ Ⓓ	
19 Ⓐ Ⓑ Ⓒ Ⓓ	
20 Ⓐ Ⓑ Ⓒ Ⓓ	
21 Ⓐ Ⓑ Ⓒ Ⓓ	
22 Ⓐ Ⓑ Ⓒ Ⓓ	
23 Ⓐ Ⓑ Ⓒ Ⓓ	
24 Ⓐ Ⓑ Ⓒ Ⓓ	
25 Ⓐ Ⓑ Ⓒ Ⓓ	

CUT HERE

243

SECTION III

READING COMPREHENSION AND VOCABULARY

1 Ⓐ Ⓑ Ⓒ Ⓓ	26 Ⓐ Ⓑ Ⓒ Ⓓ	51 Ⓐ Ⓑ Ⓒ Ⓓ
2 Ⓐ Ⓑ Ⓒ Ⓓ	27 Ⓐ Ⓑ Ⓒ Ⓓ	52 Ⓐ Ⓑ Ⓒ Ⓓ
3 Ⓐ Ⓑ Ⓒ Ⓓ	28 Ⓐ Ⓑ Ⓒ Ⓓ	53 Ⓐ Ⓑ Ⓒ Ⓓ
4 Ⓐ Ⓑ Ⓒ Ⓓ	29 Ⓐ Ⓑ Ⓒ Ⓓ	54 Ⓐ Ⓑ Ⓒ Ⓓ
5 Ⓐ Ⓑ Ⓒ Ⓓ	30 Ⓐ Ⓑ Ⓒ Ⓓ	55 Ⓐ Ⓑ Ⓒ Ⓓ
6 Ⓐ Ⓑ Ⓒ Ⓓ	31 Ⓐ Ⓑ Ⓒ Ⓓ	56 Ⓐ Ⓑ Ⓒ Ⓓ
7 Ⓐ Ⓑ Ⓒ Ⓓ	32 Ⓐ Ⓑ Ⓒ Ⓓ	57 Ⓐ Ⓑ Ⓒ Ⓓ
8 Ⓐ Ⓑ Ⓒ Ⓓ	33 Ⓐ Ⓑ Ⓒ Ⓓ	58 Ⓐ Ⓑ Ⓒ Ⓓ
9 Ⓐ Ⓑ Ⓒ Ⓓ	34 Ⓐ Ⓑ Ⓒ Ⓓ	59 Ⓐ Ⓑ Ⓒ Ⓓ
10 Ⓐ Ⓑ Ⓒ Ⓓ	35 Ⓐ Ⓑ Ⓒ Ⓓ	60 Ⓐ Ⓑ Ⓒ Ⓓ
11 Ⓐ Ⓑ Ⓒ Ⓓ	36 Ⓐ Ⓑ Ⓒ Ⓓ	
12 Ⓐ Ⓑ Ⓒ Ⓓ	37 Ⓐ Ⓑ Ⓒ Ⓓ	
13 Ⓐ Ⓑ Ⓒ Ⓓ	38 Ⓐ Ⓑ Ⓒ Ⓓ	
14 Ⓐ Ⓑ Ⓒ Ⓓ	39 Ⓐ Ⓑ Ⓒ Ⓓ	
15 Ⓐ Ⓑ Ⓒ Ⓓ	40 Ⓐ Ⓑ Ⓒ Ⓓ	
16 Ⓐ Ⓑ Ⓒ Ⓓ	41 Ⓐ Ⓑ Ⓒ Ⓓ	
17 Ⓐ Ⓑ Ⓒ Ⓓ	42 Ⓐ Ⓑ Ⓒ Ⓓ	
18 Ⓐ Ⓑ Ⓒ Ⓓ	43 Ⓐ Ⓑ Ⓒ Ⓓ	
19 Ⓐ Ⓑ Ⓒ Ⓓ	44 Ⓐ Ⓑ Ⓒ Ⓓ	
20 Ⓐ Ⓑ Ⓒ Ⓓ	45 Ⓐ Ⓑ Ⓒ Ⓓ	
21 Ⓐ Ⓑ Ⓒ Ⓓ	46 Ⓐ Ⓑ Ⓒ Ⓓ	
22 Ⓐ Ⓑ Ⓒ Ⓓ	47 Ⓐ Ⓑ Ⓒ Ⓓ	
23 Ⓐ Ⓑ Ⓒ Ⓓ	48 Ⓐ Ⓑ Ⓒ Ⓓ	
24 Ⓐ Ⓑ Ⓒ Ⓓ	49 Ⓐ Ⓑ Ⓒ Ⓓ	
25 Ⓐ Ⓑ Ⓒ Ⓓ	50 Ⓐ Ⓑ Ⓒ Ⓓ	

CUT HERE

ANSWER SHEET FOR PRACTICE TEST 6
(Remove This Sheet and Use it to Mark Your Answers)

SECTION I

LISTENING COMPREHENSION

1 Ⓐ Ⓑ Ⓒ Ⓓ	26 Ⓐ Ⓑ Ⓒ Ⓓ
2 Ⓐ Ⓑ Ⓒ Ⓓ	27 Ⓐ Ⓑ Ⓒ Ⓓ
3 Ⓐ Ⓑ Ⓒ Ⓓ	28 Ⓐ Ⓑ Ⓒ Ⓓ
4 Ⓐ Ⓑ Ⓒ Ⓓ	29 Ⓐ Ⓑ Ⓒ Ⓓ
5 Ⓐ Ⓑ Ⓒ Ⓓ	30 Ⓐ Ⓑ Ⓒ Ⓓ
6 Ⓐ Ⓑ Ⓒ Ⓓ	31 Ⓐ Ⓑ Ⓒ Ⓓ
7 Ⓐ Ⓑ Ⓒ Ⓓ	32 Ⓐ Ⓑ Ⓒ Ⓓ
8 Ⓐ Ⓑ Ⓒ Ⓓ	33 Ⓐ Ⓑ Ⓒ Ⓓ
9 Ⓐ Ⓑ Ⓒ Ⓓ	34 Ⓐ Ⓑ Ⓒ Ⓓ
10 Ⓐ Ⓑ Ⓒ Ⓓ	35 Ⓐ Ⓑ Ⓒ Ⓓ
11 Ⓐ Ⓑ Ⓒ Ⓓ	36 Ⓐ Ⓑ Ⓒ Ⓓ
12 Ⓐ Ⓑ Ⓒ Ⓓ	37 Ⓐ Ⓑ Ⓒ Ⓓ
13 Ⓐ Ⓑ Ⓒ Ⓓ	38 Ⓐ Ⓑ Ⓒ Ⓓ
14 Ⓐ Ⓑ Ⓒ Ⓓ	39 Ⓐ Ⓑ Ⓒ Ⓓ
15 Ⓐ Ⓑ Ⓒ Ⓓ	40 Ⓐ Ⓑ Ⓒ Ⓓ
16 Ⓐ Ⓑ Ⓒ Ⓓ	41 Ⓐ Ⓑ Ⓒ Ⓓ
17 Ⓐ Ⓑ Ⓒ Ⓓ	42 Ⓐ Ⓑ Ⓒ Ⓓ
18 Ⓐ Ⓑ Ⓒ Ⓓ	43 Ⓐ Ⓑ Ⓒ Ⓓ
19 Ⓐ Ⓑ Ⓒ Ⓓ	44 Ⓐ Ⓑ Ⓒ Ⓓ
20 Ⓐ Ⓑ Ⓒ Ⓓ	45 Ⓐ Ⓑ Ⓒ Ⓓ
21 Ⓐ Ⓑ Ⓒ Ⓓ	46 Ⓐ Ⓑ Ⓒ Ⓓ
22 Ⓐ Ⓑ Ⓒ Ⓓ	47 Ⓐ Ⓑ Ⓒ Ⓓ
23 Ⓐ Ⓑ Ⓒ Ⓓ	48 Ⓐ Ⓑ Ⓒ Ⓓ
24 Ⓐ Ⓑ Ⓒ Ⓓ	49 Ⓐ Ⓑ Ⓒ Ⓓ
25 Ⓐ Ⓑ Ⓒ Ⓓ	50 Ⓐ Ⓑ Ⓒ Ⓓ

SECTION II

STRUCTURE AND WRITTEN EXPRESSION

1 Ⓐ Ⓑ Ⓒ Ⓓ	26 Ⓐ Ⓑ Ⓒ Ⓓ
2 Ⓐ Ⓑ Ⓒ Ⓓ	27 Ⓐ Ⓑ Ⓒ Ⓓ
3 Ⓐ Ⓑ Ⓒ Ⓓ	28 Ⓐ Ⓑ Ⓒ Ⓓ
4 Ⓐ Ⓑ Ⓒ Ⓓ	29 Ⓐ Ⓑ Ⓒ Ⓓ
5 Ⓐ Ⓑ Ⓒ Ⓓ	30 Ⓐ Ⓑ Ⓒ Ⓓ
6 Ⓐ Ⓑ Ⓒ Ⓓ	31 Ⓐ Ⓑ Ⓒ Ⓓ
7 Ⓐ Ⓑ Ⓒ Ⓓ	32 Ⓐ Ⓑ Ⓒ Ⓓ
8 Ⓐ Ⓑ Ⓒ Ⓓ	33 Ⓐ Ⓑ Ⓒ Ⓓ
9 Ⓐ Ⓑ Ⓒ Ⓓ	34 Ⓐ Ⓑ Ⓒ Ⓓ
10 Ⓐ Ⓑ Ⓒ Ⓓ	35 Ⓐ Ⓑ Ⓒ Ⓓ
11 Ⓐ Ⓑ Ⓒ Ⓓ	36 Ⓐ Ⓑ Ⓒ Ⓓ
12 Ⓐ Ⓑ Ⓒ Ⓓ	37 Ⓐ Ⓑ Ⓒ Ⓓ
13 Ⓐ Ⓑ Ⓒ Ⓓ	38 Ⓐ Ⓑ Ⓒ Ⓓ
14 Ⓐ Ⓑ Ⓒ Ⓓ	39 Ⓐ Ⓑ Ⓒ Ⓓ
15 Ⓐ Ⓑ Ⓒ Ⓓ	40 Ⓐ Ⓑ Ⓒ Ⓓ
16 Ⓐ Ⓑ Ⓒ Ⓓ	
17 Ⓐ Ⓑ Ⓒ Ⓓ	
18 Ⓐ Ⓑ Ⓒ Ⓓ	
19 Ⓐ Ⓑ Ⓒ Ⓓ	
20 Ⓐ Ⓑ Ⓒ Ⓓ	
21 Ⓐ Ⓑ Ⓒ Ⓓ	
22 Ⓐ Ⓑ Ⓒ Ⓓ	
23 Ⓐ Ⓑ Ⓒ Ⓓ	
24 Ⓐ Ⓑ Ⓒ Ⓓ	
25 Ⓐ Ⓑ Ⓒ Ⓓ	

ANSWER SHEET FOR PRACTICE TEST 6
(Remove This Sheet and Use it to Mark Your Answers)

SECTION III

READING COMPREHENSION AND VOCABULARY

1 Ⓐ Ⓑ Ⓒ Ⓓ	26 Ⓐ Ⓑ Ⓒ Ⓓ	51 Ⓐ Ⓑ Ⓒ Ⓓ
2 Ⓐ Ⓑ Ⓒ Ⓓ	27 Ⓐ Ⓑ Ⓒ Ⓓ	52 Ⓐ Ⓑ Ⓒ Ⓓ
3 Ⓐ Ⓑ Ⓒ Ⓓ	28 Ⓐ Ⓑ Ⓒ Ⓓ	53 Ⓐ Ⓑ Ⓒ Ⓓ
4 Ⓐ Ⓑ Ⓒ Ⓓ	29 Ⓐ Ⓑ Ⓒ Ⓓ	54 Ⓐ Ⓑ Ⓒ Ⓓ
5 Ⓐ Ⓑ Ⓒ Ⓓ	30 Ⓐ Ⓑ Ⓒ Ⓓ	55 Ⓐ Ⓑ Ⓒ Ⓓ
6 Ⓐ Ⓑ Ⓒ Ⓓ	31 Ⓐ Ⓑ Ⓒ Ⓓ	56 Ⓐ Ⓑ Ⓒ Ⓓ
7 Ⓐ Ⓑ Ⓒ Ⓓ	32 Ⓐ Ⓑ Ⓒ Ⓓ	57 Ⓐ Ⓑ Ⓒ Ⓓ
8 Ⓐ Ⓑ Ⓒ Ⓓ	33 Ⓐ Ⓑ Ⓒ Ⓓ	58 Ⓐ Ⓑ Ⓒ Ⓓ
9 Ⓐ Ⓑ Ⓒ Ⓓ	34 Ⓐ Ⓑ Ⓒ Ⓓ	59 Ⓐ Ⓑ Ⓒ Ⓓ
10 Ⓐ Ⓑ Ⓒ Ⓓ	35 Ⓐ Ⓑ Ⓒ Ⓓ	60 Ⓐ Ⓑ Ⓒ Ⓓ
11 Ⓐ Ⓑ Ⓒ Ⓓ	36 Ⓐ Ⓑ Ⓒ Ⓓ	
12 Ⓐ Ⓑ Ⓒ Ⓓ	37 Ⓐ Ⓑ Ⓒ Ⓓ	
13 Ⓐ Ⓑ Ⓒ Ⓓ	38 Ⓐ Ⓑ Ⓒ Ⓓ	
14 Ⓐ Ⓑ Ⓒ Ⓓ	39 Ⓐ Ⓑ Ⓒ Ⓓ	
15 Ⓐ Ⓑ Ⓒ Ⓓ	40 Ⓐ Ⓑ Ⓒ Ⓓ	
16 Ⓐ Ⓑ Ⓒ Ⓓ	41 Ⓐ Ⓑ Ⓒ Ⓓ	
17 Ⓐ Ⓑ Ⓒ Ⓓ	42 Ⓐ Ⓑ Ⓒ Ⓓ	
18 Ⓐ Ⓑ Ⓒ Ⓓ	43 Ⓐ Ⓑ Ⓒ Ⓓ	
19 Ⓐ Ⓑ Ⓒ Ⓓ	44 Ⓐ Ⓑ Ⓒ Ⓓ	
20 Ⓐ Ⓑ Ⓒ Ⓓ	45 Ⓐ Ⓑ Ⓒ Ⓓ	
21 Ⓐ Ⓑ Ⓒ Ⓓ	46 Ⓐ Ⓑ Ⓒ Ⓓ	
22 Ⓐ Ⓑ Ⓒ Ⓓ	47 Ⓐ Ⓑ Ⓒ Ⓓ	
23 Ⓐ Ⓑ Ⓒ Ⓓ	48 Ⓐ Ⓑ Ⓒ Ⓓ	
24 Ⓐ Ⓑ Ⓒ Ⓓ	49 Ⓐ Ⓑ Ⓒ Ⓓ	
25 Ⓐ Ⓑ Ⓒ Ⓓ	50 Ⓐ Ⓑ Ⓒ Ⓓ	

PRACTICE TEST 1

SECTION 1: LISTENING COMPREHENSION

Time: Approximately 30 Minutes
50 Questions

For Practice Test 1, insert your listening comprehension cassette in your tape player. Begin on side 1. On the actual TOEFL you will be given extra time to go on to the next page when you finish a page in the listening comprehension section. In the following test, however, you will have only the 12 seconds given after each question. Turn the page as soon as you have marked your answer. Start the cassette now.

Part A

DIRECTIONS

For each problem in Part A, you will hear a short statement. The statements will be *spoken* just one time. They will not be written out for you, and you must listen carefully in order to understand what the speaker says.

When you hear a statement, read the four sentences in your test book and decide which one is closest in meaning to the statement you have heard. Then, on your answer sheet, find the number of the problem and mark your answer.

1. (A) Sally went to the wrong class.
   (B) Sally was late for class because she got lost.
   (C) Sally missed the class.
   (D) Sally had some trouble finding the class, but she arrived on time.

2. (A) Jane is going on vacation.
   (B) Jane is leaving her job temporarily for health reasons.
   (C) During the summer, Jane often misses work because of illness.
   (D) Jane is sick of working all the time.

3. (A) Henry arrived at work on time this morning.
   (B) Henry was two hours late this morning.
   (C) Henry worked late today.
   (D) Henry was an hour late for work this morning.

4. (A) I'm not sure which type of flowers Jane sent me.
   (B) Jane received many kinds of flowers.
   (C) I received many kinds of flowers from Jane.
   (D) I appreciate Jane's sending me flowers when I was ill.

5. (A) William slept all the way from Georgia to New York.
   (B) George didn't sleep at all on the trip.
   (C) William was half asleep all the time that he was driving.
   (D) William didn't sleep at all on the trip.

6. (A) Too many people came to the meeting.
   (B) There were not enough people at the meeting to inspect the documents.
   (C) We had expected more people to come to the meeting.
   (D) There were not enough seats for all the people.

7. (A) The professor said he was sorry that he had not announced the test sooner.
   (B) The professor was sorry that he had forgotten to bring the tests to class.
   (C) The professor was sorry that he hadn't given the test earlier.
   (D) The professor said he was sorry that he had not given the results of the test sooner.

8. (A) Mary is taking a leave of absence from her job because of her health.
   (B) Mary is not going to return to her job.
   (C) Mary is right to quit her job.
   (D) Mary did very good work, but now she is quitting her job.

9. (A) John will be able to buy groceries.
   (B) John doesn't have enough money to buy groceries.
   (C) John wouldn't buy groceries even if he had enough money.
   (D) John can't find his grocery money.

10. (A) Harry sold no magazines.
    (B) Harry sold only one magazine.
    (C) Harry has never sold as many magazines as he sold today.
    (D) Harry sold five magazines at one house.

11. (A) Eighty people came to the rally.
    (B) Forty people came to the rally.
    (C) One hundred sixty people came to the rally.
    (D) One hundred people came to the rally.

12. (A) We are going to meet Fred and Mary at the movies if we have time.
    (B) We went to the movies with Fred and Mary, but the theater was closed.
    (C) We couldn't meet Fred and Mary at the movies because we didn't have any money.
    (D) Fred and Mary were supposed to meet us at the movies, but their car broke down.

13. (A) Frank told the contractor to do the work in spite of the cost.
    (B) Frank told the contractor that the price was too high.
    (C) Frank cannot afford the work on his house.
    (D) Frank repaired his own house.

14. (A) I studied last night because I had to.
    (B) I tried to study last night, but the material was too hard.
    (C) I couldn't study last night because I was very tired.
    (D) I studied last night because I was bored.

15. (A) John was supposed to give the awards at the banquet, but he didn't.
    (B) John was given an award, but he refused it.
    (C) John didn't go to the banquet.
    (D) John went to the awards banquet, but he refused to give a speech.

16. (A) Edna goes to a movie every year.
    (B) Edna hasn't gone to a movie yet this year, but last year she did.
    (C) Edna doesn't go to a movie unless she has the time.
    (D) Edna hasn't seen a movie for a long time.

17. (A) He is out of sugar.
    (B) He puts only sugar in his coffee.
    (C) There isn't enough sugar in his coffee.
    (D) He likes sugar, but the coffee he is drinking has too much.

18. (A) Arnold was embarrassed because his date wanted to pay for her own meal.
    (B) Arnold had less than $15.
    (C) Arnold didn't want his date to know how much the food cost.
    (D) Arnold didn't want to pay for his date's meal.

19. (A) George didn't have $1,000 for the man.
    (B) George wanted more than $1,000 for the car.
    (C) George agreed to take $1,000 for his car.
    (D) George thought that $1,000 was too much to pay for a used car.

20. (A) Harvey turned around to answer the teacher's question.
    (B) Harvey is an intelligent student.
    (C) Harvey must have been embarrassed.
    (D) Harvey looked in the red book for the answer to the question.

GO ON TO PART B

Part B

DIRECTIONS

In Part B, you will hear 15 short conversations between two speakers. At the end of each conversation, a third voice will ask a question about what was said. The question will be *spoken* just one time. After you hear a conversation and the question about it, read the four possible answers and decide which one would be the best answer to the question you have heard. Then, on your answer sheet, find the number of the problem and mark your answer.

21. (A) She's tired of teaching.   (C) She's changing jobs.
    (B) She was dismissed from her   (D) The school is too hot.
        job.

22. (A) She got up later than usual.   (C) She forgot her class.
    (B) The bus was late.   (D) Her clock was wrong.

23. (A) $39   (B) $35   (C) $4   (D) $5

24. (A) She thinks his lectures are boring.
    (B) She thinks his tests are too long.
    (C) She doesn't like his choice of test questions.
    (D) She doesn't think he prepares well enough.

25. (A) getting a suntan   (C) taking a bath
    (B) swimming   (D) watching for an eclipse

26. (A) looking for water   (C) looking for something
    (B) planting something   (D) getting dirty

27. (A) a movie   (C) a soccer game
    (B) a documentary   (D) a comedy

28. (A) America   (B) England   (C) Switzerland   (D) Sweden

29. (A) 2:50   (B) 2:15   (C) 3:50   (D) 3:15

30. (A) The woman will go home for dinner.
    (B) The woman won't go to the concert.
    (C) The man and woman will eat together.
    (D) Both of them will go home before going to the concert.

31. (A) Wiwtner   (B) Wittner   (C) Wittmer   (D) Witner

32. (A) 7:55   (B) 7:45   (C) 7:50   (D) 8:00

33. (A) $17.50   (B) $19.95   (C) $35   (D) $70

34. (A) 5   (B) 3   (C) 2   (D) 8

35. (A) on a train   (C) on a plane
    (B) on a boat   (D) on a bus

GO ON TO PART C

Part C

DIRECTIONS

In this part of the test, you will hear several short talks and/or conversations. After each talk or conversation, you will be asked some questions. The talks and questions will be *spoken* just one time. They will not be written out for you, so you will have to listen carefully in order to understand and remember what the speaker says.

When you hear a question, read the four possible answers in your test book and decide which one would be the best answer to the question you have heard. Then, on your answer sheet, find the number of the problem and fill in the space that corresponds to the letter of the answer you have chosen.

36. (A) Spain   (C) Florida
    (B) Latin America   (D) America

37. (A) soccer   (C) football
    (B) handball   (D) horse racing

38. (A) Jai alai is one of the fastest-moving games.
    (B) Jai alai requires a great deal of skill and endurance.
    (C) Jai alai can be played as singles or doubles.
    (D) It is illegal to bet on Florida jai alai games.

39. (A) baseball   (C) handball
    (B) Ping-Pong   (D) badminton

40. (A) in a clothing store   (C) at a bank
    (B) in customs   (D) in a liquor store

41. (A) 1   (B) 2   (C) 3   (D) 4

42. (A) four weeks   (C) four months
    (B) three weeks   (D) two months

43. (A) plants   (B) rum   (C) meat   (D) $100

44. (A) multiple telegraph   (C) aviation
    (B) telephone   (D) acoustics

45. (A) acoustical science   (C) adventure
    (B) aviation   (D) architecture

46. (A) He worked very hard, but never achieved success.
    (B) He spent so many years working in aviation because he wanted to be a pilot.
    (C) He dedicated his life to science and the well-being of mankind.
    (D) He worked with the deaf so that he could invent the telephone.

47. (A) Bell was born in the eighteenth century.
    (B) Bell worked with the deaf.
    (C) Bell experimented with the science of acoustics.
    (D) Bell invented a multiple telegraph.

48. (A) 100   (B) 25   (C) 35   (D) 50

49. (A) He wrote an adventure novel.
    (B) He was a spy.
    (C) He was a bullfighter.
    (D) He wrote about bullfighting.

50. (A) a thrilling novel of espionage
    (B) an account of bullfighting
    (C) a history of Spain
    (D) a biography of Ernest Hemingway

STOP. THIS IS THE END OF THE LISTENING COMPREHENSION SECTION.

SECTION II: STRUCTURE AND WRITTEN EXPRESSION

Time: 25 Minutes
40 Questions

Part A

DIRECTIONS

Each sentence in Part A is an incomplete sentence. Four words or phrases, marked (A), (B), (C), (D), are given beneath each sentence. You are to choose the *one* word or phrase that best completes the sentence. Then, on your answer sheet, find the number of the problem and mark your answer.

1. After the funeral, the residents of the apartment building
   _____.
   - (A) sent faithfully flowers all weeks to the cemetery
   - (B) sent to the cemetery each week flowers faithfully
   - (C) sent flowers faithfully to the cemetery each week
   - (D) sent each week faithfully to the cemetery flowers

2. Because the first pair of pants did not fit properly, he asked for
   _____.
   - (A) another pants   (C) the others ones
   - (B) others pants   (D) another pair

3. The committee has met and _____.
   - (A) they have reached a decision
   - (B) it has formulated themselves some opinions
   - (C) its decision was reached at
   - (D) it has reached a decision

4. Alfred Adams has not _____.
   - (A) lived lonelynessly in times previous
   - (B) never before lived sole
   - (C) ever lived alone before
   - (D) before lived without the company of his friends

5. John's score on the test is the highest in the class; _____.
   - (A) he should study last night
   - (B) he should have studied last night
   - (C) he must have studied last night
   - (D) he must had to study last night

6. Henry will not be able to attend the meeting tonight because
   _____.
   - (A) he must to teach a class   (C) of he will teach a class
   - (B) he will be teaching a class (D) he will have teaching a class

7. Having been served lunch, _____.
    (A) the problem was discussed by the members of the committee
    (B) the committee members discussed the problem
    (C) it was discussed by the committee members the problem
    (D) a discussion of the problem was made by the members of the committee

8. Florida has not yet ratified the Equal Rights Amendment, and _____.
    (A) several other states hasn't either
    (B) neither has some of the others states
    (C) some other states also have not either
    (D) neither have several other states

9. The chairman requested that _____.
    (A) the members studied more carefully the problem
    (B) the problem was more carefulnessly studied
    (C) with more carefulness the problem could be studied
    (D) the members study the problem more carefully

10. California relies heavily on income from fruit crops, and _____.
    (A) Florida also   (C) Florida is as well
    (B) Florida too   (D) so does Florida

11. The professor said that _____.
    (A) the students can turn over their reports on the Monday
    (B) the reports on Monday could be received from the students by him
    (C) the students could hand in their reports on Monday
    (D) the students will on Monday the reports turn in

12. This year will be difficult for this organization because _____.
    (A) they have less money and volunteers than they had last year
    (B) it has less money and fewer volunteers than it had last year
    (C) the last year it did not have as few and little volunteers and money
    (D) there are fewer money and volunteers that in the last year there were

13. The teachers have had some problems deciding _____.
    (A) when to the students they shall return the final papers
    (B) when are they going to return to the students the final papers
    (C) when they should return the final papers to the students
    (D) the time when the final papers they should return for the students

14. She wanted to serve some coffee to her guests; however, _____.

    (A) she hadn't many sugar

    (B) there was not a great amount of the sugar

    (C) she did not have much sugar

    (D) she was lacking in amount of the sugar

15. There has not been a great response to the sale, _____?

    (A) does there   (B) hasn't there   (C) hasn't it   (D) has there

GO ON TO PART B

Part B

DIRECTIONS

Each sentence in Part B has four words or phrases underlined. The four underlined parts of the sentence are marked (A), (B), (C), (D). You are to identify the *one* underlined word or phrase that should be corrected or rewritten. Then, on your answer sheet, find the number of the problem and mark your answer.

16. The main office of the factory can be found in Maple
     A   B C
Street in New York City.
     D

17. Because there are less members present tonight than there
             A   B
were last night, we must wait until the next meeting to vote.
  C   D

18. David is particularly fond of cooking, and he
           A   B
often cooks really delicious meals.
    C   D

19. The progress made in space travel for the early 1960s is remarkable.
     A   B   C   D

20. Sandra has not rarely missed a play or concert since
           A   B   C
she was seventeen years old.
        D

21. The governor has not decided how to deal with the new
   A   B   C
problems already.
      D

22. There was a very interesting news on the radio this
      A   B   C
    morning about the earthquake in Italy.
             D

23. The professor had already given the homework assignment
                                    A
    when he had remembered that Monday was a holiday.
             B   C   D

24. Having been beaten by the police for striking an officer,
                 A   B
    the man will cry out in pain.
      C   D

25. This table is not sturdy enough to support a television,
                 A   B
    and that one probably isn't neither.
       C   D

26. The bridge was hitting by a large ship during a sudden storm last week.
            A   B   C   D

27. The company representative sold to the manager a sewing
       A   B   C
    machine for forty dollars.
         D

28. The taxi driver told the man to don't allow his disobedient
       A   B   C
    son to hang out the window.
       D

29. These televisions are quite popular in Europe, but those ones are not.
               A   B   C   D

30. Harvey seldom pays his bills on time, and his brother does too.
           A   B   C   D

31. The price of crude oil used to be a great deal lower
       A   B   C
    than now, wasn't it?
         D

32. When an university formulates new regulations, it
       A   B   C
    must relay its decision to the students and faculty.
       D

33. Jim was upset last night because he had to do too many homeworks.
          A   B   C   D

34. There is some scissors in the desk drawer in the
        A   B   C   D
    bedroom if you need them.

35. The Board of Realtors doesn't have any informations
                                          A
    about the increase in rent for this area.
        B   C   D

36. George is not enough intelligent to pass this economics
                   A   B   C   D
    class without help.

37. There were so much people trying to leave the burning building
              A   B   C
    that the police had a great deal of trouble controlling them.
        D

38. John lived in New York since 1960 to 1975, but he
              A   B
    is now living in Detroit.
        C   D

39. The fire began in the fifth floor of the hotel, but it
                   A   B   C
    soon spread to adjacent floors.
        D

40. Mrs. Anderson bought last week a new sports car; however,
                        A   B
    she has yet to learn how to operate the manual gearshift.
        C   D

STOP. THIS IS THE END OF THE STRUCTURE AND WRITTEN EXPRESSION
SECTION. IF YOU FINISH BEFORE TIME IS UP, CHECK YOUR WORK ON PARTS A
AND B OF THIS SECTION ONLY. DO NOT WORK ON ANY OTHER SECTION OF THE
TEST.

SECTION III: READING COMPREHENSION AND VOCABULARY

Time: 45 Minutes
60 Questions

Part A

DIRECTIONS

Each sentence in Part A has a word or phrase underlined. Below each sentence are four other words or phrases. You are to choose the *one* word or phrase which would *best keep the meaning* of the original sentence if it were substituted for the underlined word.

1. Plato's teachings had a profound effect on Aristotle.
   - (A) depth
   - (B) affection
   - (C) affliction
   - (D) influence

2. The superintendent was the principal speaker at the school board meeting.
   - (A) only
   - (B) main
   - (C) outstanding
   - (D) strongest

3. The campers heard a strange rustling in the trees.
   - (A) stealing
   - (B) pillaging
   - (C) movement
   - (D) fight

4. He was an exemplary prisoner despite his past experience.
   - (A) model
   - (B) sample
   - (C) honest
   - (D) humble

5. The hotel manager became suspicious of those people who were loitering in the lobby.
   - (A) bustling
   - (B) sleeping
   - (C) meddling
   - (D) loafing

6. We decided to pay for the furniture on the installment plan.
   - (A) cash and carry
   - (B) piece by piece
   - (C) monthly payment
   - (D) credit card

7. Boys' Clubs do not deprive poor children of the opportunity to participate in sports.
   - (A) deny
   - (B) retract
   - (C) improvise
   - (D) dilute

8. The supervisor dictated a <u>memo</u> to her secretary.
   (A) letter
   (B) note
   (C) report
   (D) research paper

9. Picasso was a <u>well-known</u> cubist painter.
   (A) artistic
   (B) colorful
   (C) celebrated
   (D) knowledgeable

10. The <u>inquiry</u> concerning the accident was handled by the chief of police.
    (A) gossip
    (B) inquisitiveness
    (C) investigation
    (D) recording

11. The department chairman refused to authorize the <u>requisition</u>.
    (A) request
    (B) transfer
    (C) grant
    (D) project

12. It is <u>imperative</u> that they arrive on time for the lecture.
    (A) necessary
    (B) suggested
    (C) hoped
    (D) intended

13. The counterfeit bills were a good <u>facsimile</u> of the real ones.
    (A) factorial
    (B) reproduction
    (C) identification
    (D) similarity

14. The Montforts have decided to take a cruise, so they went to the travel agency for some <u>brochures</u>.
    (A) questions
    (B) inquisition
    (C) price lists
    (D) pamphlets

15. Scott <u>seized</u> the opportunity to present his proposal to the director.
    (A) realized
    (B) grasped
    (C) rendered
    (D) delivered

16. The <u>boundary</u> between Canada and the United States has been unfortified for over one hundred years.
    (A) border
    (B) bridge
    (C) water
    (D) diplomatic relations

17. While they were away on vacation, they allowed their mail to <u>accumulate</u> at the post office.
    (A) be delivered
    (B) pile up
    (C) get lost
    (D) be returned

18. The professor tried to <u>stimulate</u> interest in archaeology by taking his students on expeditions.
    (A) simulate
    (B) fake
    (C) encourage
    (D) diminish

19. John's unsportsmanlike behavior caused him to be <u>ostracized</u> by the other members of the country club.
    (A) shunned
    (B) excelled
    (C) readmitted
    (D) wavered

20. As a result of the accident, the police <u>revoked</u> his driver's license.
    (A) reconsidered
    (B) exorcised
    (C) canceled
    (D) investigated

21. After listening to the testimony, the members of the jury delivered their <u>verdict</u>.
    (A) sentence
    (B) decision
    (C) cross-examination
    (D) foreman

22. The children were <u>frolicking</u> in the park.
    (A) running playfully
    (B) gloating
    (C) sulking
    (D) endangering

23. <u>Efficient</u> air service has been made available through modern technology.
    (A) affluent
    (B) modern
    (C) inexpensive
    (D) effective

24. Fear of pirate <u>raids</u> caused the Spaniards to fortify their coastline.
    (A) invasions
    (B) ships
    (C) arms
    (D) investigations

25. Nearly half of the town's inhabitants are descendants of <u>indigenous</u> civilizations.
    (A) native
    (B) backward
    (C) hard-working
    (D) poor

26. That area of the country is <u>laced</u> with large and often dangerous rivers.
    (A) criss-crossed
    (B) decorated
    (C) ornate
    (D) diluted

27. After a long lunch hour, business <u>resumes</u> as usual.
    (A) responds
    (B) delays
    (C) continues
    (D) resurfaces

28. Twenty-five percent of Ecuador's population speak Quechua <u>exclusively</u>.
    (A) mainly
    (B) only
    (C) voluptuously
    (D) still

29. The Chinese people worship their <u>ancestors</u>.
    (A) fossils
    (B) elders
    (C) forefathers
    (D) heirs

30. Under the major's able <u>leadership</u>, the soldiers found safety.
    (A) guidance   (C) flagship
    (B) intensity   (D) ability

GO ON TO PART B

Part B

DIRECTIONS

In Part B, the questions are based on a variety of reading material (single sentences, paragraphs, advertisements, and the like). You are to choose the *one* best answer, (A), (B), (C), or (D), to each question. Then, on your answer sheet, find the number of the problem and mark your answer. Answer all questions following a passage on the basis of what is *stated* or *implied* in that passage.

Questions 31 through 36 are based on the following reading.

The Stone Age was a period of history which began in approximately 2 million B.C. and lasted until 3000 B.C. Its name was derived from the stone tools and weapons that modern scientists found. This period was divided into the Paleolithic, Mesolithic, and Neolithic Ages. During the first period, (2 million to 8000 B.C.) the fist hatchet and use of fire for heating and cooking were developed. As a result of the Ice Age, which evolved about 1 million years into the Paleolithic Age, people were forced to seek shelter in caves, wear clothing, and develop new tools.

During the Mesolithic Age (8000 to 6000 B.C.) people made crude pottery and the first fish hooks, took dogs hunting, and developed a bow and arrow, which was used until the fourteenth century A.D.

The Neolithic Age (6000 to 3000 B.C.) saw humankind domesticating sheep, goats, pigs, and cattle, being less nomadic than in previous eras, establishing permanent settlements, and creating governments.

31. Into how many periods was the Stone Age divided?
    (A) 2   (B) 3   (C) 4   (D) 5

32. Which of the following was developed earliest?
    (A) the fish hook   (C) the bow and arrow
    (B) the fist hatchet   (D) pottery

33. Which of the following developments is *not* related to the conditions of the Ice Age?
    (A) farming   (C) living indoors
    (B) clothing   (D) using fire

34. Which period lasted longest?
   (A) Paleolithic
   (B) Ice Age
   (C) Mesolithic
   (D) Neolithic

35. Which of the following periods saw people develop a more communal form of living?
   (A) Paleolithic
   (B) Ice Age
   (C) Mesolithic
   (D) Neolithic

36. The author states that the Stone Age was so named because
   (A) it was very durable
   (B) the tools and weapons were made of stone
   (C) there was little vegetation
   (D) the people lived in caves

Questions 37 through 41 are based on the following reading.

Hot boning is an energy saving technique for the meat processing industry. It has received considerable attention in recent years when increased pressure for energy conservation has accentuated the need for more efficient methods of processing the bovine carcass. Cooling of an entire carcass requires a considerable amount of refrigerated space, since bone and trimmable fat are cooled along with the muscle. It is also necessary to space the carcasses adequately in the refrigerated room for better air movement and prevention of microbial contamination, thus adding to the volume requirements for carcass chillers.

Conventional handling of meat involves holding the beef sides in the cooler for 24 to 36 hours before boning. Chilling in the traditional fashion is also associated with a loss of carcass weight ranging from 2% to 4% due to evaporation of moisture from the meat tissue.

Early excision, or hot boning, of muscle prerigor followed by vacuum packaging has several potential advantages. By removing only the edible muscle and fat prerigor, refrigeration space and costs are minimized, boning labor is decreased and storage yields increased. Because hot boning often results in toughening of meat, a more recent approach, hot boning following electrical stimulation, has been used to reduce the necessary time of rigor mortis. Some researchers have found this method beneficial in maintaining tender meat, while others have found that the meat also becomes tough after electrical stimulation.

37. Which of the following was *not* mentioned as a drawback of the conventional methods of boning?
   (A) storage space requirements
   (B) energy waste
   (C) loss of carcass weight
   (D) toughness of meat

38. Hot boning is becoming very popular because
    (A) it causes meat to be very tender
    (B) it helps conserve energy and is less expensive than conventional methods
    (C) meat tastes better when the bone is adequately seared along with the meat
    (D) it reduces the weight of the carcass

39. *Carcass chiller* means most nearly
    (A) a refrigerator for the animal body
    (B) a method of boning meat
    (C) electrical stimulation of beef
    (D) early excision

40. *Early excision* means most nearly
    (A) vacuum packaging   (C) carcass chilling
    (B) hot boning   (D) electrical stimulation

41. The toughening of meat during hot boning has been combatted by
    (A) following hot boning with electrical stimulation
    (B) tenderizing the meat
    (C) using electrical stimulation before hot boning
    (D) removing only the edible muscle and fat prerigor

Questions 42 through 46 are based on the following reading.

In 1920, after some thirty-nine years of problems with disease, high costs, and politics, the Panama Canal was officially opened, finally linking the Atlantic and Pacific Oceans by allowing ships to pass through the fifty-mile canal zone instead of traveling some seven thousand miles around Cape Horn. It takes a ship approximately eight hours to complete the trip through the canal and costs an average of fifteen thousand dollars, one-tenth of what it would cost an average ship to round the Horn. More than fifteen thousand ships pass through its locks each year.

The French initiated the project but sold their rights to the United States. The latter will control it until the end of the twentieth century when Panama takes over its duties.

42. Who currently controls the Panama Canal?
    (A) France   (C) Panama
    (B) United States   (D) Canal Zone

43. In approximately what year will a different government take control of the Panama Canal?
    (A) 2000   (B) 2100   (C) 3001   (D) 2999

44. On the average, how much would it cost a ship to travel around Cape Horn?
    (A) $1,500   (C) $150,000
    (B) $15,000   (D) $1,500,000

45. In what year was construction probably begun on the canal?
    (A) 1881   (B) 1920   (C) 1939   (D) 1999

46. What can be inferred from this reading?
    (A) This is a costly project which should be reevaluated.
    (B) Despite all the problems involved, the project is beneficial.
    (C) Many captains prefer to sail around Cape Horn because it is less expensive.
    (D) Due to all the problems, three governments have had to control the canal over the years.

Questions 47 through 51 are based on the following reading.

In 776 B.C. the first Olympic Games were held at the foot of Mount Olympus to honor the Greeks' chief god, Zeus. The Greeks emphasized physical fitness and strength in their education of youth. Therefore, contests in running, jumping, discus and javelin throwing, boxing, and horse and chariot racing were held in individual cities, and the winners competed every four years at Mount Olympus. Winners were greatly honored by having olive wreaths placed on their heads and having poems sung about their deeds. Originally these were held as games of friendship, and any wars in progress were halted to allow the games to take place.

The Greeks attached so much importance to these games that they calculated time in four-year cycles called "Olympiads" dating from 776 B.C.

47. Which of the following is *not* true?
    (A) Winners placed olive wreaths on their own heads.
    (B) The games were held in Greece every four years.
    (C) Battles were interrupted to participate in the games.
    (D) Poems glorified the winners in song.

48. Why were the Olympic Games held?
    (A) to stop wars   (C) to crown the best athletes
    (B) to honor Zeus   (D) to sing songs about the athletes

49. Approximately how many years ago did these games originate?
    (A) 776 years   (C) 2,277 years
    (B) 1,205 years   (D) 2,760 years

50. Which of the following contests was *not* mentioned?
    (A) discus throwing   (C) skating
    (B) boxing   (D) running

51. What conclusion can we draw about the ancient Greeks?
    (A) They liked to fight.
    (B) They were very athletic.
    (C) They liked a lot of ceremony.
    (D) They couldn't count, so they used "Olympiads" for dates.

Questions 52 through 54 are based on the following reading.

Tampa, Florida, owes a great deal of its growth and prosperity to a Cuban cigar manufacturer named Vicente Martínez Ybor. When the Cuban Revolution broke out in 1869, he was forced to flee his country and moved his business to south Florida. Sixteen years later, serious problems caused him to seek a better location along the west coast of the state. His original land purchase of sixteen blocks expanded to more than one hundred acres near Tampa. This newly developed area was called Ybor City in his honor. With the demand for factory workers for Ybor's business, the surrounding areas expanded and thrived.

52. Where is Ybor City located?
    (A) south Florida   (C) west Florida
    (B) Cuba   (D) in the Florida countryside

53. In what year was Ybor forced to leave south Florida?
    (A) 1854   (B) 1869   (C) 1885   (D) 1895

54. Why will people probably continue to remember Ybor's name?
    (A) He suffered a great deal.
    (B) An area was named in his honor.
    (C) He was a Cuban revolutionary.
    (D) He was forced to flee his homeland.

Questions 55 through 58 are based on the following reading.

Lichens are a unique group of complex, flowerless plants growing on rocks and trees. There are thousands of kinds of lichens, which come in a wide variety of colors. They are composed of algae and fungi which unite to satisfy the needs of the lichens.

The autotrophic green algae produce all their own food through a process called photosynthesis and provide the lichen with nutritional elements. On the other hand, the heterotrophic fungus, which depends on other elements to provide its food, not only absorbs and stores water for the plant, but also helps protect it. This union by which two dissimilar organisms live together is called "symbiosis."

This sharing enables lichens to resist the most adverse environmental conditions found on earth. They can be found in some very unlikely places such as the polar ice caps as well as in tropical zones, in dry areas as well as in wet ones, on mountain peaks and along coastal areas.

The lichen's strong resistance to its hostile environment and its ability to live in harmony with such environments is one example that humanity should consider in trying to solve its own problems.

55. Which of the following is *not* true?
    (A) Lichens are not simple plants.
    (B) The lichen habitat is limited to the polar ice caps.
    (C) Lichens can resist a hostile environment.
    (D) Heterotrophic plants depend on other elements to supply their food.

56. What can be said about autotrophic plants and heterotrophic plants?
    (A) They produce their food in the same manner.
    (B) Heterotrophic plants produce all their own food.
    (C) Autotrophic plants need other elements to supply their food.
    (D) Their methods of food production are completely different.

57. Which of the following conclusions could be made about lichens?
    (A) They are found worldwide and are complex plants made up of algae and fungi.
    (B) They are found worldwide and are simple plants, symbiotic in nature.
    (C) They are found worldwide and are compound plants made up entirely of algae.
    (D) Although found worldwide, lichens are found mostly as a simple plant form in the tropics.

58. Which of the following directly relates to algae?
    (A) It offers protection to lichens.
    (B) It supplies water for lichens.
    (C) It supplies its own food.
    (D) It is dependent on other plants for its food supply.

Directions for questions 59 and 60

For each of these questions, choose the answer that is *closest in meaning* to the original sentence. Note that several of the choices may be factually correct, but you should choose the one that is the *closest restatement of the given sentence*.

59. Even though Julie is a champion swimmer, she still practices every day.
    (A) Julie practices swimming every day despite the fact that she's a champion swimmer.
    (B) Even though Julie practices every day, she's still a champion swimmer.
    (C) If Julie practices every day, she'll be a champion swimmer.
    (D) Julie swims every day; consequently she's a champion swimmer.

60. Mrs. Sylvester will retire next month after teaching chemistry for twenty years.
    (A) Twenty years after teaching chemistry, Mrs. Sylvester will retire.
    (B) After she has finished teaching chemistry for twenty years, Mrs. Sylvester will retire.
    (C) Having taught chemistry for twenty years, Mrs. Sylvester will retire next month.
    (D) It will be twenty years next month since Mrs. Sylvester retired.

STOP. THIS IS THE END OF THE EXAMINATION. IF YOU FINISH BEFORE TIME IS UP, CHECK YOUR WORK ON PARTS A AND B OF THE READING COMPREHENSION AND VOCABULARY SECTION ONLY. DO NOT RETURN TO ANY OTHER SECTION OF THE TEST.

PRACTICE TEST 2

SECTION 1: LISTENING COMPREHENSION

Time: Approximately 30 Minutes
50 Questions

For Practice Test 2, restart your listening comprehension cassette immediately following Practice Test 1 on side 1. On the actual TOEFL you will be given extra time to go on to the next page when you finish a page in the listening comprehension section. In the following test, however, you will have only the 12 seconds given after each question. Turn the page as soon as you have marked your answer. Start the cassette now.

Part A

DIRECTIONS

For each problem in Part A, you will hear a short statement. The statements will be *spoken* just one time. They will not be written out for you, and you must listen carefully in order to understand what the speaker says.

When you hear a statement, read the four sentences in your test book and decide which one is closest in meaning to the statement you have heard. Then, on your answer sheet, find the number of the problem and mark your answer.

1. (A) John believes that Swiss cheese is no longer delicious.
   (B) John says that the Swiss cheese makes delicious butter.
   (C) Swiss cheese is the best cheese in John's opinion.
   (D) There are many better cheeses than Swiss in John's eyes.

2. (A) The game is temporarily delayed because of rain.
   (B) There will be no game if it rains.
   (C) There will be a game regardless of the weather.
   (D) It rains every time there is a game.

3. (A) The class began at 1:45. (C) The class began at 1:00.
   (B) The professor arrived at 1:15. (D) The class will begin at 2:00.

4. (A) Mary works in a nursery.
   (B) Mary's children stay in a nursery while she works.
   (C) Mary takes her children to work with her.
   (D) Mary's children are ill today.

5. (A) She knew the answer to the question.
   (B) She had read the material, but she didn't know the answer.
   (C) She was not prepared for class.
   (D) Even though she hadn't read the material, she knew the answer.

6. (A) Thirty people returned the evaluation forms.
   (B) Sixty people filled out the evaluation forms.
   (C) Eight people returned their forms.
   (D) Only thirty people received the evaluation forms.

7. (A) Peter is a professional musician.
   (B) Peter is very talented, but he will never be a professional musician because he doesn't practice.
   (C) Peter practices every day, but he will never be a professional musician.
   (D) Peter doesn't want to be a professional musician because he wants to practice law.

8. (A) If the weather is nice, we intend to spend the weekend at home.
   (B) If the nice weather holds out, we'll spend the weekend in the country.
   (C) If the weather were nicer, we would spend the weekend in the country.
   (D) If the weather gets nicer, we'll spend the weekend in the country.

9. (A) Dan and his family will move to Florida when he quits his job here.
   (B) As soon as Dan's new job in Florida is confirmed, he and his family will move there.
   (C) Dan wants to move to Florida, but he can't find a job there.
   (D) Dan plans to move to Florida when he retires.

10. (A) Only the seven-year-old boy saw the terrible accident.
    (B) No one at all saw the seven-year-old's terrible accident.
    (C) The seven-year-old boy saw no one in the accident.
    (D) No one in the terrible accident saw the seven-year-old boy.

11. (A) My father doesn't like fishing on a hot, summer day.
    (B) Although my father likes fishing, he doesn't want to do it on a hot, summer day.
    (C) Fishing is my father's favorite enjoyment on a hot, summer day.
    (D) My father loves to eat hot fish for breakfast in the summer.

12. (A) Louise writes and speaks Spanish equally well.
    (B) Louise both writes and speaks Spanish, but she writes better.
    (C) Even though Louise writes Spanish, she speaks it better.
    (D) Louise doesn't like to write Spanish, but she speaks it.

13. (A) When the production had begun, the actors realized that they should have practiced more.
    (B) Before the production began, the actors reviewed their lines one more time.
    (C) Although the actors had practiced for months, the production was a flop.
    (D) The actors went to the theater in two separate cars.

14. (A) Ms. Daly gave the class an assignment.
    (B) Ms. Daly gave the students a hand with their assignments.
    (C) Ms. Daly asked the students to turn in their assignments.
    (D) Ms. Daly asked the students to raise their hands if they wanted to ask a question about the assignment.

15. (A) Peter and Lucy missed the homework assignment, but they turned it in later.
    (B) Peter and Lucy hate each other since their argument.
    (C) Peter and Lucy caught a baby squirrel, but they soon let it go.
    (D) Peter and Lucy had an argument, but now they are friends again.

16. (A) This morning I woke up after 7:30.
    (B) My alarm clock did not work this morning.
    (C) This morning I woke up at 7:30, but I usually wake up earlier.
    (D) I slept over at a friend's house last night.

17. (A) If we go on vacation, Mary will stay at our house.
    (B) After we return from vacation, we are going to buy a dog.
    (C) Mary will take care of our dog while we are on a vacation.
    (D) Mary will be very tired after the long vacation.

18. (A) John arrived at 9:00.
    (B) John arrived at 8:00.
    (C) John should have arrived at 8:00, but he didn't.
    (D) John arrived too late to eat.

19. (A) The game of golf originated in the United States.
    (B) The game of golf is very popular in Scotland.
    (C) The game of golf originated in the United States, but now it is more popular in Scotland.
    (D) The game of golf originated in Scotland, but now it is more popular in the United States.

20. (A) I saw my aunt and uncle thirteen years ago.
    (B) My aunt and uncle arrived thirty years ago.
    (C) I haven't seen my aunt and uncle for thirty years.
    (D) I see my aunt and uncle once every thirteen years.

GO ON TO PART B

Part B

DIRECTIONS

In Part B, you will hear 15 short conversations between two speakers. At the end of each conversation, a third voice will ask a question about what was said. The question will be *spoken* just one time. After you hear a conversation and the question about it, read the four possible answers and decide which one would be the best answer to the question you have heard. Then, on your answer sheet, find the number of the problem and mark your answer.

21. (A) $100   (B) $115   (C) $126   (D) $150

22. (A) They both liked it.
    (B) Neither liked it.
    (C) The mother didn't like it, but the father did.
    (D) The mother didn't like it because it wasn't in English.

23. (A) a taxi   (B) a plane   (C) a boat   (D) a bus

24. (A) a supermarket   (C) a drugstore
    (B) a department store   (D) a car repair shop

25. (A) The teacher postponed the conference.
    (B) There won't be a test this afternoon.
    (C) The students will be attending the conference.
    (D) The students took a science test that afternoon.

26. (A) The program was on too late.
    (B) The rain didn't let up until after the speech.
    (C) He doesn't like the president.
    (D) He had a late class.

27. (A) lawyer-client   (C) dentist-patient
    (B) doctor-patient   (D) bank teller-customer

28. (A) 4:45   (B) 5:15   (C) 5:45   (D) 8:45

29. (A) She's not hungry.
    (B) She's at the dentist's.
    (C) The food tastes like an old shoe.
    (D) She's in too much pain.

30. (A) $3.75   (B) $3.25   (C) $7.50   (D) $15.00

31. (A) packing her own groceries
    (B) not enough variety in meats
    (C) the unreasonable prices
    (D) the attitude of the employees

32. (A) Spain   (B) Sweden   (C) Scotland   (D) Switzerland

33. (A) sail a boat   (C) catch a horse
    (B) hang clothes   (D) fish

34. (A) 12:15   (B) 1:00   (C) 1:10   (D) 12:30

35. (A) home economics   (C) microbiology
    (B) business administration (D) history

GO ON TO PART C

Part C

DIRECTIONS

In this part of the test, you will hear several short talks and/or conversations. After each talk or conversation, you will be asked some questions. The talks and questions will be *spoken* just one time. They will not be written out for you, so you will have to listen carefully in order to understand and remember what the speaker says.

When you hear a question, read the four possible answers in your test book and decide which one would be the best answer to the question you have heard. Then, on your answer sheet, find the number of the problem and fill in the space that corresponds to the letter of the answer you have chosen.

36. (A) She was sick.
    (B) She couldn't make up her mind as to which countries she should visit.
    (C) She couldn't think of a topic for her composition.
    (D) She was totally disorganized.

37. (A) that she take a cruise   (C) that she ride a camel
    (B) that she try to get organized (D) that she write about her trip

38. (A) Hungary   (B) North Africa   (C) Egypt   (D) The Holy Land

39. (A) to pack his bags for his trip (C) He's not feeling well.
    (B) to write his own composition   (D) to pick up some photographs

40. (A) Nathaniel Bacon and his friends fought against Indian marauders.
    (B) Bacon and his friends were Piedmont farmers.
    (C) Bacon and a few farmers marched on the capital to protest the Indian raids.
    (D) Governor Berkeley did not listen to the demands of the farmers.

41. (A) less than 1 year   (C) 10 years
    (B) 5 years   (D) 23 years

42. (A) He was killed by Indians.
    (B) Governor Berkeley had him hanged.
    (C) He succumbed to malaria.
    (D) He was accidentally shot by one of the farmers.

43. (A) type his paper
    (B) help him with his research
    (C) present his findings at the July conference
    (D) verify his findings

44. (A) He's about to leave for a new job.
    (B) He wants to present it at a conference.
    (C) His employer has requested it.
    (D) It's very important for his livelihood.

45. (A) July   (B) September   (C) May   (D) February

46. (A) death of its sculptor   (C) disinterest in the project
    (B) lack of funds   (D) too many Indian raids

47. (A) Abraham Lincoln   (C) Thomas Jefferson
    (B) Franklin Roosevelt   (D) George Washington

48. (A) 27 years old   (C) 60 years old
    (B) 41 years old   (D) 74 years old

49. (A) They bear little resemblance to the people they represent.
    (B) The figures are gigantic, but too serious.
    (C) They portray the characteristics of the people they represent.
    (D) Because they are old and weatherbeaten, the faces are disfigured.

50. (A) This magnificent work of art is located very high in the Black
        Hills.
    (B) Four American presidents have been sculpted as a lasting memorial
        to their leadership.
    (C) It took fourteen years to complete the project.
    (D) Gutzon Borglum was near retirement age when he began this
        project.

STOP. THIS IS THE END OF THE LISTENING COMPREHENSION SECTION.

SECTION II: STRUCTURE AND WRITTEN EXPRESSION

Time: 25 Minutes
40 Questions

Part A

DIRECTIONS

Each sentence in Part A is an incomplete sentence. Four words or phrases, marked (A), (B), (C), (D), are given beneath each sentence. You are to choose the *one* word or phrase that best completes the sentence. Then, on your answer sheet, find the number of the problem and mark your answer.

1. Captain Henry, _____ crept slowly through the underbrush.
    (A) being remote from the enemy,
    (B) attempting to not encounter the enemy,
    (C) trying to avoid the enemy,
    (D) not involving himself in the enemy,

2. Tommy was one _____.
    (A) of the happy childs of his class
    (B) of the happiest child in the class
    (C) child who was the happiest of all the class
    (D) of the happiest children in the class

3. _____ he began to make friends more easily.
    (A) Having entered school in the new city, it was found that
    (B) After entering the new school,
    (C) When he had been entering the new school,
    (D) Upon entering into the new school,

4. It is very difficult to stop the cultivation of marijuana because _____.

    (A) it grows very carelessly   (C) it grows well with little care
    (B) of it's growth without   (D) it doesn't care much to grow
        attention

5. The fact that space exploration has increased dramatically in the past thirty years _____.
    (A) is an evidence of us wanting to know more of our solar system
    (B) indicates that we are very eager to learn all we can about our solar system
    (C) how we want to learn more about the solar system
    (D) is pointing to evidence of our intention to know a lot more about what is called our solar system

6. Many of the current international problems we are now facing _____.
   - (A) linguistic incompetencies
   - (B) are the result of misunderstandings
   - (C) are because of not understanding themselves
   - (D) lacks of the intelligent capabilities of understanding each other

7. Mr. Roberts is a noted chemist _____.
   - (A) as well as an effective teacher
   - (B) and too a very efficient teacher
   - (C) but he teaches very good in addition
   - (D) however he teaches very good also

8. Public television stations are different from commercial stations _____.
   - (A) because they receive money differently and different types of shows
   - (B) for money and program types
   - (C) in the areas of funding and programming
   - (D) because the former receives money and has programs differently from the latter

9. Manufacturers often sacrifice quality _____.
   - (A) for a larger profit margin
   - (B) in place of to earn more money
   - (C) to gain more quantities of money
   - (D) and instead earn a bigger amount of profit

10. Automobile production in the United States _____.
    - (A) have taken slumps and rises in recent years
    - (B) has been rather erratic recently
    - (C) has been erratically lately
    - (D) are going up and down all the time

11. A major problem in the construction of new buildings _____.
    - (A) is that windows have been eliminated while air conditioning systems have not been perfected
    - (B) is they have eliminated windows and still don't have good air conditioning
    - (C) is because windows are eliminated but air conditioners don't work good
    - (D) is dependent on the fact that while they have eliminated windows, they are not capable to produce efficient air conditioning systems

12. John said that no other car could go _____.
    - (A) so fast like his car
    - (B) as fast like his car
    - (C) as fast like the car of him
    - (D) as fast as his car

13. Her grades have improved, but only _____.
    (A) in a small amount   (C) minimum
    (B) very slightly   (D) some

14. While attempting to reach his home before the storm, _____.
    (A) the bicycle of John broke down
    (B) it happened that John's bike broke down
    (C) the storm caught John
    (D) John had an accident on his bicycle

15. The changes in this city have occurred _____.
    (A) with swiftness   (C) fastly
    (B) rapidly   (D) in rapid ways

GO ON TO PART B

Part B

DIRECTIONS

Each sentence in Part B has four words or phrases underlined. The four underlined parts of the sentences are marked (A), (B), (C), (D). You are to identify the *one* underlined word or phrase that should be corrected or rewritten. Then, on your answer sheet, find the number of the problem and mark your answer.

16. The officials object to them wearing long dresses for
                        A   B   C
    the inaugural dance at the country club.
                         D

17. Janet is finally used to cook on an electric stove
                            A
    after having a gas one for so long.
       B   C   D

18. He knows to repair the carburetor without taking the whole car apart.
        A   B   C   D

19. Stuart stopped to write his letter because he had to
                  A   B
    leave for the hospital.
       C   D

20. She must retyping the report before she hands it in
              A   B   C
    to the director of financing.
       D

21. How much times did Rick and Jennifer have to do the experiment
         A   B
before they obtained the results they had been expecting.
                        C   D

22. Each of the students in the accounting class has to type
                   A   B
their own research paper this semester.
 C   D

23. Mrs. Stevens, along with her cousins from New Mexico,
                       A   B
are planning to attend the festivities.
 C   D

24. They are going to have to leave soon, and so do we.
         A   B   C   D

25. All the students are looking forward spending their
            A   B   C   D
free time relaxing in the sun this summer.

26. Dresses, skirts, shoes, and children's clothing
                                    A
are advertised at great reduced prices this weekend.
     B   C   D

27. Mary and her sister just bought two new winters coats
              A   B   C   D
at the clearance sale.

28. A lunch of soup and sandwiches do not appeal to all of
 A   B   C   D
the students.

29. Some of us have to study their lessons more carefully if
              A   B   C
we expect to pass this examination.
         D

30. Mr. Peters used to think of hisself as the only
                    A   B   C
president of the company.
         D

31. The instructor advised the students for the procedures
                                    A   B
to follow in writing the term paper.
 C   D

32. Although both <u>of them</u> <u>are trying</u> <u>to get</u> the scholarship,
              A   B   C
    she has the <u>highest</u> grades.
              D

33. The new technique <u>calls for</u> <u>heat</u> the mixture before
                 A   B
    <u>applying</u> it to the <u>wood</u>.
      C   D

34. The pilot <u>and the crew</u> <u>divided</u> the life preservers
              A   B
    <u>between</u> the twenty <u>frantic passengers</u>.
      C   D

35. <u>A</u> five-thousand-dollars reward <u>was offered</u>
   A   B   C
    <u>for the capture</u> of the escaped criminals.
        D

36. The <u>equipment</u> <u>in the office</u> was <u>badly</u> in need of
         A   B   C
    <u>to be repaired</u>.
       D

37. <u>A</u> liter is <u>one of the</u> metric <u>measurements</u>, <u>aren't they</u>?
   A   B   C   D

38. We thought he <u>is</u> planning <u>to go on vacation</u> <u>after</u>
              A   B   C
    <u>the first</u> of the month.
      D

39. There <u>are</u> a large supply <u>of pens</u> and notebooks
       A   B
    <u>in the storeroom</u> <u>to the left</u> of the library entrance.
      C   D

40. The president refuses <u>to accept</u> <u>either</u> of the four
                  A   B
    new proposals <u>made by</u> the contractors.
      C   D

STOP. THIS IS THE END OF THE STRUCTURE AND WRITTEN EXPRESSION SECTION. IF YOU FINISH BEFORE TIME IS UP, CHECK YOUR WORK ON PARTS A AND B OF THIS SECTION ONLY. DO NOT WORK ON ANY OTHER SECTION OF THE TEST.

SECTION III: READING COMPREHENSION AND VOCABULARY

Time: 45 Minutes
60 Questions

Part A

DIRECTIONS

Each sentence in Part A has a word or phrase underlined. Below each sentence are four other words or phrases. You are to choose the *one* word or phrase which would *best keep the meaning* of the original sentence if it were substituted for the underlined word.

1. Larry was so absorbed in his novel that he forgot about his dinner cooking in the oven.
   (A) engrossed   (C) enlivened
   (B) obliged   (D) excelled

2. Having come from an affluent society, Dick found it difficult to adjust to a small country town.
   (A) affable   (C) overpopulated
   (B) wealthy   (D) large

3. The question was discarded because it was ambiguous.
   (A) incorrect   (C) vague
   (B) biased   (D) dull

4. Most students abhor lengthy exams at the end of the year.
   (A) detest   (C) nullify
   (B) regret   (D) negate

5. The news of the president's death astonished the world.
   (A) alerted   (C) atoned
   (B) admonished   (D) astounded

6. King Midas's greed led him to spend a life of grief.
   (A) cruelty   (C) warning
   (B) wealth   (D) avarice

7. A multitude of people attended the fund-raising presentation in the mall.
   (A) small number   (C) huge crowd
   (B) select group   (D) large herd

8. The new building was to be <u>octagonal</u> in shape.
   (A) five sided   (C) seven sided
   (B) six sided   (D) eight sided

9. Mark cannot talk well because he has a speech <u>impediment</u>.
   (A) skeptic   (C) imposition
   (B) defect   (D) aspect

10. Our final assignment for the English class is to give an <u>impromptu</u> speech.
    (A) eloquent   (C) technical
    (B) unprepared   (D) unbiased

11. The <u>rigor</u> exhibited by the general was totally unwarranted.
    (A) calisthenics   (C) march
    (B) severity   (D) cleanliness

12. The people interviewed for the survey were <u>randomly</u> selected.
    (A) carefully   (C) indiscriminately
    (B) carelessly   (D) thoughtfully

13. Lyndon Johnson <u>succeeded</u> John Kennedy as president of the United States.
    (A) overruled   (C) followed
    (B) preceded   (D) assisted

14. The foreign countries' attempt at a <u>blockade</u> of the port was unsuccessful.
    (A) expedition   (C) landing
    (B) opening   (D) closure

15. When he was director of the company, his first <u>accomplishment</u> was to bring about better working conditions.
    (A) accumulation   (C) defeat
    (B) achievement   (D) job

16. During the American colonial period, the capable leaders <u>instilled</u> a spirit of nationalism in the colonists.
    (A) insatiated   (C) implanted
    (B) extirpated   (D) extracted

17. Because the details of the project were rather <u>hazy</u>, we decided to reject the proposal.
    (A) dubious   (C) lucrative
    (B) unobtainable   (D) vague

18. Many weak and <u>incompetent</u> rulers were overthrown by more powerful forces.
    (A) incapable   (C) clever
    (B) impulsive   (D) greedy

19. The passengers on the boat were <u>mesmerized</u> by the motion of the sea.
    (A) paralyzed   (C) nauseated
    (B) hypnotized   (D) reverberated

20. Allowing fields to lie <u>fallow</u> is one means of restoring fertility.
    (A) unplanted   (C) watered
    (B) plowed   (D) seeded

21. The guests at the luau enjoyed it very much but refused to eat the <u>raw</u> fish.
    (A) marinated   (C) rotten
    (B) fresh   (D) uncooked

22. American <u>legend</u> says that Johnny Appleseed planted apple orchards throughout Ohio.
    (A) almanac   (C) history
    (B) myth   (D) record

23. After a long, hard struggle, we <u>gradually</u> succeeded in having people accept the truth of our theory.
    (A) slowly   (C) suddenly
    (B) momentarily   (D) graciously

24. Exchanges of language and culture were a direct result of <u>commerce</u>.
    (A) embargo   (C) stagnation
    (B) trade   (D) schooling

25. That artist did not achieve acclaim because he was <u>an imitator</u>, not a creator.
    (A) a distorter   (C) an originator
    (B) a copier   (D) a burglar

26. The powerful ruler <u>suppressed</u> a rebellion and punished the instigators.
    (A) initiated   (C) quashed
    (B) supported   (D) reinstated

27. During the war, many foreign lands were <u>confiscated</u> by the government.
    (A) owned   (C) bartered
    (B) sequestrated   (D) sold

28. That <u>vast</u> region was irrigated by the large river and its many tributaries.
    (A) arid   (C) enormous
    (B) miniscule   (D) damp

29. The television station was <u>inundated</u> with calls protesting the distasteful program.
    (A) harassed   (C) probated
    (B) modulated   (D) flooded

30. The dog saw his <u>reflection</u> in the pool of water.
    (A) image   (C) imagination
    (B) bone   (D) leash

GO ON TO PART B

Part B

DIRECTIONS

In Part B, the questions are based on a variety of reading material (single sentences, paragraphs, advertisements, and the like). You are to choose the *one* best answer, (A), (B), (C), or (D), to each question. Then, on your answer sheet, find the number of the problem and mark your answer. Answer all questions following a passage on the basis of what is *stated* or *implied* in that passage.

Questions 31 through 37 are based on the following reading.

Napoleon Bonaparte's ambition to control all the area around the Mediterranean Sea led him and his French soldiers to Egypt. After losing a naval battle, they were forced to remain there for three years. In 1799, while constructing a fort, a soldier discovered a piece of stele (stone pillar bearing an inscription) known as the Rosetta stone. This famous stone, which would eventually lead to the deciphering of ancient Egyptian hieroglyphics dating to 3100 B.C., was written in three languages: hieroglyphics (picture writing), demotic (a shorthand version of hieroglyphics), and Greek. Scientists discovered that the characters, unlike those in English, could be written from right to left and in other directions as well.

Twenty-three years after discovery of the Rosetta stone, Jean François Champollion, a French philologist, fluent in several languages, was able to decipher the first word—Ptolemy—name of an Egyptian ruler. This name was written inside an oval called a "cartouche." Further investigation revealed that cartouches contained names of important people of that period. Champollion painstakingly continued his search and was able to increase his growing list of known phonetic signs. He and an Englishman, Thomas Young, worked independently of each other to unravel the deeply hidden mysteries of this strange language. Young believed that sound values could be assigned to the symbols, while Champollion insisted that the pictures represented words.

31. How many years elapsed between the date of the oldest hieroglyphics deciphered by means of the Rosetta stone and the stone's discovery?
    (A) 1,301   (B) 1,799   (C) 3,100   (D) 4,899

32. Which of the following languages was *not* written on the Rosetta stone?
    (A) French   (B) demotic   (C) Greek   (D) hieroglyphics

33. Which of the following statements is *not* true?
    (A) Cartouches contained names of prominent people of the period.
    (B) Champollion and Young worked together in an attempt to decipher the hieroglyphics.
    (C) One of Napoleon's soldiers discovered the Rosetta stone.
    (D) Thomas Young believed that sound values could be assigned to the symbols.

34. When was the first word from the Rosetta stone deciphered?
    (A) 3100 B.C.   (B) 1766   (C) 1799   (D) 1822

35. What was the first word that was deciphered from the Rosetta stone?
    (A) cartouche   (B) Ptolemy   (C) demotic   (D) Champollion

36. Why were Napoleon's soldiers in Egypt in 1799?
    (A) They were celebrating a naval victory.
    (B) They were looking for the Rosetta stone.
    (C) They were waiting to continue their campaign.
    (D) They were trying to decipher the hieroglyphics.

37. Who was responsible for deciphering the first word?
    (A) Champollion   (B) Young   (C) Ptolemy   (D) Napoleon

Questions 38 through 43 are based on the following passage.

Sequoyah was a young Cherokee Indian, son of a white trader and an Indian squaw. At an early age, he became fascinated by "the talking leaf," an expression that he used to describe the white man's written records. Although many believed this "talking leaf" to be a gift from the Great Spirit, Sequoyah refused to accept that theory. Like other Indians of the period, he was illiterate, but his determination to remedy the situation led to the invention of a unique 86-character alphabet based on the sound patterns that he heard.

His family and friends thought him mad, but while recuperating from a hunting accident, he diligently and independently set out to create a form of communication for his own people as well as for other Indians. In 1821, after twelve years of work, he had successfully developed a written language that would enable thousands of Indians to read and write.

Sequoyah's desire to preserve words and events for later generations has caused him to be remembered among the important inventors. The giant redwood trees of California, called "sequoias" in his honor, will further imprint his name in history.

38. What is the most important reason that Sequoyah will be remembered?
    (A) California redwoods were named in his honor.
    (B) He was illiterate.
    (C) He created a unique alphabet.
    (D) He recovered from his madness and helped mankind.

39. How did Sequoyah's family react to his idea of developing his own "talking leaf"?
    (A) They arranged for his hunting accident.
    (B) They thought he was crazy.
    (C) They decided to help him.
    (D) They asked him to teach them to read and write.

40. What prompted Sequoyah to develop his alphabet?
    (A) People were writing things about him that he couldn't read.
    (B) He wanted to become famous.
    (C) After his hunting accident, he needed something to keep him busy.
    (D) He wanted the history of his people preserved for future generations.

41. The word *illiterate* means most nearly
    (A) fierce   (C) abandoned
    (B) poor   (D) unable to read or write

42. How would you describe Sequoyah?
    (A) determined   (B) mad   (C) backwards   (D) meek

43. Which of the following is *not* true?
    (A) Sequoyah developed a form of writing with the help of the Cherokee tribe.
    (B) Sequoyah was a very observant young man.
    (C) Sequoyah spent twelve years developing his alphabet.
    (D) Sequoyah was honored by having some trees named after him.

Questions 44 through 46 are based on the following reading.

The mighty, warlike Aztec nation felt that its existence depended upon human sacrifices. The sun would not shine, the crops would not grow, and wars would not be won if the gods were not appeased. As brutal as the ceremonies were, the victims (usually taken from among captives from battles) accepted their fate passively, having been previously indoctrinated and heavily sedated.

44. Why did the Aztecs offer human sacrifices?
    (A) They were cruel and inhuman.
    (B) They believed they had to pacify the gods.
    (C) They wanted to force the citizens to obey.
    (D) They wanted to deter crime.

45. Before the sacrifices, the victims were
    (A) tortured and harassed   (C) brainwashed and drugged
    (B) fed and entertained   (D) interrogated and drugged

46. In what manner did the victims accept their destiny?
    (A) submissively   (C) violently
    (B) rebelliously   (D) notoriously

Questions 47 through 51 are based on the following passage.

Petroleum products, such as gasoline, kerosine, home heating oil, residual fuel oil, and lubricating oils, come from one source—crude oil found below the earth's surface, as well as under large bodies of water, from a few hundred feet below the surface to as deep as 25,000 feet into the earth's interior. Sometimes crude oil is secured by drilling a hole through the earth, but more dry holes are drilled than those producing oil. Pressure at the source or pumping forces crude oil to the surface.

Crude oil wells flow at varying rates, from ten to thousands of barrels per hour. Petroleum products are always measured in 42-gallon barrels.

Petroleum products vary greatly in physical appearance: thin, thick, transparent or opaque, but regardless, their chemical composition is made up of only two elements: carbon and hydrogen, which form compounds called hydrocarbons. Other chemical elements found in union with the hydrocarbons are few and are classified as impurities. Trace elements are also found, but these are of such minute quantities that they are disregarded. The combination of carbon and hydrogen forms many thousands of compounds which are possible because of the various positions and joinings of these two atoms in the hydrocarbon molecule.

The various petroleum products are refined from the crude oil by heating and condensing the vapors. These products are the so-called light oils, such as gasoline, kerosine, and distillate oil. The residue remaining after the light oils are distilled is known as heavy or residual fuel oil and is used mostly for burning under boilers. Additional complicated refining processes rearrange the chemical structure of the hydrocarbons to produce other products, some of which are used to upgrade and increase the octane rating of various types of gasolines.

47. Which of the following is *not* true?
    (A) Crude oil is found below land and water.
    (B) Crude oil is always found a few hundred feet below the surface.
    (C) Pumping and pressure force crude oil to the surface.
    (D) A variety of petroleum products is obtained from crude oil.

48. Many thousands of hydrocarbon compounds are possible because
    (A) the petroleum products vary greatly in physical appearance
    (B) complicated refining processes rearrange the chemical structure
    (C) the two atoms in the molecule assume many positions
    (D) the pressure needed to force it to the surface causes molecular transformation

49. Which of the following is true?
    (A) The various petroleum products are produced by filtration.
    (B) Heating and condensation produce the various products.
    (C) Chemical separation is used to produce the various products.
    (D) Mechanical means such as the centrifuge are used to produce the various products.

50. How is crude oil brought to the surface?
    (A) expansion of the hydrocarbons
    (B) pressure and pumping
    (C) vacuum created in the drilling pipe
    (D) expansion and contraction of the earth's surface

51. Which of the following is *not* listed as a light oil?
    (A) distillate oil   (C) lubricating oil
    (B) gasoline   (D) kerosine

Questions 52 through 57 are based on the following passage.

An election year is one in which all four numbers are evenly divisible by four (1944, 1948, etc.) Since 1840, American presidents elected in years ending in zero have been destined to die in office. William H.

Harrison, the man who served the shortest term, died of pneumonia several weeks after his inauguration.

Abraham Lincoln was one of four presidents who were assassinated. He was elected in 1860, and his untimely death came just five years later.

James A. Garfield, a former Union army general from Ohio, was shot during his first year in office (1881) by a man to whom he wouldn't give a job.

While in his second term of office (1901), William McKinley, another Ohioan, attended the Pan-American Exposition at Buffalo, New York. During the reception, he was assassinated while shaking hands with some of the guests.

Three years after his election in 1920, Warren G. Harding died in office. Although it was never proved, many believe he was poisoned.

Franklin D. Roosevelt had been elected four times (1932, 1936, 1940, and 1944), the only man to serve so long a term. He had contracted polio in 1921 and died of the illness in 1945.

John F. Kennedy, the last of the line, was assassinated in 1963, only three years after his election.

Will 1980's candidate suffer the same fate?

52. Which of the following was *not* an election year?
   (A) 1960   (B) 1930   (C) 1888   (D) 1824

53. Which president served the shortest term in office?
   (A) Abraham Lincoln   (C) William McKinley
   (B) Warren G. Harding   (D) William H. Harrison

54. Which of the following is true?
   (A) All presidents elected in years ending in zero have died in office.
   (B) Only presidents from Ohio have died in office.
   (C) Franklin D. Roosevelt completed four terms as president.
   (D) Four American presidents have been assassinated.

55. How many presidents elected in years ending in zero since 1840 have died in office?
   (A) 7   (B) 5   (C) 4   (D) 3

56. In this reading, what does *inauguration* mean?
   (A) election   (C) swearing-in ceremonies
   (B) acceptance speech   (D) campaign

57. Which of the following was *not* assassinated?
   (A) John F. Kennedy   (C) Abraham Lincoln
   (B) Franklin D. Roosevelt   (D) James A. Garfield

Directions for questions 58 through 60

For each of these questions, choose the answer that is *closest in meaning* to the original sentence. Note that several of the choices may be factually correct, but you should choose the one that is the *closest restatement of the given statement.*

58. Unintentionally, some cities are squeezing out the middle class by forcing them to support the poor.
    (A) Unintentionally the poor are supporting a movement to squeeze the middle class out of some cities.
    (B) The middle class in some cities is unfortunately squeezing out the support of the poor.
    (C) In some cities, the middle class is forcing the poor to support them.
    (D) By being forced to support the poor, the middle class is unintentionally being squeezed out of some cities.

59. The current was black and mindless, with a beauty that almost masked its danger.
    (A) Although it appeared dangerous, the current had a beauty that was only black and mindless.
    (B) The current was black and mindless but not as dangerous as it seemed.
    (C) Although the current was black and mindless, its beauty nearly disguised the danger.
    (D) Despite its danger, the blackness and mindlessness of the current made it more beautiful.

60. Despite the breathtaking natural beauty of the crystalline Great Lakes during the winter, man is reluctant to venture into this snowy wonderland.
    (A) Even though the crystalline Great Lakes are breathtaking in the winter, man is afraid to explore this snowy wonderland.
    (B) Man is reluctant to venture into the snowy wonderland in the winter because of the breathtaking natural beauty of the crystalline Great Lakes.
    (C) Man is reluctant to venture into the crystalline Great Lakes during the winter because it makes breathing difficult.
    (D) Although reluctant to venture into the crystalline Great Lakes, man does so to appreciate their breathtaking natural beauty.

STOP. THIS IS THE END OF THE EXAMINATION. IF YOU FINISH BEFORE TIME IS UP, CHECK YOUR WORK ON PARTS A AND B OF THE READING COMPREHENSION AND VOCABULARY SECTION ONLY. DO NOT RETURN TO ANY OTHER SECTION OF THE TEST.

PRACTICE TEST 3

SECTION 1: LISTENING COMPREHENSION

Time: Approximately 30 Minutes
50 Questions

For Practice Test 3, restart your listening comprehension cassette immediately following Practice Test 2 on side 2. On the actual TOEFL you will be given extra time to go on to the next page when you finish a page in the listening comprehension section. In the following test, however, you will have only the 12 seconds given after each question. Turn the page as soon as you have marked your answer. Start the cassette now.

Part A

DIRECTIONS

For each problem in Part A, you will hear a short statement. The statements will be *spoken* just one time. They will not be written out for you, and you must listen carefully in order to understand what the speaker says.

When you hear a statement, read the four sentences in your test book and decide which one is closest in meaning to the statement you have heard. Then, on your answer sheet, find the number of the problem and mark your answer.

1. (A) Mary's car is being repaired at the gas station.
   (B) Frank is going to the gas station to pick up Mary's car.
   (C) Mary had her gas tank filled with gasoline.
   (D) Mary's car isn't working properly because of the type of gasoline that she is using.

2. (A) Although they knew there was going to be a meeting, they didn't come.
   (B) They didn't want to attend the meeting, but they did anyway.
   (C) They didn't know about the meeting.
   (D) They didn't let anybody know about the meeting, so nobody attended.

3. (A) Martha is Barbara's mother.
   (B) Martha and Barbara are sisters.
   (C) Martha is older than Barbara.
   (D) Martha is younger than Barbara.

289

4. (A) John made the best grade in his class.
   (B) John is an exceptionally good student.
   (C) John's classmates receive good grades, but John doesn't.
   (D) John is one of the better students in his class.

5. (A) The dean was asked to question several students.
   (B) The humanities professor questioned several students.
   (C) The humanities professor was able to answer the students' questions.
   (D) The humanities professor has asked the dean a question about some students.

6. (A) The time is now 6:45.   (C) The time is now 7:45.
   (B) The time is now 7:15.   (D) The time is now 7:20.

7. (A) You should ask him how long it will take to repair the car.
   (B) I advise you not to repair the car until he agrees on the cost.
   (C) I advise you not to allow him to repair the car before you have a cost estimate.
   (D) I'm sure he is going to overcharge you if you let him repair the car.

8. (A) Henry went to the movies because he didn't want to work.
   (B) Henry didn't go to the movies because he had too much work to do.
   (C) Although Henry had a lot of work to do, he went to the movies.
   (D) Henry never goes to the movies if he has work to do.

9. (A) Jane watched TV last night instead of working on her paper.
   (B) Jane didn't watch TV last night because she had to write a paper.
   (C) Jane wrote her paper last night while she was watching TV.
   (D) Jane wasn't able to write her paper last night because she was tired after watching TV.

10. (A) John admired the deer's beauty from his bedroom window.
    (B) John closed the door quickly.
    (C) John shot a deer with a rifle.
    (D) John took a photograph of a deer.

11. (A) James lost the library's new books.
    (B) James is going to the new library to look for some books.
    (C) James may keep the library books for two more weeks.
    (D) James had to pay a late fee for the books.

12. (A) The woman found $240 in the street.
    (B) The woman had $54 in her purse.
    (C) The woman realized that she had $240 in her purse.
    (D) The woman needed only $18, but she had $54.

13. (A) Henry is afraid to start smoking because of the hazardous effects.
    (B) Henry is afraid he'll become fat if he stops smoking.
    (C) Henry is afraid that he will become more nervous if he stops smoking.
    (D) Henry doesn't realize the possible dangers of smoking.

14. (A) John would rather eat apple pie than strawberry pie.
    (B) John doesn't get apple pie often enough.
    (C) John would rather eat strawberry pie than apple pie.
    (D) John's wife likes strawberry pie, but John doesn't.

15. (A) We have to be at the airport at 6:30.
    (B) We have to be at the airport at 5:55.
    (C) We have to be at the airport at 6:00.
    (D) We have to be at the airport at 6:45.

16. (A) Harry studies every day, but he's not doing well in school.
    (B) Harry is so lazy that he rarely passes his classes.
    (C) Harry hasn't studied for a while, but he thinks he'll pass all his classes.
    (D) Harry probably won't pass because he hasn't studied.

17. (A) Mary injured Anne.
    (B) Mary had to run downtown last week.
    (C) Mary went downtown to exercise.
    (D) Mary met Anne downtown unexpectedly.

18. (A) Our meat wasn't tender.
    (B) The speaker at the banquet didn't have a good character.
    (C) We found it difficult to meet new people at the banquet.
    (D) We had to cut the banquet meeting short.

19. (A) John never forgets when he has a meeting.
    (B) It seems that John forgot about our meeting.
    (C) John should have cancelled the meeting.
    (D) John has to come to the meeting.

20. (A) James missed the bus this morning.
    (B) James's alarm clock didn't go off this morning.
    (C) James forgot that he had a class this morning.
    (D) James didn't wake up in time to get to school on time this morning.

GO ON TO PART B

Part B

DIRECTIONS

In Part B, you will hear 15 short conversations between two speakers. At the end of each conversation, a third voice will ask a question about what was said. The question will be *spoken* just one time. After you hear a conversation and the question about it, read the four possible answers and decide which one would be the best answer to the question you have heard. Then, on your answer sheet, find the number of the problem and mark your answer.

21. (A) $29   (B) $50   (C) $25   (D) $30

22. (A) She'll go to the concert.
    (B) She'll watch her neighbors' children.
    (C) She'll go to a military dinner.
    (D) She'll visit her neighbor.

23. (A) vegetables   (B) fruit   (C) meat   (D) cookies

24. (A) April   (B) May   (C) June   (D) July

25. (A) Philadelphia   (B) Chapmans   (C) Doctors   (D) Arizona

26. (A) Ray will have a class at 1:00.
    (B) Ray will go to the library at 2:00.
    (C) Ray will go home immediately after his class.
    (D) Ray will go home around 3:00.

27. (A) Joe and Nancy couldn't afford a honeymoon.
    (B) Joe and Nancy went to Puerto Rico.
    (C) Joe and Nancy went to St. Augustine.
    (D) Joe and Nancy are still planning on going to Puerto Rico.

28. (A) The first hot dogs came from Germany.
    (B) Hot dogs originated in the United States.
    (C) Some hot dogs are made from reindeer meat.
    (D) Even countries like Finland have a food similar to hot dogs.

29. (A) gas station   (C) lost and found department
    (B) police station   (D) bar

30. (A) Jason Daniels isn't home right now.
    (B) The caller dialed the wrong number.
    (C) Jason Daniels can't come to the phone right now.
    (D) Jason Daniels doesn't want to speak to the caller.

31. (A) She's on a committee.   (C) She exercises too much.
    (B) She's been working late.   (D) She's trying to budget her sleep.

32. (A) better   (B) sick   (C) fine   (D) tired

33. (A) No, because it's not for sale.
    (B) Yes, because he has plenty of money.
    (C) Yes, if he borrows the money from the woman.
    (D) No, because he didn't bring enough money.

34. (A) Europe   (B) here   (C) Canada   (D) California

35. (A) The bus has broken down and will not arrive.
    (B) The bus was in a terrible accident.
    (C) The bus will probably arrive at 9:15.
    (D) The bus may arrive tonight, but the man isn't sure.

GO ON TO PART C

Part C

DIRECTIONS

In this part of the test, you will hear several short talks and/or conversations. After each talk or conversation, you will be asked some questions. The talks and questions will be *spoken* just one time. They will not be written out for you, so you will have to listen carefully in order to understand and remember what the speaker says.

When you hear a question, read the four possible answers in your test book and decide which one would be the best answer to the question you have heard. Then, on your answer sheet, find the number of the problem and fill in the space that corresponds to the letter of the answer you have chosen.

36. (A) 2   (B) 5   (C) 3   (D) 7

37. (A) The men attracted the attention of a private airplane.
    (B) They ran out of gas.
    (C) Some fishermen spotted them.
    (D) Their families finally found them.

38. (A) They knew that they had run out of fuel.
    (B) Their families had reported them missing.
    (C) They hadn't met the private airplane that came to meet them.
    (D) It was starting to get dark.

39. (A) 15 miles   (C) 2 miles
    (B) 7½ miles   (D) 5 miles

40. (A) He was crazy.
    (B) They thought he was dead.
    (C) He had many broken bones.
    (D) He fell out of a plane.

41. (A) on a plane   (C) on the ground
    (B) on television   (D) in a hospital

42. (A) He fell out of a plane.
    (B) His two parachutes didn't open.
    (C) He fell while walking.
    (D) A parachute fell on him.

43. (A) He died.
    (B) He jumped from a plane again.
    (C) He broke his leg.
    (D) He went crazy.

44. (A) aluminum   (B) steel   (C) aging   (D) burnable

45. (A) It would burn on reentry to the earth's atmosphere.
    (B) It would collide with aircraft on reentry.
    (C) It might cause considerable damage.
    (D) It will not survive its atmospheric descent.

46. (A) The pieces would be concentrated in one area.
    (B) The Skylab would not completely burn before reentry.
    (C) There could be considerable property damage.
    (D) Some 400 to 500 pieces might survive reentry.

47. (A) dentist–patient   (C) teacher–student
    (B) doctor–patient   (D) pharmacist–customer

48. (A) in a few days   (C) very slowly
    (B) before leaving the office   (D) soon enough

49. (A) some medicine   (C) exhaling slowly
    (B) some tests   (D) filling her lungs with air

50. (A) She does not have enough air in her lungs.
    (B) She's exhaling too slowly.
    (C) She didn't do well in her tests.
    (D) She has a little congestion.

STOP. THIS IS THE END OF THE LISTENING COMPREHENSION SECTION.

SECTION II: STRUCTURE AND WRITTEN EXPRESSION

Time: 25 Minutes
40 Questions

Part A

DIRECTIONS

Each sentence in Part A is an incomplete sentence. Four words or phrases, marked (A), (B), (C), (D), are given beneath each sentence. You are to choose the *one* word or phrase that best completes the sentence. Then, on your answer sheet, find the number of the problem and mark your answer.

1. The attorney told his client that _____.
   (A) they had little chance of winning the case
   (B) the case was of a small chance to win
   (C) it was nearly impossible to win him the case
   (D) the case had a minimum chance to be won by him

2. One of the professor's greatest attributes is _____.
   (A) when he gives lectures
   (B) how in the manner that he lectures
   (C) the way to give lectures
   (D) his ability to lecture

3. The bank sent a notice to its customers which contained _____.
   (A) a remembrance that interest rates were to raise the following month
   (B) a reminder that a raise in interest rates was the month following
   (C) to remember that the interest rates were going up next month
   (D) a reminder that the interest rates would rise the following month

4. _____ was the day before yesterday.
   (A) The France's Independence Day
   (B) The day of the French independence
   (C) French's Independence Day
   (D) France's Independence Day

5. It was not until she had arrived home _____ remembered her appointment with the doctor.
   (A) when she   (C) and she
   (B) that she   (D) she

6. George would certainly have attended the proceedings _____.
   - (A) if he didn't get a flat tire
   - (B) if the flat tire hadn't happened
   - (C) had he not had a flat tire
   - (D) had the tire not flattened itself

7. _____ received law degrees as today.
   - (A) Never so many women have
   - (B) Never have so many women
   - (C) The women aren't ever
   - (D) Women who have never

8. The students liked that professor's course because _____.
   - (A) there was few if any homework
   - (B) not a lot of homework
   - (C) of there wasn't a great amount of homework
   - (D) there was little or no homework

9. George _____ he could improve his test scores, but he did not have enough time to study.
   - (A) knew to
   - (B) knew how
   - (C) knew how that
   - (D) knew how to

10. _____ he would have come to class.
   - (A) If Mike is able to finish his homework
   - (B) Would Mike be able to finish his homework
   - (C) If Mike could finish his homework
   - (D) If Mike had been able to finish his homework

11. Lee contributed fifty dollars, but he wishes he could contribute _____.
   - (A) one other fifty dollars
   - (B) the same amount also
   - (C) another fifty
   - (D) more fifty dollars

12. The people at the party were worried about Janet because no one was aware _____ she had gone.
   - (A) where that
   - (B) of where
   - (C) of the place where
   - (D) the place

13. Fred's yearly income since he changed professions has _____.
   - (A) nearly tripled
   - (B) got almost three times bigger
   - (C) almost grown by three times
   - (D) just about gone up three times

14. Nancy hasn't begun working on her Ph.D. _____ working on her master's.
    (A) still because she is yet
    (B) yet as a result she is still
    (C) yet because she is still
    (D) still while she is already

15. The director of this organization must know _____.
    (A) money management, selling, and able to satisfy the stockholders
    (B) how to manage money, selling his product, and be able to satisfy stockholders
    (C) how to manage money, sell his product, and satisfy the stockholders
    (D) money management, selling, the idea of being able to satisfy the stockholders

GO ON TO PART B

Part B

DIRECTIONS

Each sentence in Part B has four words or phrases underlined. The four underlined parts of the sentence are marked (A), (B), (C), (D). You are to identify the *one* underlined word or phrase that should be corrected or rewritten. Then, on your answer sheet, find the number of the problem and mark your answer.

16. She wishes that we didn't send her the candy yesterday
                         A   B
    because she's on a diet.
         C   D

17. They are planning on attending the convention next month,
               A   B   C
    and so I am.
         D

18. Today was such beautiful day that I couldn't bring myself
                  A   B
    to complete all my chores.
         C   D

19. While they were away at the beach, they allowed
      A   B
    their neighbors use their barbeque grill.
         C   D

20. The artist tried <u>stimulate</u> <u>interest</u> in painting <u>by taking</u>
                       A   B   C
    his students <u>to the</u> museums.
                 D

21. Mumps <u>are</u> a very <u>common disease</u> <u>which</u> <u>usually</u> affects children.
          A   B   C   D

22. Nancy said <u>that</u> she <u>went</u> <u>to</u> the supermarket <u>before coming</u> home.
                A   B C   D

23. <u>Before</u> she moved here, Arlene had <u>been</u> president <u>of the</u>
    A   B   C
    organization <u>since</u> four years.
                   D

24. Each <u>of the</u> nurses <u>report</u> to the operating room when
         A   B
    <u>his or her name</u> <u>is called</u>.
        C   D

25. The <u>athlete</u>, together <u>with</u> <u>his</u> coach and several relatives,
        A   B   C
    <u>are</u> traveling to the Olympic Games.
    D

26. Professor Duncan <u>teaches</u> <u>both</u> <u>anthropology</u> as well as
                    A   B   C
    sociology <u>each fall</u>.
           D

27. My brother is <u>in</u> California <u>on</u> vacation, but I wish he
               A   B
    <u>was</u> here so that he could help <u>me repair my car</u> .
    C   D

28. I <u>certainly</u> appreciate <u>him</u> <u>telling us</u> about the delay in
     A   B   C
    <u>delivering</u> the materials because we had planned to
    D
    begin work tomorrow.

29. The chemistry instructor explained the experiment <u>in</u>
                                              A
    <u>such of a way</u> that it <u>was</u> <u>easily understood</u>.
        B   C   D

30. Rudolph Nureyev <u>has become</u> one of the <u>greatest</u> <u>dancer</u>
                    A   B   C
    that the ballet world has <u>ever known</u>.
                             D

31. He has less friends in his classes now than he had last year.
           A   B   C   D

32. The town we visited was a four-days journey from our
                          A   B

    hotel, so we took the train instead of the bus.
               C   D

33. The influence of the nation's literature, art, and
                         A

    science have captured widespread attention.
            B   C   D

34. The leader emphasized the need for justice and equality
                          A   B

    between his people.
       C   D

35. Many of the population in the rural areas is composed of
    A   B   C

    manual laborers.
           D

36. Several people have apparent tried to change the man's mind,
                      A   B   C

    but he refuses to listen.
                    D

37. Keith is one of the most intelligent boys of the science class.
                    A   B   C   D

38. The girls were sorry to had missed the singers when they
                  A   B   C

    arrived at the airport.
       D

39. When Keith visited Alaska, he lived in a igloo in the
                                  A   B

    winter months as well as in the spring.
           C   D

40. The harder he tried, the worst he danced before the
                    A   B   C

    large audience.
    D

STOP. THIS IS THE END OF THE STRUCTURE AND WRITTEN EXPRESSION
SECTION. IF YOU FINISH BEFORE TIME IS UP, CHECK YOUR WORK ON PARTS A
AND B OF THIS SECTION ONLY. DO NOT WORK ON ANY OTHER SECTION OF THE
TEST.

SECTION III: READING COMPREHENSION AND VOCABULARY

Time: 45 Minutes
60 Questions

Part A

DIRECTIONS

Each sentence in Part A has a word or phrase underlined. Below each sentence are four other words or phrases. You are to choose the *one* word or phrase which would *best keep the meaning* of the original sentence if it were substituted for the underlined word.

1. The fourth year sociology class was a homogeneous group of university students.
   - (A) uniform
   - (B) dreary
   - (C) unrelated
   - (D) distinguishable

2. The tornado caused irreparable damage to the Florida citrus crop.
   - (A) irresolute
   - (B) irresponsible
   - (C) irrecoverable
   - (D) irregular

3. The discontented students retaliated by boycotting the school cafeteria.
   - (A) rewarded
   - (B) vindicated
   - (C) took revenge
   - (D) fluctuated

4. The spy used a fictitious name while dealing with the enemy.
   - (A) funny
   - (B) false
   - (C) real
   - (D) foreign

5. John didn't enjoy the rock concert because he thought the tempo was bad.
   - (A) audience
   - (B) rhythm
   - (C) singer
   - (D) weather

6. The flowers on the table were a manifestation of the child's love for his mother.
   - (A) a demonstration
   - (B) an infestation
   - (C) a combination
   - (D) a satisfaction

7. Marvin's doctor said he was obese and had to take immediate measures to correct the problem.
   - (A) anemic
   - (B) tired
   - (C) corpulent
   - (D) petulant

8. Frank condoned his brother's actions because he knew he meant well.
   - (A) overlooked
   - (B) praised
   - (C) condemned
   - (D) satisfied

9. John's unabashed behavior caused great concern among his teachers.
   - (A) terrible
   - (B) unembarrassed
   - (C) cowardly
   - (D) unforgivable

10. Many new medicines today eradicate diseases before they become too widespread.
    - (A) wipe out
    - (B) identify
    - (C) prolong
    - (D) suspend

11. The director's spacious new office overlooked the city.
    - (A) quiet
    - (B) colorful
    - (C) roomy
    - (D) comfortable

12. The thieves were trying to perpetrate a robbery in the office building.
    - (A) view
    - (B) interfere with
    - (C) stop
    - (D) commit

13. Before the earthquake hit the area, many minor tremors were felt.
    - (A) spasms
    - (B) noises
    - (C) vibrations
    - (D) crumblings

14. When the protestor entered the meeting clad only in a beach towel, the audience was dumbfounded.
    - (A) speechless
    - (B) excited
    - (C) content
    - (D) applauding

15. Marcia's career involved a dual role for her as a counselor and a teacher.
    - (A) tiring
    - (B) dedicated
    - (C) twofold
    - (D) satisfying

16. Andy's jocular manner made him loved by all his companions.
    - (A) easygoing
    - (B) jesting
    - (C) intelligent
    - (D) artistic

17. Sally was mortified by her date's unprecedented behavior.
    - (A) eradicated
    - (B) humiliated
    - (C) overjoyed
    - (D) challenged

18. The student's wan appearance caused the teacher to send him home.
    - (A) pale
    - (B) shabby
    - (C) bellicose
    - (D) hungry

19. Nothing could <u>efface</u> the people's memory of their former leader's cruelty although many years had elapsed.
    (A) broaden
    (B) erase
    (C) edify
    (D) substantiate

20. The doctor asked the patient to <u>disrobe</u> before the examination.
    (A) take medicine
    (B) breathe deeply
    (C) relax
    (D) undress

21. The protesting crowd <u>dispersed</u> after the rally.
    (A) scattered
    (B) became violent
    (C) fought
    (D) danced

22. Because Dolly is such a good cook, she has <u>concocted</u> a great new recipe.
    (A) created
    (B) named
    (C) epitomized
    (D) baked

23. After the drops were placed in the patient's eyes, his pupils became <u>dilated</u>.
    (A) enlarged
    (B) smaller
    (C) irritated
    (D) sensible

24. Her <u>brusque</u> manner surprised all of the guests.
    (A) satirical
    (B) humorous
    (C) shameless
    (D) abrupt

25. In that organization, they place <u>emphasis</u> on mutual aid and cooperation.
    (A) reward
    (B) work
    (C) stress
    (D) pressure

26. She didn't say much, but her tone of voice <u>insinuated</u> more.
    (A) blamed
    (B) suggested
    (C) demanded
    (D) intervened

27. Jan took many <u>snapshots</u> while on vacation in Europe.
    (A) notes
    (B) gifts
    (C) photos
    (D) clothes

28. The young couple chose a <u>secluded</u> place for their picnic.
    (A) authentic
    (B) sunny
    (C) isolated
    (D) grassy

29. The <u>daring</u> young man rode through the Indian village trying to find his long-lost sister.
    (A) bold
    (B) cowardly
    (C) persistent
    (D) captured

30. The victors <u>defined</u> their terms to the conquered.

(A) dictated   (C) insinuated

(B) wrote   (D) forced

GO ON TO PART B

Part B

DIRECTIONS

In Part B, the questions are based on a variety of reading material (single sentences, paragraphs, advertisements, and the like). You are to choose the *one* best answer, (A), (B), (C), or (D), to each question. Then, on your answer sheet, find the number of the problem and mark your answer. Answer all questions following a passage on the basis of what is *stated* or *implied* in that passage.

Questions 31 through 34 are based on the following reading.

Elizabeth Blackwell was born in England in 1821, and emigrated to New York City when she was ten years old. One day she decided that she wanted to become a doctor. That was nearly impossible for a woman in the middle of the nineteenth century. After writing many letters seeking admission to medical schools, she was finally accepted by a doctor in Philadelphia. So determined was she, that she taught school and gave music lessons to earn money for her tuition.

In 1849, after graduation from medical school, she decided to further her education in Paris. She wanted to be a surgeon, but a serious eye infection forced her to abandon the idea.

Upon returning to the United States, she found it difficult to start her own practice because she was a woman. By 1857 Elizabeth and her sister, also a doctor, along with another female doctor, managed to open a new hospital, the first for women and children. Besides being the first female physician and founding her own hospital, she also established the first medical school for women.

31. Why couldn't Elizabeth Blackwell realize her dream of becoming a surgeon?

(A) She couldn't get admitted to medical school.

(B) She decided to further her education in Paris.

(C) A serious eye infection halted her quest.

(D) It was difficult for her to start a practice in the United States.

32. What main obstacle almost destroyed Elizabeth's chances for becoming a doctor?
    (A) She was a woman.
    (B) She wrote too many letters.
    (C) She couldn't graduate from medical school.
    (D) She couldn't establish her hospital.

33. How many years elapsed between her graduation from medical school and the opening of her hospital?
    (A) 8   (B) 10   (C) 19   (D) 36

34. All of the following are "firsts" in the life of Elizabeth Blackwell, *except*
    (A) she became the first female physician
    (B) she was the first woman surgeon
    (C) she and several other women founded the first hospital for women and children
    (D) she established the first medical school for women

Questions 35 through 38 are based on the following reading.

Glands manufacture and secrete necessary substances. Exocrine glands secrete their products through ducts, but endocrine glands, or ductless glands, release their products directly into the bloodstream.

One important endocrine gland is the thyroid gland. It is in the neck and has two lobes, one on each side of the windpipe. The thyroid gland collects iodine from the blood and produces thyroxine, an important hormone, which it stores in an inactive form. When thyroxine is needed by the body, the thyroid gland excretes it directly into the bloodstream. Thyroxine is combined in the body cells with other chemicals and affects many functions of the body.

The thyroid gland may be underactive or overactive, resulting in problems. An underactive thyroid causes hypothyroidism, while an overactive one causes hyperthyroidism. The former problem, called myxedema in adults and cretinism in children, causes the growth process to slow down. A cretin's body and mind do not grow to their full potential. Hyperthyroidism, on the other hand, results in extreme nervousness, an increase in heart action, and other problems.

Either hypothyroidism or hyperthyroidism may result in goiter, or an enlarged thyroid gland. A goiter will appear when the body is not getting enough iodine. Goiter is less common today, since most people use iodized salt.

35. The thyroid gland is called an endocrine gland
    (A) because it has ducts
    (B) because it has lobes
    (C) because it excretes directly into the bloodstream
    (D) because it is located in the neck

36. A cretin is
    (A) a child with hyperthyroidism
    (B) an adult with an underperforming thyroid gland
    (C) a young person with hypothyroidism
    (D) an extremely irritable child

37. Which of the following is a probable result of myxedema?
    (A) sluggishness
    (B) hyperactivity
    (C) overproduction of thyroxine
    (D) perspiration

38. A goiter is
    (A) a person with myxedema
    (B) a swollen thyroid gland
    (C) an underactive thyroid gland
    (D) a chemical

Questions 39 through 43 are based on the following reading.

A recent investigation by scientists at the U.S. Geological Survey shows that strange animal behavior might help predict future earthquakes. Investigators found such occurrences in a ten-kilometer radius of the epicenter of a fairly recent quake. Some birds screeched and flew about wildly; dogs yelped and ran around uncontrollably.

Scientists believe that animals can perceive these environmental changes as early as several days before the mishap.

In 1976 after observing animal behavior, the Chinese were able to predict a devastating quake. Although hundreds of thousands of people were killed, the government was able to evacuate millions of other people and thus keep the death toll at a lower level.

39. What prediction may be made by observing animal behavior?
    (A) an impending earthquake
    (B) the number of people who will die
    (C) the ten-kilometer radius of the epicenter
    (D) environmental changes

40. Why can animals perceive these changes when humans cannot?
    (A) Animals are smarter than humans.
    (B) Animals have certain instincts that humans don't possess.
    (C) By running around the house, they can feel the vibrations.
    (D) Humans don't know where to look.

41. Which of the following is *not* true?
    (A) Some animals may be able to sense an approaching earthquake.
    (B) By observing animal behavior scientists perhaps can predict earth-
        quakes.
    (C) The Chinese have successfully predicted an earthquake and saved
        many lives.
    (D) All birds and dogs in a ten-kilometer radius of the epicenter went
        wild before the quake.

42. In this passage, the word *evacuate* most nearly means
    (A) remove   (C) destroy
    (B) exile   (D) emaciate

43. If scientists can accurately predict earthquakes, there will be
    (A) fewer animals going crazy
    (B) a lower death rate
    (C) fewer people evacuated
    (D) fewer environmental changes

Questions 44 through 47 are based on the following reading.

As a result of the recent oil crisis, 9.9 million of California's 15
million motorists were subjected to an odd-even plan of gas rationing.
The governor signed a bill forcing motorists with license plates ending in
odd numbers to buy gas only on odd-numbered days, and those ending
in even numbers on even-numbered days. Those whose plates were all
letters or specially printed had to follow the odd-numbered plan.

Exceptions were made only for emergencies and out-of-state drivers.
Those who could not get gas were forced to walk, bike, or skate to
work.

This plan was expected to eliminate the long lines at many service
stations. Those who tried to purchase more than twenty gallons of gas or
tried to fill a more than half filled tank would be fined and possibly
imprisoned.

44. All of the following are true *except*
    (A) officials hoped that this plan would alleviate long gas lines
    (B) a gas limit was imposed
    (C) California has 9.9 million drivers
    (D) the governor signed the bill concerning gas rationing

45. Those who violated the rationing program
    (A) were forced to walk, bike, or skate to work
    (B) were fined and possibly imprisoned
    (C) had to wait in long lines
    (D) were forced to use odd-numbered days

46. The gas rationing plan was not binding on
    (A) even-numbered license plates
    (B) odd-numbered license plates
    (C) all-lettered plates
    (D) out-of-state plates

47. California was forced to adopt this plan because
    (A) a recent oil crisis necessitated it
    (B) too many drivers were filling their tanks with more than twenty
        gallons and spilling it
    (C) people were not getting enough exercise and needed to walk, bike,
        or skate
    (D) too many motorists had odd-numbered plates

Questions 48 through 52 are based on the following passage.

As far back as 700 B.C., man has talked about children being cared
for by wolves. Romulus and Remus, the legendary twin founders of
Rome, were purported to have been cared for by wolves. It is believed
that when a she-wolf loses her litter, she seeks a human child to take its
place.

This seemingly preposterous idea did not become credible until the
late nineteenth century when a French doctor actually found a naked
ten-year-old boy wandering in the woods. He did not walk erect, could
not speak intelligibly, nor could he relate to people. He only growled and
stared at them. Finally the doctor won the boy's confidence and began
to work with him. After many long years of devoted and patient
instruction, the doctor was able to get the boy to clothe and feed
himself, recognize and utter a number of words, as well as write letters
and form words.

48. The French doctor found the boy
    (A) wandering in the woods   (C) growling at him
    (B) at his doorstep   (D) speaking intelligibly

49. In this passage, the word *litter* most nearly means
    (A) garbage   (B) master   (C) offspring   (D) hair

50. The doctor was able to work with the boy because
   (A) the boy was highly intelligent
   (B) the boy trusted him
   (C) the boy liked to dress up
   (D) the boy was dedicated and patient

51. Which of the following statements is *not* true?
   (A) She-wolves have been said to substitute human children for their lost litters.
   (B) Examples of wolves' caring for human children can be found only in the nineteenth century.
   (C) The French doctor succeeded in domesticating the boy somewhat.
   (D) The young boy never was able to speak perfectly.

52. In this passage, the word *preposterous* most nearly means
   (A) dedicated   (B) scientific   (C) wonderful   (D) absurd

Directions for questions 53 and 54

   For each of these questions, choose the answer that is *closest in meaning* to the original sentence. Note that several of the choices may be factually correct, but you should choose the one that is the *closest restatement of the given sentence.*

53. Hal used to play on the country club's racquetball team.
   (A) Hal plays with the racquetball team at the country club.
   (B) Hal doesn't play racquetball any more, but still belongs to the country club.
   (C) At one time Hal played racquetball on the country club's team.
   (D) Hal used to team up with the country club and play racquetball.

54. Peter is attending a private school and is majoring in electronics.
   (A) Peter is specializing in electronics at a private school.
   (B) Peter is a major at a private electronics school.
   (C) Although Peter is attending a private school, he's majoring in electronics.
   (D) Peter's private school is letting him major in electronics.

Questions 55 through 60 are based on the following reading.

   Vibrio parahaemolyticus is a bacteria that has been isolated from sea water, shell fish, finfish, plankton and salt springs. It has been a major cause of food poisoning in Japan and the Japanese have done several studies on it. They have confirmed the presence of *V. parahaemolyticus* in the north and central Pacific with the highest abundance in inshore waters, particularly in or near large harbors.

A man named Nishio studied the relationship between the chloride content of sea water and the seasonal distribution of *V. parahaemolyticus* and concluded that while the isolation of *V. parahaemolyticus* was independent of the sodium chloride content, the distribution of *V. parahaemolyticus* in sea water was dependent on the water temperature. In fact it has been isolated in high frequencies during summer, from June to September, but was not isolated with the same frequency in winter.

Within four or five days after eating contaminated foods, a person will begin to experience diarrhea, the most common symptom; this will very often be accompanied by stomach cramps, nausea, and vomiting. Headache and fever, with or without chills, may also be experienced.

55. Which of the following locations would be most likely to have a high concentration of *Vibrio parahaemolyticus*?
    (A) a bay   (C) the middle of the ocean
    (B) a sea   (D) sediment

56. The safest time for eating seafood is probably
    (A) August   (B) November   (C) July   (D) September

57. The most common symptom of *V. parahaemolyticus* is
    (A) nausea   (B) diarrhea   (C) vomiting   (D) headache and fever

58. The incubation period for this illness is
    (A) 2 to 3 days   (C) 4 to 5 days
    (B) 3 to 4 hours   (D) several months

59. Nishio's study showed that
    (A) the presence of *V. parahaemolyticus* was dependent on neither the salt content nor the water temperature
    (B) the presence of *V. parahaemolyticus* was dependent on only the salt content
    (C) the presence of *V. parahaemolyticus* was independent of both the water temperature and the salt content
    (D) the presence of *V. parahaemolyticus* was dependent on the water temperature

60. The word *cramp* in the reading means most nearly
    (A) noises   (B) toxicity   (C) severe pain   (D) high temperature

STOP. THIS IS THE END OF THE EXAMINATION. IF YOU FINISH BEFORE TIME IS UP, CHECK YOUR WORK ON PARTS A AND B OF THE READING COMPREHENSION AND VOCABULARY SECTION ONLY. DO NOT RETURN TO ANY OTHER SECTION OF THE TEST.

PRACTICE TEST 4

SECTION 1: LISTENING COMPREHENSION

Time: Approximately 30 Minutes
50 Questions

For Practice Test 4, have friends read the script (found in Part V) aloud to you or use the cassette available by mail. (See ordering information, page 485.) On the actual TOEFL you will be given extra time to go on to the next page when you finish a page in the listening comprehension section. In the following test, however, you will have only the 12 seconds given after each question. Turn the page as soon as you have marked your answer.

Part A

DIRECTIONS

For each problem in Part A, you will hear a short statement. The statements will be *spoken* just one time. They will not be written out for you, and you must listen carefully in order to understand what the speaker says.

When you hear a statement, read the four sentences in your test book and decide which one is closest in meaning to the statement you have heard. Then, on your answer sheet, find the number of the problem and mark your answer.

1. (A) The bank closed before I could deposit my money.
   (B) If I hurry, I'll get to the bank before closing time.
   (C) I have to take some money out of the bank before it closes.
   (D) The bank is closing my account because I haven't deposited any money.

2. (A) The people were total strangers.
   (B) Dan knew the people only slightly.
   (C) Dan knew the people very well.
   (D) Dan wasn't sure whether he knew the people or not.

3. (A) I have more than enough money to pay for the book.
   (B) The book costs more than I have with me.
   (C) I have just enough money to pay for the book.
   (D) I need three more dollars to pay for the book.

4. (A) My keys are lost forever.
   (B) I expect to find my keys soon.
   (C) My keys were lost, but now I have found them.
   (D) Someone showed up with my keys soon after I had lost them.

5. (A) We attended the concert even though the tickets were expensive.
   (B) We wanted to attend the concert, but the tickets were sold out.
   (C) The tickets were so inexpensive that we attended the concert.
   (D) We couldn't afford the tickets for the concert.

6. (A) The train left at 6:15.   (C) The train left at 7:30.
   (B) The train left at 7:15.   (D) The train left at 7:45.

7. (A) Lucy didn't wear the coat, because she doesn't like red.
   (B) Lucy is allergic to wool.
   (C) Lucy wore the coat, but broke out in a rash.
   (D) Lucy couldn't wear the coat because she was in a rush.

8. (A) They managed to pull all the victims through the wreckage.
   (B) The crash victims were pulling each other through the wreckage.
   (C) None of the victims of the crash will survive.
   (D) All those involved in the accident will probably survive.

9. (A) There were so many tickets left that they had to sell them again the
       next day.
   (B) Not many showed up to purchase tickets on opening day.
   (C) There were no tickets left by noon of the opening day.
   (D) A few tickets were left for the afternoon of opening day.

10. (A) The kidnapper escaped with both the money and the child.
    (B) The kidnapper escaped with the child, but left the money.
    (C) The kidnapper left the child and took the money.
    (D) The kidnapper escaped with neither the child nor the money.

11. (A) Knowing that he lacked experience, Phil still applied.
    (B) Even though he was experienced, Phil didn't apply for the job.
    (C) Phil was highly qualified for the job, so he applied.
    (D) Phil didn't have much experience working in the fields.

12. (A) The problem could not be solved by anyone.
    (B) Everyone knew how to solve the problem.
    (C) James was the only one who couldn't solve the problem.
    (D) Only James could solve the problem.

13. (A) Mr. Cunningham works in a hardware store.
    (B) Mr. Cunningham works in a laundromat.
    (C) Mr. Cunningham works in a grocery store.
    (D) Mr. Cunningham works in a drugstore.

14. (A) The people thanked us for our response.
    (B) They were grateful because we had requested the information.
    (C) We were happy with the response to our first request.
    (D) We responded gratefully to their request.

15. (A) I'd like to have a steak and salad now.
    (B) I think I'll run out and buy a steak and salad right now.
    (C) I'm going to have steak and salad.
    (D) I'm eating a steak and salad at the moment.

16. (A) We left too late to catch the train.
    (B) The train left late.
    (C) We almost missed the train.
    (D) Because the train was late, we had no trouble catching it.

17. (A) Jane can't attend the meeting because she has too much home-
        work.
    (B) Jane completed her homework early so that she could attend the
        meeting.
    (C) Although Jane has homework due tomorrow, she plans to go to the
        meeting.
    (D) Jane refuses to attend this class because of the homework.

18. (A) Jeanette usually goes to the football games.
    (B) Jeanette hasn't seen a football game for a long time.
    (C) Jeanette doesn't like football.
    (D) Jeanette usually doesn't go to football games.

19. (A) John prefers that we wait for him.
    (B) John is happy because we didn't wait for him.
    (C) We are angry because John left before we arrived.
    (D) John doesn't want us to wait for him.

20. (A) The insurance agent has sold no policies this week.
    (B) The insurance agent has sold only one policy this week.
    (C) The insurance agent hasn't sold too many policies this week.
    (D) Last week, the insurance agent sold more policies than anybody
        else.

GO ON TO PART B

Part B

DIRECTIONS

   In Part B, you will hear 15 short conversations between two speakers. At
the end of each conversation, a third voice will ask a question about what was
said. The question will be *spoken* just one time. After you hear a conversa-

tion and the question about it, read the four possible answers and decide which one would be the best answer to the question you have heard. Then, on your answer sheet, find the number of the problem and mark your answer.

21. (A) She is jogging.   (C) She went for a walk.
    (B) She is at the store.   (D) She is getting a newspaper.

22. (A) Something happened to her car.
    (B) She was broke and couldn't afford the bus.
    (C) She got up too late to catch the bus.
    (D) Her car got stuck in the driveway.

23. (A) She got scratched in the wild berry bushes.
    (B) She got cut at the wild picnic celebration.
    (C) She was allergic to the fruit that she had eaten.
    (D) She was trying to get a suntan at the picnic.

24. (A) She doesn't like other people brushing her clothes.
    (B) She doesn't like to drink.
    (C) She doesn't like to knit.
    (D) She doesn't like being snubbed at a party.

25. (A) Bill will buy the car as soon as he gets the money.
    (B) Bill's friend is buying the car for him.
    (C) Bill can't afford to buy a new car.
    (D) Bill has already made the down payment on the car.

26. (A) She had to fly out of town.
    (B) She's sick.
    (C) She said that she'd come later.
    (D) She decided to stay home.

27. (A) 15   (B) 50   (C) 85   (D) 100

28. (A) The man doesn't have to study a foreign language.
    (B) The man just received an "A" on his test.
    (C) The man's adviser gave him some good advice.
    (D) He doesn't have to take the final exam.

29. (A) They can't afford to eat meat.
    (B) Their rent has been raised so they have to cut down on their grocery expenditures.
    (C) The cheaper grade of meat comes without fat.
    (D) They will have to cut down on expenses.

30. (A) Nobody answered at the number he called.
    (B) He needs help making a long-distance call.
    (C) He doesn't know the area code.
    (D) He was disconnected.

31. (A) Joe will lose his car because he hasn't made the payments.
    (B) The finance company is returning Joe's car.
    (C) Joe has a broken finger from falling on the pavement behind his car.
    (D) Joe's car is being repaired.

32. (A) Oscar pays his bills ahead of time.
    (B) Oscar has decided to get a loan to pay his bills.
    (C) Oscar has too many expenses and can't save any money.
    (D) Oscar's wife will have to go to work.

33. (A) The teacher reviewed a previous lesson.
    (B) The teacher presented new material.
    (C) The teacher tested the students.
    (D) The teacher made the students write in class.

34. (A) The woman is getting another job.
    (B) The woman is disappointed at not getting the job.
    (C) The woman's boss is letting her have a better job.
    (D) The woman's job is much better than she had expected.

35. (A) They are pleased.   (C) They are undecided.
    (B) They dread it.   (D) They are frustrated.

GO ON TO PART C

Part C

DIRECTIONS

In this part of the test, you will hear several short talks and/or conversations. After each talk or conversation, you will be asked some questions. The talks and questions will be *spoken* just one time. They will not be written out for you, so you will have to listen carefully in order to understand and remember what the speaker says.

When you hear a question, read the four possible answers in your test book and decide which one would be the best answer to the question you have heard. Then, on your answer sheet, find the number of the problem and fill in the space that corresponds to the letter of the answer you have chosen.

36. (A) the high cost of gasoline
    (B) overcongestion of university areas
    (C) roller skating in the streets
    (D) police roadblocks

37. (A) state law only   (C) natural law
    (B) city law only   (D) city and state law

38. (A) Roller skating in the streets is only a local problem.
    (B) Skaters are creating problems for motorists.
    (C) Police will ticket violators.
    (D) The problem is most common in college and university areas.

39. (A) new political ways   (C) new means of water travel
    (B) new methods of fishing   (D) how to trap animals

40. (A) They were plentiful in England.
    (B) They grew only in certain sections of the country.
    (C) They were preferred raw.
    (D) They did not exist in England.

41. (A) by canoe
    (B) by blazing trails through the forest
    (C) by toboggan and snowshoes
    (D) on animals

42. (A) corn   (C) building sod houses
    (B) domesticated animals   (D) trapping animals

43. (A) Spaniards   (C) other Englishmen
    (B) Indians   (D) political leaders

44. (A) The settlers were well prepared for the hardships that they would
        encounter.
    (B) The new settlers evidently found the winters severe.
    (C) The Indians taught the settlers how to build canoes.
    (D) The settlers brought tools and weapons to the new world.

45. (A) 6:45 in Baton Rouge   (C) 1:45 in Dallas
    (B) 1:45 in Atlanta   (D) 2:45 in Dallas

46. (A) smoking cigars   (C) smoking a pipe
    (B) drinking whiskey   (D) smoking cigarettes

47. (A) 3242   (B) 3224   (C) 2334   (D) 3442

48. (A) 1:45 P.M.   (B) 12 midnight   (C) 1:45 A.M.   (D) 6:45 P.M.

49. (A) tuna fish   (B) eggs   (C) bleach   (D) detergent

50. (A) It is a no-frills store.
    (B) The fresh food looked appetizing.
    (C) The lines are shorter.
    (D) There is a wide selection.

STOP. THIS IS THE END OF THE LISTENING COMPREHENSION SECTION.

SECTION II: STRUCTURE AND WRITTEN EXPRESSION

Time: 25 Minutes
40 Questions

Part A

DIRECTIONS

Each sentence in Part A is an incomplete sentence. Four words or phrases, marked (A), (B), (C), (D), are given beneath each sentence. You are to choose the *one* word or phrase that best completes the sentence. Then, on your answer sheet, find the number of the problem and mark your answer.

1. The cyclist _____ he crossed the main street.
   - (A) looked with caution after
   - (B) had looked cautiously before
   - (C) was looked cautious when
   - (D) looks cautious when

2. Here _____ notebook and report that I promised you last week.
   - (A) is the (B) are the (C) was the (D) has been a

3. Neither Jane nor her brothers _____ a consent form for tomorrow's field trip.
   - (A) need (B) needs (C) is needing (D) has need

4. Cuba is _____ sugar-growing areas in the world.
   - (A) one of the larger
   - (B) one of largest
   - (C) one of the largest
   - (D) largest

5. The skiers would rather _____ through the mountains than go by bus.
   - (A) to travel on train
   - (B) traveled by train
   - (C) travel by train
   - (D) traveling by the train

6. That magnificent _____ temple was constructed by the Chinese.
   - (A) eight-centuries-old
   - (B) eight-century's-old
   - (C) old-eight-centuries
   - (D) eight-century-old

7. There were two small rooms in the beach house, _____ served as a kitchen.
   - (A) the smaller of which
   - (B) the smallest of which
   - (C) the smaller of them
   - (D) smallest of that

8. Pioneer men and women endured terrible hardships, and _____.
   - (A) so do their children
   - (B) neither did the children
   - (C) also the childs
   - (D) so did their children

9. Last year, Matt earned _____ his brother, who has a better position.
   - (A) twice as much as
   - (B) twice more than
   - (C) twice as many as
   - (D) twice as more as

10. _____, he would have been able to pass the exam.
   - (A) If he studied more
   - (B) If he were studying to a greater degree
   - (C) Studying more
   - (D) Had he studied more

11. Mr. Duncan does not know _____ the lawn mower after they had finished using it.
   - (A) where did they put
   - (B) where they did put
   - (C) where they put
   - (D) where to put

12. The facilities of the older hospital _____.
   - (A) is as good or better than the new hospital
   - (B) are as good or better that the new hospital
   - (C) are as good as or better than the new hospital
   - (D) are as good as or better than those of the new hospital

13. Our flight from Amsterdam to London was delayed _____ the heavy fog.
   - (A) because of   (B) because   (C) on account   (D) as result

14. The teacher suggested that her students _____ experiences with ESP.
   - (A) write a composition on their
   - (B) to write composition about the
   - (C) wrote some compositions of his or her
   - (D) had written any compositions for his

15. Of the two new teachers, one is experienced and _____.
   - (A) the others are not
   - (B) another is inexperienced
   - (C) the other is not
   - (D) other lacks experience

GO ON TO PART B

Part B

DIRECTIONS

Each sentence in Part B has four words or phrases underlined. The four underlined parts of the sentence are marked (A), (B), (C), (D). You are to identify the *one* underlined word or phrase that should be corrected or rewritten. Then, on your answer sheet, find the number of the problem and mark your answer.

16. While searching for the wreckage of a unidentified aircraft,
       A   B   C

    the Coast Guard encountered severe squalls at sea.
                                     D

17. Although a number of police officers was guarding the
                                     A

    priceless treasures in the museum, the director worried that
            B

    someone would try to steal them.
              C   D

18. Since it was so difficult for American Indians to negotiate
                 A   B

    a peace treaty or declare war in their native language ,
                               C

    they used a universal understood form of sign language.
                D

19. Louis Braille designed a form of communication enabling people
                                         A

    to convey and preserve their thoughts to incorporate a series of dots
      B   C

    which were read by the finger tips.
            D

20. While verbalization is the most common form of language in
                             A

    existence, humans make use of many others systems
           B   C

    and techniques to express their thoughts and feelings.
                 D

21. The need for a well-rounded education was an idea
           A   B

    espoused by the Greeks in time of Socrates.
       C   D

22. Writers and media <u>personnel</u> sell <u>theirselves</u> best <u>by the</u>
                      A   B   C
    impression given in their verbal <u>expression</u>.
                                     D

23. <u>In the spirit</u> of the <u>naturalist</u> writers, that <u>author's</u> work
      A   B   C
    portrays man's struggle for <u>surviving</u>.
                             D

24. <u>Stephen Crane's story</u> is <u>a</u> clinical portrayal <u>of man as an animal</u>
             A   B   C
    trapped by <u>the fear</u> and hunger.
                D

25. Their silly, whiny conversation <u>on a child level</u> was meant
                                 A
    <u>to create tension</u> and <u>heighten</u> <u>Nancy's</u> fears and anxiety.
        B   C   D

26. For a long time, <u>this</u> officials <u>have been known</u> throughout
                    A   B
    the country <u>as</u> political bosses and <u>law enforcers</u>.
           C   D

27. Nora hardly <u>never</u> misses <u>an</u> opportunity <u>to play</u> <u>in</u>
              A   B   C D
    the tennis tournaments.

28. Air pollution, together <u>with</u> littering, <u>are</u> causing <u>many</u>
                      A   B   C
    problems <u>in our large</u>, industrial cities today.
             D

29. <u>Because of</u> the severe snow storm and the road blocks, <u>the</u>
      A   B
    air force <u>dropped food</u> and medical supplies <u>close the city</u>.
             C   D

30. Hummingbirds are <u>the only birds</u> capable <u>to fly</u> backward
                     A   B
    as well as <u>forward</u>, up, and down.
       C   D

31. <u>The</u> news of the president's treaty negotiations with the
    A
    foreign government <u>were</u> <u>received</u> with <u>mixed emotions</u>
                   B   C
    by the citizens <u>of both governments</u>.
                  D

32. Angie's bilingual ability and previous experience <u>were</u> the qualities
                                                        A
that which <u>helped her</u> get the job over all <u>the other</u> candidates.
   B   C   D

33. <u>Joel</u> giving up <u>smoking has</u> <u>caused him to gain</u> weight
      A   B   C
and <u>become irritable</u> with his acquaintances.
        D

34. They asked me <u>what did happen</u> <u>last night</u>, but I was
                        A   B
<u>unable</u> <u>to tell them</u>.
   C   D

35. The <u>test</u> administrator ordered <u>we</u> <u>not to open</u> our books
        A   B   C
until he <u>told us to do so</u>.
            D

36. <u>Our new</u> neighbors <u>had been living</u> in Arizona <u>since</u> ten
      A   B   C
years <u>before moving to</u> their present house.
         D

37. I <u>would of</u> attended the meeting <u>of the planning</u> committee
       A   B
last week, but I <u>had to deliver</u> a speech <u>at a convention</u>.
                     C   D

38. We are <u>suppose</u> to read <u>all of</u> chapter seven and <u>answer</u>
              A   B   C
the questions <u>for tomorrow's class</u>.
                 D

39. The explanation that <u>our</u> instructor <u>gave us</u> was different
                          A   B
<u>than</u> the one <u>yours gave you</u>.
   C   D

40. <u>In the sixteenth</u> century, Spain <u>became involved in foreign</u>
      A   B
wars with <u>several other</u> European countries and could not
             C
find the means of <u>finance</u> the battles that ensued.
                     D

STOP. THIS IS THE END OF THE STRUCTURE AND WRITTEN EXPRESSION
SECTION. IF YOU FINISH BEFORE TIME IS UP, CHECK YOUR WORK ON PARTS A
AND B OF THIS SECTION ONLY. DO NOT WORK ON ANY OTHER SECTION OF THE
TEST.

SECTION III: READING COMPREHENSION AND VOCABULARY

Time: 45 Minutes
60 Questions

Part A

DIRECTIONS

Each sentence in Part A has a word or phrase underlined. Below each sentence are four other words or phrases. You are to choose the *one* word or phrase which would *best keep the meaning* of the original sentence if it were substituted for the underlined word.

1. The house by the sea had a mysterious air of serenity about it.
   (A) melancholy   (C) sadness
   (B) joy   (D) calmness

2. The speaker emphasized the need for cooperation in the project that we were about to undertake.
   (A) accentuated   (C) discussed
   (B) downplayed   (D) displayed

3. Marsha found it difficult to cope with the loss of her job.
   (A) anticipate   (C) deal with
   (B) think about   (D) confirm

4. The number of unemployed people in our country is increasing rapidly.
   (A) licensed   (C) business
   (B) working   (D) jobless

5. Migrant workers have difficulty finding steady employment.
   (A) midget   (C) transient
   (B) diligent   (D) unmotivated

6. Christopher Columbus was the first person to navigate under the patronage of Queen Isabella of Spain.
   (A) explore   (C) work
   (B) sail   (D) circumvent

7. The sun's intense rays distorted the image on the horizon.
   (A) reflected   (C) melted
   (B) altered   (D) disrupted

8. A new government department was established to control <u>maritime</u> traffic.
   - (A) sea
   - (B) military
   - (C) highway
   - (D) air

9. His company <u>empowered</u> him to negotiate the contract.
   - (A) helped
   - (B) forbade
   - (C) authorized
   - (D) ordered

10. His <u>involuntary</u> reflexes betrayed his feelings.
    - (A) automatic
    - (B) unbelievable
    - (C) unnecessary
    - (D) unreasonable

11. The principal <u>congratulated</u> the student on his outstanding display of leadership.
    - (A) alluded
    - (B) scolded
    - (C) praised
    - (D) contacted

12. A middle-aged woman of tremendous <u>girth</u> sat down beside the other patients in the waiting room.
    - (A) prestige
    - (B) rotundity
    - (C) eloquence
    - (D) mirth

13. <u>Numbing</u> terror filled their brains as they witnessed the explosions.
    - (A) torpid
    - (B) tantalizing
    - (C) paralyzing
    - (D) sentient

14. The atmosphere in the police chief's office was electric with <u>contention</u>.
    - (A) discord
    - (B) rejoicing
    - (C) weeping
    - (D) curiosity

15. Penny's <u>impromptu</u> speech given at the state competition won her the first prize.
    - (A) interesting
    - (B) informative
    - (C) extemporaneous
    - (D) expressive

16. The slender boy <u>scaled</u> the wall like a lizard.
    - (A) balanced
    - (B) crawled
    - (C) plastered
    - (D) climbed

17. The salon was the most elegant room Madeline had ever seen, despite its <u>austerity</u>.
    - (A) flexibility
    - (B) design
    - (C) decoration
    - (D) simplicity

18. The Royal Museum contains a <u>facsimile</u> of the king's famous declaration.
    - (A) copy
    - (B) showcase
    - (C) record
    - (D) new edition

19. The raccoon is a <u>nocturnal</u> animal.
    (A) harmless   (C) marsupial
    (B) night   (D) diurnal

20. The author wrote with great <u>clarity,</u> not missing a single detail.
    (A) genius   (C) clearness
    (B) cleverness   (D) extensiveness

21. Double agents live in a <u>perpetual</u> state of fear.
    (A) perfect   (C) ceasing
    (B) constant   (D) perpetrated

22. After the alien spacecraft had hovered over the park for a short while, it <u>vanished.</u>
    (A) landed   (C) attacked
    (B) disappeared   (D) rose

23. After receiving the insulting letter, Ron became <u>furious.</u>
    (A) ghastly   (C) fulgent
    (B) resentful   (D) irate

24. Her childhood <u>poverty</u> caused Lucy to be very thrifty as she grew older.
    (A) practicality   (C) wealth
    (B) indigence   (D) shyness

25. If the crops are not <u>irrigated</u> soon, the harvest will be sparse.
    (A) watered   (C) planted
    (B) plowed   (D) fertilized

26. While in Europe on vacation, the twins <u>roamed</u> the countryside on their bikes.
    (A) rounded   (C) wandered
    (B) rocked   (D) rustled

27. The coroner was able to extract a <u>minute</u> particle of cloth from under the victim's fingernail.
    (A) infinitesimal   (C) large
    (B) significant   (D) short

28. Let's <u>suppose</u> that we are floating in a cool pool on a hot summer's day.
    (A) imagine   (C) succumb
    (B) imply   (D) suggest

29. The students' records were not readily <u>accessible</u> for their perusal.
    (A) offered   (C) acceptable
    (B) available   (D) accountable

30. Scientists say that brown genes are <u>dominant</u> and blue ones are recessive.
    (A) controlling
    (B) docile
    (C) dormant
    (D) doleful

GO ON TO PART B

Part B

DIRECTIONS

In Part B, the questions are based on a variety of reading material (single sentences, paragraphs, advertisements, and the like). You are to choose the *one* best answer, (A), (B), (C), or (D), to each question. Then, on your answer sheet, find the number of the problem and mark your answer. Answer all questions following a passage on the basis of what is *stated* or *implied* in that passage.

Questions 31 through 34 are based on the following reading.

Why would anyone want to set aside a day to honor a lowly little groundhog? The answer to that question is not certain, but a group of people get together every February 2 in Punxsutawney, Pennsylvania, to watch Punxsutawney "Pete" leave his burrow. What "Pete" does next, many believe, will indicate whether spring is just around the corner or a long way off. You see, in Pennsylvania on this date there is usually a great deal of snow on the ground, and the little animal has been hibernating during the long, cold winter. He gorged himself during the autumn months and then went into his burrow for a long sleep, his body fat helping keep him alive. But as he emerges on February 2, he looks very thin. If the sun is shining brightly and he sees his shadow, according to legend, it scares him back into his home where he will stay another six weeks. Should it be cloudy and gray, the little animal will supposedly wander around for food—a sure sign that spring is near. While many believe in the groundhog's predictions, it is unwise to accept them as factual.

31. According to this reading, why do people gather every year to observe the groundhog?
    (A) He's cute and playful, and children love to watch him.
    (B) He's looking for food and the people want to help him find it in the snow.
    (C) Many people believe him to be a harbinger of spring.
    (D) The people want to be sure he is alive after such a long winter.

32. How does the groundhog manage to stay alive during the long winter?
    (A) People set out food for him.
    (B) His stored body fat sustains him.
    (C) He wakes up on nice days and hunts for food.
    (D) It is a mystery as yet unsolved.

33. Which of the following is *not* true?
    (A) Animals have a certain instinct which helps them predict the seasons.
    (B) According to the legend, the groundhog leaves his burrow on February 2.
    (C) Groups of people in Pennsylvania wait for the groundhog's predictions.
    (D) After his long period of hibernation, the groundhog looks very thin.

34. What prediction does the groundhog supposedly make?
    (A) If he sees his shadow, it will soon be spring.
    (B) If he sees his shadow, spring will not arrive for another six weeks.
    (C) If he does not see his shadow, spring will arrive in six weeks.
    (D) If he does not see his shadow, all the snow will disappear immediately.

Questions 35 through 38 are based on the following reading.

The First Amendment to the American Constitution declares freedom of the press to all men. Although this right was not officially adopted until 1791, the famous Zenger trial of 1735 laid the groundwork for insuring this precious freedom.

John Peter Zenger emigrated as a teenager from Germany. In 1733 he began publishing the *New York Weekly Journal*. The following year, he was arrested for writing a story about the crown-appointed governor of New York. While he was imprisoned for nine months, Zenger's wife dutifully published the newpaper every day, bravely telling the truth about the corrupt government officials sent by the king to govern the colonies.

Finally Zenger's long-awaited trial took place. The hostile judge dismissed Zenger's local lawyers, making it necessary for his wife to seek out Andrew Hamilton, a prominent Philadelphia lawyer. Persuaded by Hamilton, the jury bravely returned a not-guilty verdict defying the judge's orders for a conviction.

As a result of determination and bravery on the part of the colonists, a lasting victory for freedom of the press was set by a young immigrant.

35. John Peter Zenger was a _____.
    (A) corrupt governor of New York (C) brave newspaper publisher
    (B) famous lawyer   (D) hostile judge

36. What political problem existed in the colonies at that time?
    (A) Government officials were corrupt.
    (B) Newspapers exaggerated the truth about the political officials.
    (C) Lawyers were hostile to witnesses.
    (D) All newspaper publishers were imprisoned.

37. How long did it take after the Zenger trial before the concept of freedom
    of the press was officially adopted?
    (A) 9 months   (B) 1 year   (C) 56 years   (D) 58 years

38. Which of the following is *not* true?
    (A) Despite Zenger's imprisonment, his newspaper continued to be
        published.
    (B) Andrew Hamilton encouraged the jury to fight for freedom.
    (C) The jury obeyed the judge's orders and convicted Zenger.
    (D) The king controlled the colonies through his own appointed rulers.

Questions 39 through 41 are based on the following reading.

When buying a house, you must be sure to have it checked for
termites. A termite is much like an ant in its communal habits, although
physically the two insects are distinct.

Like those of ants, termite colonies consist of different classes, each
with its own particular job. The most perfectly formed termites, both
male and female, make up the reproductive class. They have eyes, hard
body walls, and fully developed wings. A pair of reproductive termites
founds the colony. When new reproductive termites develop, they leave
to form another colony. They use their wings only this one time and then
break them off.

The worker termites are small, blind, and wingless, with soft bodies.
They make up the majority of the colony and do all the work. Soldiers
are also wingless and blind but are larger than the workers and have
hard heads and strong jaws and legs. They defend the colony and are
cared for by the workers.

The male and female of the reproductive class remain inside a
closed-in cell where the female lays thousands of eggs. The workers
place the eggs in cells and care for them.

39. How are termites like ants?
    (A) They live in communities, and each class has a specific duty.
    (B) Their bodies are the same shape.
    (C) The king and queen are imprisoned.
    (D) The females' reproductive capacities are the same.

40. Which of the following is *not* true?
    (A) All termites have eyes.
    (B) Some termites cannot fly.
    (C) Workers are smaller than soldiers.
    (D) Termites do not fly often.

41. Which of the following statements is probably true?
    (A) Thousands of termites may move together to develop a new colony.
    (B) The male and female reproductives do not venture outdoors except to form a new colony.
    (C) There are more soldiers than workers.
    (D) A worker could easily kill a soldier.

Questions 42 through 46 are based on the following reading.

In recent years, there has been an increasing awareness of the inadequacies of the judicial system in the United States. Costs are staggering both for the taxpayers and the litigants—and the litigants, or parties, have to wait sometimes many years before having their day in court. Many suggestions have been made concerning methods of ameliorating the situation, but as in most branches of government, changes come slowly.

One suggestion that has been made in order to maximize the efficiency of the system is to allow districts that have an overabundance of pending cases to borrow judges from other districts that do not have such a backlog. Another suggestion is to use pretrial conferences, in which the judge meets in his chambers with the litigants and their attorneys in order to narrow the issues, limit the witnesses, and provide for a more orderly trial. The theory behind pretrial conferences is that judges will spend less time on each case and parties will more readily settle before trial when they realize the adequacy of their claims and their opponents' evidence. Unfortunately, at least one study has shown that pretrial conferences actually use more judicial time than they save, rarely result in pretrial settlements, and actually result in higher damage settlements.

Many states have now established another method, small-claims courts, in which cases over small sums of money can be disposed of with considerable dispatch. Such proceedings cost the litigants almost nothing. In California, for example, the parties must appear before the judge without the assistance of counsel. The proceedings are quite informal and there is no pleading—the litigants need to make only a one-sentence statement of their claim. By going to this type of court, the plaintiff waives any right to a jury trial and the right to appeal the decision.

In coming years, we can expect to see more and more innovations in the continuing effort to remedy a situation which must be remedied if the citizens who have valid claims are going to be able to have their day in court.

42. The pretrial conference, in theory, is supposed to do all of the following *except*
    (A) narrow the issues   (C) save judicial time
    (B) cause early settlements   (D) increase settlement costs

43. What is the main topic of the passage?
    (A) All states should follow California's example in using small-claims courts in order to free judges for other work.
    (B) The legislature needs to formulate fewer laws so that the judiciary can catch up on its older cases.
    (C) Nobody seems to care enough to attempt to find methods for making the judicial system more efficient.
    (D) While there are many problems with the court system, there are viable suggestions for improvement.

44. The word *litigants* means most nearly
    (A) jury members   (C) parties in a lawsuit
    (B) commentators   (D) taxpayers

45. Which of the following is true about small-claims courts?
    (A) It is possible to have one's case heard by a jury if he or she is dissatisfied with the court's decision.
    (B) The litigants must plead accurately and according to a strict form.
    (C) The decision may not be appealed to a higher court.
    (D) The parties may not present their cases without an attorney's help.

46. What can we assume from the passage?
    (A) Most people who feel they have been wronged have a ready remedy in courts of law.
    (B) Many people would like to bring a case to court, but are unable to because of the cost and time required.
    (C) The judicial system in the United States is highly acclaimed for its efficiency.
    (D) Pretrial conferences will someday probably have replaced trials completely.

Questions 47 through 50 are based on the following reading.

In 1971, the great Persian Empire celebrated the 2500th anniversary of its founding. Its founder was Cyrus the Great, who proclaimed himself the King of Kings. His son Cambyses succeeded him, conquering Egypt and expanding the empire. Darius I followed Cambyses and was probably the most famous of this long line of kings. Under his rule, the empire stretched as far as India. Governors were placed in charge of the provinces. Extensive systems of roads and waterways improved communication throughout the realm. He was one of a few ancient rulers who permitted his subjects to worship as they wished. The magnificent city of Persepolis, founded under his direction in 518 B.C., was a ceremonial center then as well as in the 1970's.

47. Who is considered the founder of the Persian Empire?
    (A) Persepolis   (B) Cyrus   (C) Darius I   (D) Cambyses

48. In what year was the Persian Empire founded?
    (A) 2500 B.C.   (B) 518 B.C.   (C) 529 B.C.   (D) 971 A.D.

49. Who was the predecessor of Cambyses?
    (A) Egypt   (B) Darius I   (C) Persepolis   (D) Cyrus

50. Which of the following best describes the empire under Darius I?
    (A) ceremonial   (C) punitive
    (B) bellicose   (D) progressive

Questions 51 through 54 are based on the following reading.

In an effort to produce the largest, fastest, and most luxurious ship afloat, the British built the *Titanic*. It was so superior to anything else on the seas that it was dubbed "unsinkable." So sure of this were the owners that they provided lifeboats for only 950 of its possible 3,500 passengers.

Many passengers were aboard the night it rammed an iceberg, only two days at sea and more than half way between England and the New York destination. Because the luxury liner was traveling so fast, it was impossible to avoid the ghostly looking iceberg. An unextinguished fire also contributed to the ship's submersion. Panic increased the number of casualties as people jumped into the icy water or fought to be among the few to board the lifeboats. Four hours after the mishap, another ship, the *Carpathia,* rescued the survivors—less than a third of those originally aboard.

The infamous *Titanic* enjoyed only two days of sailing glory on its maiden voyage in 1912 before plunging into 12,000 feet of water near the coast of Newfoundland, where it lies today.

51. Which of the following is *not* true?
    (A) Only a third of those aboard perished.
    (B) The *Carpathia* rescued the survivors.
    (C) The *Titanic* sank near Newfoundland.
    (D) The *Titanic* was the fastest ship afloat in 1912.

52. Which of the following did *not* contribute to the large death toll?
    (A) panic   (B) fire   (C) speed   (D) *Carpathia*

53. How many days was the Titanic at sea before sinking?
    (A) 2   (B) 4   (C) 6   (D) 12

54. The word *unextinguished* means most nearly the same as
    (A) indestructable   (C) undiscovered
    (B) uncontrollable   (D) unquenched

Questions 55 through 58 are based on the following reading.

The Great Pyramid of Giza, a monument of wisdom and prophecy, was built as a tomb for Pharaoh Cheops in 2720 B.C. Despite its antiquity, certain aspects of its construction make it one of the truly great wonders of the world. The four sides of the pyramid are aligned almost exactly on true north, south, east, and west—an incredible engineering feat. The ancient Egyptians were sun worshipers and great astronomers, so computations for the Great Pyramid were based on astronomical observations.

Explorations and detailed examinations of the base of the structure reveal many intersecting lines. Further scientific study indicates that these represent a type of time line of events—past, present, and future. Many of the events have been interpreted and found to coincide with known facts of the past. Others are prophesied for future generations and are presently under investigation.

Was this superstructure made by ordinary beings, or one built by a race far superior to any known today?

55. Approximately how long ago was the Great Pyramid constructed?
    (A) 640 years   (B) 2,720 years   (C) 4,000 years   (D) 4,700 years

56. On what did the ancient Egyptians base their calculations?
    (A) observation of the celestial bodies
    (B) advanced technology
    (C) advanced tools of measurement
    (D) knowledge of the earth's surface

57. Why was the Great Pyramid constructed?
    (A) as a solar observatory   (C) as a tomb for the pharoah
    (B) as a religious temple   (D) as an engineering feat

58. Why is the Great Pyramid of Giza considered one of the seven wonders
    of the world?
    (A) It is perfectly aligned with the four cardinal points of the compass
        and contains many prophecies.
    (B) It was selected as the tomb of Pharaoh Cheops.
    (C) It was built by a super race.
    (D) It is very old.

Directions for questions 59 and 60

For each of these questions, choose the answer that is *closest in
meaning* to the original sentence. Note that several of the choices may
be factually correct, but you should choose the one that is the *closest
restatement of the given sentence.*

59. Parents have become increasingly concerned about the television view-
    ing habits of their children—so much so that families are beginning to
    censor the programs that enter their homes.
    (A) Families watch television together more often now than in the past
        so that they can decide whether shows are desirable or not.
    (B) Families with televisions are not as close as families without
        televisions because the former bicker more over program choices.
    (C) Although parents worry about the programs that their children
        watch, they find it very difficult because censorship is not what it
        used to be.
    (D) Because of their concern over the television programs that are
        aired, many parents are deciding which programs they will allow
        their children to watch.

60. Children reared in poverty tend, on the average, to do poorly on tests of
    intelligence.
    (A) Impoverished children are generally not as intelligent as rich
        children.
    (B) Behind the poverty trend is an assumption that children are stupid.
    (C) Children from poor families have a tendency to fare badly on
        intelligence tests.
    (D) Intelligence tests are poorly administered to poor children.

STOP. THIS IS THE END OF THE EXAMINATION. IF YOU FINISH BEFORE TIME IS
UP, CHECK YOUR WORK ON PARTS A AND B OF THE READING COMPREHENSION
AND VOCABULARY SECTION ONLY. DO NOT RETURN TO ANY OTHER SECTION OF
THE TEST.

PRACTICE TEST 5

SECTION 1: LISTENING COMPREHENSION

Time: Approximately 30 Minutes
50 Questions

For Practice Test 5 have friends read the script (found in Part V) aloud to you or use the cassette available by mail. (See ordering information, page 485.) On the actual TOEFL you will be given extra time to go on to the next page when you finish a page in the listening comprehension section. In the following test, however, you will have only the 12 seconds given after each question. Turn the page as soon as you have marked your answer.

Part A

DIRECTIONS

For each problem in Part A, you will hear a short statement. The statements will be *spoken* just one time. They will not be written out for you, and you must listen carefully in order to understand what the speaker says.

When you hear a statement, read the four sentences in your test book and decide which one is closest in meaning to the statement you have heard. Then, on your answer sheet, find the number of the problem and mark your answer.

1. (A) John probably called his office at 9:50.
   (B) John had to call his office at 9:15.
   (C) John wasn't supposed to call his office before 9:15.
   (D) John was supposed to call his office at 9:50.

2. (A) Please give me your hand.
   (B) Would you help me carry these packages?
   (C) Please remove your hands from those packages.
   (D) My hand is stuck under the packages.

3. (A) Every week, there are three direct flights from Atlanta to Chicago.
   (B) Next week, the three flights from Atlanta to Chicago will be stopped.
   (C) Three planes which travel from Atlanta to Chicago each week make nine stops enroute.
   (D) The number of planes that travel from Atlanta to Chicago will be reduced within the next three weeks.

4. (A) Mr. Roberts is pleased because his family is coming up from South America to see him for vacation.
   (B) Mr. Roberts is considering several maps to decide where to go on his vacation.
   (C) Mr. Roberts is rather excited because he has a vacation soon.
   (D) Mr. Roberts is coming up to see us on his vacation.

5. (A) Louise is trying to find a new typing job.
   (B) Louise is looking for somebody to type her research paper.
   (C) Louise is trying to find somebody to move her typewriter to another table.
   (D) Louise has accepted employment as a typist.

6. (A) Maria is angry because there is too much chlorine in the pool.
   (B) The chlorine in the swimming pool bothers Maria's eyes.
   (C) According to Maria, the correct amount of chlorine is essential to a clean swimming pool.
   (D) Maria doesn't believe that there is enough chlorine in the pool.

7. (A) The coat cost $20 on sale.
   (B) Ted said that he had bought a coat for $20, but he was lying.
   (C) The coat actually cost $2 less than the advertised price.
   (D) The coat actually cost $2 more than the advertised price.

8. (A) There was a fire alarm at 2:20 yesterday.
   (B) Because of a fire, class was cancelled.
   (C) The class began at 2:20 because it was delayed by a fire drill.
   (D) The fire drill was postponed until 2:20 so the students could finish class first.

9. (A) Sandra returned the shoes and took a pair of pants instead.
   (B) Sandra took the shoes back to the store and got some different ones.
   (C) One of Sandra's shoes didn't fit properly so she returned them both.
   (D) Because of a problem with the heel of her shoes, Sandra returned them.

10. (A) John didn't go to class because he didn't know there was going to be a test.
    (B) John didn't want to take the test, so he skipped class.
    (C) John went to class although he didn't want to take the test.
    (D) John was happy that yesterday's test was postponed.

11. (A) They were supposed to arrive at 12:15, but they're late.
    (B) They arrived at 11:45.
    (C) They didn't arrive until 12:15.
    (D) After a delay of a quarter of an hour, they arrived at 12 o'clock.

12. (A) Janet was not able to read her assignment because she broke her glasses.
    (B) Janet could have read the assignment if she hadn't had to wash dishes.
    (C) Janet won't go to class tomorrow because she must go to the optometrist.
    (D) Because she cut herself on some broken glass, Janet didn't do her homework.

13. (A) Anne sold all the tickets to the show last week.
    (B) Anne is a policewoman.
    (C) Anne received a citation last week for driving too fast.
    (D) Anne received an award for her good driving habits.

14. (A) They arrived at 3 o'clock because they had been delayed two hours.
    (B) They finally arrived at 5 o'clock.
    (C) They were supposed to arrive at 2 o'clock, but they were delayed three hours.
    (D) They had planned to arrive at 11 o'clock.

15. (A) Drive for 90 miles on East Highway 16, and then turn left and go 50 miles more.
    (B) Go east on Highway 90 for 60 miles and then go north on Highway 50.
    (C) Travel east on Highway 19 for 16 miles; after that, drive 50 miles on North Highway.
    (D) After you travel for 90 miles on East Highway 90, go right on Highway 15.

16. (A) This project will be cancelled as a result of mismanagement of funds.
    (B) They probably made an error in figuring the expenses for this project.
    (C) They must give a complete report on the estimated costs of this project.
    (D) They have to charge the calculations to the company office.

17. (A) Jane was able to go to the conference because her employer paid her expenses.
    (B) Jane couldn't go to the conference because her boss wouldn't pay her while she was away.
    (C) Although Jane's employer had offered to pay her expenses to the conference, she didn't go.
    (D) Jane's boss refused to give her money to attend the conference, but she went anyway.

18. (A) John uses some strange methods when he studies.
    (B) John receives very good grades although he doesn't study.
    (C) John is very fond of studying dangerous situations.
    (D) It's too bad that John dislikes studying.

19. (A) George has entered the university hospital for treatment.
    (B) George met his wife while she was working as a nurse at the university hospital.
    (C) George wants to find a place close to the university to keep his children during the day.
    (D) George likes the university because it has a good nursing program.

20. (A) Although Janet doesn't like television, her husband watches it every night.
    (B) Janet refuses to let her husband watch television.
    (C) Although Janet hates television, her husband is a TV salesman.
    (D) Janet's husband refuses to have the TV repaired.

GO ON TO PART B

Part B

DIRECTIONS

In Part B, you will hear 15 short conversations between two speakers. At the end of each conversation, a third voice will ask a question about what was said. The question will be *spoken* just one time. After you hear a conversation and the question about it, read the four possible answers and decide which one would be the best answer to the question you have heard. Then, on your answer sheet, find the number of the problem and mark your answer.

21. (A) a love story
    (B) one about jail escapes and mental hospitals
    (C) one that is very realistic and touching
    (D) one that is not realistic or sentimental

22. (A) They were extremely displeased.
    (B) They found it extremely sad.
    (C) They thought it was shocking, but very funny.
    (D) They became angry at the promiscuity.

23. (A) to the beach   (C) to a movie theater
    (B) to a play   (D) to a restaurant

24. (A) He's dying.
    (B) He doesn't hear too well.
    (C) He was at a party.
    (D) He was reading something important.

25. (A) The Kehoes got a bargain.
    (B) John bought a new house.
    (C) The Kehoes bought a house out of the country.
    (D) Mr. Kehoe is a real estate agent.

26. (A) The food spoiled.
    (B) The group was shameful.
    (C) The weather was bad.
    (D) The program director wanted to have it on another day.

27. (A) Sebring High School   (C) Melrose Community College
    (B) Clark High School   (D) Enrold College

28. (A) The class thought the demonstration was too complex.
    (B) Too many students showed up.
    (C) The professor didn't show up.
    (D) The professor cancelled it.

29. (A) Monday, Wednesday, and Friday
    (B) Saturday and Sunday
    (C) Tuesday, Thursday, and Sunday
    (D) Monday, Friday, and Saturday

30. (A) a bicycle   (C) a shirt
    (B) a game   (D) baseball shoes

31. (A) It's more direct.   (C) It's faster.
    (B) There's a traffic jam.   (D) It's less expensive.

32. (A) He got a one-way plane ticket.
    (B) He went the wrong direction on a one-way street.
    (C) He made an improper turn.
    (D) He slowed down at the wrong time.

33. (A) Susan Flannigan rings a bell.
    (B) Her name sounds familiar.
    (C) Susan Flannigan is ringing the bell now.
    (D) Her name sounds melodic.

34. (A) Roy's standing in line for a gold medal.
    (B) Roy was the best, so he got a gold medal.
    (C) Nobody's better than Roy at getting gold medals.
    (D) Roy probably won't win a gold medal.

35. (A) $3.00   (B) $3.75   (C) $3.25   (D) $4.00

GO ON TO PART C

Part C

DIRECTIONS

In this part of the test, you will hear several short talks and/or conversations. After each talk or conversation, you will be asked some questions. The talks and questions will be *spoken* just one time. They will not be written out for you, so you will have to listen carefully in order to understand and remember what the speaker says.

When you hear a question, read the four possible answers in your test book and decide which one would be the best answer to the question you have heard. Then, on your answer sheet, find the number of the problem and fill in the space that corresponds to the letter of the answer you have chosen.

36. (A) mechanic   (C) TV repairman
    (B) policeman   (D) car salesman

37. (A) broken fuel pump   (C) dirty oil
    (B) dirty carburetor   (D) leaky radiator

38. (A) He was struck by lightning.
    (B) He was very old.
    (C) He was in a car accident.
    (D) He fell down in his yard.

39. (A) his wife   (B) a tree   (C) a clock   (D) lightning

40. (A) Edwards had been blind for nine years.
    (B) Edwards was unconscious for twenty minutes after the lightning had struck him.
    (C) Doctors believe that Edwards was never really blind or deaf.
    (D) Edwards awoke with his face in a puddle of water.

41. (A) hiding from the storm under a tree
    (B) climbing a tree
    (C) driving a car
    (D) lying on the ground

42. (A) He regained his sight from a head injury when he fell from a tree.
    (B) He was happy after his wife entered his room for the first time in nine years.
    (C) The lightning took the feeling from his legs and gave feeling in his eyes.
    (D) Because the blow that blinded him was very severe, it took another very severe blow to restore his sight.

43. (A) All her expenses will be paid.
    (B) She'll earn a great deal of money.
    (C) She can practice her Spanish.
    (D) She can spend her free time at the beach.

44. (A) one week   (C) six weeks
    (B) immediately   (D) a few hours

45. (A) swim suit   (C) passport
    (B) a Spanish dictionary (D) money

46. (A) two   (B) three   (C) four   (D) five

47. (A) cotton   (B) nylon   (C) grains   (D) rayon

48. (A) It is the smallest state in size.
    (B) It was the first to discover nylon.
    (C) It was the first to ratify the Constitution.
    (D) It was the "bread basket" in colonial days.

49. (A) Irish   (B) Swedish   (C) English   (D) Dutch

50. (A) It was at the heart of the country.
    (B) It was extremely small.
    (C) They sold baskets which they made by hand.
    (D) They produced corn, wheat, and other grains, which were sold throughout the country.

STOP. THIS IS THE END OF THE LISTENING COMPREHENSION SECTION.

SECTION II: STRUCTURE AND WRITTEN EXPRESSION

Time: 25 Minutes
40 Questions

Part A

DIRECTIONS

Each sentence in Part A is an incomplete sentence. Four words or phrases, marked (A), (B), (C), (D), are given beneath each sentence. You are to choose the *one* word or phrase that best completes the sentence. Then, on your answer sheet, find the number of the problem and mark your answer.

1. I understand that the governor is considering a new proposal _____.
    - (A) what would eliminate unnecessary writing in government
    - (B) who wants to cut down on the amount of writing in government
    - (C) that would eliminate unnecessary paperwork in government
    - (D) to cause that the amount of papers written in government offices will be reduced

2. The doctor told his receptionist that he would return _____.
    - (A) as early as it would be possible
    - (B) at the earliest that it could be possible
    - (C) as soon as possible
    - (D) at the nearest early possibility

3. George belongs to the _____.
    - (A) class of the upper middle
    - (B) upper middle class
    - (C) class from the center up
    - (D) high medium class

4. A good student must know _____.
    - (A) to study hard
    - (B) to be a good student
    - (C) how to study effectively
    - (D) the way of efficiency in study

5. Jane changed her major from French to business _____.
    - (A) with hopes to be able easier to locate employment
    - (B) hoping she can easier get a job
    - (C) with the hope for being able to find better a job
    - (D) hoping to find a job more easily.

6. He has received several scholarships _____.
   - (A) not only because of his artistic but his academic ability
   - (B) for both his academic ability as well as his artistic
   - (C) because of his academic and artistic ability
   - (D) as resulting of his ability in the art and the academy

7. Harvey will wash the clothes, _____.
   - (A) iron the shirts, prepare the meal, dusting the furniture
   - (B) ironing the shirts, preparing the meal, and dusting the furniture
   - (C) iron the shirts, prepare the meal, and dust the furniture
   - (D) to iron the shirts, prepare the meal, and dust the furniture

8. _____ that new information to anyone else but the sergeant.
   - (A) They asked him not to give
   - (B) They asked him to don't give
   - (C) They asked him no give
   - (D) They asked him to no give

9. _____, he would have signed his name in the corner.
   - (A) If he painted that picture
   - (B) If he paints that picture
   - (C) If he had painted that picture
   - (D) If he would have painted that picture

10. The doctor insisted that his patient _____.
    - (A) that he not work too hard for three months
    - (B) take it easy for three months
    - (C) taking it easy inside of three months
    - (D) to take some vacations for three months

11. The manager was angry because somebody _____.
    - (A) had allowed the photographers to enter the building
    - (B) had let the photographers to enter into the building
    - (C) permitting the photographers enter the building
    - (D) the photographers let into the building without the proper documentations

12. Richard was asked to withdraw from graduate school because _____.
    - (A) they believed he was not really able to complete research
    - (B) he was deemed incapable of completing his research
    - (C) it was decided that he was not capable to complete the research
    - (D) his ability to finish the research was not believed or trusted

13. The committee members resented _____.
    - (A) the president that he did not tell them about the meeting
    - (B) the president not to inform them of the meeting
    - (C) the president's not informing them of the meeting
    - (D) that the president had failed informing themselves that there was going to be a meeting

14. _____ did Arthur realize that there was danger.
    (A) Upon entering the store
    (B) When he entered the store
    (C) After he had entered the store
    (D) Only after entering the store

15. The rabbit scurried away in fright _____.
    (A) when it heard the movement in the bushes
    (B) the movement among the bushes having been heard
    (C) after it was hearing moving inside of the bushes
    (D) when he has heard that something moved in the bushes

GO ON TO PART B

Part B

DIRECTIONS

Each sentence in Part B has four words or phrases underlined. The four underlined parts of the sentence are marked (A), (B), (C), (D). You are to identify the *one* underlined word or phrase that should be corrected or rewritten. Then, on your answer sheet, find the number of the problem and mark your answer.

16. Neither of the <u>girls</u> <u>have</u> turned in the term papers <u>to the</u> instructor <u>yet</u>.
              A   B   C   D

17. <u>After studying</u> <u>all the new</u> materials, the student <u>was able</u>
        A   B   C
    to <u>rise</u> his test score by twenty-five points.
        D

18. The book <u>that</u> you <u>see</u> <u>laying</u> on the table <u>belongs to</u> the teacher.
             A   B C   D

19. I suggest <u>that</u> he <u>goes</u> <u>to the</u> doctor as soon as he
              A   B   C
    <u>returns from</u> taking the exam.
         D

20. She is <u>looking</u> forward to <u>go</u> to Eurpoe after she
          A   B
    <u>finishes</u> her studies <u>at the</u> university.
      C   D

21. They said <u>that</u> the man <u>jumped</u> <u>off of</u> the bridge and
              A   B   C
    <u>plunged into</u> the freezing water.
        D

22. Mr. Anderson used to <u>jogging</u> in the <u>crisp morning</u> air
    <u>during</u> the <u>winter months</u>, but now he has stopped.
    A — jogging, B — crisp morning air, C — during, D — winter months

22. Mr. Anderson used to <u>jogging</u> in the <u>crisp morning</u> air
$$\overset{A}{\qquad}\qquad\overset{B}{\qquad}$$
    <u>during</u> the <u>winter months</u>, but now he has stopped.
$$\overset{C}{\qquad}\qquad\overset{D}{\qquad}$$

23. The volume four of our encyclopedia set has been missing
    A — volume, B — our, C — has been missing
    for two months.
    D — for

24. I do not know where <u>could he have</u> <u>gone</u> <u>so early</u> <u>in the</u> morning.
    A — could he have, B — gone, C — so early, D — in the

25. The people tried <u>of defending</u> <u>their</u> village, but they
    A — of defending, B — their
    were finally <u>forced</u> <u>to retreat.</u>
    C — forced, D — to retreat

26. The professor was <u>considering</u> <u>postponing</u> the examination
    A — considering, B — postponing
    until <u>the following week</u> <u>because</u> the students' confusion.
    C — the following week, D — because

27. <u>Having lost</u> the election, the presidential candidate intends
    A — Having lost
    <u>supporting</u> the opposition <u>despite</u> <u>the objections</u> of his staff.
    B — supporting, C — despite, D — the objections

28. The congressman, accompanied <u>by</u> secret service agents
    A — by
    and aides, <u>are</u> preparing <u>to enter</u> the convention hall
    B — are, C — to enter
    <u>within the next</u> few minutes.
    D — within the next

29. <u>Because</u> the <u>torrential</u> rains that <u>had devastated</u> the area, the governor
    A — Because, B — torrential, C — had devastated
    sent the National Guard <u>to assist in</u> the clean-up operation.
    D — to assist in

30. Lack <u>of sanitation</u> in restaurants <u>are</u> a major <u>cause of</u>
    A — of sanitation, B — are, C — cause of
    disease <u>in some areas of</u> the country.
    D — in some areas of

31. <u>Had the committee members</u> considered the alternatives
    A — Had the committee members
    <u>more carefully,</u> they would have realized that the
    B — more carefully
    <u>second was</u> better <u>as the first.</u>
    C — second was, D — as the first

32. Malnutrition is a major cause of death in those countries where the
                   A   B
    cultivation of rice have been impeded by recurrent drought.
                       C   D

33. The decision to withdraw all support from the activities of the
                   A   B
    athletes are causing an uproar among the athletes' fans.
            C   D

34. Underutilized species of fish has been proposed as a
    A   B   C
    solution to the famine in many underdeveloped countries.
             D

35. Because the residents had worked so diligent to renovate
    A   B   C   D
    the old building, the manager had a party.

36. John's wisdom teeth were troubling him, so he went to a
                       A
    dental surgeon to see about having them pull.
                   B   C   D

37. Hardly he had entered the office when he realized
        A   B
    that he had forgotten his wallet.
         C   D

38. Suzy had better to change her study habits if she
         A   B
    hopes to be admitted to a good university.
         C   D

39. The teacher told the students to don't discuss the
                A   B   C
    take-home exam with each other.
                    D

40. Some bacteria are extremely harmful, but anothers are
                  A   B
    regularly used in producing cheeses, crackers,
    C
    and many other foods.
        D

STOP. THIS IS THE END OF THE STRUCTURE AND WRITTEN EXPRESSION SECTION. IF YOU FINISH BEFORE TIME IS UP, CHECK YOUR WORK ON PARTS A AND B OF THIS SECTION ONLY. DO NOT WORK ON ANY OTHER SECTION OF THE TEST.

SECTION III: READING COMPREHENSION AND VOCABULARY

Time: 45 Minutes
60 Questions

Part A

DIRECTIONS

Each sentence in Part A has a word or phrase underlined. Below each sentence are four other words or phrases. You are to choose the *one* word or phrase which would *best keep the meaning* of the original sentence if it were substituted for the underlined word.

1. It was inevitable that the smaller company should merge with the larger.
   - (A) urgent
   - (B) unavoidable
   - (C) important
   - (D) necessary

2. The government is engaged in a project to pacify the hostile element of society.
   - (A) poor
   - (B) antagonistic
   - (C) delinquent
   - (D) reticent

3. Ray is indulging in his favorite hobby, that of collecting military statues.
   - (A) quenching
   - (B) expediting
   - (C) discarding
   - (D) engaging

4. Recent border confrontations between the two military groups lend credence to the rumors of an impending war.
   - (A) enterprises
   - (B) consequences
   - (C) conferences
   - (D) disputes

5. Marcia and Bill were the recipients of the president's scholarship for fine arts.
   - (A) creators
   - (B) donors
   - (C) receivers
   - (D) instigators

6. The ancient Greek temple is perched on top of Athens' highest hill.
   - (A) paramount
   - (B) seen
   - (C) viewed
   - (D) located

7. Most of the wounded passengers were quickly removed from the aircraft.
   - (A) unconscious
   - (B) injured
   - (C) deceased
   - (D) distressed

8. During the conference, the speaker tried to <u>convey</u> his feelings concerning the urgency of a favorable decision.
   (A) summon   (C) impose
   (B) usurp   (D) communicate

9. The <u>coveted</u> Oscar was won by the best performing actor.
   (A) much desired   (C) outstanding
   (B) rewarding   (D) highly regarded

10. The high mountain climate is cold and <u>inhospitable</u>.
    (A) rainy   (C) uninviting
    (B) stormy   (D) intense

11. The old hotel has recently been <u>renovated</u>.
    (A) repainted   (C) refurnished
    (B) refurbished   (D) reiterated

12. An unsuccessful attempt was made to <u>salvage</u> the yacht and its contents.
    (A) save   (C) sink
    (B) surface   (D) submerge

13. Egyptian authorities are trying to prevent their historical monuments from <u>succumbing</u> to the ravages of time.
    (A) sustaining   (C) yielding
    (B) devaluating   (D) enduring

14. The art students were <u>enthralled</u> by the sheer beauty of the portrait which hung before them.
    (A) stimulated   (C) shocked
    (B) entrenched   (D) captivated

15. Monique had to exercise great care at this <u>crucial</u> stage of her experiment.
    (A) critical   (C) final
    (B) scientific   (D) initial

16. It was difficult to apprehend the criminal because of the <u>sketchy</u> details supplied by the witness.
    (A) complicated   (C) artistic
    (B) gruesome   (D) vague

17. A feeling of sadness <u>permeated</u> the atmosphere.
    (A) quieted   (C) stilled
    (B) pervaded   (D) stifled

18. The *Titanic* lies buried in its <u>aqueous</u> tomb.
    (A) watery   (C) glorious
    (B) subterranean   (D) unknown

19. The disinterred mummy was found to be in an advanced stage of disintegration.
    (A) glorification   (C) decomposition
    (B) saturation   (D) preservation

20. The scientist tried to fuse the two tubes, but found it impossible to do.
    (A) separate   (C) bend
    (B) unite   (D) straighten

21. His final remarks had a tremendous impact on the audience.
    (A) effect   (C) uplift
    (B) collision   (D) uproar

22. The recent medical breakthrough was the culmination of many long years of experimentation.
    (A) result   (C) abyss
    (B) climax   (D) cultivation

23. The densely populated area was a breeding place for infectious diseases.
    (A) meagerly   (C) sparsely
    (B) improperly   (D) heavily

24. Few countries today enjoy prosperous economies.
    (A) static   (C) flourishing
    (B) stable   (D) poor

25. The test site region encompassed a ten-square-mile area.
    (A) overlooked   (C) surveyed
    (B) owned   (D) encircled

26. After World War II, Russia emerged as a world power.
    (A) surrendered   (C) fought
    (B) came forth   (D) dismissed

27. Part of the county area was annexed to the city in recent months.
    (A) joined   (C) dispensed
    (B) separated   (D) revoked

28. His replies were inconsistent with his previous testimony.
    (A) contradicted   (C) were compatible with
    (B) incorporated   (D) enhanced

29. The students arrived promptly at 9 o'clock for their biology class.
    (A) hurriedly   (C) quickly
    (B) punctually   (D) sleepily

30. Her only chance to elude her pursuer was to mingle with the crowd.
    (A) friend   (C) follower
    (B) lawyer   (D) captor

GO ON TO PART B

Part B

DIRECTIONS

In Part B, the questions are based on a variety of reading material (single sentences, paragraphs, advertisements, and the like). You are to choose the *one* best answer, (A), (B), (C), or (D), to each question. Then, on your answer sheet, find the number of the problem and mark your answer. Answer all questions following a passage on the basis of what is *stated* or *implied* in that passage.

Questions 31 through 35 are based on the following reading.

The food we eat seems to have profound effects on our health. Although science has made enormous steps in making food more fit to eat, it has, at the same time, made many foods unfit to eat. Some research has shown that perhaps eighty percent of all human illnesses are related to diet and forty percent of cancer is related to the diet as well, especially cancer of the colon. Different cultures are more prone to contract certain illnesses because of the food that is characteristic in these cultures. That food is related to illness is not a new discovery. In 1945, government researchers realized that nitrates and nitrites, commonly used to preserve color in meats, and other food additives, caused cancer. Yet, these carcinogenic additives remain in our food, and it becomes more difficult all the time to know which things on the packaging labels of processed food are helpful or harmful. The additives which we eat are not all so direct. Farmers often give penicillin to beef and poultry, and because of this, penicillin has been found in the milk of treated cows. Sometimes similar drugs are administered to animals not for medicinal purposes, but for financial reasons. The farmers are simply trying to fatten the animals in order to obtain a higher price on the market. Although the Food and Drug Administration (FDA) has tried repeatedly to control these procedures, the practices continue.

31. How has science done a disservice to mankind?
    (A) Because of science, disease caused by contaminated food has been virtually eradicated.
    (B) It has caused a lack of information concerning the value of food.
    (C) As a result of scientific intervention, some potentially harmful substances have been added to our food.
    (D) The scientists have preserved the color of meats, but not of vegetables.

32. What are nitrates used for?
   (A) They preserve flavor in packaged foods.
   (B) They preserve the color of meats.
   (C) They are the objects of research.
   (D) They cause the animals to become fatter.

33. What does FDA mean?
   (A) Food Direct Additives
   (B) Final Difficult Analysis
   (C) Food and Drug Administration
   (D) Federal Dairy Additives

34. The word *carcinogenic* means most nearly the same as
   (A) trouble-making
   (B) color-retaining
   (C) money-making
   (D) cancer-causing

35. Which of the following statements is *not* true?
   (A) Drugs are always given to animals for medical reasons.
   (B) Some of the additives in our food are added to the food itself and some are given to the living animals.
   (C) Researchers have known about the potential hazards of food additives for over thirty-five years.
   (D) Food may cause forty percent of cancer in the world.

Questions 36 through 38 are based on the following reading selection.

Because Egyptians believed in life after death, they mummified the body to preserve it from decay. The ancients left no written accounts as to the execution of this process, so scientists have had to examine mummies and establish their own theories. The embalming process might have taken up to seventy days for nobles and only a few for the poor. Certain compounds of salts, spices, and resins were used to preserve the corpse, which was later wrapped in a fine linen cloth and then encased in a wooden box before being placed in a sarcophagus.

36. How have we been able to learn about the mummification process?
   (A) Accurate records have been handed down to us.
   (B) Interviews with embalmers who still use the process have revealed the secret.
   (C) After studying mummies, scientists have developed their own theories.
   (D) Chemical analysis of the compounds has led us to an explanation of the method used.

37. How would you describe the embalming process?
   (A) lengthy and complicated
   (B) short and simple
   (C) strict and unfaltering
   (D) wild and terrifying

38. Which of the following statements is *not* true?
   (A) Bodies were preserved as a matter of religious belief.
   (B) All mummification took seventy days to complete.
   (C) Special compounds were used to embalm the bodies.
   (D) It has been difficult to determine the process used.

Questions 39 through 43 are based on the following reading.

A tapeworm is a parasite that lives in the intestines of humans and animals. Some tapeworms attach themselves to the intestinal wall by means of suckers in their heads. Others float freely in the intestines and absorb food through the walls of their bodies.

A tapeworm consists of numerous segments. When a new segment forms, older ones move to the back of the animal. Each segment contains hermaphroditic sexual organs (that is, organs of male and female). The uterus of each segment fills with eggs, which develop into embryos. Generally, when the egg is ready to hatch, the segment breaks off and is eliminated through the host's excretory system. These embryos continue their development only if ingested by an intermediate host.

One may be infected by tapeworms by eating undercooked beef, pork, or fish. Symptoms include irregular appetite, abdominal discomfort, anemia, weakness, and nervousness.

39. Which of the following statements can we assume from the passage is *not* true?
   (A) An embryo will cease to develop if not ingested by a host.
   (B) A tapeworm will continue to live even when segments break off.
   (C) The segment farthest back on the tail is the oldest.
   (D) Tapeworms always float freely in the digestive system.

40. A hermaphrodite is
   (A) a tapeworm
   (B) a segment containing an embryo
   (C) a being that contains male and female sexual organs
   (D) an animal made of segments

41. Which of the following is probably *not* a symptom of tapeworm infestation?
   (A) unusual eating habits
   (B) excitability
   (C) deficiency of red blood cells
   (D) euphoria

42. Which of the following statements is true?
    (A) A tapeworm uterus contains one egg.
    (B) Overcooked beef is a cause of tapeworms.
    (C) A male tapeworm must always be ingested before reproduction will occur.
    (D) Tapeworms vary in their method of ingesting food.

43. What would be the best title for this reading passage?
    (A) Parasites
    (B) Reproduction of the Tapeworm
    (C) The Tapeworm, a Harmful Parasite
    (D) Segmented Parasites

Questions 44 through 48 are based on the following reading.

After inventing dynamite, Swedish-born Alfred Nobel became a very rich man. However, he foresaw its universally destructive powers too late. Nobel preferred not to be remembered as the inventor of dynamite, so in 1895, just two weeks before his death, he created a fund to be used for awarding prizes to people who had made worthwhile contributions to mankind. Originally there were five awards: literature, physics, chemistry, medicine, and peace. Economics was added in 1968, just sixty-seven years after the first awards ceremony.

Nobel's original legacy of nine million dollars was invested, and the interest on this sum is used for the awards which vary from $30,000 to $125,000.

Every year on December 10, the anniversary of Nobel's death, the awards (gold medal, illuminated diploma, and money) are presented to the winners. Sometimes politics plays an important role in the judges' decisions. Americans have won numerous science awards, but relatively few literature prizes.

No awards were presented from 1940 to 1942 at the beginning of World War II. Some people have won two prizes, but this is rare; others have shared their prizes.

44. When did the first award ceremony take place?
    (A) 1895   (B) 1901   (C) 1962   (D) 1968

45. Why was the Nobel prize established?
    (A) to recognize worthwhile contributions to humanity
    (B) to resolve political differences
    (C) to honor the inventor of dynamite
    (D) to spend money

46. In which area have Americans received the most awards?
    (A) literature
    (B) peace
    (C) economics
    (D) science

47. Which of the following statements is *not* true?
   (A) Awards vary in monetary value.
   (B) Ceremonies are held on December 10 to commemorate Nobel's invention.
   (C) Politics can play an important role in selecting the winners.
   (D) A few individuals have won two awards.

48. In how many fields are prizes bestowed?
   (A) 2   (B) 5   (C) 6   (D) 10

Questions 49 through 52 are based on the following newspaper advertisement.

3 BR apt., start Aug. 1, close to univ., pool, part. furn. w/ washer/ dryer, cent. A/C, $150 + 1/3 util., nonsmoker, 1st, last, + $100 dep.

49. In what section of the newspaper will you find this advertisement?
   (A) editorial   (C) classified
   (B) entertainment   (D) real estate

50. What restriction is mentioned in the ad?
   (A) Renter must not smoke.
   (B) Renter must bring all his or her furniture.
   (C) Renter must share bedroom.
   (D) Renter will be close to the university.

51. Which of the following statements is *not* true?
   (A) The tenant will have to pay only $150 per month.
   (B) Washer and dryer are provided.
   (C) Occupation date is August 1st.
   (D) Renter will need to provide some furniture.

52. How much will the renter need to pay initially before moving into the apartment?
   (A) $150   (B) $400   (C) $100   (D) $250

Questions 53 through 57 are based on the following reading selection.

Ever since humans have inhabited the earth, they have made use of various forms of communication. Generally, this expression of thoughts and feelings has been in the form of oral speech. When there is a language barrier, communication is accomplished through sign language in which motions stand for letters, words, and ideas. Tourists, the deaf, and the mute have had to resort to this form of expression. Many of these symbols of whole words are very picturesque and exact and can be used internationally; spelling, however, cannot.

Body language transmits ideas or thoughts by certain actions, either intentionally or unintentionally. A wink can be a way of flirting or indicating that the party is only joking. A nod signifies approval, while shaking the head indicates a negative reaction.

Other forms of nonlinguistic language can be found in Braille (a system of raised dots read with the fingertips), signal flags, Morse code, and smoke signals. Road maps and picture signs also guide, warn, and instruct people.

While verbalization is the most common form of language, other systems and techniques also express human thoughts and feelings.

53. Which of the following best summarizes this passage?
    (A) When language is a barrier, people will find other forms of communication.
    (B) Everybody uses only one form of communication.
    (C) Nonlinguistic language is invaluable to foreigners.
    (D) Although other forms of communication exist, verbalization is the fastest.

54. Which of the following statements is *not* true?
    (A) There are many forms of communication in existence today.
    (B) Verbalization is the most common form of communication.
    (C) The deaf and mute use an oral form of communication.
    (D) Ideas and thoughts can be transmitted by body language.

55. Which form other than oral speech would be most commonly used among blind people?
    (A) picture signs   (C) body language
    (B) Braille   (D) signal flags

56. How many different forms of communication are mentioned here?
    (A) 5   (B) 7   (C) 9   (D) 11

57. Sign language is said to be very picturesque and exact and can be used internationally *except* for _____ .
    (A) spelling   (B) ideas   (C) whole words   (D) expressions

Directions for questions 58 through 60

For each of these questions, choose the answer that is *closest* in meaning to the original sentence. Note that several of the choices may be factually correct, but you should choose the one that is the *closest restatement of the given sentence.*

58. A family's photograph album is generally about the extended family, and often it is all that remains of it.

    (A) A photograph is generally an extension of the family, and the family cannot survive the presence of it.

    (B) The remains of a family generally contain an extended photograph album.

    (C) The photograph albums of most families generally contain photographs of parents, grandparents, aunts, uncles, cousins, and children, and the photographs generally remain after the people have died.

    (D) The family is the focus of most photograph albums, and these albums can always be found among the extended family's remains.

59. Perhaps we have failed to perceive that earth's biosphere is the brunt of our technological advances because the technological revolution descended upon us so precipitately, and we have been so busy basking luxuriantly in the benefits that we haven't bothered to think about the morning after.

    (A) We have always realized that our technological advances were occurring at a more rapid rate than our earth could handle, yet we weren't prepared, heretofore, to forego our enjoyment of the benefits.

    (B) Because we did not understand that technology was affecting our country's precipitation processes, we have been the brunt of a terrible joke.

    (C) We have revolutionized technology so rapidly that we have enjoyed a greater prosperity without having to concern ourselves with possible adverse effects on our fellow countrymen.

    (D) It is possible that, because we so quickly found ourselves in a technological revolution, and were enjoying the benefits to such a degree, we did not realize the possible effects on the earth's biosphere.

60. Animal experiments suggest that good nutrition during the first three years of human life is crucial.

    (A) Experiments have proven that it is very important for a human baby under three years of age to have some nutrition.

    (B) Because of the experiments with animals, researchers believe that good nutrition for infants is very important.

    (C) If animals are deprived of health food for three years, they will not be healthy.

    (D) If infant humans do not eat good food for three years, they will act like animals.

STOP. THIS IS THE END OF THE EXAMINATION. IF YOU FINISH BEFORE TIME IS UP, CHECK YOUR WORK ON PARTS A AND B OF THE READING COMPREHENSION AND VOCABULARY SECTION ONLY. DO NOT RETURN TO ANY OTHER SECTION OF THE TEST.

PRACTICE TEST 6

SECTION 1: LISTENING COMPREHENSION

Time: Approximately 30 Minutes
50 Questions

For Practice Test 6 have friends read the script (found in Part V) aloud to you or use the cassette available by mail. (See ordering information, page 485.) On the actual TOEFL you will be given extra time to go on to the next page when you finish a page in the listening comprehension section. In the following test, however, you will have only the 12 seconds given after each question. Turn the page as soon as you have marked your answer.

Part A

DIRECTIONS

For each problem in Part A, you will hear a short statement. The statements will be *spoken* just one time. They will not be written out for you, and you must listen carefully in order to understand what the speaker says.

When you hear a statement, read the four sentences in your test book and decide which one is closest in meaning to the statement you have heard. Then, on your answer sheet, find the number of the problem and mark your answer.

1. (A) We may cause Mary to be late.
   (B) Mary will be here shortly.
   (C) We will probably be late if Mary doesn't arrive soon.
   (D) Mary probably forgot the appointment.

2. (A) The program will begin at 20 minutes to 9:00.
   (B) The president is supposed to make a speech soon.
   (C) The program cut off the president's speech.
   (D) The program began at 9:20.

3. (A) We will go to a party either Friday or Saturday night.
   (B) We will go to a party if the weather is good.
   (C) We will go to a party on both Friday and Saturday nights.
   (D) We will not go to the party because of the weather.

4. (A) Helen hates fish.
   (B) Helen often fishes with her husband, but she doesn't like it.
   (C) Helen hates her husband after he has been fishing.
   (D) Helen likes fish, but her husband likes to fish too much.

5. (A) It was hard for me to learn so much material.
   (B) I learned the difficult extremes.
   (C) I wasn't able to materialize the difficulties.
   (D) I found the material after a difficult search.

6. (A) Bob studied because it was a nice day.
   (B) Bob didn't study because it was a very nice day.
   (C) Bob studied in spite of the beautiful weather.
   (D) Bob likes to study when the weather is nice.

7. (A) Susan found a hard seat because the theater was dark.
   (B) Susan couldn't find a seat in the dark.
   (C) Because the theater was dark, Susan couldn't seat her friends.
   (D) Susan had some difficulty finding a seat.

8. (A) Rick enjoys painting puzzles.
   (B) Rick's expression puzzled the girl.
   (C) Rick was somewhat confused by the girl's expression.
   (D) Rick expressed the girl's face in a puzzle.

9. (A) After the class had begun, some of the brazen students entered the room.
   (B) There were three dozen students in the class after it had begun.
   (C) There were 24 students in the class after it had begun.
   (D) The dozen people in the room were doubling as students.

10. (A) Alice was in a grocery store.   (C) Alice was in a car repair shop.
    (B) Alice was on the highway.   (D) Alice was on a farm.

11. (A) George likes listening to all kinds of music.
    (B) George prefers music to studying rocks.
    (C) George prefers Beethoven to rock music.
    (D) George doesn't like Beethoven as much as he likes rock music.

12. (A) John must exhaust the runner.
    (B) John was probably very tired after running.
    (C) The rum made John sleepy.
    (D) John must run after the thief.

13. (A) Bill expected the professor to contradict himself.
    (B) Bill had expected the professor to cancel the class.
    (C) Bill was contrary with the professor.
    (D) Bill hadn't expected the professor to cancel class, but he did.

14. (A) You can probably see Dr. Jones tomorrow afternoon.
    (B) Tomorrow at noon Dr. Jones will see you.
    (C) Dr. Jones may see you now, but he'll be too busy tomorrow.
    (D) You must pay your last bill if you want to see Dr. Jones.

15. (A) Suzy's friends have very bad habits.
    (B) Suzy doesn't have many friends because she is spiteful.
    (C) Suzy has many friends although she has bad habits.
    (D) Bad people are avoided by Suzy.

16. (A) The houses are too simple to cost so much.
    (B) It is easy to pay for a nice house.
    (C) We don't have enough money for a new house because of the high prices.
    (D) We can afford a new house now, but not next year.

17. (A) Bob bought an expensive stereo from the catalog.
    (B) Bob could have saved a lot of money if he had bought the stereo from the catalog.
    (C) Bob didn't buy a stereo because it was too expensive.
    (D) Bob bought a cheap stereo but now he wishes he had bought a better one.

18. (A) George is an art dealer.
    (B) George is a baker.
    (C) George is a car salesman.
    (D) George is a pharmacist.

19. (A) Registration should have closed yesterday, but it will close in two days.
    (B) Registration closes two days from now.
    (C) Registration closed two days ago.
    (D) Registration for the class is late.

20. (A) Jane didn't know that we had changed plans.
    (B) Our change in plans didn't affect Jane's plans.
    (C) Jane didn't tell us when she changed plans.
    (D) Jane didn't know that they had changed the schedule of the planes.

GO ON TO PART B

Part B

DIRECTIONS

In Part B, you will hear 15 short conversations between two speakers. At the end of each conversation, a third voice will ask a question about what was said. The question will be *spoken* just one time. After you hear a conversation and the question about it, read the four possible answers and decide which one would be the best answer to the question you have heard. Then, on your answer sheet, find the number of the problem and mark your answer.

21. (A) Mark is fond of rare meat.
    (B) Mark is angry at the chef.
    (C) Mark dislikes rare meat.
    (D) Mark doesn't want his meat cooked medium rare.

22. (A) The man doesn't like skim milk.
    (B) The milk has turned bad.
    (C) The man's check-cashing card has expired.
    (D) The milk may turn sour if we don't drink it within the next five days.

23. (A) in a butcher shop   (C) in a drugstore
    (B) in a bakery   (D) in an ice-cream store

24. (A) Henry won the trophy.   (C) Henry sprained his ankle.
    (B) Henry fell off a bicycle. (D) Henry broke his arm.

25. (A) He has other plans.
    (B) He has a bad personality.
    (C) He thinks it will be frightening.
    (D) He doesn't have enough time.

26. (A) in the winter   (C) in September
    (B) in July   (D) in April

27. (A) It has been in her family a long time.
    (B) It is a family disgrace.
    (C) Her mother doesn't like it.
    (D) Her boyfriend gave it to her.

28. (A) It was cleaned.
    (B) There was a large sale.
    (C) The employees had to work very late.
    (D) There was a robbery.

29. (A) skip his lunch   (C) be a bad boy
    (B) go to a game   (D) eat too fast

30. (A) He thinks she has good taste in clothes.
    (B) He doesn't think her choice is suitable for the occasion.
    (C) He thinks the skirt is pretty, but he doesn't like the blouse.
    (D) He thinks it is too elegant.

31. (A) Louie is at school.   (C) Louie is bowling.
    (B) Louie is playing baseball. (D) Louie doesn't like sports.

32. (A) Jack didn't visit them.
    (B) Jack will not visit them because it's not on his way.
    (C) They hope Jack will visit them.
    (D) They are sure that Jack will visit them if he doesn't run out of time.

33. (A) She'll count the votes on the proposal.
    (B) She'll support the man's proposal.
    (C) She'll make the proposal herself.
    (D) She'll back out of the proposal.

34. (A) playing the piano   (C) typing
    (B) making a photocopy   (D) taking a picture

35. (A) at the jewelry store   (C) from a machine
    (B) from the purchaser   (D) down the hall

GO ON TO PART C

Part C

DIRECTIONS

In this part of the test, you will hear several short talks and/or conversations. After each talk or conversation, you will be asked some questions. The talks and questions will be *spoken* just one time. They will not be written out for you, so you will have to listen carefully in order to understand and remember what the speaker says.

When you hear a question, read the four possible answers in your test book and decide which one would be the best answer to the question you have heard. Then, on your answer sheet, find the number of the problem and fill in the space that corresponds to the letter of the answer you have chosen.

36. (A) a duck   (C) a chameleon
    (B) a skunk   (D) a rabbit

37. (A) their bite   (C) their odor
    (B) their pigmentation   (D) their quills

38. (A) claws   (B) sting   (C) bite   (D) pigmentation

39. (A) There was not much wind.
    (B) There was no way of controlling them.
    (C) It was hard to get off the ground.
    (D) They were too heavy.

40. (A) Germany   (B) France   (C) United States   (D) England

41. (A) a French clockmaker   (C) Hindenberg
    (B) von Zeppelin   (D) Blimp

42. (A) Germany   (B) England   (C) United States   (D) France

43. (A) The airships were used for wartime purposes.
    (B) They were afraid because of the tragedy of the *Hindenberg*.
    (C) The newer models were too small.
    (D) They were difficult to control.

44. (A) elephants   (C) bears
    (B) rabbits   (D) tigers

45. (A) butterflies   (C) spiders
    (B) snakes   (D) turtles

46. (A) disease   (C) size
    (B) speed   (D) fur

47. (A) beasts   (C) carnivorous
    (B) herbivorous   (D) dinosaurs

48. (A) 150 years ago   (C) 16 million years ago
    (B) 60 million years ago   (D) 150 million years ago

49. (A) by excavating sites
    (B) by reconstructing skeletons
    (C) by observing them closely
    (D) by living with them

50. (A) Scientists have studied them for centuries.
    (B) They were meat eating as well as plant eating.
    (C) They wandered the earth for millions of years.
    (D) They lived on land, in the sea, and in the sky.

STOP. THIS IS THE END OF THE LISTENING COMPREHENSION SECTION.

SECTION II: STRUCTURE AND WRITTEN EXPRESSION

Time: 25 Minutes
40 Questions

Part A

DIRECTIONS

Each sentence in Part A is an incomplete sentence. Four words or phrases, marked (A), (B), (C), (D), are given beneath each sentence. You are to choose the *one* word or phrase that best completes the sentence, Then, on your answer sheet, find the number of the problem and mark your answer.

1. George did not do well in the class because _____.
   - (A) he studied bad
   - (B) he was not good studywise
   - (C) he was a badly student
   - (D) he failed to study properly

2. This university's programs _____ those of Harvard.
   - (A) come second after
   - (B) are second only to
   - (C) are first except for
   - (D) are in second place from

3. The more she worked, _____.
   - (A) the less she achieved
   - (B) she achieved not enough
   - (C) she did not achieve enough
   - (D) she was achieving less

4. _____ the best car to buy is a Mercedes Benz.
   - (A) Because of its durability and economy,
   - (B) Because it lasts a long time, and it is very economical,
   - (C) Because of its durability and it is economical,
   - (D) Because durably and economywise it is better than all the others,

5. When Henry arrived home after a hard day at work, _____.
   - (A) his wife was sleeping
   - (B) his wife slept
   - (C) his wife has slept
   - (D) his wife has been sleeping

6. He gave _____.
   - (A) to the class a tough assignment
   - (B) the class a tough assignment
   - (C) a tough assignment for the class
   - (D) an assignment very tough to the class

7. People all over the world are starving _____.
   (A) greater in numbers
   (B) in more numbers
   (C) more numerously
   (D) in greater numbers

8. It was not until she arrived in class _____ realized she had forgotten her book.
   (A) and she
   (B) when she
   (C) she
   (D) that she

9. John has not been able to recall where _____.
   (A) does she live
   (B) she lives
   (C) did she live
   (D) lived the girl

10. Ben would have studied medicine if he _____ to a medical school.
    (A) could be able to enter
    (B) had been admitted
    (C) was admitted
    (D) were admitted

11. He entered a university _____.
    (A) when he had sixteen years
    (B) when sixteen years were his age
    (C) at the age of sixteen
    (D) at age sixteen years old

12. The jurors were told to _____.
    (A) talk all they wanted
    (B) make lots of expressions
    (C) speak freely
    (D) talk with their minds open

13. Those students do not like to read novels _____ text books.
    (A) in any case
    (B) forgetting about
    (C) leaving out of the question
    (D) much less

14. He _____ looked forward to the new venture.
    (A) eagerly
    (B) with great eagerness
    (C) eagernessly
    (D) in a state of increasing eagerness

15. The families were told to evacuate their houses immediately _____.
    (A) at the time when the water began to go up
    (B) when the water began to rise
    (C) when up was going the water
    (D) in the time when the water raised

GO ON TO PART B

Part B

DIRECTIONS

Each sentence in Part B has four words or phrases underlined. The four underlined parts of the sentence are marked (A), (B), (C), (D). You are to identify the *one* underlined word or phrase that should be corrected or rewritten. Then, on your answer sheet, find the number of the problem and mark your answer.

16. <u>Most</u> Americans would not be happy <u>without</u> <u>a</u> color
       A   B   C
    television, two cars, and <u>working at</u> an extra job.
                                  D

17. The lion has <u>long</u> been <u>a</u> symbol of strength, power,
     A   B   C
    and <u>it is very cruel.</u>
          D

18. <u>All</u> the scouts got <u>theirselves</u> ready for <u>the</u> long camping
     A   B   C
    trip by spending their weekends <u>living</u> in the open.
                             D

19. Nobody <u>had known</u> before <u>the</u> presentation that Sue and her
            A   B
    sister <u>will receive</u> <u>the</u> awards for outstanding scholarship.
           C   D

20. In 1927 Charles Lindbergh <u>was</u> the first <u>to fly</u> solo
                      A   B
    nonstop from New York to Paris <u>in</u> <u>such short time.</u>
                          C   D

21. <u>Until</u> his last class at the university in 1978, Bob
     A
    always <u>turns</u> in <u>all of</u> his assignments <u>on time.</u>
           B   C   D

22. When I last saw Janet, she <u>hurried</u> to her next class on
         A   B
    <u>the other</u> side of the campus and <u>did not have</u> time to talk.
       C   D

23. <u>Before we returned</u> from swimming in the river near the
             A
    camp, someone <u>had stole</u> our clothes, and we had to walk
                 B
    <u>back</u> with our towels <u>around</u> us.
     C   D

24. Patrick was very late <u>getting home</u> last night, and
                          A
   unfortunately <u>for him</u>, the <u>dog</u> barking woke everyone <u>up</u>.
                 B   C   D

25. He <u>has been hoped</u> for a raise for the <u>last</u> four months,
       A   B
   but his boss is reluctant <u>to give</u> him <u>one</u>.
                             C   D

26. <u>After driving</u> for twenty miles, he suddenly <u>realized</u>
    A   B
   that he <u>has been driving</u> <u>in</u> the wrong direction.
            C   D

27. <u>The</u> Department of Foreign Languages <u>are</u> not located <u>in</u>
    A   B   C
   the new building <u>opposite</u> the old one.
                     D

28. The Nobel prize winning candidate, accompanied <u>by</u> his wife
                                                   A
   and children, <u>are</u> staying in Sweden <u>until</u> <u>after</u> the presentation.
                 B   C   D

29. Neither <u>of</u> the scout leaders <u>know</u> how to trap wild
            A   B
   animals <u>or</u> how to prepare them <u>for mounting</u>.
           C   D

30. <u>Those of</u> you who signed up <u>for</u> Dr. Daniel's anthropology
    A   B
   class should get <u>their</u> books as soon <u>as possible</u>.
                     C   D

31. I put my new <u>book of zoology</u> here on <u>the</u> desk a few
                 A   B
   minutes <u>ago</u>, but <u>I cannot</u> seem to find it.
           C   D

32. <u>Marta</u> being <u>chosen</u> as the <u>most outstanding</u> student on
    A   B   C
   her campus <u>made her parents</u> very happy.
              D

33. Jane said she would <u>borrow</u> <u>me</u> her new movie camera if I
                        A   B
   <u>wanted</u> to use it <u>on my trip</u> to Europe.
    C   D

34. When Cliff was sick with the flu, his mother made him
        A   B
    to eat chicken soup and rest in bed.
        C   D

35. My cousin composes not only the music, but also sings the songs for
                      A   B   C
    the major Broadway musicals.
        D

36. The geology professor showed us a sample about volcanic
    A   B   C
    rock which dated back seven hundred years.
                    D

37. The girl whom my cousin married was used to be a chorus
    A   B   C
    girl for the Rockettes in Radio City Music Hall in New York.
            D

38. Ralph has called his lawyer last night to tell him about his
              A   B
    problems, but was told that the lawyer had gone to a lecture.
                            C   D

39. Some bumper stickers are very funny and make us laugh, yet
                          A   B
    another can make us angry because of their ridiculousness.
       C   D

40. The results of the test proved to Fred and me that we
    A   B   C
    needed to study harder and watch less movies on television
                                      D
    if we wanted to receive scholarships.

STOP. THIS IS THE END OF THE STRUCTURE AND WRITTEN EXPRESSION
SECTION. IF YOU FINISH BEFORE TIME IS UP, CHECK YOUR WORK ON PARTS A
AND B OF THIS SECTION ONLY. DO NOT WORK ON ANY OTHER SECTION OF THE
TEST.

SECTION III: READING COMPREHENSION AND VOCABULARY

Time: 45 Minutes
60 Questions

Part A

DIRECTIONS

Each sentence in Part A has a word or phrase underlined. Below each sentence are four other words or phrases. You are to choose the *one* word or phrase which would *best keep the meaning* of the original sentence if it were substituted for the underlined word.

1. Mr. Jacob's <u>sole</u> objective is to make his firm a Fortune 500 company.
   - (A) only
   - (B) principal
   - (C) important
   - (D) immediate

2. The president of the company will <u>resign</u> at the end of the fiscal year.
   - (A) quit
   - (B) relocate
   - (C) reserve
   - (D) get a raise

3. Professor Johnson has a <u>thorough</u> knowledge of Egyptian hieroglyphics.
   - (A) complete
   - (B) hazy
   - (C) wonderful
   - (D) scientific

4. The detective's <u>resourcefulness</u> helped him solve the mystery.
   - (A) assistance
   - (B) skill
   - (C) family
   - (D) money

5. They have been vacationing in the country <u>recently</u>.
   - (A) suddenly
   - (B) quietly
   - (C) lately
   - (D) formerly

6. The Johnsons' new garage was <u>not wide enough</u> for the camper to fit.
   - (A) too new
   - (B) too big
   - (C) too long
   - (D) too narrow

7. The old utilities building was <u>demolished</u> and a new highrise took its place.
   - (A) renovated
   - (B) razed
   - (C) remodeled
   - (D) reconciled

8. Perhaps the customer has <u>overlooked</u> his monthly statement and not paid the bill.
   - (A) perused
   - (B) confused
   - (C) neglected
   - (D) not received

9. The current edition of that magazine discusses the ancient civilizations of Latin America.
   (A) latest   (C) running
   (B) first   (D) special

10. He is a person who understands his obligations and attends to them.
    (A) restrictions   (C) observations
    (B) annoyances   (D) duties

11. He was refused admission to the restaurant for not wearing a tie.
    (A) granted   (C) acquiesced
    (B) denied   (D) appealed

12. John was not promoted because his work did not meet the manager's expectations.
    (A) anticipations   (C) expertise
    (B) expenditures   (D) gaudiness

13. Joyce is loved by all her friends because she is very congenial.
    (A) pleasant   (C) courageous
    (B) wealthy   (D) sensitive

14. The students were given complimentary passes for the new movie.
    (A) inexpensive   (C) expensive
    (B) free   (D) good

15. Prehistoric cave art portrayed animals in motion.
    (A) enhanced   (C) criticized
    (B) hindered   (D) depicted

16. She discarded the cores after Nellie had baked the apple pie.
    (A) peels   (C) centers
    (B) seeds   (D) cartons

17. Victoria Holt and William Shakespeare are prolific writers.
    (A) productive   (C) esteemed
    (B) famous   (D) celebrated

18. After receiving her check, Suzy endorsed it and took it to the bank.
    (A) destroyed   (C) folded
    (B) signed   (D) deposited

19. After the rope had broken, the mountain climber was left dangling freely.
    (A) swinging   (C) sliding
    (B) falling   (D) wrinkling

20. The professor's <u>introductory</u> remarks concerned the development of the laser beam.
  - (A) preliminary
  - (B) final
  - (C) supplementary
  - (D) interminable

21. The speaker was asked to <u>condense</u> his presentation in order to allow his audience to ask questions.
  - (A) abbreviate
  - (B) expand
  - (C) continue
  - (D) delay

22. <u>Fragments</u> of the Dead Sea Scrolls have been found in recent years.
  - (A) aromas
  - (B) pieces
  - (C) drawings
  - (D) writers

23. We were caught in a <u>deluge</u> while returning from our vacation.
  - (A) hailstorm
  - (B) downpour
  - (C) sandstorm
  - (D) blizzard

24. The daring rescue of those stranded on the mountaintop was truly a <u>creditable</u> deed.
  - (A) hard to believe
  - (B) praiseworthy
  - (C) unusual
  - (D) risky

25. The driver of the car was <u>liable</u> for the damages caused to the passenger.
  - (A) arrested
  - (B) liberated
  - (C) legally responsible
  - (D) proposed

26. That he should ask her to marry him was rather <u>presumptuous</u> on his part.
  - (A) audacious
  - (B) stupid
  - (C) brave
  - (D) nice

27. The Lucas family <u>emigrated</u> from Switzerland before the war.
  - (A) departed
  - (B) arrived
  - (C) was exiled
  - (D) resided

28. The pianist was <u>adept</u> at playing the arpeggios.
  - (A) proficient
  - (B) adjustable
  - (C) awkward
  - (D) careful

29. The company asked for <u>additional</u> information.
  - (A) certain
  - (B) emphatic
  - (C) further
  - (D) enchanting

30. The president's <u>compassion</u> for the refugees caused him to admit a very large number of them.
    (A) friendship   (C) pity
    (B) respect   (D) hostility

GO ON TO PART B

Part B

DIRECTIONS

In Part B, the questions are based on a variety of reading material (single sentences, paragraphs, advertisements, and the like). You are to choose the *one* best answer, (A), (B), (C), or (D), to each question. Then, on your answer sheet, find the number of the problem and mark your answer. Answer all questions following a passage on the basis of what is *stated* or *implied* in that passage.

Questions 31 through 36 are based on the following passage.

Although the period that we call the Renaissance began in Italy in the fourteenth century, this idea of rebirth in learning characterized other epochs in history in different parts of the world.

In 800 A.D. Charlemagne became king of the Franks and initiated the Carolingian Renaissance, a period which saw beautiful and more modern cities patterned on Roman architecture. His improvements in instruction for boys expanded the educational system, helped maintain Roman culture, and continued a society in Western Europe, as well as created libraries (a carryover from Alexandrian Egypt of 323 B.C.).

Kievan Russia also enjoyed a period of rebirth some 200 years later under the able rule of Yaroslav the Wise. Like Charlemagne, he founded schools, established libraries, and brought about many architectural achievements.

31. Which was the earliest period of rebirth mentioned?
    (A) Russian   (C) Carolingian
    (B) Italian   (D) Roman

32. Which city did Charlemagne look upon as a model for his architectural improvements?
    (A) Kiev   (C) Carolingian
    (B) Rome   (D) Frank

33. Which of the following was *not* mentioned as a characteristic of the Renaissance movement?
    (A) maintaining the status quo   (C) architectural advances
    (B) improved education   (D) creation of libraries

34. How many centuries separated the Kievan and the Italian Renaissance?
    (A) 2   (B) 3   (C) 4   (D) 5

35. What can we assume about Yaroslav?
    (A) He was demented.   (C) He was inept.
    (B) He was a competent leader. (D) He was cruel.

36. The word *carryover* in this selection most nearly means
    (A) remnant   (C) innovation
    (B) residue   (D) barbarism

Questions 37 through 40 are based on the following reading.

Gelatin is a protein substance that comes from the skins and bones of animals. Most people know it as the substance used to make a jellylike salad or dessert. Not only is it useful in making these foods, but it is also beneficial to the consumer because of its high protein content. Gelatin is also commonly used in the photographic industry and in making medicinal capsules.

The process for producing gelatin is a long and complex one. In the processing of gelatin made from bones, which varies slightly from that of gelatin made from skin, the grease first must be eliminated. Then, the bones are soaked in a solution of hydrochloric acid in order to rid them of minerals and are washed several times in water. Next, the bones are placed in distilled water, heated to over 90°F for a few hours, placed in fresh distilled water, and then heated again at a little over 100°F. A fluid forms from this heating, and it is concentrated, chilled, and sliced. Finally, it is dried and ground. In its final form, gelatin is white, tasteless, and odorless.

37. What can we assume from this reading passage?
    (A) One could easily make gelatin at home.
    (B) It is necessary to add minerals to the gelatin.
    (C) Fat aids in making good gelatin.
    (D) Gelatin is useful for elderly and ill people because it is easy to chew and high in protein.

38. Which of the following is true?
    (A) Gelatin made from skin is produced in the same way as that made from bones.
    (B) Grease probably does not aid in producing gelatin.
    (C) The chemical used in making gelatin comes off the surface of the bones by rinsing with water.
    (D) When the gelatin is dried, it is in powder form.

39. Which of the following would be the best title for this passage?
    (A) The Process of Making   (C) Uses for Bones
        Gelatin   (D) A Great Dessert
    (B) Protein Foods

40. Which of the following industries is *not* mentioned as using gelatin?
    (A) lawn care   (C) pharmaceutical
    (B) photographic   (D) food

Questions 41 through 45 are based on the following reading.

In recent years, scientific and technological developments have drastically changed human life on our planet, as well as our views both of ourselves as individuals in society and of the universe as a whole. Maybe one of the most profound developments of the last decade is the discovery of recombinant DNA technology, which allows scientists to introduce genetic material (or genes) from one organism into another. In its simplest form, the technology requires the isolation of a piece of DNA, either directly from the DNA of the organism under study, or artificially synthesized from an RNA template, by using a viral enzyme called reverse transcriptase. This piece of DNA is then ligated to a fragment of bacterial DNA which has the capacity to replicate itself independently. The recombinant molecule thus produced can be introduced into the common intestinal bacterium *Escherishchia coli,* which can be grown in very large amounts in synthetic media. Under proper conditions, the foreign gene will not only replicate in the bacteria, but also express itself, through the process of transcription and translation, to give rise to large amounts of the specific protein coded by the foreign gene.

The technology has already been successfully applied to the production of several therapeutically important biomolecules, such as insulin, interferon, and growth hormones. Many other important applications are under detailed investigation in laboratories throughout the world.

41. Recombinant DNA technology consists primarily of
    (A) producing several therapeutically important biomolecules
    (B) giving rise to large amounts of protein
    (C) introducing genetic material from one organism into another
    (D) using a viral enzyme called reverse transcriptase

42. Recombinant DNA technology has been used in the production of all of the following biomolecules except
    (A) growth hormones   (C) interferon
    (B) *Escherishchia coli*   (D) insulin

43. Which of the following is *not* true?
    (A) The foreign gene will replicate in the bacteria, but it will not express itself through transcription and translation.
    (B) The bacterium *Escherischia coli* can be grown in large amounts in synthetic media.
    (C) Research continues in an effort to find other uses for this technology.
    (D) Recombinant DNA technology is a recent development.

44. Expression of a gene in *Escherischia coli* requires
    (A) the viral enzyme reverse transcriptase
    (B) the processes of transcription and translation
    (C) production of insulin and other biomolecules
    (D) that the bacteria be grown in a synthetic media

45. The term *recombinant* is used because
    (A) by ligation, a recombinant molecule is produced, which has the capacity of replication
    (B) the technique requires the combination of several types of technology
    (C) by ligation, a recombinant protein is produced, part of whose amino acids come from each different organism
    (D) *Escherischia coli* is a recombinant organism

Questions 46 through 49 are based on the following reading.

Of the six outer planets, Mars, commonly called the Red Planet, is the closest to Earth. Mars, 4,200 miles in diameter and 55% of the size of Earth, is 34,600,000 miles from Earth, and 141,000,000 miles from the Sun. It takes this planet, along with its two moons, Phobos and Deimos, 1.88 years to circle the Sun, compared to 365 days for the Earth.

For many years, Mars had been thought of as the planet with the man-made canals, supposedly discovered by an Italian astronomer, Schiaparelli, in 1877. With the United States spacecraft Viking I's landing on Mars in 1976, the man-made canal theory was proven to be only a myth.

Viking I, after landing on the soil of Mars, performed many scientific experiments and took numerous pictures. The pictures showed that the red color of the planet is due to the reddish, rocky Martian soil. No biological life was found, though it had been speculated by many scientists. The Viking also monitored many weather changes including violent dust storms. Some water vapor, polar ice and permafrost (frost below the surface) were found, indicating that at one time there were significant quantities of water on this distant planet. Evidence collected by the spacecraft shows some present volcanic action, though the volcanos are believed to be dormant, if not extinct.

46. Which of the following is *not* true?
    (A) Mars has two moons.
    (B) It takes longer for Mars to circle the Sun than it takes Earth.
    (C) Martian soil is rocky.
    (D) Mars is larger than Earth.

47. Man-made canals were supposedly discovered by
    (A) Viking I   (C) Phobos
    (B) Schiaparelli   (D) Martian

48. Mars has been nicknamed
    (A) Viking I   (C) Deimos
    (B) the Red Planet   (D) Martian

49. The Viking I exploration accomplished all of the following *except*
    (A) performing scientific experiments
    (B) collecting information showing volcanic action
    (C) monitoring weather conditions
    (D) discovering large quantities of polar ice and permafrost

Questions 50 through 55 are based on the following passage.

Italy enjoyed a highly developed and specialized civilization from about 264 B.C. until the fall of the Roman Empire in 476 A.D. Important contributions were made in art, science, education, religion, and architecture. Remains of Roman aqueducts and amphitheaters can still be seen in various parts of Africa and Europe today. Probably the most lasting of the Roman heritage to the world can be found in laws based on Roman legal principles as found in England, Latin America, and the United States, as well as the Roman alphabet which forms the basis of many languages among which are English, Spanish, and German.

50. During how many centuries did Italy enjoy an advanced civilization?
    (A) 3   (B) 4   (C) 6   (D) 8

51. Which of the following is considered to be the most enduring heritage of the Romans?
    (A) art   (C) law
    (B) science   (D) education

52. Where can we still find evidence of Roman architecture today?
    (A) Latin America   (C) Germany
    (B) Africa   (D) United States

53. All of the following are true *except*
    (A) Roman law was so advanced that other nations adopted Roman legal principles
    (B) some Roman-built structures are still standing
    (C) Roman superiority began to decline in the fourth century A.D.
    (D) the ancient Romans were talented in many areas

54. Which of the following languages is not given as using the Roman alphabet?
    (A) English   (B) German   (C) Russian   (D) Spanish

55. Which of the following areas was *not* mentioned as having a legal code based on the ancient Roman code?
    (A) China   (C) England
    (B) Latin America   (D) United States

Questions 56 through 58 are based on the following reading.

Article II of the United States Constitution states that only natural-born citizens of the United States who have attained the age of 35 years and who have resided in the United States for 14 years may become president. The 22nd amendment to the Constitution imposes a two-term limit for this office by declaring that a person can be elected for two four-year terms only, but that when a person acts as president for no more than two years for which he or she was not elected, such as when a vice-president succeeds a deceased president, he or she may be elected twice after completing the former president's term.

56. Which of the following could *not* become president of the United States?
    (A) a 38-year-old man born in the United States
    (B) a 40-year-old naturalized citizen who has lived in the United States for 25 years
    (C) a 45-year-old woman born of parents who were U.S. citizens
    (D) a 60-year-old woman who was born in Japan of parents who were citizens of the United States and who has lived in the United States for 20 years

57. What is the maximum number of years that a person can serve as president of the United States?

(A) 4   (B) 8   (C) 10   (D) 14

58. How long must a citizen have lived in the United States before he or she can become president?

(A) 8 years   (B) 14 years   (C) 22 years   (D) 35 years

Directions for questions 59 and 60

For each of these questions, choose the answer that is *closest in meaning* to the original sentence. Note that several of the choices may be factually correct, but you should choose the one that is the *closest restatement of the given sentence.*

59. All term papers are due tomorrow unless special arrangements are made to turn them in at a later date.

(A) Term papers can be turned in later tomorrow after making special arrangements.

(B) Unless previous arrangements are made, all term papers are due tomorrow.

(C) Special arrangements can be made tomorrow to turn in term papers at a later date.

(D) Term papers arranged for a later date can be turned in tomorrow.

60. After many long and grueling hours of practice, Rita finally became an accomplished violinist.

(A) Rita's long and grueling hours of practice helped her become an accomplished violinist.

(B) Rita accomplished many long, grueling hours of practice and became a violinist.

(C) After becoming an accomplished violinist, Rita spent many long, grueling hours of practice.

(D) Rita spent many long, grueling hours accomplishing her violin practice.

STOP. THIS IS THE END OF THE EXAMINATION. IF YOU FINISH BEFORE TIME IS UP, CHECK YOUR WORK ON PARTS A AND B OF THE READING COMPREHENSION AND VOCABULARY SECTION ONLY. DO NOT RETURN TO ANY OTHER SECTION OF THE TEST.

PART V: Listening Comprehension Scripts, Answers, and Explanations for Practice Tests 1 through 6

HOW TO USE PART V

Part V contains answers and explanations for the six practice tests, scripts for the listening comprehension sections, answer keys that are cross-referenced to grammar review pages in Part III, and scoring charts to help you see your strengths and weaknesses. In order to improve your score, you MUST analyze your mistakes and strive to avoid making the same errors again. MAKE FULL USE OF THE FOLLOWING PAGES TO IMPROVE YOUR PERFORMANCE. Follow this step-by-step procedure.

● First turn to the *answer keys* to check your results. Then turn to the *Analysis-Scoring Sheet* for the test you have taken and fill in the number of questions that you got CORRECT in each section. Follow the directions to figure your total converted score. Which section did you do best in? Which section did you worst in? The section in which you received your lowest score is the section which you must work hardest on improving.

● If you did poorly on the listening comprehension, *study the script carefully,* comparing the questions that you heard to what you read on paper. *Listen to the tape again* to see if you can now hear more clearly. If there are vocabulary items, idiomatic expressions, or grammatical constructions that are causing you to make mistakes in listening, look them up and study them again. Use your dictionary for expressions that were not covered in this guide.

● If you did poorly in the grammar section, you must *look back at the rule and study it again* until you can recognize such a problem immediately. Most grammar explanations contain a shortened version of the rule, and the answer keys are cross-referenced by page number. The page numbers refer to rules and examples in Part III that you should study again. Sometimes there are several page numbers because the sentence contains several different problems.

● There are no detailed explanations provided for the vocabulary part of the practice tests. You will learn and understand the words best by *looking them up* in a good English/English dictionary. Find the definition that matches the word *as it was used in the original sentence.* Record unfamiliar words in a notebook. It is a good idea to write your own sentence with all words that you learn so that you can practice using them. Be sure that you know all words among the four, and not just the correct answer. Try to use these words in speech and in writing whenever you can.

● For the reading comprehension questions, *look at the explanations and refer back to the reading* itself to understand why you missed the question.

The explanation will often tell you in which sentence the material necessary to answer the question can be found. Remember that generally the words in the questions and the words in the text are not exactly the same. Be sure that you understand the meaning of each reading selection and question and that you learn any new vocabulary words that you run across.

● *Always look back at questions that you missed* to see whether you could answer them correctly now that you have restudied.

CONVERTED SCORE SHEET

To use this chart, find the number in the raw score column that corresponds to your total CORRECT answers on each section. The converted score in each section is listed to the right of the raw score. Transfer each of the three converted scores to the Practice Test Analysis-Scoring Sheet that precedes the explanation section for each practice test. Follow the directions given there to determine your total converted score. The highest possible score on the tests in this guide is 673; the lowest is 223. On the actual TOEFL the scores may range from 700 to 200.

Raw Score	Converted Scores Section I	Section II	Section III	Raw Score	Converted Scores Section I	Section II	Section III
60			67	48	64		56
59			66	47	63		56
58			65	46	62		55
57			64	45	61		55
56			63	44	60		54
55			62	43	59		53
54			61	42	58		53
53			60	41	57		52
52			60	40	56	67	51
51			59	39	56	66	51
50	68		58	38	55	64	50
49	66		57	37	54	63	49

Raw Score	Converted Scores Section I	Converted Scores Section II	Converted Scores Section III	Raw Score	Converted Scores Section I	Converted Scores Section II	Converted Scores Section III
36	53	61	49	18	42	41	36
35	52	59	48	17	41	40	35
34	52	58	47	16	41	39	34
33	51	57	47	15	40	38	33
32	50	55	46	14	39	37	32
31	50	54	46	13	38	36	31
30	49	53	45	12	37	35	30
29	49	52	45	11	36	34	29
28	48	51	44	10	34	33	28
27	48	50	43	9	33	32	27
26	47	49	43	8	32	30	26
25	46	48	42	7	31	29	26
24	46	47	41	6	30	28	25
23	45	46	40	5	29	26	24
22	44	45	39	4	28	25	24
21	44	44	39	3	27	24	23
20	43	43	38	2	26	22	23
19	43	42	37	1	25	20	22

PRACTICE TEST 1

ANSWER KEY FOR PRACTICE TEST 1

After some answers in this answer key, you will find numbers in italic type. These are page numbers in Part III where you will find review material for these questions. Although any one question may involve several different rules and concepts, these page numbers refer to important areas you should review if you have missed a question or are not sure of the material involved. Make full use of these page number references and of the index to direct your personal review.

Section I: Listening Comprehension

1. (B)	11. (C)	21. (B)	31. (B)	41. (B)
2. (B)	12. (C)	22. (A)	32. (A)	42. (A)
3. (D)	13. (A)	23. (C)	33. (B)	43. (B)
4. (D)	14. (C)	24. (C)	34. (C)	44. (B)
5. (D)	15. (C)	25. (A)	35. (C)	45. (B)
6. (C)	16. (D)	26. (B)	36. (A)	46. (C)
7. (A)	17. (B)	27. (C)	37. (D)	47. (A)
8. (B)	18. (B)	28. (B)	38. (D)	48. (B)
9. (B)	19. (B)	29. (A)	39. (C)	49. (A)
10. (A)	20. (C)	30. (C)	40. (B)	50. (A)

Section II: Structure and Written Expression

1. (C) *39*
2. (D) *48*
3. (D) *64*
4. (C) *84*
5. (C) *105*
6. (B) *90, 120*
7. (B) *161–162*
8. (D) *49, 82*
9. (D) *141*
10. (D) *81*
11. (C) *156*
12. (B) *43, 64*
13. (C) *78*
14. (C) *43*
15. (D) *80*
16. (C) *213*
17. (A) *43*
18. (D) *172*
19. (D) *56*
20. (A) *84*

21. (D) *56*
22. (B) *43*
23. (B) *58*
24. (D) *156, 161*
25. (D) *82*
26. (A) *130*
27. (B) *169*
28. (C) *85*
29. (C) *50*
30. (D) *82*
31. (D) *99*
32. (A) *44*
33. (D) *43*
34. (A) *65*
35. (A) *43*
36. (A) *119*
37. (B) *43*
38. (B) *210*
39. (A) *213*
40. (A) *39*

Section III: Reading Comprehension and Vocabulary

1. (D)
2. (B)
3. (C)
4. (A)
5. (D)
6. (C)
7. (A)
8. (B)
9. (C)
10. (C)
11. (A)
12. (A)

13. (B)
14. (D)
15. (B)
16. (A)
17. (B)
18. (C)
19. (A)
20. (C)
21. (B)
22. (A)
23. (D)
24. (A)

25. (A)
26. (A)
27. (C)
28. (B)
29. (C)
30. (A)
31. (B)
32. (B)
33. (A)
34. (A)
35. (D)
36. (B)

37. (D)
38. (B)
39. (A)
40. (B)
41. (C)
42. (B)
43. (A)
44. (C)
45. (A)
46. (B)
47. (A)
48. (B)

49. (D)
50. (C)
51. (B)
52. (C)
53. (C)
54. (B)
55. (B)
56. (D)
57. (A)
58. (C)
59. (A)
60. (C)

PRACTICE TEST 1: ANALYSIS-SCORING SHEET

Use the chart below to spot your strengths and weaknesses in each test section and to arrive at your total converted score. Fill in your number of correct answers for each section in the space provided. Refer to the Converted Score Sheet on page 378 to find your converted score for each section and enter those numbers on the chart. Find the sum of your converted scores, multiply that sum by 10, and divide by 3.

Example:	If raw scores are	then	converted scores are
Section I:	33		51
Section II:	26		49
Section III:	38		50

Sum of Converted Scores   150

Times 10 = 1,500

Divided by 3 =   500 = Total
Converted
Score

This will give you the approximate score that you would obtain if this were an actual TOEFL. Remember that your score here may possibly be higher than the score that you might receive on an actual TOEFL simply because you are studying the elements of the test shortly before taking each test. The score is intended only to give you a general idea of approximately what your actual score will be.

	Total Possible	Total Correct	Converted Score
Section I: Listening Comprehension	50		
Section II: Structure and Written Expression	40		
Section III: Reading Comprehension and Vocabulary	60		
TOTALS	150		

Sum of Converted Scores _____

Times 10 = _____

Divided by 3 = _____ = Total Converted Score

SECTION 1: LISTENING COMPREHENSION SCRIPT

Part A

1. Sally couldn't find the classroom until after the class had begun.
2. Jane is taking a sick leave from work for the summer.
3. Henry is supposed to be at work at 8 o'clock, but he arrived at 9 this morning.
4. It certainly was kind of Jane to send me flowers when I was sick.
5. William drove George's car from Georgia to New York without stopping to sleep.
6. Fewer people came to the meeting than we had expected.
7. The professor apologized for not announcing the test earlier.
8. Mary is leaving her job for good.
9. John has some money, but not enough to buy groceries.
10. Harry spent five hours knocking on doors, but he didn't sell a single magazine.
11. They expected eighty people at the rally, but twice that many showed up.
12. We were supposed to meet Fred and Mary at the movies, but we're broke.
13. The contractor said the repairs on Frank's house would be very expensive, but Frank decided to have the work done.
14. I should have studied last night, but I was too tired.
15. John refused to go to the banquet although he was going to receive an award.
16. Edna hasn't gone to a movie for years.
17. He likes sugar in his coffee, but nothing else.
18. Arnold was embarrassed to tell his date that he didn't have $15 to pay for the meal.
19. The man offered $1,000 for the car, but George shook his head.
20. Harvey's face turned bright red when the teacher asked him a question.

Part B

21. Man: Mary, why isn't Jane teaching here this term?
     Woman: She can't. She was fired.
     Third Voice: What reason was given for Jane's not teaching?

22. Man: Nancy, why were you late for class this morning?
     Woman: I overslept and missed the bus.
     Third Voice: Why was Nancy late?

23. Woman: I'd like to exchange this green tablecloth that I bought last week for the red one.

Man: Let's see now. The red one is only $10.95, and the green one was $15.

Third Voice: Approximately how much money does the clerk owe the woman?

24. Man: What do you think of Professor Conrad's class?

Woman: Well, his lectures are interesting enough, but I think he could choose more appropriate questions for the tests.

Third Voice: What does the woman *not* like about Professor Conrad's class?

25. Man: Where is Charlotte?

Woman: She's outside sunbathing.

Third Voice: Why is Charlotte outside?

26. Man: May I watch what you're doing?

Woman: Sure. You dig a hole, put in the seed, cover it with dirt, and then water it.

Third Voice: What is the woman doing?

27. Woman: Are you going to watch the movie on TV tonight?

Man: No, I think I'll watch the soccer game and then the documentary on volcanoes.

Third Voice: Which is the first program the man is planning to watch?

28. Man: Where did Suzanne come from?

Woman: She was born in Switzerland and grew up in Sweden, but now she's a citizen of England.

Third Voice: What country does Suzanne presently call her home?

29. Man: Miss, what time is flight 452 for Boston due to depart?

Woman: It leaves at 3:50, but you must check in one hour prior to departure.

Third Voice: At what time must the passenger be at the airport for flight 452?

30. Woman: I want to go to the concert tonight, but it starts at 7, and I have to work until 5. There won't be enough time to go home for dinner.

Man: I've got an idea. I'll pick you up after work and we'll eat downtown. That'll give us plenty of time to get to the concert.

Third Voice: What do we learn from this conversation?

31. Woman: Would you please spell your name for me, sir?

Man: Sure. W . . . I . . . double T . . . N . . . E . . . R.

Third Voice: What is the man's name?

32. Woman: What time does the ballet start?
    Man: At 8:30. We have 35 minutes to get there.
    Third Voice: What time is it now?

33. Man: Do you sell jogging shoes, ma'am?
    Woman: Yes, we do. They're on special this week at $19.95 a pair
                  or two pairs for $35.
    Third Voice: How much is one pair of jogging shoes?

34. Woman: Louie, how did your football team do last season?
    Man: We won three times, lost five times, and tied twice.
    Third Voice: How many times did they tie?

35. Woman: Good afternoon, I'm Roseanne your flight attendant.
                  Welcome aboard.
    Man: Hello. I've got seat A8. I hope it's by a window so that
                  I can see the view.
    Third Voice: Where did this conversation most probably take place?

Part C

Questions 36 through 39 are based on the following talk.

Although played quite well in Florida and Latin America, jai alai is not an
American game. This handball type game originated in the Basque region of
Spain. Jai alai is one of the fastest-moving ball games. In Florida it is legal to
place bets on the players, somewhat similar to betting in horse racing. Bets
are placed on a win, place, show basis—that is, first, second, and third.

Sports experts agree that jai alai requires more skill, speed, endurance,
and nerve than any other game.

36. Where did jai alai originate?
37. Betting on jai alai players is compared to betting in what other sport?
38. Which of the following is *not* true?
39. To what game is jai alai compared in the reading?

Questions 40 through 43 are based on the following conversation.

Man: How long have you been out of the country, miss? Where did
        you go?
Woman: I spent three weeks in Switzerland, and one week in Greece.
Man: Do you have any plants, meat, or alcoholic beverages to declare?
Woman: I have only two bottles of rum.
Man: How much did you spend on your purchases while you were
        away?
Woman: About $100.
Man: Please open this small suitcase for me. . . . OK, give this card
        to the official at the red desk.

40. Where did this conversation most likely take place?
41. How many countries did the woman visit?
42. How long was the woman out of the country?
43. What did the woman have to declare?

Questions 44 through 48 are based on the following talk.

Alexander Graham Bell was born in Edinburgh, Scotland, in the nineteenth century, and later came to the United States. Several members of his family did a great deal to encourage him in the field of science. His father was most instrumental by supervising his work with the deaf. While he dealt with the deaf and investigated the science of acoustics, his studies eventually led to invention of the multiple telegraph and his greatest invention—the telephone. The last quarter century of his life was dedicated to advances in aviation.

44. What was considered to be Alexander Graham Bell's greatest invention?
45. To what did Bell dedicate the last years of his life?
46. What can we conclude about Alexander Graham Bell?
47. Which of the following statements is *not* true?
48. How many years did Bell dedicate to aviation?

Questions 49 and 50 are based on the following conversation.

Man: Who wrote that exciting spy adventure novel *Topaz*?
Woman: That was Leon Uris.
Man: Didn't he also write those famous stories about bullfighting in Pamplona, Spain?
Woman: No. That was Ernest Hemingway.

49. What do we learn about Leon Uris?
50. What kind of book is *Topaz*?

This is the end of the Practice Test 1 listening comprehension section.

EXPLANATIONS FOR PRACTICE TEST 1

SECTION II: STRUCTURE AND WRITTEN EXPRESSION

Part A

1. (C) The word order should be: subject + verb + complement + modifier of manner + modifier of time.

2. (D) Choice (A) is incorrect because *another* is singular and *pants* is plural. (B) and (C) are incorrect because *other* cannot be used in the

plural form when it is functioning as an adjective. (D) is correct; *pair* is preceded by the singular article (*an* + *other* pair).

3. (D) *Committee* is singular, so the pronoun that follows it must be *it* and the verb must be *has*. Choice (B) is verbose and uses a plural reflexive pronoun, *themselves,* incorrectly. (C) is passive and thus not parallel. It also contains an unnecessary preposition, *at*.

4. (C) Choice (A) is incorrect because *lonelynessly* is not a word, and the expression *in times previous* should read *in previous times* (or better, *previously*). Choice (B) contains a double negative, *not never,* and *sole* means *only*. It does not mean *alone*. (D) is verbose.

5. (C) *Must* + perfective indicates a logical conclusion. (He made the highest score, so we assume that he studied.)

6. (B) Modal + [verb in simple form]. (Will be teaching = future progressive.) Choice (A) is incorrect because *must* should not be followed by the infinitive. (C) is incorrect because *because of* cannot be followed by a complete sentence. (D) is incorrect because *have* cannot be followed by a [verb + *ing*].

7. (B) Choices (A), (C), and (D) all have dangling participles (suggesting that the *problem, it,* or the *discussion* may have been served lunch). The subject of the participial phrase must be *the committee members*.

8. (D) Follow the negative agreement rule: *neither* + auxiliary + subject. Choice (A) is incorrect because *states* is plural and *hasn't* is singular. (B) is incorrect for the same reason, and it has *others* before a noun. (C) is incorrect because *also* is redundant when used with *either*.

9. (D) This sentence requires the subjunctive form: *requested that* + [verb in simple form]. In choice (A) the verb is in the past tense (*studied*) rather than in the simple form (*study*), and the modifier (*more carefully*) is incorrectly placed before the complement (*the problem*). (B) also contains the verb in past tense and *carefulnessly,* which is not a word.

10. (D) Use the affirmative agreement rule: *so* + auxiliary + subject. Choices (A) and (B) do not have an auxiliary, and (C) has an incorrect auxiliary (*is* instead of *does*).

11. (C) The sequence of tense should be *said ... could* (past ... past). In choice (A) *can* is present tense, and *the* usually cannot precede a day of the week. Choice (B) is passive. The passive construction is not necessary here and makes the sentence verbose. Choice (D) contains incorrect word order.

12. **(B)** *Organization* is singular and requires a singular verb, *has*. *Less* is used with non-count nouns and *fewer* with count nouns. Choice (A) contains a plural pronoun and verb, and *volunteers* should be preceded by *fewer*. (C) uses incorrect word order. (D) is incorrect because you should use *than*, not *that*, in a comparative.

13. **(C)** This is an embedded question: question word + subject + verb. Choices (A), (B), and (D) do not follow this order. (D) also has the expression *the time when*, which is redundant.

14. **(C)** Use *much* + non-count nouns. Choice (A) uses *many* instead of *much*. (B) and (D) are verbose and use *the* incorrectly (*sugar* here is general, not specific).

15. **(D)** This is a tag question. *Has* is the auxiliary in the main clause; therefore *has* must be used in the tag. The main clause is negative, so the tag should be affirmative. When *there* is used as the subject of the main clause, it must also be the subject of the tag.

Part B

NOTE: ∅ = nothing, indicating that this word or phrase should be deleted.

16. **(C)** should be *on*. *On* + the name of a street.

17. **(A)** should be *fewer*. *Members* is a count noun and must be preceded by *fewer*.

18. **(D)** should be *very*. *Really* is slang and not appropriate in formal written English.

19. **(D)** should be *since*. Use *since* + beginning time (the action began in the 1960s and continues up to the present). *During* or *in* would also be correct if the sentence were taken to mean that the progress took place *only* in the 1960s.

20. **(A)** should be *rarely*. *Rarely* is negative and cannot be used with another negative. *Not rarely* is a double negative.

21. **(D)** should be *yet*. Use *yet* in negative sentences. *Already* is used only in positive sentences.

22. **(B)** should be ∅ or *some*. *News* is a non-count noun and *a* means *one*.

23. **(B)** should be *remembered*. He gave the assignment first (past perfect), and then he remembered (simple past) that Monday was a holiday.

24. **(D)** should be *cried out*. The correct sequence of tense requires past tense. (*Having* + [verb in past participle] means past time.)

25. (D) should be *either*. Correct negative agreement is: subject + auxiliary + *not* + *either*.

26. (A) should be *was hit*. Passive voice is necessary here. *Be* + [verb in past principle]. (The ship *hit* the bridge.)

27. (B) should be *the manager*. Subject + verb + indirect object + direct object. There should be *no* preposition.

28. (C) should be *not to allow*. This is a negative indirect command: verb + (*not*) + infinitive.

29. (C) should be *those*. It is incorrect to say *these ones* or *those ones* although it is possible to say *this one* or *that one*.

30. (D) should be *doesn't either*. *Seldom* is negative and must be followed by negative agreement, not positive agreement.

31. (D) should be *didn't it*. *Used to* indicates a past habit and uses *did* when an auxiliary is needed.

32. (A) should be *a*. Use this indefinite article before words beginning with a consonant sound.

33. (D) should be *much homework*. *Homework* can never be plural, and it is non-count, so it must be preceded by *much*.

34. (A) should be *are*. *Scissors* is plural and must be used with a plural verb.

35. (A) should be *information*. This noun can never be plural. It is non-count.

36. (A) should be *intelligent enough*. Adjective + *enough*.

37. (B) should be *many*. *People* is a plural count noun.

38. (B) should be *from*. *From* a time *to* a time.

39. (A) should be *on*. Always use this preposition with the floor of a building because a floor is a surface.

40. (A) should be *a new sports car last week*. The complement (*a new sports car*) should precede the modifier (*last week*).

SECTION III: READING COMPREHENSION AND VOCABULARY

Part B

31. (B) The three periods are Paleolithic, Mesolithic, and Neolithic.

32. **(B)** The fist hatchet was developed between 2 million B.C. and 8000 B.C., during the first period.

33. **(A)** Farming was never mentioned.

34. **(A)** The Paleolithic Age lasted over 1 million years, the Mesolithic 2,000 years, and the Neolithic 3,000 years.

35. **(D)** The last paragraph says that the people became less nomadic and established permanent settlements during the Neolithic period.

36. **(B)** Sentence 2 says, "its name was derived from the stone tools and weapons that modern scientists found."

37. **(D)** Choices (A), (B), and (C) were drawbacks (disadvantages) of the *conventional method* of boning. Only choice (D), toughness of meat, was given as a drawback of hot boning.

38. **(B)** The first paragraph concerns the fact that hot boning is an energy-saving technique, and the last paragraph says that refrigeration space and costs are minimized by hot boning.

39. **(A)** A *carcass* is a *body*. To *chill* means to *cool*.

40. **(B)** *Early excision* means *hot boning*. Paragraph 3 says "early excision, or hot boning," which indicates that they mean the same thing.

41. **(C)** The last paragraph states, "hot boning following electrical stimulation has been used to reduce the necessary time of rigor mortis. . . ."

42. **(B)** The last sentence says that the United States currently controls the canal.

43. **(A)** The last sentence tells us that Panama will take control of the canal at the end of the twentieth century, or about the year 2000.

44. **(C)** Sentence 2 says that it costs fifteen thousand dollars to travel through the canal and ten times that amount ($150,000) to go around Cape Horn.

45. **(A)** Sentence 1 suggests that 1920 was thirty-nine years after the canal construction was begun (1920 − 39 = 1881).

46. **(B)** Because of lower costs and shorter traveling time, we can assume that the project has been beneficial.

47. **(A)** They did not place the olive wreaths on their *own* heads.

48. **(B)** The first sentence says, "the first Olympic Games were held . . . to honor the Greeks' chief god, Zeus."

49. **(D)** Add a B.C. date to an A.D. date to get the total length of time. 776 + 1985 (approximately) = 2,760 (approximately). Notice that the question says *approximately* and that none of the other answers are close.

50. **(C)** Sentence 3 lists the contests. Skating is the only choice *not* mentioned.

51. **(B)** This is an inference question. While it is mentioned in the passage that wars were suspended for the games, nothing suggests that the Greeks *liked* to fight (choice A). Nor does the passage necessarily suggest that they *liked* a lot of ceremony (choice C), only that there were ceremonies concerning the olive wreaths. Because they "calculated time in four-year cycles," it *could not be inferred* that they couldn't count (choice D). Because the whole passage concerns athletics, choice (B) is the logical answer.

52. **(C)** We are told in sentence 3 that Ybor moved his business from south Florida to west Florida.

53. **(C)** Sentence 3 says that Ybor moved his business to west Florida sixteen years after 1869 (1869 + 16 = 1885).

54. **(B)** It can be inferred from the reading that Ybor will be remembered because Ybor City was named in his honor.

55. **(B)** Lichens are found in many locations in addition to the polar ice caps, as is stated in paragraph 3.

56. **(D)** Paragraph 2 states that autotrophic plants produce their own food and heterotrophic plants depend on other sources. Thus, their methods of food production are completely different.

57. **(A)** Paragraph 1 says, "they are composed of algae and fungi" and that they are "complex" plants. Paragraph 3 lists the wide range of places in which they may be found.

58. **(C)** As an autotrophic plant, algae supplies its own food.

59. **(A)** Julie is a champion swimmer *now,* and she still practices every day. Choice **(B)** suggests that she is a champion *in spite of* the practice. Choice **(C)** suggests that she is *not* a champion now, and choice **(D)** that she is a champion *because* she swims every day *now.* None of these are suggested by the original sentence.

60. **(C)** *After teaching* is the same as *having taught.* She has been teaching for twenty years, but now she is going to retire. The other choices suggest ideas not given in the original sentence: Choice (A) that it has been twenty years since she taught, choice (B) that she will finish some day but not now, and choice (D) that she retired twenty years ago.

PRACTICE TEST 2

Section I: Listening Comprehension

1. (C)	11. (C)	21. (B)	31. (A)	41. (A)
2. (C)	12. (A)	22. (C)	32. (B)	42. (C)
3. (A)	13. (B)	23. (D)	33. (D)	43. (A)
4. (B)	14. (C)	24. (C)	34. (B)	44. (B)
5. (C)	15. (D)	25. (B)	35. (B)	45. (C)
6. (A)	16. (A)	26. (D)	36. (C)	46. (B)
7. (B)	17. (C)	27. (A)	37. (D)	47. (B)
8. (B)	18. (C)	28. (C)	38. (A)	48. (D)
9. (B)	19. (D)	29. (D)	39. (B)	49. (C)
10. (A)	20. (C)	30. (C)	40. (C)	50. (C)

Section II: Structure and Written Expression

1. (C) *172*
2. (D) *43, 117, 172*
3. (B) *161*
4. (C) *68, 172*
5. (B) *43*
6. (B) *158*
7. (A) *107, 143*
8. (C) *166*
9. (A)
10. (B) *60, 107*
11. (A) *72, 107, 158*
12. (D) *109*
13. (B) *107*
14. (D) *162*
15. (B) *107, 172*
16. (B) *75*
17. (A) *99*
18. (A) *144*
19. (A) *71*
20. (A) *91*

21. (A) *43*
22. (C) *62*
23. (C) *61*
24. (D) *81*
25. (C) *72*
26. (D) *107*
27. (D) *118*
28. (C) *61*
29. (B)
30. (B) *69*
31. (A)
32. (D) *116*
33. (B) *72*
34. (C) *204*
35. (B) *118*
36. (D) *76*
37. (D) *80*
38. (A) *156*
39. (A) *61*
40. (B)

Section III: Reading Comprehension and Vocabulary

1. (A)
2. (B)
3. (C)
4. (A)
5. (D)
6. (D)
7. (C)
8. (D)
9. (B)
10. (B)
11. (B)
12. (C)

13. (C)
14. (D)
15. (B)
16. (C)
17. (D)
18. (A)
19. (B)
20. (A)
21. (D)
22. (B)
23. (A)
24. (B)

25. (B)
26. (C)
27. (B)
28. (C)
29. (D)
30. (A)
31. (D)
32. (A)
33. (B)
34. (D)
35. (B)
36. (C)

37. (A)
38. (C)
39. (B)
40. (D)
41. (D)
42. (A)
43. (A)
44. (B)
45. (C)
46. (A)
47. (B)
48. (C)

49. (B)
50. (B)
51. (C)
52. (B)
53. (D)
54. (D)
55. (A)
56. (C)
57. (B)
58. (D)
59. (C)
60. (A)

PRACTICE TEST 2: ANALYSIS-SCORING SHEET

Use the chart below to spot your strengths and weaknesses in each test section and to arrive at your total converted score. Fill in your number of correct answers for each section in the space provided. Refer to the Converted Score Sheet on page 378 to find your converted score for each section and enter those numbers on the chart. Find the sum of your converted scores, multiply that sum by 10, and divide by 3.

Example: If raw scores are   then   converted scores are
Section I: 33   51
Section II: 26   49
Section III: 38   50
                    Sum of Converted Scores   150
                       Times 10 = 1,500
                  Divided by 3 =   500 = Total
                                       Converted
                                        Score

This will give you the approximate score that you would obtain if this were an actual TOEFL. Remember that your score here may possibly be higher than the score that you might receive on an actual TOEFL simply because you are studying the elements of the test shortly before taking each test. The score is intended only to give you a general idea of approximately what your actual score will be.

	Total Possible	Total Correct	Converted Score
Section I: Listening Comprehension	50		
Section II: Structure and Written Expression	40		
Section III: Reading Comprehension and Vocabulary	60		
TOTALS	150		

Sum of Converted Scores _____
Times 10 = _____
Divided by 3 = _____ = Total Converted Score

SECTION 1: LISTENING COMPREHENSION SCRIPT

Part A

1. According to John, there's no better cheese than Swiss cheese.
2. The game will be held, rain or shine.
3. The class should have begun at 1:15, but the professor was half an hour late.
4. Mary takes her children to a nursery on her way to work.
5. Had she read the material, she would have been prepared for class.
6. Sixty people received evaluation forms on the summer lecture series, but only half returned them.
7. Peter has the potential to be a professional musician, but he's too lazy to practice.
8. We're planning on spending the weekend in the country as long as the weather stays nice.
9. Dan and his family will move to Florida when his job confirmation comes through.
10. No one but the seven-year-old boy saw the terrible accident.
11. My father likes nothing better than fishing on a hot, summer day.
12. Louise writes Spanish as well as she speaks it.
13. The actors went over their lines once more before the production began.
14. Ms. Daly asked the students to hand in their assignments.
15. Peter and Lucy had a quarrel, but they soon made up.
16. I usually wake up at 7:30, but this morning I overslept.
17. While we're on vacation, Mary will look after the dog.
18. John was supposed to be here at 8 o'clock, but he's late.
19. Although the game of golf originated in Scotland, it is probably more popular in the United States than anywhere else.
20. It's been thirty years since I have seen my aunt and uncle.

Part B

21. Man: Where are you going on vacation this summer?
    Woman: I've heard about a nice place called the Swiss Chalet. It's $18 a day or $115 a week.
    Third Voice: How much would it cost to stay at the Swiss Chalet for a week?

22. Man: How did your parents like the play they attended last week?
    Woman: My mother thought the language was terrible, but my father liked it.
    Third Voice: What did the woman's parents think about the play?

23. Woman: Do you make connections with the Maple Avenue line?
    Man: Yes, ma'am. Pay your fare and I'll give you a free
                transfer and call you before we get to Maple Avenue.
    Third Voice: Where did this conversation most probably take place?

24. Woman: May I have this prescription filled here? I have a
                terrible headache.
    Man: Yes, but you'll have a 15-minute wait.
    Third Voice: Where did this conversation most probably take place?

25. Woman: Aren't we supposed to have a science test this afternoon?
    Man: It was postponed because the teacher had to attend a
                conference.
    Third Voice: What do we learn from this conversation?

26. Woman: Did you listen to the president's State of the Union
                message on television last night?
    Man: I couldn't because my political science lecture let out
                too late.
    Third Voice: Why didn't the man listen to the president's speech?

27. Woman: Do you think I have a chance of proving my case?
    Man: Definitely, and we're going to sue for injuries as well.
    Third Voice: What is the probable relationship between the man and
                woman?

28. Woman: What time did yesterday's second baseball game start?
    Man: It was supposed to start at a quarter to 5, but it was
                delayed an hour because they had to play four extra
                innings in the first game.
    Third Voice: At what time did the game finally start?

29. Man: Marie's not eating her supper tonight. What's the matter
                with her?
    Woman: She went to the dentist and had braces put on her teeth.
                She says it hurts too much to chew.
    Third Voice: Why isn't Marie going to eat?

30. Woman: We went to that new restaurant last night and had two
                steak dinners for the price of one.
    Man: John told me you had a delicious and filling meal all
                for $7.50.
    Third Voice: What is the regular price for one steak dinner?

31. Man: Have you been to that new supermarket that just
                opened?
    Woman: Yes. The prices are quite reasonable. They have a great

variety even in meats and vegetables, but you have to
bag your own groceries.

Third Voice: What is the one drawback of the new store according to
the woman?

32. Woman: Where did you and Sue go on your vacation?
    Man: We spent three days in Scotland, one week in Spain, and
                five days in Switzerland.
    Third Voice: Which of the following countries was *not* mentioned?

33. Man: Can you help me? I haven't done this before.
    Woman: It's easy. All you do is put the worm on the hook,
                loosen the line, and cast it.
    Third Voice: What is the woman showing the man how to do?

34. Woman: Don't take too long at the snack bar. It's a quarter
                after 12.
    Man: It's OK. We have 45 minutes before the plane leaves.
    Third Voice: What time is their departure scheduled?

35. Man: I heard Marilyn's going to college. What's she studying?
    Woman: She's taking courses in statistics, economics, and
                accounting.
    Third Voice: What career does Marilyn probably plan to follow?

Part C

Questions 36 through 39 are based on the following conversation.

Man: You don't look too happy. What seems to be the problem?
Woman: I've got to write a long composition for my English class, and I
        just can't come up with any ideas, and it's due tomorrow.
Man: That shouldn't be too difficult. Remember those pictures you
        were showing me last week? The ones from your cruise last
        winter.
Woman: Sure. I've got them here someplace.
Man: Why don't you write about your impressions of the pyramids in
        Egypt and the camel ride you took.
Woman: That sounds like a good idea. I can also tell about our visit to
        North Africa, the Holy Land, and all of the historical, biblical
        places we visited.
Man: Well, now that you're feeling better about this, I think I'll be
        on my way. I've got to finish my composition too.
Woman: Thanks for your help. Once I get organized, it won't be so
        difficult.

36. What was the woman's problem?

37. What does the man suggest?
38. Which of the following places did the woman *not* visit?
39. Why does the man have to leave?

Questions 40 through 42 are based on the following reading.

Nathaniel Bacon was a man determined to protect his property against Indian raids. He encouraged other Piedmont farmers to do likewise. After Governor Berkeley of Virginia had refused to help them, Bacon and his friends banded together and destroyed a group of attackers in April of 1676. Governor Berkeley declared them traitors, and they assembled a group of some 500 people and marched on Jamestown, the capital, to insist on the governor's assistance. Berkeley later ordered them all arrested. Because of this, the farmers burned Jamestown and took control of the government. The governor fled.

The fight, which was known as Bacon's Rebellion, lasted almost a year. Bacon contracted malaria and died in October of 1676, leaving the farmers at the mercy of Governor Berkeley. Twenty-three of them were hanged at his request.

40. Which of the following is *not* true?
41. Approximately how long were Bacon and the farmers able to fight off the governor?
42. How did Nathanial Bacon die?

Questions 43 through 45 are based on the following conversation.

Woman: Alan, you've been so busy lately that we don't see you anymore.
Man: I've been trying to finish this research project so that I can present my findings at the annual conference in July.
Woman: But that's two months away. You've still got lots of time.
Man: Not really. You see, I've finished all the research, and I've just about organized all my notes, but it will take me almost two months to type them.
Woman: Well, if that's your only problem, I can type up your paper in less than two weeks.

43. What does the woman offer to do for the man?
44. Why does the man need to finish the paper?
45. What month is it now?

Questions 46 through 50 are based on the following reading.

Towering over the Black Hills of South Dakota at 6,000 feet above sea level can be seen the majestic and lifelike figures of four of America's greatest presidents. Gutzon Borglum spent fourteen years carving these gargantuan busts in Mount Rushmore as a lasting tribute to American leadership. In 1927 Borglum began this monumental task when he was sixty years old, a time when most men are preparing for their retirement, and not for a lengthy project. Upon Borglum's death, his son continued the project until the funding ran out.

Of the four presidents, George Washington's bust is the most prominent, looking as serious as we tend to think of him. Behind him is Thomas Jefferson, who bears a friendlier visage. Teddy Roosevelt is tucked off into the corner next to the last of the four, Abraham Lincoln, whose bust is the least complete.

It is unbelievable that such a monumental masterpiece should sit in a now quiet area, once the scene of deadly battles between the Sioux Indians and the white man.

46. Why was work on Mount Rushmore finally discontinued?
47. Which of the following presidents is *not* represented in this magnificent sculpture?
48. How old was Gutson Borglum when he died?
49. How can the figures of Mount Rushmore best be described?
50. Which of the following is *not* true?

This is the end of the Practice Test 2 listening comprehension section.

EXPLANATIONS FOR PRACTICE TEST 2

SECTION II: STRUCTURE AND WRITTEN EXPRESSION

Part A

1. (C) In choice (A), the verb *being* is incorrect because it suggests that Captain Henry is *now* remote from the enemy. If this were true, he would not need to creep through the underbrush. (B) is incorrect because the infinitive *to encounter* is split by the particle *not*. (D) uses incorrect vocabulary. One can "involve oneself in something," but one cannot "involve oneself in a person or people."

2. (D) Choice (A) incorrectly uses *childs*. *Children* is the correct plural of *child*. (B) is incorrect because a plural noun is required after *one of the*. Choice (C) is verbose.

3. (B) Choice (A) is in error because it contains a dangling participle, suggesting that *it* entered school. (C) contains an improper use of the past perfect progressive (*had been entering*). (D) incorrectly uses *enter into;* use *enter* + noun. (Exception: It is correct to *enter into* an agreement or contract.)

4. **(C)** In choice (A) *carelessly* is misused. *Carelessly* is the opposite of *carefully* and can be used only with people or animals. In (B) *it's* is an error. *It's* means *it is*. It is not the same as the possessive pronoun *its*. (D) is incorrect because only a person can *care* about something. *Care* indicates the presence of feelings, which plants (marijuana) do not have.

5. **(B)** Choice (A) is incorrect because *evidence* is a non-count noun, so a singular article cannot be used with it. Also, you should use a possessive form before a gerund (*our wanting*). (C) is incorrect because it is an incomplete sentence. After *the fact,* which is the subject of the sentence, a verb is necessary (the verb *has* in this case is part of a relative clause). Choice (D) is verbose.

6. **(B)** Choice (A) is a sentence fragment. It has no main verb. (C) uses *themselves* incorrectly. It has no antecedent. Choice (D) has no sensible meaning.

7. **(A)** Choice (B) contains an incorrect inclusive (*too*). *Also* would be correct here. Choices (C) and (D) should say *teaches well*. A verb is modified by an adverb.

8. **(C)** Choice (A) uses improper word choice and is not parallel. The verb *receive* refers only to *money*. Another verb would be necessary for *different types of shows* (such as, *broadcast* different types of shows). (B) uses improper word choice and order. (D) is verbose, and *differently from* should be *different from*.

9. **(A)** Choice (B) is incorrect because the proper form is: preposition + [verb + *ing*]. Choice (C) has improper word choice. We do not speak of *quantities of money*. Choice (D) is incorrect because *amount of profit* is redundant, and *bigger* is too informal for written English. It would be correct if it said *earn a larger profit*.

10. **(B)** The subject of this sentence is singular (*production*). Choice (A) incorrectly uses a plural verb (*have*). Choice (C) is incorrect because *be* is a linking verb and cannot be modified by the adverb *erratically*. (D) also uses a plural verb with a singular subject. Also, *going up and down* is too informal for written English.

11. **(A)** In choice (B), the pronoun *they* has no antecedent. Choice (C) is incorrect because verbs are modified by adverbs. In this case, the word should be *well,* not *good*. (D) is verbose, has no antecedent for the pronoun *they,* and should read *capable of producing. Capable* + *of* + [verb + *ing*].

12. **(D)** In an equal comparison use *as . . . as*.

13. **(B)** *Improved* is a verb and must be modified by an adverb.

14. **(D)** Choices (A), (B), and (C) all contain dangling participles, suggesting that the *bicycle, it,* or the *storm* is attempting to reach home.

15. **(B)** Choices (A) and (D) are verbose. Choice (C) uses *fastly,* which is not a word.

Part B

16. **(B)** should be *their*. Use a possessive adjective before a gerund.

17. **(A)** should be *cooking. Be used to* + [verb + *ing*].

18. **(A)** should be *knows how. Know how* + [verb in infinitive].

19. **(A)** should be *writing. Stop* + [verb + *ing*].

20. **(A)** should be *retype*. Modal + [verb in simple form].

21. **(A)** should be *many*. *Times* is a plural count noun and thus cannot be modified by *much*.

22. **(C)** should be *his*. *Each* is singular and must be followed by a singular verb and pronoun.

23. **(C)** should be *is*. *Mrs. Stevens* is a singular subject and requires a singular verb. The phrase beginning with *along with* has no effect on the number of the verb.

24. **(D)** should be *so are*. The auxiliary in the main sentence is *are*. The positive agreement must contain the same auxiliary.

25. **(C)** should be *forward to spending. Look forward to* + [verb + *ing*].

26. **(D)** should be *greatly*. Adverb + adjective + noun.

27. **(D)** should be *winter*. When a noun functions as an adjective, it cannot be plural. (*Winter* is the adjective and *coats* is the noun.)

28. **(C)** should be *does*. The singular subject *lunch* requires the singular verb *does*.

29. **(B)** should be *our*. For agreement of pronouns use *us . . . our*.

30. **(B)** should be *himself. Hisself* is not a word.

31. **(A)** should be *on*. One *advises* someone *on* something.

32. **(D)** should be *higher*. Use the comparative, not the superlative, when only two entities are mentioned.

33. **(B)** should be *heating*. Use a gerund [verb + *ing*] after a preposition (*for*).

34. **(C)** should be *among*. Use *among* for three or more entities and *between* for two entities.

35. **(B)** should be *dollar*. When a noun functions as an adjective, it cannot be plural.

36. **(D)** should be *repair*. *In need of* + noun.

37. **(D)** should be *isn't it*. *A liter* is singular, so the tag must also be singular.

38. **(A)** should be *was*. The correct sequence of tense is *thought* (past) . . . *was* (past).

39. **(A)** should be *is*. The subject is singular (*supply*) and must take a singular verb (*is*).

40. **(B)** should be *any*. *Either* is used for only two items, *any* for three or more.

SECTION III: READING COMPREHENSION AND VOCABULARY

Part B

31. **(D)** Add the date of the oldest hieroglyphic deciphered (3100 B.C.) to the date given for the discovery (1799). 3100 + 1799 = 4,899.

32. **(A)** Three languages, hieroglyphics, demotic, and Greek, are mentioned at the end of the first paragraph. The only choice *not* mentioned is (A), French.

33. **(B)** Paragraph 2, sentence 5, states that they worked *independently* of each other. *Independently* means the opposite of *together*.

34. **(D)** The reading says that they discovered the stone in 1799 and that twenty-three years later Young deciphered the first word. 1799 + 23 = 1822.

35. **(B)** Paragraph 2, sentence 1, says that the word was *Ptolemy*.

36. **(C)** The words "they were forced to remain there for three years" indicate that they were waiting to continue their campaign. This is an inference question. Note that choice (A) is contradicted by paragraph 1, sentence 2, which tells us they lost the battle. Choices (B) and (D) are contradicted by the fact that the stone was discovered by accident during the construction of a fort.

37. (A) Paragraph 2, sentence one, states that Champollion deciphered the first word.

38. (C) The entire reading, especially the last paragraph, indicates that Sequoya will be remembered because he created a new alphabet. Although he will also be remembered because the redwoods were named after him, this would not be the *most important* reason.

39. (B) Paragraph 2, sentence 1, says, "his family and friends thought him mad."

40. (D) Paragraph 3, sentence 1, says that he desired "to preserve words and events for later generations." Those words and events would be the history of his people.

41. (D) *Illiterate* means *not literate, not able to read or write.*

42. (A) The fact that he spent 12 years developing this written alphabet, despite obstacles, demonstrates his determination.

43. (A) Paragraph 2, sentence 1, says that he worked *independently,* which means that he had the help of no one. Choice (A) is the only choice that is *not* true. Choices (C) and (D) are specifically stated in the passage. Choice (B) should be inferred from the facts given, such as Sequoyah's basing his alphabet on sound patterns he heard, and his early observation of the "talking leaf."

44. (B) Sentences 1 and 2 indicate that the Aztecs believed that they must offer human sacrifices to appease, or pacify, the gods.

45. (C) The last sentence tells us that the victims were indoctrinated (brainwashed) and heavily sedated (drugged).

46. (A) The last sentence says that they accepted their fate passively, or submissively.

47. (B) Paragraph 1, sentence 1 says that crude oil is found "from a few hundred feet beneath the surface to as deep as 25,000 feet." Thus (B), "always found a few hundred feet," is *not* true.

48. (C) Paragraph 3, last sentence, specifically states this as the reason for the many thousands of compounds. Complicated refining processes (B) are mentioned as producing other products, but not thousands of compounds.

49. (B) Paragraph 4, sentence 1, gives heating and condensation as the methods of producing products.

50. **(B)** The last sentence of paragraph 1 says, "pressure at the source or pumping forces crude oil to the surface." Although choices (A), (C), and (D), might conceivably produce pressure, they are not as complete as (B) because they do not include pumping and are not specifically mentioned in the reading.

51. **(C)** Paragraph 4, sentence 2, lists examples of light oils as gasoline, kerosine, and distillate oil. Lubricating oil is mentioned in the first sentence of the reading, but we are not told whether it is classified as a light or heavy oil.

52. **(B)** Paragraph 1, sentence 1, says that an election year is one that is evenly divisible by four. Of the choices given, only (B), 1930, is *not* evenly divisible by four, leaving a remainder of two.

53. **(D)** The last sentence of paragraph 1 tells us that William H. Harrison served the shortest term.

54. **(D)** Paragraphs 2, 3, 4, and 7 give the names of the four American presidents assassinated. Choice (A) is not true because the reading gives information only about presidents *since* 1840. (C) is not true because, although Roosevelt was elected four times, he died during the fourth term.

55. **(A)** The entire reading answers this question. The presidents mentioned are Harrison, Lincoln, Garfield, McKinley, Harding, Roosevelt, and Kennedy.

56. **(C)** *Inauguration* means *swearing-in ceremonies,* a ceremonial induction into office.

57. **(B)** Paragraph 6 tells us that Roosevelt died of polio; he was not assassinated.

58. **(D)** The original sentence does not suggest that the poor support a movement. Consequently, choice (A) is incorrect. The words *unintentionally* and *support* in (A) are contradictory. *Support* is an active word suggesting something that is *intentional.* Choice (B) is the opposite of the original sentence, suggesting that the middle class will remain in the cities and that they are squeezing out the *support,* not another class. Choice (C) also is opposite in meaning. It states that the poor are supporting the middle class.

59. **(C)** Choice (A) is incorrect because this sentence says only that the current "appeared dangerous," while the original sentence indicates that the current actually *was* dangerous. (B) also indicates that the

current was not dangerous. (D) suggests that the current was beautiful *because* it was "black and mindless," a meaning not included in the original sentence.

60. (A) Choice (B) is incorrect because the beauty is not what makes one reluctant to explore; rather, there is some implied danger. Choice (C) is incorrect because *breathtaking* means *inspiring awe* and has nothing to do with making breathing difficult. Choice (D) indicates that man *does* enter this area, and the original sentence does not indicate that this is true.

PRACTICE TEST 3

ANSWER KEY FOR PRACTICE TEST 3

After some answers in this answer key, you will find numbers in italic type. These are page numbers in Part III where you will find review material for these questions. Although any one question may involve several different rules and concepts, these page numbers refer to important areas you should review if you have missed a question or are not sure of the material involved. Make full use of these page number references and of the index to direct your personal review.

Section I: Listening Comprehension

1. (C)	11. (C)	21. (D)	31. (B)	41. (B)
2. (C)	12. (C)	22. (B)	32. (C)	42. (B)
3. (C)	13. (B)	23. (B)	33. (C)	43. (B)
4. (C)	14. (C)	24. (D)	34. (C)	44. (A)
5. (A)	15. (A)	25. (A)	35. (C)	45. (C)
6. (C)	16. (C)	26. (D)	36. (C)	46. (A)
7. (C)	17. (D)	27. (C)	37. (A)	47. (B)
8. (B)	18. (A)	28. (B)	38. (B)	48. (B)
9. (A)	19. (B)	29. (A)	39. (B)	49. (A)
10. (D)	20. (D)	30. (B)	40. (C)	50. (D)

Section II: Structure and Written Expression

1. (A)
2. (D)
3. (D) *147*
4. (D) *46*
5. (B)
6. (C) *95*
7. (B) *171*
8. (D) *43, 120*
9. (B) *95*
10. (D) *95*
11. (C) *48*
12. (B) *165*
13. (A)
14. (C) *56*
15. (C) *144, 167*
16. (A) *97*
17. (D) *81*
18. (A) *123*
19. (D) *71*
20. (A) *71*

21. (A) *43*
22. (B) *58, 156*
23. (D) *56*
24. (B) *62*
25. (D) *62*
26. (B) *143*
27. (C) *97*
28. (B) *75*
29. (B) *123*
30. (C) *117*
31. (A) *43*
32. (B) *118*
33. (C) *62*
34. (C) *204*
35. (A) *43*
36. (B) *107*
37. (C) *117*
38. (B)
39. (B) *44*
40. (B) *115*

Section III: Reading Comprehension and Vocabulary

1. (A)
2. (C)
3. (C)
4. (B)
5. (B)
6. (A)
7. (C)
8. (A)
9. (B)
10. (A)
11. (C)
12. (D)

13. (C)
14. (A)
15. (C)
16. (B)
17. (B)
18. (A)
19. (B)
20. (D)
21. (A)
22. (A)
23. (A)
24. (D)

25. (C)
26. (B)
27. (C)
28. (C)
29. (A)
30. (A)
31. (C)
32. (A)
33. (A)
34. (B)
35. (C)
36. (C)

37. (A)
38. (B)
39. (A)
40. (B)
41. (D)
42. (A)
43. (B)
44. (C)
45. (B)
46. (D)
47. (A)
48. (A)

49. (C)
50. (B)
51. (B)
52. (D)
53. (C)
54. (A)
55. (A)
56. (B)
57. (B)
58. (C)
59. (D)
60. (C)

PRACTICE TEST 3: ANALYSIS-SCORING SHEET

Use the chart below to spot your strengths and weaknesses in each test section and to arrive at your total converted score. Fill in your number of correct answers for each section in the space provided. Refer to the Converted Score Sheet on page 378 to find your converted score for each section and enter those numbers on the chart. Find the sum of your converted scores, multiply that sum by 10, and divide by 3.

Example: If raw scores are   then   converted scores are

Section I:	33	51
Section II:	26	49
Section III:	38	50

Sum of Converted Scores   150
Times 10 = 1,500
Divided by 3 =   500 = Total
Converted
Score

This will give you the approximate score that you would obtain if this were an actual TOEFL. Remember that your score here may possibly be higher than the score that you might receive on an actual TOEFL simply because you are studying the elements of the test shortly before taking each test. The score is intended only to give you a general idea of approximately what your actual score will be.

	Total Possible	Total Correct	Converted Score
Section I: Listening Comprehension	50		
Section II: Structure and Written Expression	40		
Section III: Reading Comprehension and Vocabulary	60		
TOTALS	150		

Sum of Converted Scores _____

Times 10 = _____

Divided by 3 = _____ = Total Converted Score

SECTION 1: LISTENING COMPREHENSION SCRIPT

Part A

1. Mary went to the gas station to have her tank filled.
2. They would have come to the meeting if they had known about it.
3. Martha was born before Barbara was.
4. Most students in the class score eighty percent and above, but John is the exception.
5. The humanities professor asked the dean to question several students.
6. John was supposed to arrive at 6:15, but he's an hour and a half late.
7. Be sure to get an estimate before you let him repair your car.
8. If Henry hadn't had so much work to do, he would have gone to the movies.
9. Jane should have worked on her paper last night, but she watched TV instead.
10. John focused on the deer and snapped the shutter.
11. James had the library books renewed.
12. The woman needed $54, but she was pleased to find that she had $240 in her purse.
13. Henry is afraid he'll gain weight if he stops smoking.
14. John prefers strawberry pie, but his wife always bakes apple pie.
15. It's a quarter to 5. We have an hour and 45 minutes to get to the airport.
16. Although Harry hasn't studied in weeks, he's sure he'll pass his classes.
17. Mary ran into Anne downtown last week.
18. The meat at the banquet was so tough we could hardly cut it.
19. John must have forgotten about our meeting.
20. James was late for school this morning because he overslept.

Part B

21. Man: Operator, I'd like to place a call to Athens, Greece. How much will it cost?

    Woman: $9 for the first three minutes and $3 for each additional minute.

    Third Voice: How much would a ten-minute call cost?

22. Man: Are you going to the concert tonight?

    Woman: No. I promised to babysit for my neighbors while they go to a military dinner.

    Third Voice: What will the woman do tonight?

23. Man: What's in that big bag over there?

    Woman: I bought some apples, peaches, pears, and grapes.

    Third Voice: What did the woman buy?

24. **Man:** I thought Francie and Mike were getting married in June.

    Woman: No, that's when his cousin's wedding is. They're getting married the following month.

    Third Voice: When are Francie and Mike getting married?

25. **Man:** Did you hear that the Chapmans sold their house and are moving to Arizona?

    Woman: Yes, and the man who bought the house is a doctor from Philadelphia.

    Third Voice: From where did the new owner come?

26. **Woman:** Ray, are you going straight home after school today?

    Man: No. I have a class until 1 o'clock, and after that I'm going to spend a couple of hours at the library before going home.

    Third Voice: What is Ray going to do this afternoon?

27. **Woman:** Where did Joe and Nancy go for their honeymoon?

    Man: They were going to go to Puerto Rico, but they couldn't afford it, so they went to St. Augustine for one week instead.

    Third Voice: Where did Joe and Nancy go on their honeymoon?

28. **Woman:** Did you know that the hot dog did not originate in the United States, but in Germany?

    Man: Yes, and they even have something similar to it in Finland. It's made out of reindeer meat.

    Third Voice: Which of the following is *not* true about the hot dog?

29. **Woman:** This doesn't look at all familiar. We must be lost. We'd better get some directions.

    Man: Let's pull in here. While I'm filling the tank, you ask about the directions and get me a soft drink.

    Third Voice: Where will the man and woman go for assistance?

30. **Man:** May I speak to Jason Daniels please?

    Woman: Nobody by that name works here.

    Third Voice: What do we learn from this conversation?

31. **Man:** Martha, you look tired.

    Woman: I am. I've been working on the budget report for the finance committee for three days and nights.

    Third Voice: Why is the woman tired?

32. **Woman:** John, how are you? I heard you were sick.

    Man: They must have confused me with somebody else. I've never felt better.

Third Voice: How does John feel?

33. Man: I'd like to buy this table, but I'm $20 short.
    Woman: I'll lend you the money if you can pay me back by
               Friday.
    Third Voice: Can the man buy the table?

34. Man: Has George returned from Europe yet?
    Woman: Yes, but he was only here for three days before his
               company sent him to Canada.
    Third Voice: Where is George now?

35. Woman: Excuse me. When will the 7:15 bus arrive?
    Man: It's been delayed two hours because a bridge was broken.
    Third Voice: What do we learn from this conversation?

Part C

Questions 36 through 39 are based on the following news story.

Two men and a thirteen-year-old boy are safe now after being rescued
from their tiny boat which had been adrift in the Gulf of Mexico for
twenty-four hours. After their families had reported them missing, the Coast
Guard began searching, but the men were rescued after waving frantically at
a private airplane flying overhead. It turned out that they had drifted only
seven and a half miles from where their engine had broken down.

36. How many people were in the boat?
37. How were they finally rescued?
38. Why did the authorities begin to search for the boat?
39. How far had the boat drifted?

Questions 40 through 43 are based on the following conversation.

Man: Did you see that TV program last night about the sky diver whose
       parachutes didn't open after he had jumped from his plane?
Woman: No, I didn't. Did he die?
Man: No. It's really unbelievable how he could have survived such a
       free fall, much less live to tell about it on television!
Woman: What happened?
Man: Neither of his chutes opened as he plummeted to the ground.
       When they found him, they thought he was dead. Doctors said
       he'd never walk again, but he proved them wrong.
Woman: How long was he recuperating?
Man: He spent eighteen months in the hospital while his bones were
       mending, most of which were broken. He was no sooner dis-
       charged than he went back and jumped out of a plane again.
Woman: Gee, some people sure do crazy things!

40. Why was the man in the hospital?
41. Where did the interview take place?
42. What caused the man's accident?
43. What happened to the man soon after he was released from the hospital?

Questions 44 through 46 are based on the following news story.

NASA officials have expressed a great deal of concern recently over the descent of Skylab, a satellite which is slowly making its way back to earth and is expected to reenter our atmosphere within the next two weeks. The aluminum Skylab is not expected to disintegrate on reentry. In fact, it is feared that some 400 to 500 pieces, some weighing up to 1,000 pounds, could survive reentry. These pieces would not all land in one area, but would be spread over hundreds of miles causing a great deal of damage to property and endangering human lives. At this point, we just don't know where or when it will come down or how much damage it might cause.

44. From what type of material is Skylab made?
45. Which of the following statements is true?
46. Which of the following statements is *not* true?

Questions 47 through 50 are based on the following conversation.

Woman: What do you think? Am I OK?
Man: Well, there is some congestion. I want to do some tests.
Woman: How soon will I get the results?
Man: Oh, you'll have the results before you leave the office, and here is some medicine that I believe will help you.

47. What is the probable relationship between these two speakers?
48. When will the woman receive the results of the tests?
49. What does the man feel will help the woman?
50. What is the woman's problem?

This is the end of the Practice Test 3 listening comprehension section.

EXPLANATIONS FOR PRACTICE TEST 3

SECTION II: STRUCTURE AND WRITTEN EXPRESSION

Part A

1. (A) Choice (B) includes improper word choice and order. (C) is incorrect because it is not possible to say "win him the case." Correct form is "win the case for him." (D) is incorrect because *minimum* is a noun and cannot modify another noun (*chance*); it is not clear to whom

him refers, and the order is not correct.

2. **(D)** Choices (A) and (B) are in error because it is not correct to say "an attribute is *when*" or "an attribute is *how*"; an attribute is a static quality. Choice (C) would be correct if it said, "the way he gives lectures."

3. **(D)** Choice (A) uses incorrect vocabulary choice. *Remembrance* has a sentimental meaning; it should be *reminder*. Also, the verb *rise,* not *raise* should be used. (B) should read *the following month,* not *the month following*. (The adjective precedes the noun.) Also, *rise,* not *raise,* is required. (C) is incorrect because the verb *contained* must be followed by a noun, not a verb.

4. **(D)** Choice (A) incorrectly uses *the* before a singular country name. (B) uses improper word order and also uses *the* incorrectly. (C) is in error because *French* when used as an adjective cannot be made possessive.

5. **(B)** The expression should read, "It was *not until . . . that.*" To use *when* (choice A) is redundant.

6. **(C)** In choice (A) there is improper use of the past conditional. (B) includes improper vocabulary choice. A flat tire does not *happen*. (D) makes improper use of the reflexive *itself*. A tire, being inanimate, could not flatten itself.

7. **(B)** The correct structure is adverbial (*never*) + auxiliary (*have*) + subject (*so many women*) + verb (*received*).

8. **(D)** Choice (A) is incorrect because *homework* is a non-count noun and *few* cannot be used with non-count nouns. (B) is incorrect because a complete sentence is required after *because*. Choice (C) is verbose. Also, *because of* cannot be followed by a complete sentence.

9. **(B)** *Know how* in this sentence means "to have a practical understanding of something." It is not correct to use *to* after *know how* unless it is followed by a verb.

10. **(D)** Choices (A), (B), and (C) are all incorrect past conditions.

11. **(C)** Choice (A) includes improper word choice. *One other* should be *another*. Choice (B) uses *also*. *Also* does not mean the same as *again,* which is the meaning conveyed by the sentence. (D) uses incorrect word order. It should say *fifty dollars more*.

12. **(B)** Choices (A) and (D) are incorrect because the adjective *aware* must be followed by *of* before a noun or noun phrase. Choice (C) uses *of,* but *the place where* is redundant.

13. **(A)** Choices (B), (C), and (D) are all too informal for written English and are verbose.

14. **(C)** *Still, yet,* and *already* are misused in the other answer choices.

15. **(C)** Choices (A) and (D) omit the word *how,* which must follow *know* before a verb. Only choice (C) uses parallel construction (*how to manage . . . sell . . . satisfy*).

Part B

NOTE: ∅ = nothing, indicating that this word or phrase should be deleted.

16. **(A)** should be *hadn't sent.* A past wish must be followed by the past perfect.

17. **(D)** should be *so am I.* For affirmative agreement use *so* + auxiliary + subject.

18. **(A)** should be *such a beautiful.* Cause and effect: *such* + *a* + adjective + singular count noun.

19. **(D)** should be *to use. Allow* + indirect object + infinitive.

20. **(A)** should be *to stimulate.* Use *try* + infinitive.

21. **(A)** should be *is. Mumps* is a non-count noun.

22. **(B)** should be *had gone.* The past perfect is necessary to show that this action (going to the supermarket) occurred before the other action (coming home).

23. **(D)** should be *for.* Use *for* + duration of time.

24. **(B)** should be *reports. Each* + singular verb.

25. **(D)** should be *is. Athlete* is the subject and is singular.

26. **(B)** should be ∅. *Both* and *as well as* are redundant if they are used together; use either *both . . . and* or *as well as* alone.

27. **(C)** should be *were.* This is a present wish. The verb *be* must be in the plural past tense form in a present wish because it is contrary to fact.

28. **(B)** should be *his.* Possessive forms must be used before a gerund.

29. **(B)** should be *such a way.* Cause and effect: *such* + *a* + singular count noun + *that.*

30. **(C)** should be *dancers.* After *one of the* there must be a plural noun.

31. **(A)** should be *fewer. Friends* is a plural count noun, so *less* is incorrect.

32. (B) should be *four-day*. *Four-day* here functions as an adjective modifying the noun *journey,* so it cannot be plural.

33. (C) should be *has*. The subject, *influence,* is singular and thus requires a singular verb, *has*.

34. (C) should be *among*. Use *between* when there are only two entities, *among* when there are more than two.

35. (A) should be *much*. *Population* is a non-count noun, so *many* cannot modify it.

36. (B) should be *apparently*. Verbs are always modified by adverbs, not adjectives.

37. (C) should be *in*. After *one of the* + superlative + noun + . . ., use *in* + singular count noun.

38. (B) should be *to have missed*. This is a perfect infinitive.

39. (B) should be *an*. Use *an* before words beginning with vowel sounds.

40. (B) should be *worse*. This is a double comparative: *the harder . . . the worse. Worst* is superlative.

SECTION III: READING COMPREHENSION AND VOCABULARY

Part B

31. (C) Paragraph 2, sentence 2, says that "a serious eye infection forced her to abandon the idea." Choice (A) is contradicted by the information given. She *did* get admitted to medical school. We are told she was finally accepted. Choices (B) and (D) are true statements, but they have nothing to do with her not becoming a surgeon.

32. (A) Paragraph 1 says that it was a "near impossibility" for a woman at this time to become a doctor. This answer can also be inferred from the fact that she was the first female physician.

33. (A) Paragraph 2 tells us that she graduated in 1849 and paragraph 3 that the hospital was opened in 1857. 1857 − 1849 = 8.

34. (B) The question asks for the one choice that was *not* a first in Elizabeth Blackwell's life. The passage states that she did *not* become a surgeon because of an eye infection.

35. (C) We are told in paragraph 1 that endocrine glands have no ducts and release their products directly into the bloodstream.

36. (C) Paragraph 3, sentences 2 and 3, says that cretinism occurs in children as a result of hypothyroidism, or underactive thyroid gland.

37. (A) Paragraph 3, sentence 3, tells us that myxedema occurs in adults and causes the growth process to slow down. We can infer that this would result in sluggishness, or lethargy.

38. (B) We are told in paragraph 4, sentence 1, that a goiter is an enlarged, or swollen, thyroid gland.

39. (A) Paragraph 2 says, "animals can perceive these environmental changes." Although choice (D) is "environmental changes," the question asks what *predictions* might be made, and as the first sentence says, "strange animal behavior might help *predict* future [impending] earthquakes."

40. (B) This is an inference question. Reasons for the animals' perceptions are not specifically given in the reading, but we can assume that animals are able to predict these occurrences because they have some instincts that humans do not possess. None of the other choices are reasonable or are suggested in any way by the reading.

41. (D) The reading says that "*some* birds . . . flew about wildly," not *all* birds.

42. (A) Even if you are not familiar with the word *evacuate,* you would know that to keep the death toll down, people would have to be *moved away* (removed) from the area.

43. (B) It can be inferred that if scientists can predict earthquakes, they will have enough warning to lead people to safety, thus lowering the death rate.

44. (C) You are asked to choose the one statement that is *not* true. Choices (A) and (B) are stated in paragraph 3 and (D) in paragraph 1. Choice (C) is *not* true because the first sentence of the reading says that California has 15 million motorists; only 9.9 million of them were affected by the rationing plan.

45. (B) The only punishments mentioned in the reading are *fine* and *possible imprisonment*. See the last sentence of the reading.

46. (D) Paragraph 2, sentence 1, says that *exceptions* (meaning *not included* in the plan) were made for out-of-state drivers. Out-of-state drivers would have out-of-state license plates.

47. (A) The reading begins, "As a result of the recent oil crisis . . ." *Result of* means that the crisis *necessitated* it (made it necessary).

48. (A) Paragraph 2, sentence 1, states that the boy was found wandering in the woods. While it is true that the boy growled at people, choice (C), we are not told that he growled at the doctor when he was found.

49. (C) The word *offspring* means *children*. *Litter* is used to indicate the offspring of multiparous animals (animals that give birth to a number of offspring each pregnancy).

50. (B) Paragraph 2, sentence 4, says that "the doctor won the boy's confidence and began to work with him." You should infer that the ability to work with him was the result of the boy's confidence (trust).

51. (B) Sentence 1 indicates that wolves have been said to care for human children as far back as 700 B.C. Choice (C) is true. *Domesticating* means to *tame* or *make fit for living in human society*. The doctor was successful in getting the boy to clothe and feed himself and speak and write to some degree. Choice (D) is true because *a number of words* does not indicate that he could speak *perfectly*.

52. (D) In this sentence the word *preposterous* is being contrasted to the word *credible*. Since *credible* means *believable*, you can determine that *preposterous* means the opposite, *absurd* (totally unbelievable).

53. (C) *Used to* indicates a past time habit. Therefore, choice (A) is incorrect because *plays* is present tense. (B) is incorrect because there is nothing in the original sentence to indicate that Hal is still a member of the club. (D) uses the verbal idiom *team up* in a way that does not mean the same as the original sentence.

54. (A) Choice (B) is incorrect because the sentence does not say that Peter is a *major*, but that he is *majoring in electronics*, which has a very different meaning. Also, (B) indicates that the school teaches *only* electronics. (C) is incorrect because it includes the word *although*, indicating a contrast that the original sentence does not contain. (D) changes the meaning of the sentence, suggesting that the school is doing Peter some special favor.

55. (A) The last sentence of paragraph 1 states that *Vibrio* is found in highest abundance in inshore waters, particularly near harbors (a harbor is similar to a bay).

56. (B) The last sentence of paragraph 2 states that *Vibrio* is not isolated as frequently in winter as it is during warmer months. November is the coldest month listed.

57. (B) The first sentence of paragraph 3 gives diarrhea as the most common symptom.

58. (C) An incubation period means the time between an infection's entry into an organism and the exhibiting of the first symptoms. The first sentence of paragraph 3 says that the first symptom occurs "within four or five days."

59. (D) Paragraph 2, sentence 1, states, "the distribution of *V. parahaemolyticus* in sea water was *dependent* on the water temperature," but "*independent* of the sodium chloride content." Sodium chloride is salt.

60. (C) Since stomach cramps are given as a symptom of the infection, you can assume they would be unpleasant. (C) is the most logical choice. Although high temperature would also be unpleasant, it would not normally be associated with the stomach.

PRACTICE TEST 4

ANSWER KEY FOR PRACTICE TEST 4

After some answers in this answer key, you will find numbers in italic type. These are page numbers in Part III where you will find review material for these questions. Although any one question may involve several different rules and concepts, these page numbers refer to important areas you should review if you have missed a question or are not sure of the material involved. Make full use of these page number references and of the index to direct your personal review.

Section I: Listening Comprehension

1. (B)	11. (A)	21. (B)	31. (A)	41. (C)
2. (B)	12. (D)	22. (A)	32. (C)	42. (B)
3. (B)	13. (A)	23. (C)	33. (A)	43. (A)
4. (B)	14. (C)	24. (D)	34. (B)	44. (A)
5. (D)	15. (A)	25. (C)	35. (A)	45. (C)
6. (C)	16. (C)	26. (B)	36. (C)	46. (D)
7. (B)	17. (C)	27. (C)	37. (D)	47. (B)
8. (D)	18. (A)	28. (A)	38. (A)	48. (C)
9. (C)	19. (D)	29. (D)	39. (A)	49. (D)
10. (C)	20. (A)	30. (D)	40. (D)	50. (B)

Section II: Structure and Written Expression

1. (B) *52, 54, 156, 172*
2. (B) *60–61*
3. (A) *63*
4. (C) *116–117*
5. (C) *100*
6. (D) *118*
7. (A) *116, 135*
8. (D) *43, 82*
9. (A) *43, 114*
10. (D) *95*
11. (C) *78*
12. (D) *60, 112*
13. (A) *120*
14. (A) *141*
15. (C) *48*
16. (C) *44*
17. (A) *65*
18. (D) *107*
19. (C)
20. (C) *48*
21. (D) *45*
22. (B) *69*
23. (D)
24. (D) *45*
25. (A)
26. (A) *43*
27. (A) *84*
28. (B) *60*
29. (D)
30. (B) *72*
31. (B) *60*
32. (B) *135*
33. (A) *75*
34. (A) *78*
35. (B) *67, 85*
36. (C) *56*
37. (A) *91, 95*
38. (A) *103*
39. (C) *110*
40. (D) *72, 219*

Section III: Reading Comprehension and Vocabulary

1. (D)
2. (A)
3. (C)
4. (D)
5. (C)
6. (B)
7. (B)
8. (A)
9. (C)
10. (A)
11. (C)
12. (B)
13. (C)
14. (A)
15. (C)
16. (D)
17. (D)
18. (A)
19. (B)
20. (C)
21. (B)
22. (B)
23. (D)
24. (B)
25. (A)
26. (C)
27. (A)
28. (A)
29. (B)
30. (A)
31. (C)
32. (B)
33. (A)
34. (B)
35. (C)
36. (A)
37. (C)
38. (C)
39. (A)
40. (A)
41. (B)
42. (D)
43. (D)
44. (C)
45. (C)
46. (B)
47. (B)
48. (C)
49. (D)
50. (D)
51. (A)
52. (D)
53. (A)
54. (D)
55. (D)
56. (A)
57. (C)
58. (A)
59. (D)
60. (C)

PRACTICE TEST 4: ANALYSIS-SCORING SHEET

Use the chart below to spot your strengths and weaknesses in each test section and to arrive at your total converted score. Fill in your number of correct answers for each section in the space provided. Refer to the Converted Score Sheet on page 378 to find your converted score for each section and enter those numbers on the chart. Find the sum of your converted scores, multiply that sum by 10, and divide by 3.

Example: If raw scores are   then   converted scores are

Section I:	33	51
Section II:	26	49
Section III:	38	50

Sum of Converted Scores   150

Times 10 = 1,500

Divided by 3 =   500 = Total

Converted

Score

This will give you the approximate score that you would obtain if this were an actual TOEFL. Remember that your score here may possibly be higher than the score that you might receive on an actual TOEFL simply because you are studying the elements of the test shortly before taking each test. The score is intended only to give you a general idea of approximately what your actual score will be.

	Total Possible	Total Correct	Converted Score
Section I: Listening Comprehension	50		
Section II: Structure and Written Expression	40		
Section III: Reading Comprehension and Vocabulary	60		
TOTALS	150		

Sum of Converted Scores _____

Times 10 = _____

Divided by 3 = _____ = Total Converted Score

SECTION 1: LISTENING COMPREHENSION SCRIPT

Part A

1. I have to hurry to deposit this money before the bank closes.
2. Dan hardly knew the people he was going to visit.
3. The book costs $15.95, and I have only $14.50.
4. I can't find my keys, but I'm sure that they will turn up soon.
5. We would have attended the concert if the tickets had not been so expensive.
6. The train was supposed to depart at 6:15, but it was an hour and a quarter late.
7. Lucy couldn't wear the wool coat because it made her break out in a rash.
8. It looks as if all the crash victims will pull through.
9. So many people showed up to purchase the tickets on opening day that they were sold out by noon.
10. The kidnapper escaped with the money but returned the child.
11. Despite his inexperience in the field, Phil applied for the job.
12. No one but James knew how to solve the problem.
13. Mr. Cunningham sells tools, nails, and plumbing materials.
14. The response to our initial request was gratifying.
15. I could sure go for a steak and salad now.
16. Had we left any later, we would have missed the train.
17. Jane plans to attend the meeting in spite of the homework she needs to complete for tomorrow.
18. Jeanette rarely misses a football game.
19. John would rather that we didn't wait for him, but I plan to anyway.
20. The insurance agent hasn't sold a single policy this week.

Part B

21. **Man:** Where is Diane?
    Woman: She ran out of milk and went out to get some.
    Third Voice: Where is Diane?

22. **Man:** What happened to you? You're so late.
    Woman: My car broke down on the highway, and I had to walk.
    Third Voice: Why did the woman have to walk?

23. **Man:** Why are you wearing that cream all over your arms?
    Woman: I ate too many wild berries at the picnic last week, and I broke out in a rash.
    Third Voice: What happened to the woman?

24. **Man:** We missed you at Dale's party last night. What happened?

Woman: I'm not going to any celebrations with that group because they're so tightly knit that they brush everyone else off.

Third Voice: Why didn't the woman attend Dale's party?

25. Woman: Bill, are you still planning to buy that nice red sports car you looked at last week?

Man: I'm afraid that's impossible because I haven't been able to come up with the cash, and someone else has already made a down payment on it.

Third Voice: What do we learn from this conversation?

26. Man: Gail is supposed to be here at the meeting tonight. Where is she?

Woman: She came down with the flu and had to stay home.

Third Voice: Why didn't Gail attend the meeting?

27. Man: How many people will be coming to the reunion on Saturday?

Woman: We had to cross off fifteen names from our original list of one hundred.

Third Voice: How many people do they expect to attend the reunion?

28. Woman: Why do you look so happy this morning?

Man: I just came from my adviser's office and found out that the college board has done away with the foreign language requirement for graduation.

Third Voice: What do we learn from this conversation?

29. Man: Why are you buying that cheaper grade of meat, Cindy?

Woman: Bob didn't get a cost-of-living raise, so we have to do without a few things now.

Third Voice: What do we learn from this conversation?

30. Man: Operator, we've been cut off. Would you please help me get my party again?

Woman: I'll try to connect you again with that area code.

Third Voice: What is the man's problem?

31. Man: I hear that Joe's car is being repossessed by the finance company.

Woman: Yes, he's fallen behind in the payments.

Third Voice: What do we learn from this conversation?

32. Man: What's the matter with Oscar?

Woman: He's got so many bills that his wife says that he will never get ahead.

Third Voice: What do we learn from this conversation?

33. Woman: What did you do in class today?
    Man: The teacher went over last Friday's lesson.
    Third Voice: What did the teacher do?

34. Woman: Not getting that job was a big letdown.
    Man: Don't worry. Something better will come along.
    Third Voice: What do we learn from this conversation?

35. Man: How do the Finleys feel about moving to New Mexico?
    Woman: They're really looking forward to it.
    Third Voice: What is their reaction to moving?

Part C

Questions 36 through 38 are based on the following talk.

In an effort to fight the soaring costs of gasoline and public transportation, many athletic students have taken to roller skating. This means of transportation is creating traffic problems and is presenting a safety hazard for skaters as well as motorists in college and university areas throughout the country.

If skaters do not return to the sidewalk, but insist on causing a dilemma for drivers, the police will issue the violators $15 citations for disregarding a city as well as a state ordinance.

36. What is the latest problem motorists are facing in many cities?
37. On what grounds is roller skating in the streets forbidden?
38. Which of the following is *not* true?

Questions 39 through 44 are based on the following talk.

When the early settlers, especially the English, arrived in the New World, the hardships and dangers awaiting them were totally unexpected. Had it not been for some friendly Indians, the colonists never would have survived the terrible winters. They knew nothing about planting crops, hunting animals, building sod houses, or making clothing from animal skins. Life in England had been much simpler, and this new life was not like what the Spanish explorers had reported.

The settlers did introduce iron tools, muskets for hunting, domesticated animals, and political ways to the Indians. In exchange, the settlers learned to build canoes for water transportation and snowshoes and toboggans for winter traveling. The Indians also taught them to blaze trails through the forest, to hunt large animals and trap smaller ones, and to spear fish in the lakes and streams.

The natives also introduced to the settlers typical foods such as turkey, corn, squash, beans, and pumpkin. Everything possible was done in order to make their new settlement resemble the homes they had left behind.

39. Which of the following did the new settlers teach the Indians?
40. What can we assume about corn, squash, and pumpkin?
41. How did the Indians teach the settlers to travel in the winter?
42. Which of the following was *not* introduced to the settlers by the Indians?
43. Whose earlier explorations and findings had misguided the English into believing that life in the New World would not be so difficult?
44. Which of the following is *not* true?

Questions 45 through 48 are based on the following announcement.

Welcome aboard the Luxury Cruise bus to Dallas, Baton Rouge, and Atlanta. We are scheduled to arrive in Dallas at 1:45 this afternoon. There will be a fifteen-minute rest stop at that time. We will have a thirty-minute dinner stop in Baton Rouge at 6:45 for those of you who are continuing on to Atlanta. We should arrive in Atlanta at 1:45 tomorrow morning. Please remember the number of your bus for reboarding. That number is 3224.

This coach is air-conditioned for your comfort. Please remember that smoking of cigarettes is permitted only in the last six rows, and the smoking of any other material is prohibited, as is the drinking of alcoholic beverages.

Thank you for traveling with us. Have a pleasant trip.

45. At what time and in what city will the passengers have a fifteen-minute rest stop?
46. Which of the following is permitted in the last six rows?
47. What is the number of the bus?
48. At what time is the bus supposed to arrive at its final destination?

Questions 49 and 50 are based on the following conversation.

Man: I can't believe it. Today I went shopping at the store near my house instead of my usual store, and the prices were fantastic!
Woman: Is it one of those no-frills stores?
Man: No, they just had some good sales, and the produce looked better than it has recently at my regular store.
Woman: What kinds of things were on sale?
Man: I got a dozen large eggs for 59¢, beer for $1.69, tuna fish for 79¢, and bleach for 43¢. I bought a lot of food for less than $50.
Woman: Where is this store? I might try it too.
Man: It's the one on the corner of 16th Avenue and Main Street.

49. Which of the following items did the man *not* buy on sale?
50. What was one advantage of this store over his regular store?

This is the end of the Practice Test 4 listening comprehension section.

EXPLANATIONS FOR PRACTICE TEST 4

SECTION II: STRUCTURE AND WRITTEN EXPRESSION

Part A

1. (B) Choice (A) is verbose, using *with caution* rather than *cautiously*. Also, it would make no sense to look cautiously *after* crossing the street. Choice (A) also uses simple past when past perfect is required. Choice (C) is passive and the sentence does not call for a passive meaning. Also, using the adjective *cautious* would indicate that *look* in the sentence is a stative verb meaning *appear*, and that is not the meaning of the sentence. (D) uses an incorrect sequence of tense. The verb *crossed* is in the past.

2. (B) The subject *notebook and report* is plural, and choices (A), (C), and (D) all contain singular verbs.

3. (A) The plural verb *need* is required here because if there is a plural noun after *nor*, the verb must be plural.

4. (C) Choice (A) is incorrect because the superlative, not the comparative, must be used when more than two are expressed. Choices (B) and (D) are incorrect because the definite article *the* must be used before the superlative.

5. (C) The correct form is *would rather* + [verb in simple form].

6. (D) *Eight-century-old* is functioning as an adjective and cannot be plural.

7. (A) Use the comparative when only two entities are involved. Choice (B) incorrectly uses the superlative. Choice (C) would be correct if *the smaller of them* began a new sentence, but it is not correct after the comma. (D) incorrectly uses the relative pronoun *that*, which cannot be used with the preposition.

8. (D) Choice (A) includes an incorrect sequence of tense; *do* should be *did* to agree with *endured*. (B) uses negative agreement, and the sentence is positive. Choice (C) includes incorrect use of affirmative agreement. Also, the correct plural of *child* is *children*.

9. (A) This is a multiple number comparative. Choice (C) is also a multiple number comparative, but one earns *money*. *Money* is a non-count noun, and thus the sentence requires *much*.

10. (D) This is a past condition. The correct sequence is *had studied . . . would have been able*. (B) is verbose.

11. (C) The correct structure for an embedded question is question word + subject + verb. Choices (A) and (B) incorrectly include *did*, and choice (D) incorrectly uses the infinitive *to put*.

12. (D) Choice (A) is incorrect because the subject *facilities* is plural and requires a plural verb. Choice (B) uses an incorrect comparative. It should be *better than*. Choices (A), (B), and (C) all use an illogical comparison. They seem to compare the *facilities* with the *new hospital*. Choice (D) is correct; *those of* = *the facilities of*.

13. (A) Choices (B), (C), and (D) are all missing necessary prepositions, because *of, on account of, as a result of* (notice that a necessary article was left out here as well).

14. (A) In this subjunctive construction use *suggest that* + [verb in simple form].

15. (C) Choice (A) incorrectly uses *others*, which implies that there are more than one other. The sentence says there are two teachers. Choice (B) incorrectly uses *another*, which indicates the indefinite. A specific is required here. (D) is incorrect because in this sentence *other* requires the article *the*.

Part B

16. (C) should be *an*. Use *an* before a word beginning with a vowel sound.

17. (A) should be *were guarding*. Use *a number of* + plural verb.

18. (D) should be *universally*. An adjective (*understood*) is always modified by an adverb, never by another adjective.

19. (C) should be *by incorporating*. This indicates the method by which they convey and preserve their thoughts.

20. (C) should be *other systems*. *Other* cannot be plural when it appears before a noun.

21. (D) should be *in the time of*. This sentence calls for specific time, *the* time of Socrates.

22. (B) should be *themselves*. The word *theirselves* does not exist.

23. (D) should be *survival*. A noun, not a gerund, is necessary here after the preposition *for*.

24. (D) should be *fear*. In this sentence *fear* is indefinite and cannot be modified by the definite article *the*.

25. **(A)** should be *on a child's level* or *on a childish level*. Before a noun, *child* must be possessive (*child's*) or it must be in adjective form (*childish*).

26. **(A)** should be *these*. *These* is the plural of *this*. The plural form is required here before the plural noun *officials*.

27. **(A)** should be *hardly ever*. *Hardly never* is a double negative and should be avoided.

28. **(B)** should be *is*. *Air pollution* is a singular subject and requires a singular verb.

29. **(D)** should be *close to the city*. *Close to* means *near*.

30. **(B)** should be *of flying*. The adjective *capable* requires the preposition *of* + [verb + *ing*].

31. **(B)** should be *was*. *News* is a non-count noun and requires a singular verb.

32. **(B)** should be *which* or *that*. *That which* is redundant here because they are both relative pronouns. One or the other should be used, but not both.

33. **(A)** should be *Joel's*. Use the possessive before a gerund.

34. **(A)** should be *what happened*. For embedded questions, use question word + subject + verb. This is a subject question, so the question word (*what*) is also the subject.

35. **(B)** should be *us*. Use the object pronoun after a verb. The sentence is an indirect command.

36. **(C)** should be *for*. Use *for* + duration of time.

37. **(A)** should be *would have*. The conditional perfect uses *would* + *have* + [verb in past participle]. *Would of* is never correct.

38. **(A)** should be *supposed to*. Use *be* + *supposed to* (means *should*).

39. **(C)** should be *from*. Always use *different from*.

40. **(D)** should be *of financing*. The noun *means* requires the preposition *of* + [verb + *ing*].

SECTION III: READING COMPREHENSION AND VOCABULARY

Part B

31. (C) *Harbinger* means *forerunner* or *precursor* (one that comes before). Sentence 3 says that what the groundhog does, people believe, "will indicate whether spring is just around the corner or a long way off." In other words, what he does *comes before* spring.

32. (B) Sentence 5 tells us that the groundhog ate a large amount of food before going to sleep and that his body fat keeps him alive.

33. (A) Choices (B), (C), and (D) are true according to the reading. They are specifically mentioned. Choice (A) might be true, but the reading gives nothing to support it. The reading concerns the *legend* of the *groundhog* (a single animal), not the *instincts* of *animals*.

34. (B) Sentence 7 tells us that if the groundhog sees his shadow, "it scares him back into his home for another six weeks." Since the reading goes on to say that if the animal *stays out* of his home, it is a sure sign that spring has arrived, you must assume that his *returning* to hibernation is a sign of spring's six-week delay. Choice (D) is not correct because the fact that spring will arrive soon would not necessarily mean that all the snow will disappear immediately.

35. (C) Paragraph 2 tells us that he published the *New York Weekly Journal,* a newspaper his wife continued to publish while he was imprisoned.

36. (A) Paragraph 2, last sentence, specifically speaks of "corrupt government officials."

37. (C) Paragraph 1, last sentence, says that the right (freedom of the press) was adopted in 1791 and that the Zenger trial was in 1735. $1791 - 1735 = 56.$

38. (C) You are asked for the one choice that is *not* true. Choice (A) is true. It is mentioned in paragraph 2. Choice (B) is true. We are told that the jury was "persuaded" by Hamilton. And it should be obvious that they were fighting "for freedom" because the entire reading concerns freedom of the press. Choice (D) is true. We are told in paragraph 2 that the king sent corrupt officials "to govern the colonies."

39. (A) The first paragraph says that termites and ants have similar communal habits but that they are physically different. Answers (C) and (D) are not suggested in the reading.

40. **(A)** We are told that the reproductive termites have eyes but that the workers and soldiers are blind. (B), (C), and (D) are true because only the reproductives fly, and fly only one time, and soldiers are larger than workers.

41. **(B)** The male and female reproductives, it is implied in paragraph 2, fly only to develop a new colony. (A) is not true because the reading indicates that a pair of reproductives flies alone.

42. **(D)** In sentences 2 and 3 of paragraph 2, all of the other choices are given as purposes of the pretrial conference.

43. **(D)** The word *viable* means *workable* or *practical*. Although the pretrial conference, according to the reading, has not been as workable as had been hoped, the small-claims court is given as a viable suggestion for improvement. And the last paragraph suggests that more innovations will be proposed in a continuing effort to find remedies. Nowhere in the passage is it suggested that all states should follow California's example, choice (A), that the legislature should formulate fewer laws, choice (B), or that no one cares, choice (C). In fact the entire reading concerns suggested remedies of those who are concerned.

44. **(C)** Paragraph 1, sentence 2, says, "and the litigants, or parties, have to wait. . . . " This indicates that *litigant* is another word for *party* in this context.

45. **(C)** The last sentence of paragraph 3 indicates that a litigant waives (gives up) his or her right to a jury trial and the right to appeal.

46. **(B)** The second sentence of paragraph 1 says that "costs are staggering" (overwhelming) and litigants "have to wait sometimes many years." And the last sentence of the reading says that the problems "must be remedied if the citizens who have valid claims are going to be able to have their day in court."

47. **(B)** Sentence 2 says that Cyrus the Great was the founder.

48. **(C)** Sentence 1 says that the empire celebrated its 2500th anniversary in 1971 (1971 A.D. − 2500 years = 529 B.C.). Answer (B) is incorrect because the last sentence says that that was the year Persepolis was founded.

49. **(D)** Sentence 3 says that Cambyses succeeded Cyrus. *Predecessor* means one who comes before.

50. **(D)** The entire reading indicates that the empire was progressive.

51. **(A)** The last sentence of paragraph 2 tells us that only one-third of the people were rescued, so it could not be true that only one-third of the people perished (died).

52. **(D)** The panic of the people, the fire on the ship, and the speed at which the ship was moving are all mentioned as contributing to the disaster. The *Carpathia,* however, was the rescue ship.

53. **(A)** Paragraph 2, sentence 1, and paragraph 3 indicate this is true. "Only two days at sea" and "two days of sailing glory on its maiden voyage" both indicate that it had traveled only two days.

54. **(D)** To *extinguish* is to put out a fire; *unextinguished* means that the fire was not stopped (was *unquenched*).

55. **(D)** The first sentence of the reading says that the Great Pyramid was built in 2720 B.C. + 1985 (approximately) A.D. = 4,705. Choice (D), 4,700, is the closest to this answer.

56. **(A)** The last sentence of paragraph 1 says that they based their calculations on astronomical observations (observation of the celestial bodies).

57. **(C)** Paragraph 1, sentence 1, tells us that it was built "as a tomb for Pharaoh Cheops." Although the Egyptians did observe the solar system (A), a tomb would have some connection with religious observances (B), and the pyramid was an engineering feat (D), none of these are given as the reason for the pyramid's construction.

58. **(A)** Sentences 2 and 3 of the first paragraph imply that the pyramid is a great wonder of the world because its four sides align with true north, south, east and west.

59. **(D)** Choice (A) is incorrect because the original sentence says nothing about the families watching television *together*. Choice (B) indicates that families with televisions argue (bicker) more than those without, which is not at all what the original sentence says. Choice (C) is incorrect because the original sentence says nothing about formal censorship; it is speaking of a censorship by the family itself.

60. **(C)** Choice (A) is incorrect because the original sentence simply tells how the children fare on tests; it does not say that they are less intelligent. In choice (B), *tend* is not the same as *trend*. The wording of this sentence is so mixed up that it is not even similar in meaning to the first sentence. Choice (D) is incorrect because the original sentence says nothing about the administration of the tests.

PRACTICE TEST 5

After some answers in this answer key, you will find numbers in italic type. These are page numbers in Part III where you will find review material for these questions. Although any one question may involve several different rules and concepts, these page numbers refer to important areas you should review if you have missed a question or are not sure of the material involved. Make full use of these page number references and of the index to direct your personal review.

Section I: Listening Comprehension

1. (D)	11. (C)	21. (B)	31. (C)	41. (A)
2. (B)	12. (A)	22. (C)	32. (B)	42. (D)
3. (A)	13. (C)	23. (D)	33. (B)	43. (B)
4. (C)	14. (D)	24. (B)	34. (D)	44. (A)
5. (A)	15. (B)	25. (A)	35. (A)	45. (C)
6. (B)	16. (B)	26. (C)	36. (A)	46. (B)
7. (D)	17. (A)	27. (C)	37. (C)	47. (B)
8. (C)	18. (D)	28. (D)	38. (C)	48. (C)
9. (B)	19. (C)	29. (C)	39. (C)	49. (A)
10. (A)	20. (A)	30. (A)	40. (C)	50. (D)

Section II: Structure and Written Expression

1. (C) *135*
2. (C) *172*
3. (B)
4. (C) *144*
5. (D) *107, 155*
6. (C) *142–143*
7. (C) *166–168*
8. (A) *85*
9. (C) *95*
10. (B) *141*
11. (A) *134*
12. (B) *72–73, 158*
13. (C) *69, 71, 75*
14. (D) *171*
15. (A) *54, 155, 167*
16. (B) *62*
17. (D) *147*
18. (C) *147–148*
19. (B) *141*
20. (B) *72*

21. (C)
22. (A) *99*
23. (A) *46–47*
24. (A) *78*
25. (A) *71*
26. (D) *120*
27. (B) *71*
28. (B) *60*
29. (A) *120*
30. (B) *60*
31. (D) *111*
32. (C) *60*
33. (C) *60*
34. (B) *60*
35. (C) *107*
36. (D) *133*
37. (A) *171*
38. (B) *103*
39. (B) *85*
40. (B) *48*

Section III: Reading Comprehension and Vocabulary

1. (B)
2. (B)
3. (D)
4. (D)
5. (C)
6. (D)
7. (B)
8. (D)
9. (A)
10. (C)
11. (B)
12. (A)
13. (C)
14. (D)
15. (A)
16. (D)
17. (B)
18. (A)
19. (C)
20. (B)
21. (A)
22. (B)
23. (D)
24. (C)
25. (D)
26. (B)
27. (A)
28. (A)
29. (B)
30. (C)
31. (C)
32. (B)
33. (C)
34. (D)
35. (A)
36. (C)
37. (A)
38. (B)
39. (D)
40. (C)
41. (D)
42. (D)
43. (C)
44. (B)
45. (A)
46. (D)
47. (B)
48. (C)
49. (C)
50. (A)
51. (A)
52. (B)
53. (A)
54. (C)
55. (B)
56. (C)
57. (A)
58. (C)
59. (D)
60. (B)

PRACTICE TEST 5: ANALYSIS-SCORING SHEET

Use the chart below to spot your strengths and weaknesses in each test section and to arrive at your total converted score. Fill in your number of correct answers for each section in the space provided. Refer to the Converted Score Sheet on page 378 to find your converted score for each section and enter those numbers on the chart. Find the sum of your converted scores, multiply that sum by 10, and divide by 3.

Example: If raw scores are   then   converted scores are

Section I:	33	51
Section II:	26	49
Section III:	38	50

Sum of Converted Scores   150
Times 10 = 1,500
Divided by 3 =   500 = Total
Converted
Score

This will give you the approximate score that you would obtain if this were an actual TOEFL. Remember that your score here may possibly be higher than the score that you might receive on an actual TOEFL simply because you are studying the elements of the test shortly before taking each test. The score is intended only to give you a general idea of approximately what your actual score will be.

	Total Possible	Total Correct	Converted Score
Section I: Listening Comprehension	50		
Section II: Structure and Written Expression	40		
Section III: Reading Comprehension and Vocabulary	60		
TOTALS	150		

Sum of Converted Scores _____

Times 10 = _____

Divided by 3 = _____ = Total Converted Score

SECTION I: LISTENING COMPREHENSION SCRIPT

Part A

1. John should have called his office at 9:50.
2. Could you give me a hand with these packages?
3. There are three nonstop flights from Atlanta to Chicago each week.
4. Mr. Roberts is looking forward to his upcoming vacation.
5. Louise is searching for a new job as a typist.
6. Maria's eyes are irritated from the chlorine in the pool.
7. The ad said that the coat was on sale for $20, but it was actually $22.
8. Class was supposed to begin at 2 o'clock, but because of the fire drill, it began 20 minutes late.
9. Sandra exchanged the shoes for a different pair.
10. Had John known about the test, he wouldn't have missed class.
11. It was a quarter after 12 when they finally arrived.
12. Because her glasses broke, Janet couldn't read her assignment.
13. Anne got a speeding ticket last week.
14. Because of the three-hour delay, it was almost 2 o'clock before they arrived.
15. Travel 60 miles east on Highway 90, and then turn north on Highway 50.
16. They must have miscalculated the costs of this project.
17. Jane couldn't have attended the conference if her boss hadn't paid her way.
18. It's a pity that John hates to study.
19. George is trying to find a nursery near the university.
20. Janet dislikes television, but her husband watches it nightly.

Part B

21. Man: I'd love to see a different type of movie for a change. I'm tired of movies about prison breaks and insane asylums.
    Woman: I agree; let's go see that new movie at the Center Theater. I hear it's a realistic and touching story of two young lovers.
    Third Voice: What kind of movie does the man *not* want to see?

22. Woman: Did you see the tears of laughter on the faces of everyone in the theater?
    Man: Yes, the play certainly raised some eyebrows, but it was nothing less than hilarious.
    Third Voice: According to the man and woman, how did the audience react to the play?

23. Man: The Green Dolphin sounds like a nice place to eat.
    Woman: OK, let's go there. I hear that they have a complete
                   menu and a warm atmosphere.
    Third Voice: Where are the man and woman going?

24. Man: Do you think your grandfather heard our plans
                   for the surprise party?
    Woman: No, he's partially deaf.
    Third Voice: Why does the woman think the grandfather doesn't
                   know about the party?

25. Woman: John, did you hear about the house that the Kehoes
                   bought in the country?
    Man: Yes, and Chuck said that they got a very good deal on it.
    Third Voice: What do we learn from this conversation?

26. Man: The program director said that we'd have to postpone
                   the outing until Saturday because of inclement weather.
    Woman: It's a shame because all the food has already been
                   ordered and will probably spoil.
    Third Voice: Why was the outing postponed?

27. Man: I thought you said that Bob went to Sebring High School.
    Woman: No, he used to attend Clark High School, but after
                   graduation last year, he enrolled in Melrose Community
                   College where his is presently studying.
    Third Voice: Where does Bob go to school now?

28. Woman: Why didn't you have your geology class today?
    Man: Only three out of a class of twenty-five showed up. Since
                   the professor had planned to present a complex
                   demonstration, he decided to cancel the class until
                   everybody was present.
    Third Voice: Why didn't the geology class meet today?

29. Woman: I hear that your son's working part-time at the
                   department store.
    Man: Yes. He works Monday, Wednesday, and Friday from 3
                   to 7 and all day Saturday.
    Third Voice: Which days does the man's son *not* work?

30. Man: Have you bought Jerry's birthday gifts yet?
    Woman: I've found the baseball shoes, a shirt, and a game, but
                   not the bicycle.
    Third Voice: Which of the following items has the woman *not* bought?

31. **Woman:** Since it's the rush hour, let's take the subway.

    Man: OK. It's not as direct as the bus, but it's faster and there will be less chance of a traffic jam.

    Third Voice: Why do the man and woman decide to take the subway?

32. **Man:** I heard Harry got a ticket yesterday. What did he do?

    Woman: He drove down a one-way street the wrong way.

    Third Voice: Why did Harry get a ticket?

33. **Woman:** Do you know Susan Flannigan?

    Man: That name rings a bell, but I'm not sure.

    Third Voice: What do we learn from this conversation?

34. **Man:** Roy doesn't stand a chance of winning a gold medal in the Olympics.

    Woman: True, but he's doing his best.

    Third Voice: What do we learn from this conversation?

35. **Man:** How much does it cost to bowl here?

    Woman: It's usually 75¢ a game, but today there's a special— 60¢ a game.

    Third Voice: How much will it cost to bowl five games today?

Part C

Questions 36 and 37 are based on the following conversation.

Man: Well, your radiator is leaking, your fuel pump is broken, and your carburetor is dirty.

Woman: How long will the repairs take?

Man: I can probably have it as good as new in four days.

36. What can we assume the man does for a living?

37. Which of the following was *not* mentioned as a problem?

Questions 38 through 42 are based on the following reading.

Robert Edwards was blinded in an automobile accident nine years ago. He was also partially deaf because of old age. Last week, he was strolling near his home when a thunderstorm approached. He took refuge under a tree and was struck by lightning. He was knocked to the ground and woke up some 20 minutes later, lying face down in water below a tree. He went into the house and lay down in bed. A short time later, he awoke; his legs were numb and he was trembling, but, when he opened his eyes, he could see the clock across the room fading in and out in front of him. When his wife entered, he saw her for the first time in nine years. Doctors confirm that he has regained his sight and hearing apparently from the flash of lightning, but they are unable to explain the occurrence. The only possible explanation offered by one doctor was that, since Edwards lost his sight as a result of trauma in a terrible accident, perhaps the only way it could be restored was by another trauma.

38. What caused Robert Edwards's blindness?
39. What was the first thing that he saw after being struck by lightning?
40. Which of the following statements is *not* true?
41. What was Edwards doing when he was struck by lightning?
42. What was the reason given by one doctor that Edwards regained his sight?

Questions 43 through 45 are based on the following conversation.

Woman: Have you heard that Nancy's boss wants her to accept
          a six-week assignment in Acapulco?
Man: She'll really like that, especially since all of her
          expenses will be paid and she can practice her Spanish.
Woman: Yes, but most of all, she'll get to spend her leisure hours
          soaking up the sun on those lovely beaches.
Man: When will she be leaving?
Woman: Since she doesn't need a passport, it'll probably be in
          about a week.
Man: That doesn't give her much time to get organized.

43. Which of the following was *not* mentioned as a reason for Nancy's enjoying her new assignment?
44. How soon will Nancy be leaving?
45. What is the one thing Nancy will *not* need for this trip?

Questions 46 through 50 are based on the following reading.

Delaware was considered the first state of the United States because it was the first to accept the Constitution, in December, 1787. It is a very small state, second only to Rhode Island. Another important fact about Delaware is that nylon, that light-weight, yet strong fiber of the twentieth century, was invented there. In colonial days, Delaware was part of the "bread basket" area, raising wheat, corn, and other grains for national consumption.

In 1638, a group of Swedish settlers set up a colony along the Delaware River and lived there peacefully until 1655 when the Dutch, who disliked the Swedes, settled there. Later, it was taken over by the English, and finally became independent in 1776.

46. How many nations controlled the territory called Delaware before its independence in 1776?
47. What important twentieth-century fiber was invented in Delaware?
48. Why is Delaware considered the first state of the United States?

49. Which of the following did *not* at any time control the Delaware territory?
50. Why was this area known as the "bread basket?"

This is the end of the Practice Test 5 listening comprehension section.

EXPLANATIONS FOR PRACTICE TEST 5

SECTION II: STRUCTURE AND WRITTEN EXPRESSION

Part A

1. (C) Choice (A) is incorrect. *What* is not a relative pronoun, and thus cannot follow a noun in this way. Choice (B) incorrectly uses the pronoun *who,* which may be used only for people. The noun immediately before it is *proposal.* (D) is verbose.

2. (C) Choices (A), (B), and (D) are all verbose.

3. (B) To speak of societal classes we have only the following choices: lower class, lower-middle class, middle class, upper-middle class, and upper class.

4. (C) Choices (A) and (B) are incorrect because the correct form is *know how* + [verb in infinitive]. Choice (D) is verbose, using a poor choice of vocabulary in "way of efficiency in study."

5. (D) Choice (A) uses improper word order. Also, *easier* should be *easily* (the adverb) to modify the verb, and "with hopes *to be* able" should be "with hopes *of being* able." (B) uses improper sequence of tense; *can* should be *could.* And, as in (A), *easier* should be *easily.* Choice (C) is incorrect because the proper idiom is *hope of,* not *hope for.*

6. (C) Choice (A) should read *not only . . . but also.* (B) is redundant. You should not say *both . . . as well as,* and the choice does not include the necessary noun (*ability, skill, talent,* etc.) after *artistic.* (D) is verbose and uses poor vocabulary choice.

7. (C) Choices (A), (B), and (D) lack parallel structure. Correct structure is *will* + [verb in simple form]: *will wash . . . iron . . . prepare . . . dust.*

8. (A) The correct form for the negative indirect command is verb + indirect object + *not* + infinitive.

9. (C) The past condition requires *if . . .* past perfect *. . .* modal + perfective.

10. (B) For the subjunctive use *insisted that* + [verb in simple form]. Choice (A) would be correct if it did not include *that he,* which is redundant when used with *that his patient.*

11. (A) Choice (B) is incorrect because it says *let ... to enter.* It must be *let* + [verb in simple form], "*let* the photographers *enter.*" In choice (C), *permitting* is in the gerund form, and a verb in the past perfect is needed. Also *permit,* like *allow,* must be followed by the infinitive, not the simple form. (D) uses incorrect word order; the verb is after the complement.

12. (B) Choice (A) is incorrect because there is no antecedent for the pronoun *they.* Choice (C) is verbose and should read either *capable of completing* or *able to complete.* (D) is also verbose and uses improper word choice. You cannot "trust" ability.

13. (C) Choice (A) is incorrect because the committee members did not resent the *president;* they resented *his not informing them.* If the sentence meant that they resented the president, it would have to say, " ... resented the president *for not informing ...* " (B) is not correct because this wording would also indicate that they resented the president himself, but *resent* here must be followed by [verb + *ing*]. (D) is verbose. It also should use *fail* + infinitive (*failed to inform*). Also, in choice (D), *themselves* is an improper use of the reflexive; *them* would be correct.

14. (D) This sentence involves the use of an adverbial at the beginning of a sentence. Correct form is adverbial + auxiliary + subject + verb. The auxiliary *did* is in the main sentence before the subject *Arthur,* so (D) is the only possible answer, as it begins with the adverbial *only.*

15. (A) Choice (B) is incorrect because it does not use parallel structure. Active voice ... active voice is needed. Choice (C) makes improper use of the past progressive. (D) is verbose and makes improper use of the present perfect. Correct sequence of tense is *scurried ... heard.*

Part B

NOTE: ∅ = nothing, indicating that this word or phrase should be deleted.

16. (B) should be *has. Neither* must be followed by a singular verb.

17. (D) should be *raise.* Use *raise* + complement (*his test score* is the complement). *Rise* does not take a complement.

18. (C) should be *lying.* Use *lay* + complement. There is no complement in this sentence, so the verb *lie,* not *lay,* is required.

19. (B) Should be *go*. The correct subjunctive form is *suggest that* + [verb in simple form].

20. (B) should be *going*. *Look forward to* + [verb + *ing*].

21. (C) should be ∅. The preposition *of* is not necessary after the preposition *off*.

22. (A) should be *jog*. Correct usage is *used to* + [verb in simple form] (Mr. Anderson *used to jog* . . .) or *be used to* + [verb + *ing*] (Mr. Anderson *was used to jogging* . . .).

23. (A) should be *volume*. Use noun + cardinal number or *the* + ordinal number + noun. It is correct to say *volume four* or *the fourth volume*.

24. (A) should be *he could have*. This is an embedded question: question word + subject + verb.

25. (A) should be *to defend*. Use *try* + infinitive.

26. (D) should be *because of*. Use *because* + sentence and *because of* + noun phrase. *The students' confusion* is only a noun phrase.

27. (B) should be *to support*. *Intend* + infinitive.

28. (B) should be *is*. *Congressman* is a singular subject and requires a singular verb.

29. (A) should be *because of*. Use *because of* + noun phrase. Note that "that had devastated the area" is a relative clause; therefore, "the torrential rains" is only a noun phrase, not a sentence.

30. (B) should be *is*. *Lack* is a singular subject and requires a singular verb.

31. (D) should be *than the first*. The correct comparison is *better than*.

32. (C) should be *has*. *Cultivation* is a singular subject and requires a singular verb.

33. (C) should be *is causing*. *Decision* is a singular subject and requires a singular verb.

34. (B) should be *have been*. *Species* (in this sentence) is a plural subject and requires a plural verb. *Species* may also be singular, but if that had been the case in this sentence, *underutilized* would have been preceded by *an*.

35. (C) should be *diligently*. The verb *had worked* should be modified by an adverb, not an adjective.

36. (D) should be *pulled*. The correct construction is *have* + complement + [verb in past participle]. This is the rule for passive causatives.

37. (A) should be *Hardly had he*. For an adverbial at the beginning of a sentence use adverbial + auxiliary + subject + verb.

38. (B) should be *change*. *Had better* + [verb in simple form].

39. (B) should be *not to*. For the negative indirect command use verb + *not* + infinitive.

40. (B) should be *others*. *An* means *one;* here *others* must be plural because it is functioning as a pronoun. It is *never* possible to say *anothers*.

SECTION III: READING COMPREHENSION AND VOCABULARY

Part B

31. (C) *Disservice* means *harm*. Sentence 2 says that science has made many foods unfit to eat. The reading later gives nitrates and nitrites as harmful substances that have been added to food.

32. (B) Sentence 6 says that nitrates are used as color preservers in meat.

33. (C) In the last sentence, the letters FDA follow the title Food and Drug Administration.

34. (D) *Carcinogenic* means *cancer-causing*. Sentence 6 states that nitrates and nitrites cause cancer. The following sentence begins, "Yet, these carcinogenic additives . . . " You can assume that the word *these* refers to the cancer-causing additives mentioned in the previous sentence.

35. (A) Sentences 10 and 11 tell us that drugs are not *always* administered for medicinal reasons.

36. (C) Choice (A) is not correct because the passage states that the Egyptians left "no written accounts." Modern embalmers still using these methods (B) are not mentioned at all, nor is chemical analysis (D). Sentence 2 does state specifically that scientists "have had to examine mummies and establish their own theories," choice (C).

37. (A) This is an inference question. The reading does not specifically describe the embalming process in any of these ways. However, you can assume that the process was not "short and simple" (B) because in some cases it took seventy days. A process would not be "strict and unfaltering" (C); those would be qualities more likely ascribed to a person. There is nothing at all in the reading to suggest that the embalming would be either "wild" or "terrifying" (D). Because of the several steps

involved and the time mentioned, however, it would seem logical that the process is "lengthy and complicated," choice (A).

38. (B) You are asked for the one choice that is *not* true. Choice (A) is true because the belief in a "life after death," mentioned in the first sentence, indicates a religious belief. Choice (C) is true. The compounds are listed as being made up of salt, spices, and resins. (D) is not specifically mentioned, but you should assume that it has been difficult to determine the process, since there are no written accounts available. Choice (B), however, is false. Sentence 3 says, "up to seventy days for nobles and *only a few* for the poor," so embalming did not *always* take seventy days to complete.

39. (D) The second sentence states that some tapeworms attach themselves to the intestinal wall; thus they do *not* float freely.

40. (C) Paragraph 2, sentence 3, says that a hermaphrodite is a being with male and female sexual organs.

41. (D) Euphoria is not mentioned as a symptom. Irregular appetite, nervousness, and anemia, which mean the same as answers (A), (B), and (C), are mentioned.

42. (D) We are told in paragraph 1 that some tapeworms attach themselves to the intestinal wall to feed, while others float freely and absorb food through their body walls.

43. (C) The reading gives general information about a particular parasite, the tapeworm.

44. (B) The last sentence of paragraph 1 says, "Economics was added in 1968, just sixty-seven years after the first awards ceremony." 1968 − 67 = 1901.

45. (A) The third sentence of paragraph 1 says that the prize was established to recognize "worthwhile contributions to mankind" (humanity).

46. (D) The last sentence of paragraph 3 says that Americans have won "numerous science awards."

47. (B) Choice (A) is true. The awards vary from $30,000 to $125,000. We are told specifically that politics sometimes play an important role in the selection (C) and that some people have won two prices, although that is rare (unusual). If it is rare, then only *a few* will have done so (D). (B) is not true. The date December 10 is not important in commemorating his invention, but is the anniversary of his death.

48. **(C)** Paragraph 1, sentence 4, says that there were originally five awards, and economics was added in 1968. The total, then, is six.

49. **(C)** This is the type of advertisement that would appear in the classified section.

50. **(A)** A *restriction* is a *limitation*. It refers to something that is *not allowed*. The prefix *non* could alert you to the fact that smoking is not allowed.

51. **(A)** Choices (B) and (C) are specifically mentioned in the advertisement. You can assume choice (D) to be true because the ad says *part. furn.* (which means *partially furnished*). If the apartment is only partially furnished, the renter will have to supply some furniture. But the renter will have to pay *more* than $150 per month. The rent is $150 + ½ *util.* (utilities—such as gas, light, phone, and water).

52. **(B)** The renter must pay the first month's rent (*1st*), the last month's rent (*last*), and a deposit (*dep.*) of $100. $150 + $150 + $100 = $400.

53. **(A)** You are asked to choose the best *summary* of the passage, which means the statement that best tells the *general idea*. Choice (B) is the opposite of what the reading says. Choices (C) and (D) *may* be true, but they are too specific to give the general idea of the entire passage. And while you might assume that verbalization is the fastest form of communication, the reading does not mention this.

54. **(C)** The deaf, although they cannot hear, sometimes can speak, but the mute, by definition, cannot speak. Therefore, they could not themselves use *oral* communication.

55. **(B)** Blind people cannot see, so choices (A), (C), and (D) would not be used by them. Braille is read with the fingertips (paragraph 3).

56. **(C)** There are nine forms of communication listed in the reading: oral speech, sign language, body language, Braille, signal flags, Morse code, smoke signals, road maps, and picture signs.

57. **(A)** The last sentence of paragraph 1 says that these symbols (sign language) *cannot* be used internationally for spelling.

58. **(C)** The *extended family* is the combination of parents, grandparents, aunts, uncles, cousins, etc. Choice (A) is incorrect because "the family cannot survive the presence of it" has no meaning that corresponds with the original sentence; also notice that *extension* is not used in the same way as *extended* in the original sentence. Choice (B) is incorrect because

remains is used in the original sentence as a verb, not a noun, and the meaning changes completely. Also notice that rather than speaking of an *extended family,* this sentence speaks of an *extended album.* Choice (D) also uses *remains* incorrectly.

59. (D) Choice (A) is incorrect because it says, "we have always realized" it; the original sentence does not say that. Choice (B) says, "we have been the brunt of a terrible joke," and the original does not say that. Choice (C) is incorrect because it says, "without having to concern ourselves." It is not that we did not have to, but that we failed to perceive the dangers.

60. (B) Choice (A) is incorrect because *some nutrition* is obviously necessary just to survive and is not the same as *good nutrition.* In choice (C), the sentence is certainly true, but it does not relate the experiments concerning *human life* as the original sentence does. Choice (D) is incorrect because there is nothing in the original sentence indicating that the human children will act like animals.

PRACTICE TEST 6

ANSWER KEY FOR PRACTICE TEST 6

After some answers in this answer key, you will find numbers in italic type. These are page numbers in Part III where you will find review material for these questions. Although any one question may involve several different rules and concepts, these page numbers refer to important areas you should review if you have missed a question or are not sure of the material involved. Make full use of these page number references and of the index to direct your personal review.

Section I: Listening Comprehension

1. (C)	11. (C)	21. (C)	31. (C)	41. (A)
2. (D)	12. (B)	22. (B)	32. (B)	42. (A)
3. (A)	13. (D)	23. (A)	33. (B)	43. (B)
4. (B)	14. (A)	24. (C)	34. (C)	44. (B)
5. (A)	15. (C)	25. (C)	35. (C)	45. (D)
6. (B)	16. (C)	26. (B)	36. (A)	46. (D)
7. (D)	17. (B)	27. (A)	37. (D)	47. (D)
8. (C)	18. (B)	28. (D)	38. (A)	48. (B)
9. (C)	19. (C)	29. (D)	39. (B)	49. (B)
10. (A)	20. (A)	30. (B)	40. (C)	50. (A)

Section II: Structure and Written Expression

1. (D) *107, 172–173*	21. (B) *53–54*
2. (B)	22. (B) *54–55*
3. (A) *115*	23. (B) *58–59*
4. (A) *167, 172–173*	24. (C) *75*
5. (A) *54*	25. (A) *57–58*
6. (B) *169*	26. (C) *155*
7. (D)	27. (B) *60*
8. (D)	28. (B) *61*
9. (B) *78*	29. (B) *63*
10. (B) *95*	30. (C) *160*
11. (C)	31. (A)
12. (C) *172*	32. (A) *75*
13. (D)	33. (A) *207*
14. (A) *172*	34. (C) *133*
15. (B) *147, 165*	35. (A) *142*
16. (D) *167*	36. (C) *219*
17. (D) *167*	37. (C) *99*
18. (B) *69*	38. (A) *53, 55–56*
19. (C) *155*	39. (C) *48*
20. (D) *122*	40. (D) *43*

Section III: Reading Comprehension and Vocabulary

1. (A)	13. (A)	25. (C)	37. (D)	49. (D)
2. (A)	14. (B)	26. (A)	38. (B)	50. (D)
3. (A)	15. (D)	27. (A)	39. (A)	51. (C)
4. (B)	16. (C)	28. (A)	40. (A)	52. (B)
5. (C)	17. (A)	29. (C)	41. (C)	53. (C)
6. (D)	18. (B)	30. (C)	42. (B)	54. (C)
7. (B)	19. (A)	31. (C)	43. (A)	55. (A)
8. (C)	20. (A)	32. (B)	44. (B)	56. (B)
9. (A)	21. (A)	33. (A)	45. (A)	57. (C)
10. (D)	22. (B)	34. (B)	46. (D)	58. (B)
11. (B)	23. (B)	35. (B)	47. (B)	59. (B)
12. (A)	24. (B)	36. (A)	48. (B)	60. (A)

PRACTICE TEST 6: ANALYSIS-SCORING SHEET

Use the chart below to spot your strengths and weaknesses in each test section and to arrive at your total converted score. Fill in your number of correct answers for each section in the space provided. Refer to the Converted Score Sheet on page 378 to find your converted score for each section and enter those numbers on the chart. Find the sum of your converted scores, multiply that sum by 10, and divide by 3.

Example: If raw scores are   then   converted scores are
Section I: 33   51
Section II: 26   49
Section III: 38   50
                                                          _____
                    Sum of Converted Scores   150
                              Times 10 = 1,500
                    Divided by 3 =   500 = Total
                                                Converted
                                                Score

This will give you the approximate score that you would obtain if this were an actual TOEFL. Remember that your score here may possibly be higher than the score that you might receive on an actual TOEFL simply because you are studying the elements of the test shortly before taking each test. The score is intended only to give you a general idea of approximately what your actual score will be.

	Total Possible	Total Correct	Converted Score
Section I: Listening Comprehension	50		
Section II: Structure and Written Expression	40		
Section III: Reading Comprehension and Vocabulary	60		
TOTALS	150		

Sum of Converted Scores _____

Times 10 = _____

Divided by 3 = _____ = Total Converted Score

SECTION I: LISTENING COMPREHENSION SCRIPT

Part A

1. If Mary doesn't come soon, we will probably be late.
2. The program was supposed to begin at 9 o'clock, but the president's speech delayed it 20 minutes.
3. I can't remember whether we are going to a party on Friday or Saturday night.
4. Helen dislikes going fishing with her husband even though she goes quite often.
5. I found it extremely difficult to learn all that material.
6. If it hadn't been such a nice day, Bob would have studied.
7. Susan could hardly find a seat in the dark theater.
8. Rick was puzzled by the expression on the girl's face.
9. Before the class began, a dozen students were in the room, but soon the number doubled.
10. Alice slowly pushed her cart down the aisle choosing cans of vegetables.
11. George would rather listen to Beethoven than rock music.
12. John must have been exhausted after that run.
13. Contrary to what Bill had expected, the professor cancelled the class.
14. Dr. Jones should be free to see you after noon tomorrow.
15. In spite of her bad habits, Suzy has a lot of friends.
16. Houses are so expensive now that we simply can't afford to buy one.
17. Bob bought a stereo for $363 in a store, but he could have gotten it for $270 from the catalog.
18. George sells doughnuts, pastry, and cake in his store.
19. It's too late to register for the class. Registration closed the day before yesterday.
20. Jane didn't know about our change in plans.

Part B

21. Woman: Mark can't stand rare meat.
    Man: I know. I ordered medium well. We'll send it back.
    Third Voice: What do we learn from this conversation?

22. Man: Ugh, this milk is sour!
    Woman: It should be good. The expiration date is five days away.
    Third Voice: What are the man and woman talking about?

23. Man: How would you like your two pounds of pork chops sliced?
    Woman: Medium thin will be fine.
    Third Voice: Where does this conversation most probably take place?

24. Man: Which of the boys is Henry Adams?
    Woman: The one with the green sweater using the crutches.
    Third Voice: What is the probable reason for Henry's using crutches?

25. Woman: Have you seen that movie about the girl who had sixteen
                  different personalities?
    Man: No, and I don't plan to. It sounds scary.
    Third Voice: Why doesn't the man want to see the movie?

26. Woman: That famous science fiction writer Isaac Asimov's new
                  book is coming out in July.
    Man: We probably won't be able to find a library copy until
                  September.
    Third Voice: When will Asimov's book be published?

27. Man: Where did you get that lovely necklace? I haven't seen
                  you wear it.
    Woman: It was packed away until last week. It's a family heir-
                  loom.
    Third Voice: What do we learn about the necklace?

28. Woman: Did you hear that the neighborhood convenience store
                  was held up last night?
    Man: Yes, I heard it on the radio this morning.
    Third Voice: What happened at the convenience store last night?

29. Mother: Don't gulp down your lunch. It's not good for you.
    Boy: OK, Mom, but the boys will be here any minute, and I
                  don't want to miss the game.
    Third Voice: What did the mother ask her son *not* to do?

30. Woman: Do you think this skirt goes well with this blouse?
    Man: Yes, but I think your red dress would be more elegant
                  for the reception.
    Third Voice: What does the man think of the woman's choice of
                  clothing?

31. Man: Where is Louie?
    Woman: He was supposed to play baseball, but it was cancelled,
                  so he went bowling instead.
    Third Voice: What do we learn from this conversation?

32. Woman: I wish Jack were coming to visit us.
    Man: He won't be able to because it's out of his way.
    Third Voice: What do we learn from this conversation?

33. Man: Will you back me up on this new curriculum proposal?
    Woman: You can count on me!
    Third Voice: What does the woman say she'll do?

34. Man: Could you show me that once more?
    Woman: Sure. Put the paper into the machine, set your margin,
                  put your fingers on the keys. Now you're ready.
    Third Voice: What is the woman doing?

35. Man: Miss, can you give me change for a dollar?
    Woman: I'm sorry, sir. I'm not allowed to give change without
                  a purchase. If you go across the hall, you'll find a
                  change machine in front of the jewelry store.
    Third Voice: Where does the woman suggest that the man get change?

Part C

Questions 36 through 38 are based on the following talk.

Adaptation is the process by which living things adjust to changes in their environment—ways of finding food, protecting themselves from their enemies, and reproducing.

The protective adaptations vary with each species of animal depending on its individual needs and environment.

Many animals possess colors that help them blend in with their surroundings. Polar bears and white rabbits can easily move undetected amidst the winter snows. Many butterflies' colors make it difficult to find them among the trees. Chameleons can change colors to disguise themselves on rocks, trees, and wood chips.

Snakes bite; bees and wasps sting; skunks emit a pungent odor; and porcupines eject painful quills into their attackers.

36. Which of the following was *not* mentioned as possessing a protective device?
37. What makes porcupines unique?
38. Which of the following protective devices was *not* mentioned in this talk?

Questions 39 through 43 are based on the following talk.

Almost two centuries ago, humans enjoyed their first airborne ride in a cloth balloon. Passengers rode in a basket fastened below the balloon. These brave adventurers depended solely on the wind velocity and direction to move them about because of the lack of a steering mechanism.

In 1852, a French clockmaker flew the first controllable balloon a distance of seventeen miles.

Germany began producing and using airships about forty-six years later with its famous Zeppelins, named in honor of their inventor, Count von Zeppelin. The largest and probably most famous of Germany's airships was the *Hindenberg,* which could travel at eighty-five miles per hour.

Later, the two countries bordering on the English Channel, Great Britain and France, built smaller airships called "blimps." The latter airships were intended for patrolling the coast and observing submarine activity, while the former served as passenger and cargo ships.

After the *Hindenberg* burned in 1937, more and more people shied away from this form of transportation.

39. Why was it difficult to fly in the air-filled balloons of two hundred years ago?
40. Which of the following countries was *not* involved in the production of airships?
41. Who flew the first controllable airship?
42. Which country used these airships for passenger and cargo transport?
43. Why did fewer people travel on airships after 1937?

Questions 44 through 46 are based on the following talk.

All living, self-propelled beings do not enjoy the same lifespan. Scientists have discovered that the faster a living thing grows and moves during its life, the shorter its life will be. Animals producing many offspring will have shorter lives than those that produce only a few. Larger animals live longer than smaller ones. Some species live several weeks, while others can enjoy more than a one-hundred-year existence.

Disease and other environmental conditions are capable of wiping out a particular species in a given area.

44. Based on the information of this talk, which of the following will probably live only a short time?
45. Which of the following can be expected to live the longest?
46. Which was *not* mentioned as a cause for shortening an animal's lifespan?

Questions 47 through 50 are based on the following talk.

It was not until one hundred and fifty years ago that scientists learned about the existence of dinosaurs. Thanks to an English doctor and his wife, the door was opened to this zoological study. Reasoning that the reptiles' tremendous size must have made them terrible creatures, scientists combined two Greek words, *deimos,* meaning *terrible,* and *sauros,* meaning *lizards,* to form the word *dinosaur.*

After many years of study, they determined that these beasts roamed the earth for millions of years, and ceased to exist some sixty million years ago.

Unbelievable as it may seem, not all dinosaurs were carnivorous, that is, meat eating. Many were herbivorous, or vegetarians.

By reassembling the bones found at excavation sites, scientists have been able to reconstruct the skeletons and learn a great deal about the dinosaurs' living conditions. They have learned that dinosaurs inhabited not only the land, but also the water and sky.

47. By what name did scientists refer to these creatures?
48. When do scientists believe that the last of the dinosaurs disappeared?
49. How have scientists been able to learn of the living conditions of these animals?
50. Which of the following is *not* true of these animals?

This is the end of the Practice Test 6 listening comprehension section.

EXPLANATONS FOR PRACTICE TEST 6

SECTION II: STRUCTURE AND WRITTEN EXPRESSION

Part A

1. (D) Choice (A) is incorrect because the verb *studied* should be modified by an adverb, *badly*. (B) is in error because it is never correct to say *wise* with a noun or verb to mean *in relation to*. (C) uses *badly*, which is an adverb and cannot modify the noun *student*.

2. (B) The expression *second only to* here means that Harvard's programs are the best, and this university's programs are second best.

3. (A) This is a double comparative. The correct form is *the more . . . the less*.

4. (A) Choice (A) contains correct parallel structure: *durability* (noun) . . . *economy* (noun). Choice (B) is verbose. *Lasts a long time* means it is *durable*. It is not necessary to use so many words. When there is a shorter answer that means the same and is grammatically correct, choose the shorter answer. Choice (C) would be correct if it said "its *durability* and *economy*" (noun/noun). Choice (D) uses *economy-wise*. It is always incorrect to use *wise* with a noun in this way.

5. (A) Past progressive: *when . . .* simple past . . . past progressive. Choice (D) would be correct if it said *had been sleeping*.

6. (B) The form should be subject + verb + indirect object + direct object. There should be *no* preposition.

7. (D) The correct expression is *in greater numbers*. This is an expression that you should memorize.

8. (D) Always after the phrase *it was not until* must appear the word *that*. To use *when* here would be redundant.

9. (B) For an embedded question use question word + subject + verb.

10. **(B)** Past condition. When the conditional perfect is used in the result clause, the past perfect must be used in the *if* clause.

11. **(C)** There are only a few possibilities for expressing age in English: (1) when he was sixteen (years old), (2) at (age) sixteen, and (3) at the age of sixteen. Choice (C) follows rule (3) and is the only correct answer.

12. **(C)** Choice (A) is verbose and too informal for written English. Choice (B) uses *make ... expressions,* which has to do with facial features, not speech, and makes no sense here. In choice (D) *with their minds open* (having open minds) is an idiom meaning to be willing to have no biases. When used in this context with *talk,* it is not logical.

13. **(D)** *Much less* is used in this context in a negative sentence to indicate that the second item mentioned is disliked even more than the first. The students dislike reading novels and dislike reading textbooks even more.

14. **(A)** Choices (B) and (D) are verbose. *Eagerly* is much more concise than either of these choices. Choice (C) uses *eagernessly,* which is not a word. It is not possible to add an adverb affix ($-ly$) to a noun affix ($-ness$).

15. **(B)** Choices (A), (C), and (D) are all verbose. In addition, choice (D) includes the wrong verb (*raised*); (A) and (D) incorrectly use *the time when.* It should be *the time that* because *the time when* is redundant; choice (C) uses incorrect word order.

Part B

NOTE: $\emptyset$ = nothing, indicating that this word or phrase should be deleted.

16. **(D)** should be $\emptyset$. Parallel structure would be adjective/noun, adjective/noun, adjective/noun. The phrase *working at* is not necessary because the verb is in the main clause.

17. **(D)** should be *cruelty.* Parallel structure requires noun (*strength*), noun (*power*), and noun (*cruelty*).

18. **(B)** should be *themselves.* The form *theirselves* does not exist.

19. **(C)** should be *would receive.* Sequence of tense should be past ... past.

20. **(D)** should be *such a short time.* Cause/effect: *such* + *a* + adjective + singular count noun.

21. **(B)** should be *turned.* He finished taking classes in 1978; therefore, the verb must be in the past tense.

22. **(B)** should be *was hurrying.* Past progressive: *when ...* past tense ... past progressive.

23. (B) should be *had stolen.* Use the past perfect: *had* + [verb in past participle].

24. (C) should be *dog's.* Use the possessive form before a gerund.

25. (A) should be *has been hoping.* Use the present perfect progressive: *has been* + [verb + *ing*].

26. (C) should be *had been driving.* The correct sequence of tense is *after driving . . . had been driving. After driving* is past in this sentence, and *has been driving* is present.

27. (B) should be *is. The Department of Foreign Languages* is singular so the verb must be singular.

28. (B) should be *is. Accompanied by* is a prepositional phrase and therefore is not part of the subject. The subject is *candidate,* which is singular.

29. (B) should be *knows. Neither* is singular and requires a singular verb.

30. (C) should be *your. Those of you* is the subject, so we must keep the same person pronoun for the possessive (*your*).

31. (A) should be *zoology book.* It is not correct to say *a book of* _____ for textbooks.

32. (A) should be *Marta's.* Use the possessive form before a gerund.

33. (A) should be *lend* or *loan.* This is incorrect vocabulary choice. (I am the receiver and Jane is the giver.)

34. (C) should be *eat.* Causative: *make* + [verb in simple form].

35. (A) should be *not only composes.* The actor does two different things, using two different verbs, *composes* and *sings. Not only* must precede the first verb because there are two verbs.

36. (C) should be *of. About* is an incorrect preposition with *sample.* It should be a *sample of* something.

37. (C) should be *used.* Use *be* + *used to* + gerund and *used to* + simple form.

38. (A) should be *called. Last night* is a specific time and requires the simple past tense, not the present perfect.

39. (C) should be *others. Another* is singular. *Others* must be plural to agree with *their.*

40. (D) should be *fewer. Movies* is a count noun, so it requires *fewer* not *less.*

SECTION III: READING COMPREHENSION AND VOCABULARY

Part B

31. **(C)** Paragraph 2 says, "In 800 A.D. Charlemagne ... initiated the Carolingian Renaissance." Although the Roman civilization is mentioned in the passage, and is older, it is not given as an example of a civilization involving rebirth.

32. **(B)** Paragraph 2 says that during the Carolingian period modern cities were patterned on Roman architecture. You could eliminate choices (C) and (D) immediately, as the question asks for a *city* and these two choices are not city names.

33. **(A)** Choices (B), (C), and (D) were specifically mentioned in the reading. If you know that *status quo* means the *existing condition,* you could realize that this would not be appropriate for a time of rebirth.

34. **(B)** The Kievan Renaissance was two hundred years after the Carolingian (800 + 200 = 1000; 1000 A.D. = eleventh century). The Italian was in the fourteenth century. 14 − 11 = 3.

35. **(B)** This is an inference question. From the fact that we are told of the *able* (competent) rule of Yaroslav, we can assume that he was in general a competent leader. Also, given his name, Yaroslav the *Wise,* one would not assume he was demented, inept, or cruel, all negative qualities.

36. **(A)** The word *carryover* means *remnant.* One can assume from the context that the libraries were something that *came from* Alexandrian Egypt. The only other choice that is close is (B) *residue.* But *residue* most often has a connotation of chemical process, and thus is not the best choice.

37. **(D)** Paragraph 1, sentences 2 and 3, states that the foods made from gelatin are *jellylike* (which would be easy to chew) and high in protein, so we can assume that gelatin would be beneficial for elderly and ill people.

38. **(B)** Paragraph 2, sentence 2, says that the grease must first be eliminated, so it probably does not aid in producing gelatin.

39. **(A)** The whole reading deals with the process of making gelatin. The other choices suggest only *details* of the passage.

40. **(A)** This is the only answer choice *not* listed in the passage.

41. **(C)** Paragraph 1, sentence 2, says that the technology "allows scientists to introduce genetic material (or genes) from one organism into anoth-

er." The key word in this question is *primarily*. Choice (D) is a *small part* of the technology. Choice (A) is a *result* of the technology. Choice (B) is the *function of the foreign gene*, and also involves only a part of the technology.

42. **(B)** Paragraph 1, sentence 5, tells us that *E. coli* is a bacteria into which the recombinant molecule can be introduced. It is not itself produced by DNA technology.

43. **(A)** Sentence 6 states that "the foreign gene will not only replicate in the bacteria, but also express itself." Thus choice (A) is the one choice that is *not* true. Choices (B) and (D) are specifically mentioned in the passage. (C) is not specifically stated, but we should assume that such important research would be ongoing.

44. **(B)** The last sentence of paragraph 1 states this fact. Choice (D) is not true because, while the reading states that *E. coli* may be produced in large amounts in synthetic media, it does not say that it *requires* synthetic media.

45. **(A)** Sentence 4 says, "This piece of DNA is then *ligated* to a fragment of bacterial DNA which has the capacity to replicate itself independently." Sentence 5 continues, "The recombinant molecule *thus* produced. . ." This means that two different molecules are ligated (joined) to produce "a recombinant molecule." Choice (B) is not true, since, although several technologies are combined, the reading does not say that the technologies are *re*combined. (C) is not true because recombination of molecules is at the level of DNA, and not at the level of their products, the proteins. (D) is not true because *E. coli* is used to obtain expression of the recombinant molecule, but it is a "common intestinal bacterium," and not a recombinant.

46. **(D)** Mars is 55% the size of Earth; therefore, it is smaller.

47. **(B)** The first sentence of paragraph 2 tells us that the canals were thought to have been discovered by Schiaparelli.

48. **(B)** If Mars is "commonly called" the Red Planet, that is its nickname.

49. **(D)** This is the only choice that is *not* true. The last paragraph states that *some* polar ice and permafrost were found, indicating that at one time there were significant quantities. Now, however, only traces are left, not large quantities.

50. **(D)** 264 B.C. is the third century B.C., and 476 A.D. is the fifth century A.D. 3 + 5 = 8.

51. **(C)** *Enduring* means *lasting*. Sentence 4 says that laws were probably the most lasting heritage.

52. **(B)** Sentence 3 says that remains can still be seen in various parts of Africa and Europe. Although Germany, choice **(C)**, is a part of Europe, the reading does not say definitely that it was one of the places where remains exist, and **(B)** is the better answer.

53. **(C)** Although the reading says that the Roman Empire fell in 476 A.D., it does not state when the decline *began*.

54. **(C)** Choices **(A)**, **(B)**, and **(D)** were specifically mentioned in the passage. Choice **(C)**, *Russian,* was not.

55. **(A)** Latin America, England, and the United States are listed as examples of countries whose legal codes are based on those of ancient Rome. China is not mentioned in the reading.

56. **(B)** We are told in sentence 1 that only natural-born citizens of the United States can become president. Naturalization involves citizenship after immigration.

57. **(C)** Sentence 2 tells us that a person can serve two four-year terms plus two years for which he or she was not elected $(4 + 4 + 2 = 10)$.

58. **(B)** Sentence 1 says that a person must reside in the United States for 14 years before being eligible to run for president.

59. **(B)** Choice **(A)** is incorrect because no special arrangements are necessary to turn the term papers in tomorrow; only if they are going to be turned in *after* tomorrow must special arrangements be made. Choice **(C)** is incorrect because the arrangements are not necessarily to be made tomorrow; they might be made today. Choice **(D)** changes the meaning of the original sentence completely.

60. **(A)** Choice **(B)** is incorrect because *accomplished* in the original sentence is used as an adjective modifying *violinist*. It tells what kind of violinist Rita is. It changes the meaning to use it as a verb, as is done in choice **(B)**. Choice **(C)** changes the time sequence; it indicates that first she became a violinist and then she practiced. In **(D)**, *accomplish* is again used incorrectly as a verb and now is describing how she practiced.

PART VI: The Writing Test

THE WRITING TEST

The writing test will appear on some administrations of TOEFL beginning with the July, 1986, administration. If you take the TOEFL at an administration where the writing test is offered, you must take that portion of the test as well. The writing test is scored by two separate readers on a scale of 1 to 6, with 1 being the poorest score and 6 being the best. If the scores given by the two readers differ by more than one point, a third reader also reviews the paper. The scores are based upon the essay as a whole; such items as vocabulary, grammar, use of examples, and organization are not scored separately. The score is reported as a separate number on the TOEFL score report.

Ability Tested

The writing test analyzes your ability to respond to an essay question under time constraints. A topic will be presented, and the student must use proper organization, grammar, vocabulary, and spelling and must provide sufficient examples.

Basic Skills Necessary

You must be able to organize and write an effective essay, using correct grammar and spelling.

General Information

The TOEFL Bulletin indicates that during the writing test, students will have the opportunity to write an essay of 200 to 300 words in 30 minutes. Examinees will not need specific or detailed knowledge of the topic presented. A lined page will be attached to the answer sheet for writing the essay. Additional paper will be provided for making notes before writing the actual essay.

In order to score well on the writing test, you should keep the following points in mind:

1. Address the assigned topic completely, being sure to answer all parts of the question asked.
2. Write a good introductory paragraph and conclusion.
3. Organize your thoughts before beginning writing and organize your paragraphs well.
4. Use correct grammar, vocabulary, and spelling. Use vocabulary and grammatical constructions that you are sure of. It is better to write simply and correctly than to try to write eloquently but make errors.

5. Keep your essay to no more than 200 or 300 words.
6. Allow enough time to write the essay well. Don't take so much time organizing your thoughts that you do not have time left to write.
7. Use specific details and avoid too many generalizations.

PLANNING YOUR ESSAY

If you have learned in composition classes a good way to organize your thoughts quickly, use the method that you already know. You should use a standard outline, a cluster outline, or some other method to organize your thoughts before you begin to write. An essay that is not properly planned will not be organized sufficiently to receive a good score. You should spend no more than 10 minutes organizing so that you have at least 20 minutes to write the essay. You will not be required to turn in your outline or other planning format, so you may use whatever is useful for you.

There are various methods of planning, and you should use the method that works best for you. The most common method is the standard outline. Each major category will be a paragraph in the essay. Study the following sample question and outline:

Some people purchase a home and others rent. Describe one or two benefits of owning a home and one or two benefits of renting. Compare the two options and explain which you think might be better for someone your age and in your situation.

Questions that must be addressed:

1. What are the benefits of owning?
2. What are the benefits of renting?
3. Which is the best for someone your age and in your situation?

STANDARD OUTLINE

I. Benefits of owning

    A. It is yours and you can do what you want
        1. Do not have to worry too much about noise
        2. Can redecorate without worrying about losing the deposit

    B. Financial reasons
        1. Interest is tax deductible
        2. Home appreciates in value

II. Benefits of renting

    A. Not tied down—if need to move, just have to worry about lease

    B. Financial reasons
      1. Do not have to come up with down payment
      2. Do not have to qualify for credit

III. Renting better for foreign student in early 20s

    A. Not tied down
      1. May transfer to another school
      2. Will return to own country after school

    B. Financial reasons
      1. Cannot afford to buy
      2. No credit

Another way of planning such an essay is with the "cluster outline." Study the following example:

CLUSTER OUTLINE

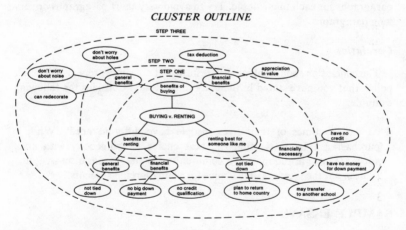

Introductory Paragraph

Every good essay has a strong opening paragraph. One method that is useful for constructing an opening paragraph is the *Generalize-Focus-Survey* structure. This is a three- or four-sentence paragraph in which the first sentence makes a generalization about the topic, the second sentence focuses on what will be discussed, and the last one or two sentences survey the details you will present in the body of the essay. Consider the following examples on the topic presented in the preceding pages:

1. *Generalize:*

   Many find it advantageous to purchase a home, but others find renting more suited to their needs.

2. *Focus:*

   While there are advantages for both options, renting is generally the best choice for young foreign students.

3. *Survey:*

   Foreign students often do not have good credit histories or enough money to buy a home and need to know that it will not be necessary to find a buyer for the home if they decide to transfer to another school or return home.

Body

The body of the essay should follow the form of your outline with separate paragraphs for each major topic. Try to avoid very short paragraphs or very long paragraphs.

Conclusion

The conclusion should sufficiently restate, but not simply repeat, the major points that you have stated in the body of the essay. Consider the following example:

At various times of their lives, people have different needs. While purchasing a home is often the best choice for somebody with an adequate income and roots in a community, for the reasons discussed, it is often not the most feasible choice for young foreign students.

SAMPLE ESSAYS

SAMPLE ESSAY 1

Introduction

Many find it advantageous to purchase a home, but others find renting more suited to their needs. While there are advantages for both options, renting is generally the best choice for young foreign students. Foreign students often do not have good credit histories or enough money to buy a home and need to know that it will not be necessary to find a buyer for the home if they decide to transfer to another school or return home.

Body Paragraph 1: Benefits of owning home

Owning a home provides a number of benefits. For example, a homeowner can make more noise than someone who lives in an apartment without having to worry that every small noise might disturb neighbors. Unlike apartment dwellers, homeowners can also put holes in walls and redecorate without being concerned about losing part or all of a security deposit. Owning is also an advantage because the interest on mortgage payments can be deducted on their income tax. In addition, real estate generally appreciates in value over the years.

Body Paragraph 2: Benefits of renting

There are also benefits to renting. A renter is tied down only by the terms of the rental agreement or lease. If a renter wants to move, it is not necessary to find a buyer. In addition, a renter does not have to provide a large down payment as does a home owner and does not have to have a good credit history.

Body Paragraph 3: Best choice for one in student's situation

A foreign student who plans to return home after college or who wishes to transfer to another school often cannot be tied down to a house. The foreign student often does not have enough money for a down payment or a credit history sufficient to borrow money to purchase a home. Consequently, renting is the answer for most young foreign students.

Conclusion

At various times of their lives, people have different needs. While purchasing a home is often the best choice for somebody with an adequate income and roots in a community, for the reasons discussed, it is often not the most feasible choice for young foreign students.

SAMPLE ESSAY 2

Topic

A writer has accused teachers and parents of causing children to develop *calcuholism*—a reliance on calculators and resulting loss of mathematical ability. Describe what you believe the writer means by *calcuholism* and what you believe causes it. Also state what you believe can be done to alleviate the problem.

Questions to Answer

1. What is *calcuholism*?
2. What causes it?
3. What can be done to alleviate it?

Standard Outline

I. What the writer means by *calcuholism*

A. The term indicates an addiction or dependency

B. Generally such a dependency is unhealthy

C. Problem—if children rely too much on calculators, they lose ability to do mathematics easily without it

II. What causes it—more technology

A. Emphasis in schools on more advanced math and technical classes that require calculators

B. Emphasis in offices on speed and efficiency—word processors and computers

C. Emphasis in industry on technologically advanced machines

III. What can be done to alleviate it

A. Schools should avoid causing students to rely on calculators

B. All should avoid becoming too dependent on the calculator
   1. Restrict use of calculators
   2. Keep up practice with actual math

Cluster Outline

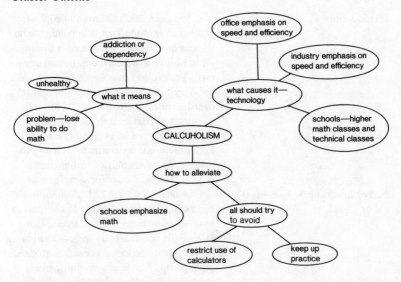

Introductory Paragraph

The type of introductory paragraph used in this essay, instead of one using the *Generalize-Focus-Survey* method, is one which follows the form of the outline in a general way.

I. It has been said that many people are victims of *calcuholism,* a dependence on the use of calculators, causing a diminished ability to do mathematics on one's own.

II. Technology in schools, offices, and industry has resulted in an unfortunate overdependence on all types of modern devices, but particularly on calculators.

III. Calcuholism can be avoided if schools and individuals concentrate on using the mind to do mathematics rather than relying on calculators for simple tasks.

Conclusion

Calcuholism has increased in recent years and will continue to increase due to advances in technology. To avoid dependency, we must do mathematics with our minds from time to time rather than with a machine.

Complete Essay

Introduction

It has been said that many people are victims of *calcuholism,* a dependence on the use of calculators, causing a diminished ability to do mathematics on one's own. Technology in schools, offices, and industry has resulted in an unfortunate overdependence on all types of modern devices, but particularly on calculators. Calcuholism can be avoided if schools and individuals concentrate on using the mind to do mathematics rather than relying on calculators for simple tasks.

Body Paragraph 1: What is it?

Obviously the term *calcuholism* has been coined with the intent to compare it to other addictions such as alcoholism. While it is not nearly as serious as alcoholism, dependence on the calculator can be harmful. Abuse of something normally beneficial may lead to a harmful reliance on it. It is not that calculators are harmful, but that overuse may cause harm by causing people to forget how to do mathematics with their own minds.

Body Paragraph 2: What causes it?

The problem arises from modern technological advances. In schools, classes become more complicated because of the technology for which students must be prepared when they graduate. Calculators are permitted and essential in many such classes. In offices, calculators, computers, and word processing systems are commonplace because they increase speed and improve efficiency. Business people may spend hours working with numbers and rarely calculate mentally. In industry as well, the emphasis on advanced machines results in individuals' solving fewer mathematical problems on their own.

Body Paragraph 3: What can be done to alleviate?

To alleviate the problem, schools should avoid allowing students to use calculators too early and should require suf-

ficient in-class work without them. All of
us should restrict our use of calculators
and strive to do math on our own so that
we will not lose our basic math skills.

Conclusion   Calcuholism has increased in recent
years and will continue to increase due to
advances in technology. To avoid dependency, we must do mathematics with our
minds from time to time rather than with
a machine.

SAMPLE ESSAY 3

Topic

The chart below shows the number of barrels of oil produced and the
number consumed by various regions of the world. What does the chart tell
you? Write one or more paragraphs that convey the information displayed in
the chart.

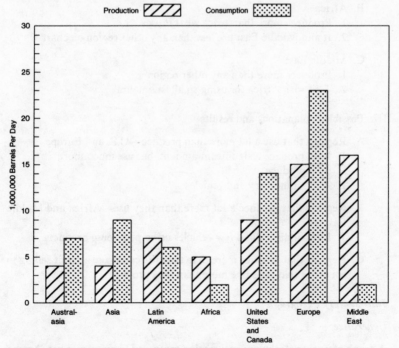

(This chart is not a completely accurate reflection of fact, but is a close representation
for illustration purposes.)

Standard Outline

I. Regions that use more than they produce

   A. Australasia and Asia—each uses about 50% more than produced

   B. Europe
     1. Uses about 75% more than produced
     2. Almost the largest producer, but also the largest user

   C. U.S. and Canada
     1. Produce 3/5 of what is used
     2. Produce twice what many other regions produce, but use the most with exception of Europe

II. Regions that produce more than they use

   A. Latin America
     1. Uses 6/7 of what it produces
     2. Biggest user of the regions that produce more than they use

   B. Africa
     1. Produces more than twice what it uses
     2. It and Middle East use less than any other region on chart

   C. Middle East
     1. Produces more than any other region
     2. Tied with Africa for using smallest amount

III. Possible explanations and results

   A. Regions that use a lot more than produce—U.S. and Europe
     1. Both produce a significant amount, but use much more than produce
     2. A lot of industry and vehicles

   B. Regions that produce a lot more than they use—Africa and Middle East
     1. Little industry and few vehicles using petroleum products

   C. Regions that produce more than they use can make a profit selling to countries that consume more than they produce

Introductory Paragraph

Generalize:

A graph of world petroleum consumption compared to petroleum use shows a tremendous difference among regions.

Focus:

Some use more than they produce, while others produce more than they use.

Survey:

Certain regions have large petroleum production but lack the industry and transportation to utilize it. They are able to make a profit by selling to regions that need it.

Conclusion

As the chart describes, certain regions produce more petroleum than they consume, and others consume more than they produce. Those with a surplus can profit by selling it to the large consumers that cannot produce all that they need.

Complete Essay

Introduction

A graph of world petroleum consumption compared to petroleum use shows a tremendous difference among regions. Some use more than they produce, while others produce more than they use. Certain regions have large petroleum production but lack the industry and transportation to utilize it. They are able to make a profit by selling to regions that need it.

Body Paragraph 1: Regions that use more

Four regions shown consume more petroleum than they produce. Both Australasia and Asia consume about fifty percent more than they produce. Europe consumes about seventy-five percent more than it produces. It is one of the largest producers but also is the largest consumer of all the regions. The United States and Canada together produce about three-fifths of what they consume; while they produce more than twice as much as many other regions, they consume the most with the exception of Europe.

Body Paragraph 2: Regions that use less than they produce

Three regions shown on the chart produce more than they consume. Latin

America produces approximately ten percent more than it consumes. It is the biggest consumer among the regions that produce more than they consume. Africa produces more than twice what it consumes, and the Middle East is the biggest producer of all. However, those two regions are tied for consuming the smallest amount.

Body Paragraph 3: Possible explanation

The United States, Canada, and Europe use a great deal more than they produce, but each produces a considerable amount. The high usage probably results from their industrial and transportation requirements. On the other hand, Africa and the Middle East produce much more than they use, which probably indicates low petroleum needs in industry and transportation.

Conclusion

As the chart describes, certain regions produce more petroleum that they consume, and others consume more than they produce. Those with a surplus can profit by selling it to the large consumers that cannot produce all that they need.

A PATTERNED PLAN OF ATTACK

Essay Writing

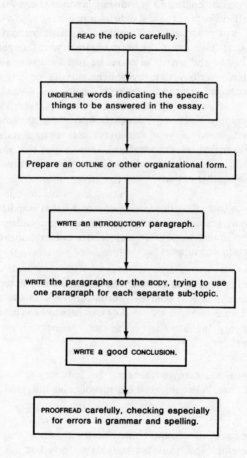

READ the topic carefully.

↓

UNDERLINE words indicating the specific things to be answered in the essay.

↓

Prepare an OUTLINE or other organizational form.

↓

WRITE an INTRODUCTORY paragraph.

↓

WRITE the paragraphs for the BODY, trying to use one paragraph for each separate sub-topic.

↓

WRITE a good CONCLUSION.

↓

PROOFREAD carefully, checking especially for errors in grammar and spelling.

SAMPLE TOPICS

Following are sample topics for practice. You should find a composition teacher who is fluent in English to grade your practice essays for you using the Essay Evaluation Form at the end of this section.

Write each of your practice essays within 30 minutes without doing any research. Find a quiet place, read the topic, organize your thoughts using no more than 10 minutes, and write the essay. Be sure to answer all questions presented in the topic. Write your essay by hand; do not type it. On the actual test, you will be required to write the essay by hand.

1. You are an employer who must decide how to handle the smoking issue in your office. Many of your employees are nonsmokers, but some, including your managers, are smokers. Devise a plan that would satisfy both groups. Explain the benefits of the plan you choose and its advantages over other options.

2. Is having a college education and a degree all that important today? Explain advantages and disadvantages to seeking a college degree as opposed to beginning work after high school and explain which of the courses of action you support.

3. In American colleges and universities, students study material from a variety of areas. Should courses concentrate only in the area of the student's future careers, or should they continue to be in many different areas? Compare the benefits of the two options and explain which position you support.

4. Being bilingual has many advantages, but it is very difficult for many people to achieve. What are some benefits of being bilingual or multilingual?

5. Some major companies in the United States are discussing the idea of having their employees work ten-hour days, forty hours a week, with three days off instead of two. What are the advantages and disadvantages of such a plan? Decide whether this plan or the standard eight-hour day and five-day week would be better for a business that you are familiar with and support your choice.

6. Students who live away from home while attending classes face the task of choosing housing accommodations. Some live in dormitories; others prefer living alone in apartments. Explain the benefits and disadvantages of the different options and support the option you prefer.

7. Some educators believe that students should receive letter grades in the courses in their major areas of concentration and pass-fail grades in all other subjects. Give the advantages and disadvantages of the two positions and explain which position you support.

8. The four charts below show various information regarding farming in the United States for the years 1900, 1925, 1950, and 1975. What do the charts tell you? Write one or more paragraphs that convey the information in the four charts.

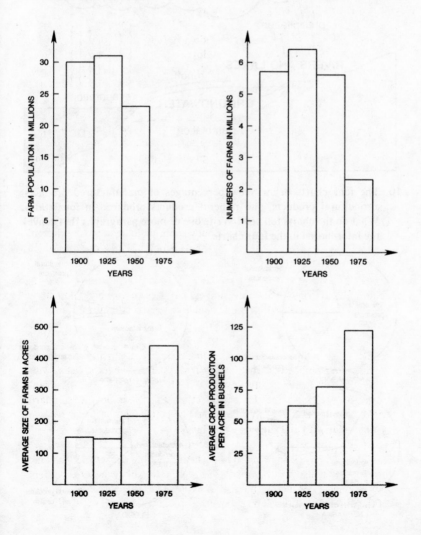

9. The diagram below shows the hydrologic cycle. What does the diagram tell you? Write one or two paragraphs that convey the information shown in the diagram.

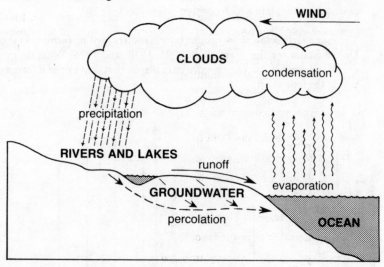

10. The four charts below show percentages of manufactured products, agricultural products, and mineral products produced in four states. What do the charts tell you? Write one or more paragraphs that convey the information in the four charts.

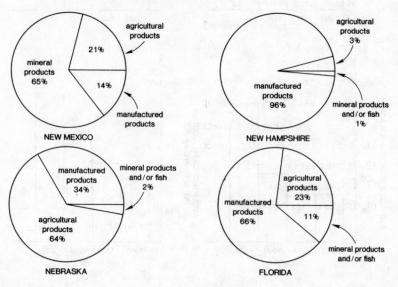

ESSAY EVALUATION FORM

Use a scale of 1 through 6 to rate the essay in each area. A rating of 1 is the lowest score possible, while a rating of 6 is the highest. In general an overall evaluation of 4, 5, or 6 may be considered a passing score by many institutions. TOEFL essays are given an *overall* score of from 1 to 6. However, this form will allow grading of your essay in a more detailed way in order for you to better analyze the areas in which you have problems.

HOW EFFECTIVELY DOES YOUR ESSAY. . .   EVALUATION

Address the Topic?

1. Does it focus on the assigned topic?   1. _____

2. Does it complete all tasks set forth by the as-   2. _____
   signment?

Organize Its Thoughts?

3. Is there an effective introduction?   3. _____

4. Are the paragraphs logically arranged?   4. _____

5. Does each paragraph focus on one main idea?   5. _____

6. Are there smooth transitions between para-   6. _____
   graphs?

7. Is there an effective closing?   7. _____

Support Its Points?

8. Are there sufficient specific details for each   8. _____
   point?

9. Are the examples given relevant to the issue   9. _____

10. Are the examples fully developed?   10. _____

Use Language Correctly?

11. Are grammar and usage correct?   11. _____

12. Is punctuation correct?   12. _____

13. Is spelling correct?   13. _____

14. Is vocabulary correct?   14. _____

TOTAL SCORE _____

TOTAL SCORE ÷ 14 = AVERAGE SCORE _____

FINAL PREPARATION: "The Final Touches"

1. Make sure that you are familiar with the testing center location and nearby parking facilities.
2. The last week of preparation should be spent primarily on reviewing strategies, techniques, and directions for each area.
3. Don't cram the night before the exam. It's a waste of time! RELAX.
4. Remember that you will be in the exam room for three hours or more, and you may bring no food with you. You may wish to eat a good breakfast. Remember that you will probably not have a break to visit a restroom, so don't drink too much before the exam.
5. Dress comfortably so that you will not be distracted. Take a light jacket if you are sensitive to cold in case the room is chilly.
6. Leave home in plenty of time to get to the exam. If you have to rush, you will feel nervous when you arrive.
7. Start off crisply, working the problems you know first, and then coming back and trying the others.
8. If you can eliminate one or more of the choices, make an educated guess. *Do not leave any spaces blank because there is no penalty for guessing.*
9. In reading passages, actively note main points, definitions, names, important conclusions, places, and numbers.
10. Make sure that you are answering "what is being asked" and that your answer is reasonable.
11. Using the SUCCESSFUL OVERALL APPROACH is the key to getting the ones right that you should get right—resulting in a good score on the TOEFL.

INDEX TO THE REVIEWS

ORDER THIS TOEFL
CASSETTE TAPE

Included with this guide is a 90-minute cassette tape to give you practice in the listening comprehension section of TOEFL Practice Tests 1, 2, and 3. Should you wish additional practice to improve your listening skills, you may order a second 90-minute cassette tape for use with Practice Tests 4, 5, and 6. To order, simply clip the coupon below and mail to

> Cliffs Notes, Inc.
> P.O. Box 80728
> Lincoln, Nebraska 68501
> U.S.A.

Your TOEFL listening comprehension cassette tape will be sent to you postpaid. (Add $1.00 per tape to be shipped outside of the United States. All foreign orders are shipped airmail.)

Cliffs Notes, Inc., P.O. Box 80728, Lincoln, Nebraska 68501, U.S.A.

Please send TOEFL cassette tape number 2 (contains listening comprehension sections for Practice Tests 4, 5, and 6).

I enclose $5.95 in check or money order (U.S. funds) for each tape ordered.

_____ tape(s) at $5.95 each	$ _____
Foreign postage at $1.00 per tape	$ _____
Total enclosed	$ _____

Name _____

Address _____

City _____ State _____ Zip _____

Country _____

485

ORDER THIS TODAY CASSETTE TAPE

Included with this guide is a 90-minute cassette tape to give you practice in the listening comprehension section of TOEFL. Practice Tests 1, 2, and 3 should be used with additional practice to improve your listening skills. You may order a second 90-minute cassette tape for use with Practice Tests 4, 5, and 6. To order, simply complete the coupon below and mail it to:

CMB Media, Inc.
P.O. Box PP 296
Lincoln, Nebraska 68501

Your TOEFL listening comprehension practice tape will be sent to you postpaid. Add $1.00 for tapes to be shipped outside of the United States. All foreign orders are airmail postpaid.

CMB Media, Inc., P.O. Box 80726, Lincoln, Nebraska 68501-0726

Please send TOEFL cassette tape number 2 (for use with listening comprehension section for Practice Tests 4, 5, and 6).

I enclose $7.25 (check or money order, U.S. funds). No cash please.

	Number of tapes ordered	
	Foreign postage ($1.00 per tape)	
	Total enclosed	

Name _____

Address _____

City _____ State _____ Zip _____

Country _____

498